CO
MATHEMATICS
FOR
IGCSE

DAVID **R**AYNER

OXFORD

OXFORD
UNIVERSITY PRESS

Great Clarendon Street, Oxford OX2 6DP

Oxford University Press is a department of the University of Oxford. It furthers the University's objective of excellence in research, scholarship, and education by publishing worldwide in

Oxford   New York

Auckland   Bangkok   Buenos Aires   Cape Town   Chennai
Dar es Salaam   Delhi   Hong Kong   Istanbul   Karachi   Kolkata
Kuala Lumpur   Madrid   Melbourne   Mexico City   Mumbai   Nairobi
São Paulo   Shanghai   Taipei   Tokyo   Toronto

Oxford is a registered trade mark of Oxford University Press
in the UK and in certain other countries

© David Rayner 2000

The author would like to thank:
Jeff Robinson for kindly vetting the material and preparing Specimen Exam Papers.
Keith Black for reporting on the first draft.
Cambridge International Examinations for kind permission to reproduce past paper questions. Cambridge International Examinations accept no responsibility for the answers to past paper questions.

The moral rights of the author have been asserted

Database right Oxford University Press (maker)

First published 2000

12 11 10 9 8 7 6

All rights reserved. No part of this publication may be reproduced, stored in a retrieval system, or transmitted, in any form or by any means, without the prior permission in writing of Oxford University Press, or as expressly permitted by law, or under terms agreed with the appropriate reprographics rights organisation. Enquiries concerning reproduction outside the scope of the above should be sent to the Rights Department, Oxford University Press, at the above address

You must not circulate this book in any other binding or cover
and you must impose this same condition on any acquirer

British Library Cataloguing in Publication Data

Data available

ISBN 0 19 914786 8

Typeset by Tech-Set Ltd.
Printed and bound in Great Britain by Bell & Bain Ltd., Glasgow

Cover photo by Corbis UK Ltd/Digital Art

Oxford University Press is a worldwide publisher of educational textbooks and we have made full use of our international reputation to bring you the most authoritative text for the Core IGCSE syllabus.

About this book

This book is designed to provide the best preparation for your IGCSE examination. It is written by a very popular and successful author, and has been vetted by the Principal Examiner for your syllabus so you can be sure it covers everything you need to know.

Finding your way around

To get the most out of this book when studying or revising, use the:
- **Edge marks** (shown on the next page) to help you find the unit you want quickly.
- **Contents list** to help you find the appropriate units.
- **Index** to find key words so you can turn to any concept straight away.

Exercises and exam questions

There are literally thousands of questions in this book, providing ample opportunities to practise the skills and techniques required in the exam.
- **Worked examples and comprehensive exercises** are one of the main features of the book. The examples show you the important skills and techniques required. The exercises are carefully graded, starting from the basics and going up to exam standard, allowing you to practise the skills and techniques.
- **Revision exercises** at the end of each unit allow you to bring together all your knowledge on a particular topic and encourage regular revision.
- **Examination exercises** at the end of each unit consist of question from past IGCSE papers. They are coded so you can tell immediately which paper they are taken from: [J 95 1] means the question is from June 95 Paper 1; [N 98 3] is from November 1998 Paper 3.
- **Specimen exam papers** at the end of the book are written by the Principal Examiner. There are two papers, corresponding to the papers you will take at the end of your course: Paper 1 and Paper 3. They give you the opportunity to practise for the real thing.
- **Revision section:** Unit 12 contains multiple choice questions to provide an extra opportunity to revise, making sure you are completely ready for your exam.
- **Answers to numerical problems** are at the end of the book so you can check your progress.

Investigations

Unit 11 provides plenty of ideas to help you gain the special skills required for the Investigation paper. Remember that you can only gain by taking this optional paper – you cannot lose marks – so it is worth developing these skills.

Contents

1	Shape and Space 1	1–36
2	Algebra 1	42–56
3	Number 1	59–100
4	Handling Data 1	104–126
5	Shape and Space 2	129–159
6	Algebra 2	166–184
7	Number 2	193–223
8	Probability	227–233
9	Shape and space 3	235–245
10	Number 3	249–265
11	Using and Applying Mathematics	269–286
12	Multiple choice tests	287–292
	Specimen Paper 1	294–296
	Specimen Paper 2	297–300
	Answers	301–332
	Index	333–335

Contents

1		**Shape and Space 1**	**1–36**
1.1		Accurate drawing	1
1.2		Angle facts	5
1.3		Angles in polygons and circles	11
1.4		Symmetry	15
1.5		Circle calculations	17
1.6		Area	26
1.7		Volume	31
		Revision exercise 1A	37
		Examination exercise 1B	39
2		**Algebra 1**	**42–56**
2.1		Sequences	42
2.2		Solving equations	44
2.3		Drawing graphs	52
		Revision exercise 2A	57
		Examination exercise 2B	58
3		**Number 1**	**59–100**
3.1		Place value	59
3.2		Arithmetic without a calculator	61
3.3		Inverse operations	62
3.4		Decimals	64
3.5		Flow diagrams	69
3.6		Properties of numbers	71
3.7		Long multiplication and division	72
3.8		Percentages	76
3.9		Map scales and ratio	80
3.10		Proportion	85
3.11		Speed, distance and time	87
3.12		Approximations	89
3.13		Metric units	91
3.14		Problems 1	93
		Revision exercise 3A	100
		Examination exercise 3B	102

4	**Handling Data 1**	104–126
4.1	Displaying data	104
4.2	Questionnaires	114
4.3	Averages	119
4.4	Frequency polygons	123
	Revision exercise 4A	127
	Examination exercise 4B	128

5	**Shape and Space 2**	129–159
5.1	Transforming shapes	129
5.2	Quadrilaterals and other polygons	143
5.3	Bearings	146
5.4	Locus	151
5.5	Pythagoras' theorem	154
5.6	Problems in area and volume	157
	Revision exercise 5A	160
	Examination exercise 5B	162

6	**Algebra 2**	166–184
6.1	Finding a rule	166
6.2	Simultaneous equations	169
6.3	Interpreting graphs	174
6.4	Brackets and factors	182
6.5	Changing the subject of a formula	183
	Revision exercise 6A	185
	Examination exercise 6B	187

7	**Number 2**	193–223
7.1	Percentage change	193
7.2	Fractions, ratio, decimals and percentage	195
7.3	Estimating	197
7.4	Measurement is approximate	201
7.5	Mental arithmetic	203
7.6	Using a calculator	213
	Revision exercise 7A	223
	Examination exercise 7B	224

8	**Probability**	227–233
8.1	One event	227
8.2	Exclusive events	231
	Revision exercise 8A	233
	Examination exercise 8B	234

9	**Shape and space 3**	235–245
9.1	Similar shapes	235
9.2	Trigonometry	238
	Revision exercise 9A	245
	Examination exercise 9B	247

10	**Number 3**	249–265
10.1	Powers and roots	249
10.2	Standard form	253
10.3	Fractions	256
10.4	Negative numbers	258
10.5	Substituting into formulas	261
10.6	Problems 3	264
	Revision exercise 10A	266
	Examination exercise 10B	267

11	**Using and Applying Mathematics**	269–286
11.1	Coursework tasks	269
11.2	Puzzles and games	274

12	**Multiple choice tests**	287–293

Specimen Paper 1	294–296
Specimen Paper 2	297–300
Answers	301–332
Index	333–335

1 SHAPE AND SPACE 1

1.1 Accurate drawing

Some questions involving bearings or irregular shapes are easy to solve by drawing an accurate diagram.

Navigators on ships use scale drawings to work out their position or their course.

To improve the accuracy of your work, follow these guidelines.

- Use a *sharp* HB pencil.
- Don't press too hard.
- If drawing an *acute* angle make sure your angle is less than 90°.
- If you use a pair of compasses make sure they are fairly stiff so the radius does not change accidently.

Exercise 1

Use a protractor and ruler to draw full size diagrams and measure the sides marked with letters.

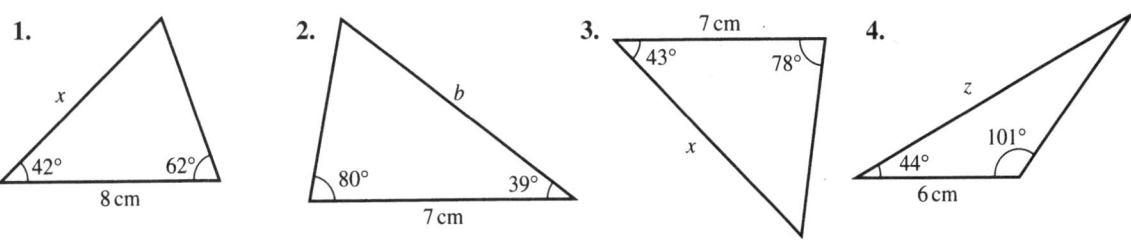

2 Shape and space 1

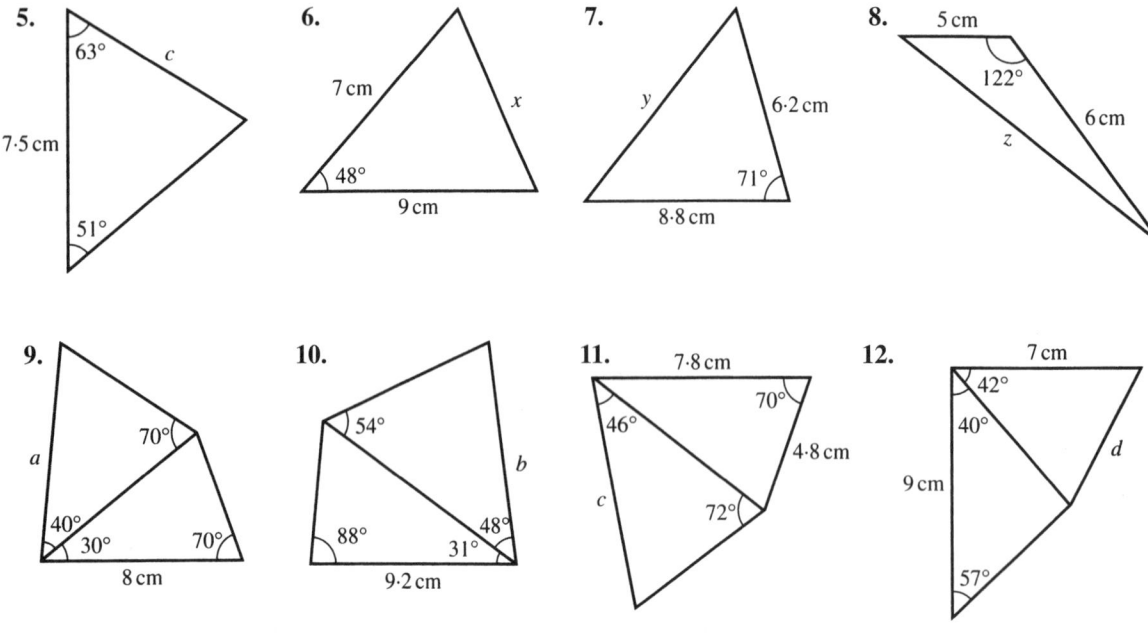

In Questions 13 to 16 construct the triangles using a pair of compasses. Measure the angles marked with letters.

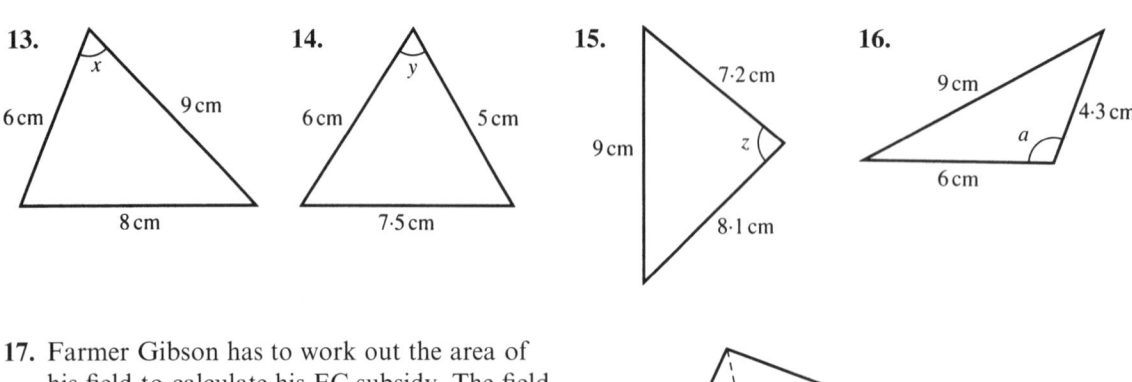

17. Farmer Gibson has to work out the area of his field to calculate his EC subsidy. The field is not a rectangle or parallelogram or any standard shape. He has measured the four sides of the field and one of the diagonals.
    (a) Make a scale drawing of the field, using a scale of 1 cm to 10 m.
    (b) Measure the lengths of the dotted lines and hence work out the total area of the field to the nearest 100 m^2.

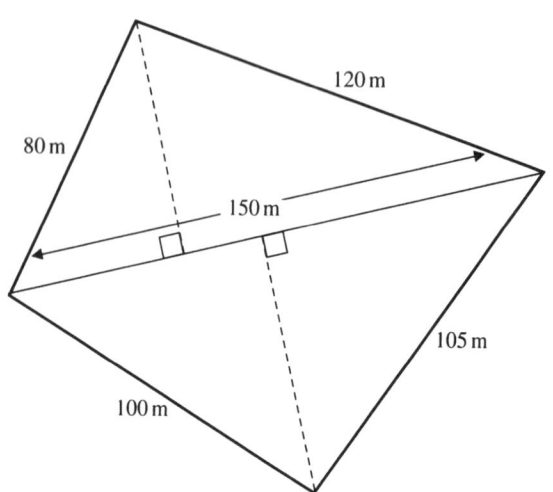

18. Make a scale drawing to calculate the area of this field, correct to the nearest 100 m².

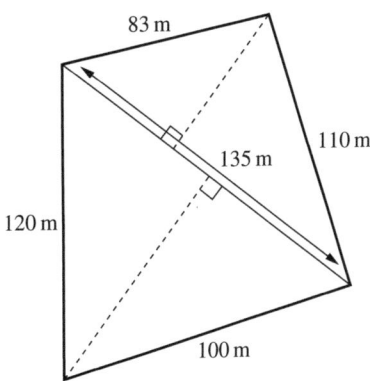

Nets

If the cube here was made of cardboard, and you cut along some of the edges and laid it out flat, you would have the *net* of the cube.

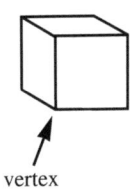

vertex

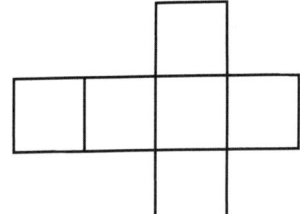

Here is the net for a square-based pyramid.

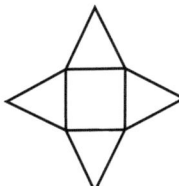

Exercise 2

1. Which of the nets below can be used to make a cube?

(a) 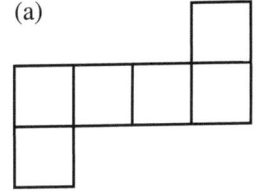 (b) 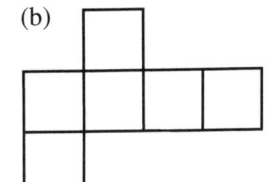 (c) 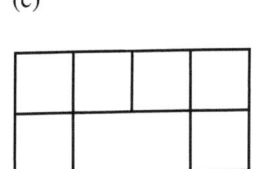 (d)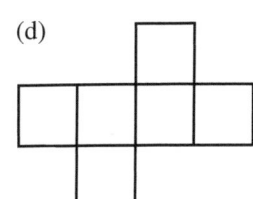

2. The numbers on opposite faces of a dice add up to 7. Take one of the possible nets for a cube from Question **1** and show the number of dots on each face.

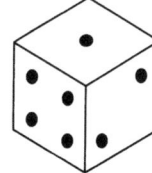

4 Shape and space 1

3. Here we have started to draw the net of a cuboid
   (a closed rectangular box) measuring 4 cm × 3 cm × 1 cm.
   Copy and then complete the net.

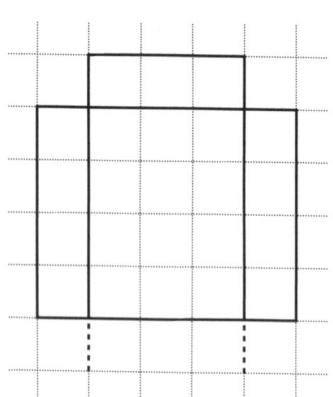

4. A cube can be dissected into three equal
   pyramids.
   Make three solids from the net shown and fit
   them together to make a cube. All lengths are
   in cm.

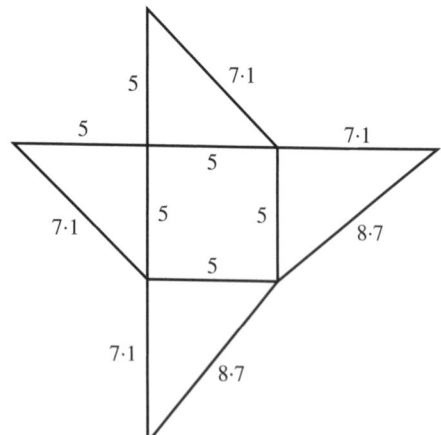

5. Describe the solid formed from each of these nets.

(a)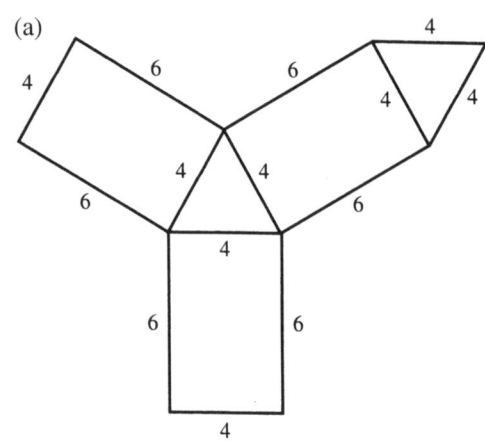

(b)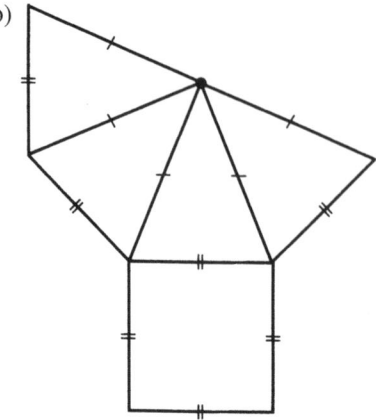

6. Sketch a possible net for each of the following:
   (a) a cuboid measuring 5 cm by 2 cm by 8 cm
   (b) a prism 10 cm long whose cross-section is a right-angled
       triangle with sides 3 cm, 4 cm and 5 cm.

7. The diagram shows the net of a pyramid. The base is shaded. The lengths are in cm.
   (a) How many edges will the pyramid have?
   (b) How many vertices will it have?
   (c) Find the lengths a, b, c, d.
   (d) Use the formula $V = \frac{1}{3}$ base area × height to calculate the volume of the pyramid.

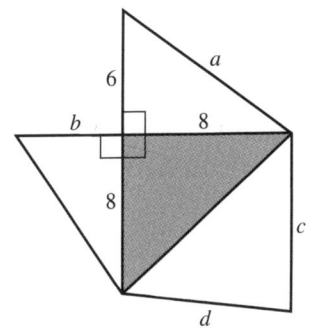

1.2 Angle facts

The angles at a point add up to 360°. The angles on a straight line add up to 180°.

Example
Find the missing angles:

(a)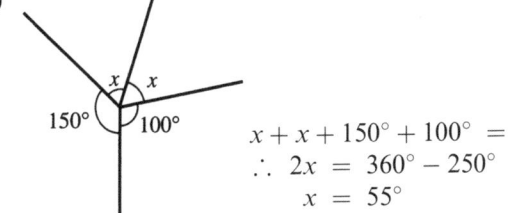

$x + x + 150° + 100° = 360°$
$\therefore 2x = 360° - 250°$
$x = 55°$

(b)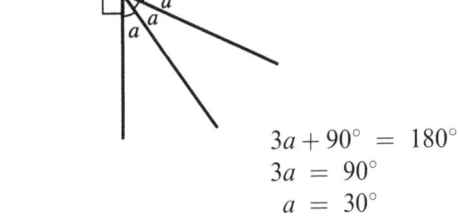

$3a + 90° = 180°$
$3a = 90°$
$a = 30°$

Exercise 3
Find the angles marked with letters. The lines AB and CD are straight.

1.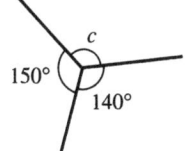
2.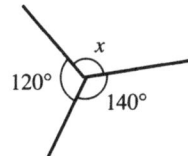
3.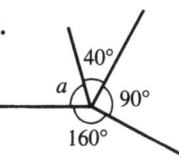
4.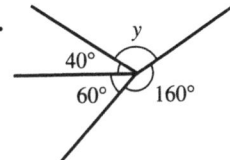
5.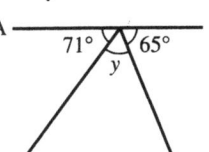
6.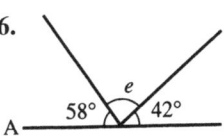
7.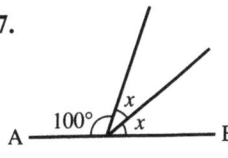
8.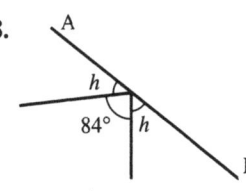
9.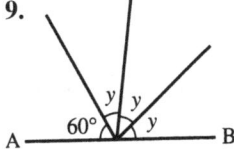
10.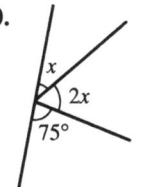
11.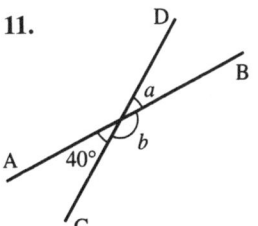
12.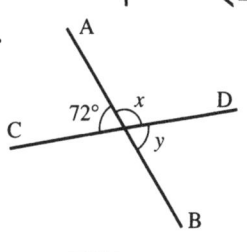

6 Shape and space 1

Triangles

The angles in a triangle add up to 180°.

Example

Find the missing angles:

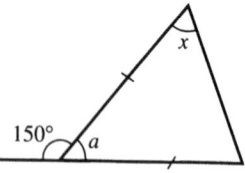

$a = 180° - 150° = 30°$
The triangle is isosceles $\therefore 2x + 30° = 180°$
$2x = 150°$
$x = 75°$

Exercise 4

Find the angles marked with letters. For the more difficult questions it is helpful to draw a diagram.

1. 2. 3. 4.

5. 6. 7. 8.

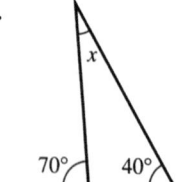

9. 10. 11. 12.

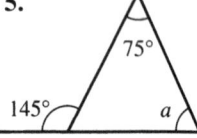 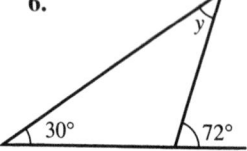 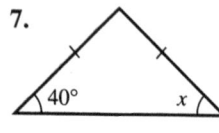 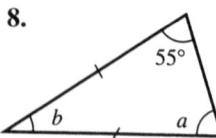

13. 14. 15. 16.

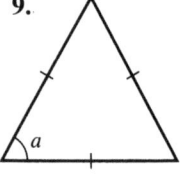 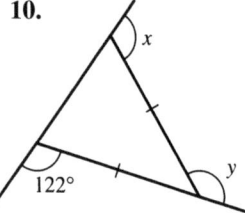 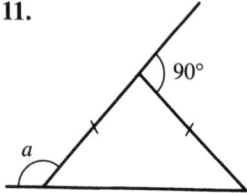 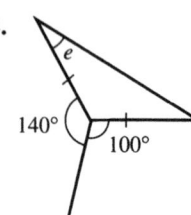

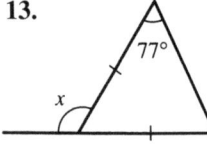 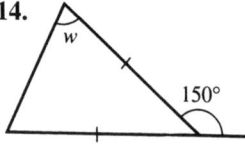 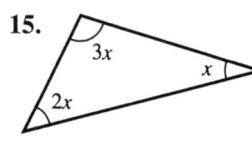 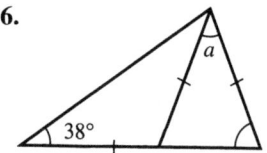

Parallel lines

When a line cuts a pair of parallel lines all the acute angles are equal and all the obtuse angles are equal.

Some people remember:
'F angles' and 'Z angles'

Exercise 5
Find the angles marked with letters.

1.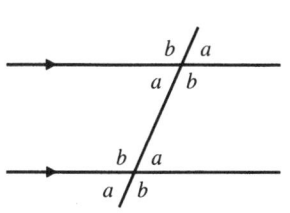

2.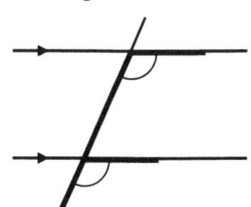

3.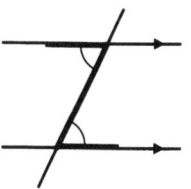

4.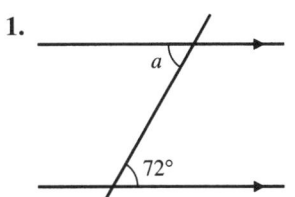

5.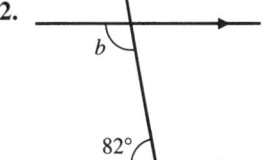

6.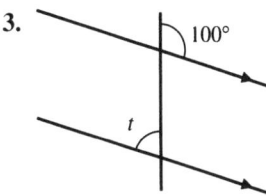

7.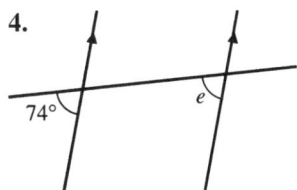

8.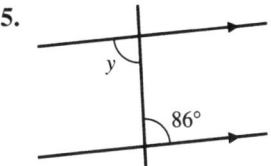

9.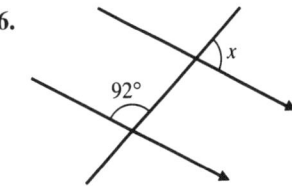

10.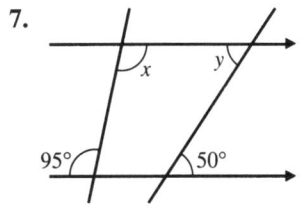

11.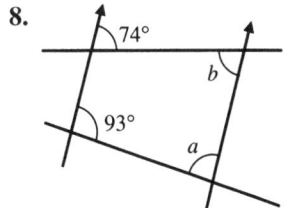

12.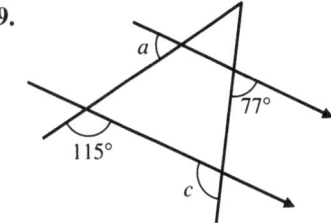

13.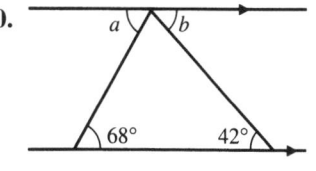

14.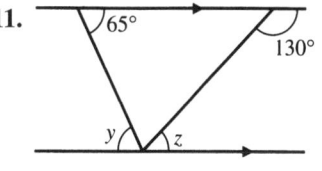

15.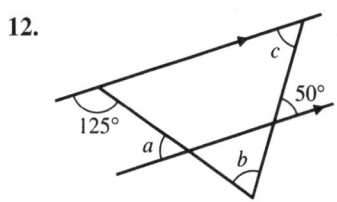

Quadrilaterals and regular polygons

The sum of the angles in a quadrilateral in 360°

Proof: The quadrilateral PQRS has been split into two triangles.

We know that $a + e + f = 180°$
and that $b + c + d = 180°$
∴ $a + b + c + d + e + f = 360°$

But the angles of the quadrilateral are $(a + b)$, c, $(d + e)$ and f.

∴ The sum of the angles in a quadrilateral is 360°.

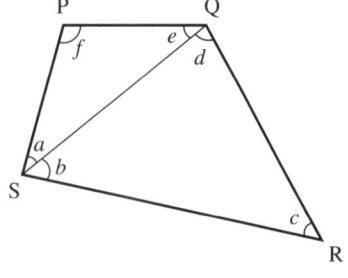

The angles at the centre of a regular polygon are equal.

Example

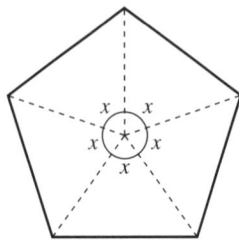

Regular pentagon:
$x + x + x + x + x = 360°$
∴ $x = 72°$

Exercise 6

Find the angles marked with letters.

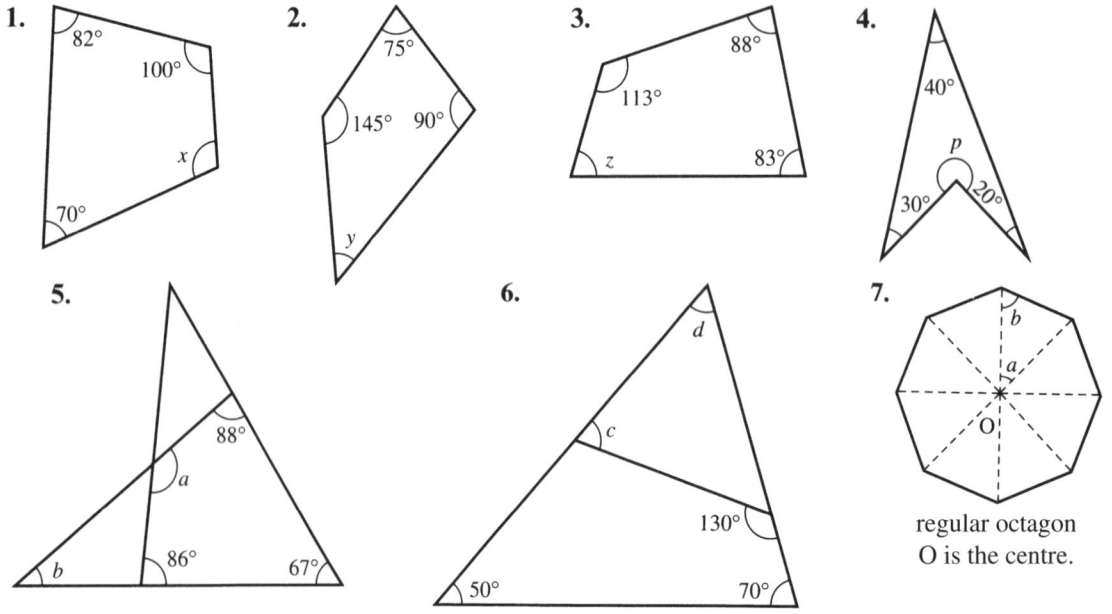

Angle facts 9

Mixed questions

The next exercise contains questions which summarise the work of the last four exercises.

Exercise 7

Find the angles marked with letters.

1.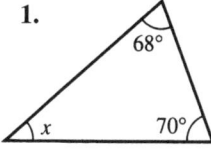
2.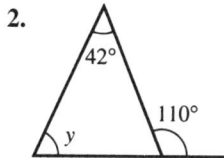
3.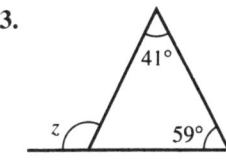
4.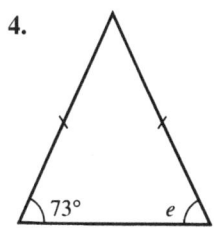

5.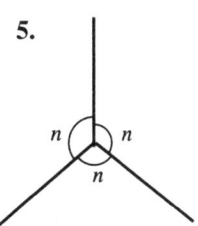
6.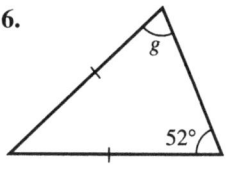
7.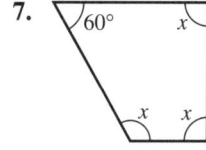
8.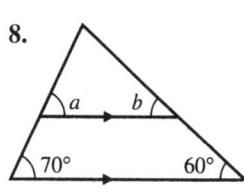

9.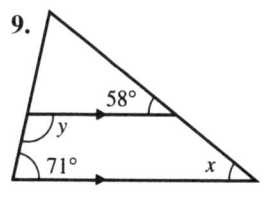
10.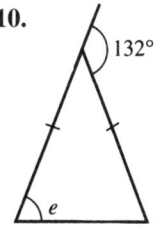
11.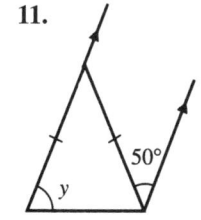
12.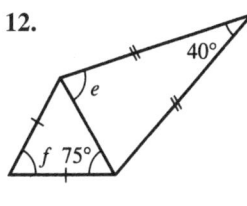

13.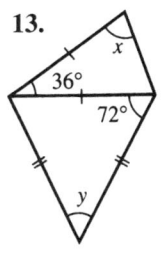
14.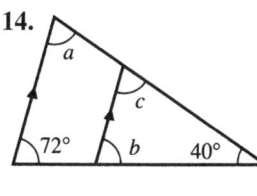
15.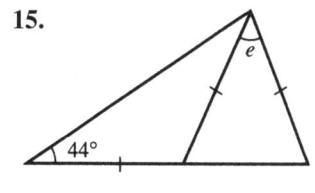
16.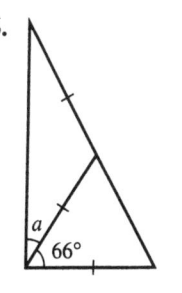

17.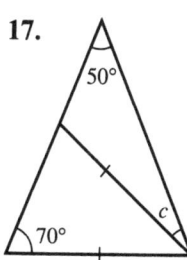
18.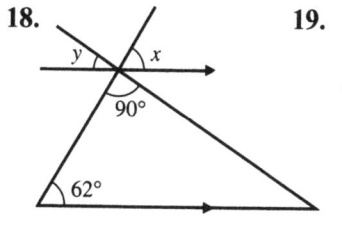
19.
20.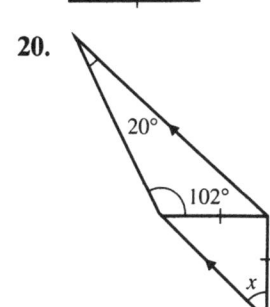

10   Shape and space 1

21.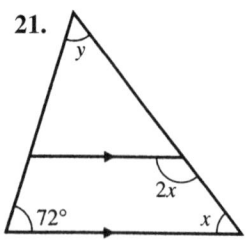

22.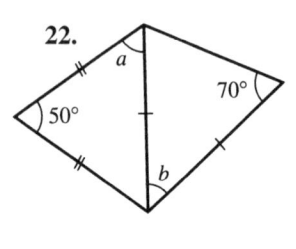

23. **24.**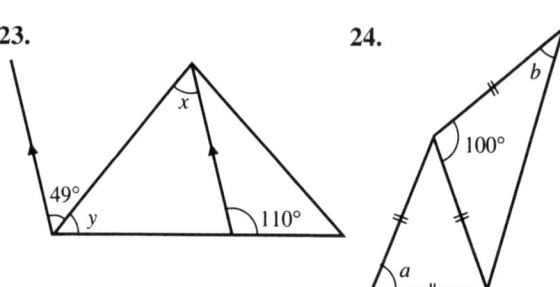

25. The diagram shows two equal squares joined to a triangle.
Find the angle *x*.

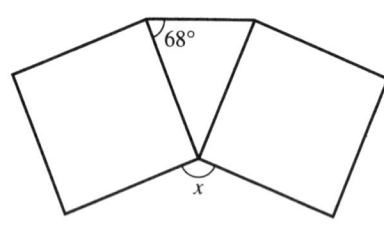

26. Find the angle *a* between the diagonals of the parallelogram.

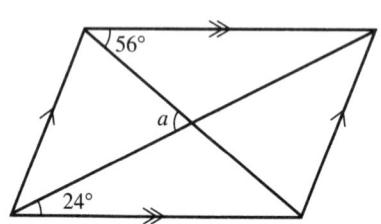

27. The diagram shows the cross-section of a roof of a chalet. PQ and RS are horizontal and ST is vertical.
Work out angles *x*, *y* and *z*.

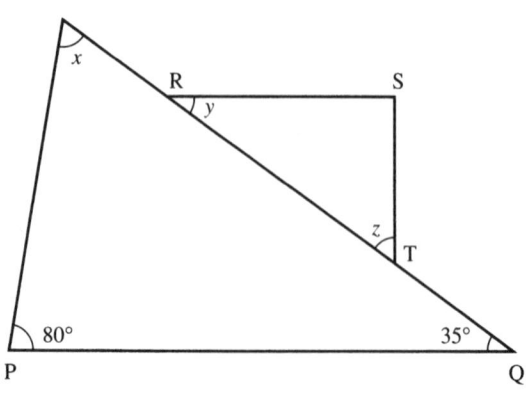

28. Given AB = AC and DA is parallel to EC, find *x*.

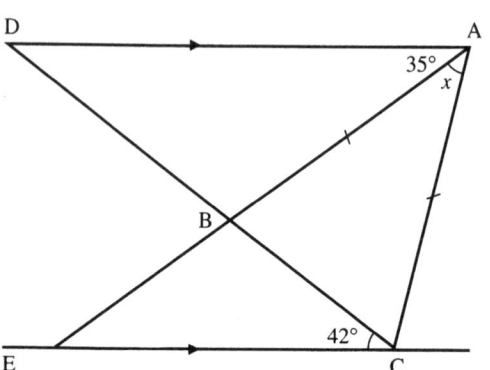

1.3 Angles in polygons and circles

Exterior angles of a polygon

The exterior angle of a polygon is the angle between a produced side and the adjacent side of the polygon. The word 'produced' in this context means 'extended'.

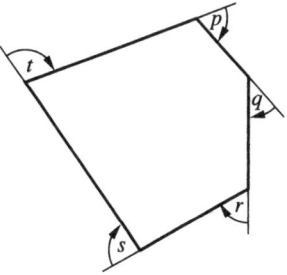

If we put all the exterior angles together we can see that the sum of the angles is 360°. This is true for any polygon.

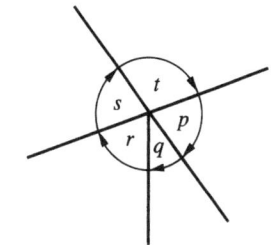

The sum of the exterior angles of a polygon = 360°

Note:
(a) In a regular polygon all exterior angles are equal.
(b) For a regular polygon with n sides, each exterior angle $= \dfrac{360°}{n}$

Example

The diagram shows a regular octagon (8 sides).

(a) Calculate the size of each exterior angle (marked e).
(b) Calculate the size of each interior angle (marked i).

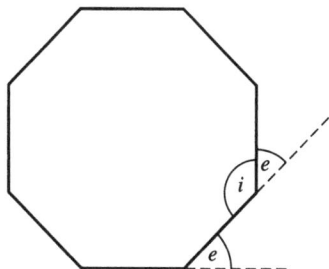

(a) There are 8 exterior angles and the sum of these angles is 360°.
∴ angle $e = \frac{360}{8} = 45°$

(b) $e + i = 180°$ (angles on a straight line)
∴ $i = 135°$

Exercise 8

1. Look at the polygon shown.
   (a) Calculate each exterior angle.
   (b) Check that the total of the exterior angles is 360°.

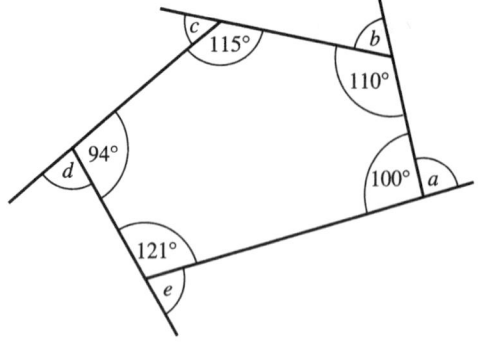

2. The diagram shows a regular decagon.
   (a) Calculate the angle *a*.
   (b) Calculate the interior angle of a regular decagon.

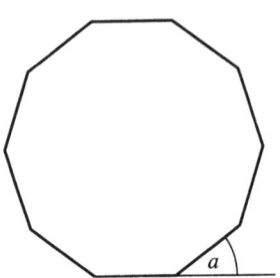

3. Find: (a) the exterior angle
         (b) the interior angle of a regular polygon with
   (i) 9 sides   (ii) 18 sides   (iii) 45 sides   (iv) 60 sides

4. Find the angles marked with letters.

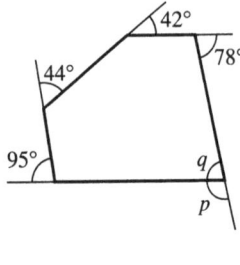
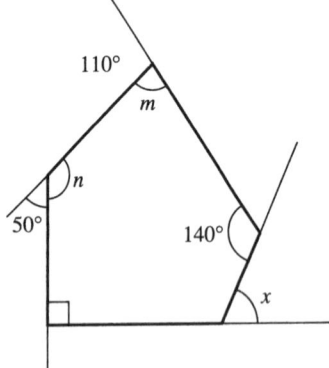

5. Each exterior angle of a regular polygon is 15°. How many sides has the polygon?

6. Each interior angle of a regular polygon is 140°. How many sides has the polygon?

7. Each exterior angle of a regular polygon is 18°. How many sides has the polygon?

8. The sides of a regular polygon subtend angles of 18° at the centre of the polygon.
   How many sides has the polygon?

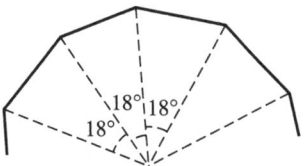

Angles in circles

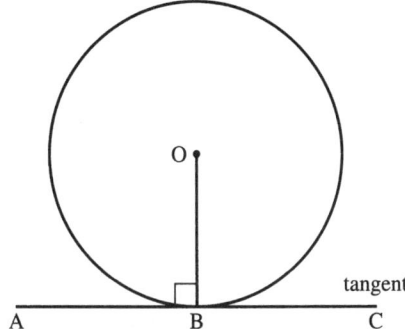

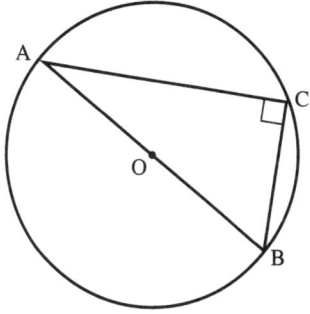

The *tangent* ABC touches the circle at B.
OB is a radius of the circle.
Angle OB̂A = 90°

AB is a diameter.
The angle at the circumference,
AĈB, is 90°.

Exercise 9

1. (a) Draw a circle with radius 5 cm and draw any diameter AB.
   (b) Draw triangles ABC, ABD, ABE and measure the angles at the circumference.

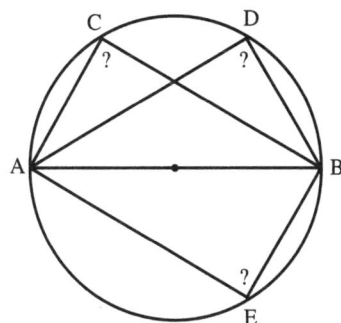

14 Shape and space 1

In Questions **2** to **13** find the angles marked with letters. Point O is the centre of the circle.

2.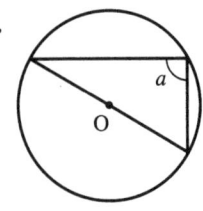

3.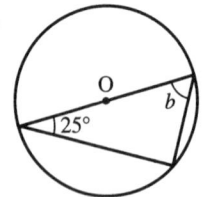

4.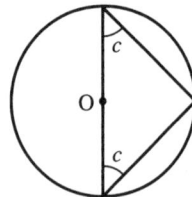

5.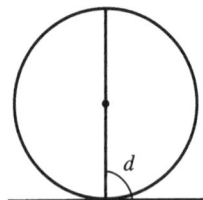

6.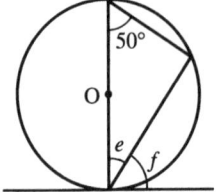

7.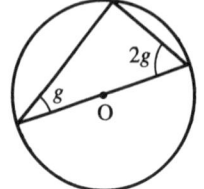

8.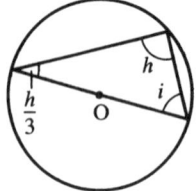

9.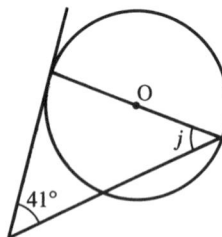

10.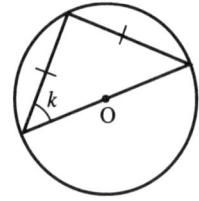

11.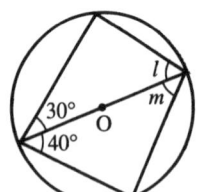

12.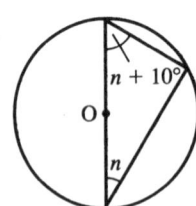

13.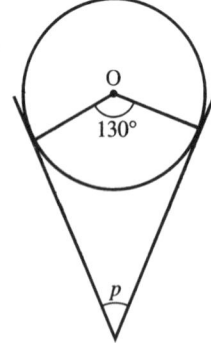

14. Draw two points A and B 10 cm apart.

    Place the corner of a piece of paper (or a set square) so that the edges of the paper pass through A and B.
    Mark the position of corner C. Slide the paper around so the edge still passes through A and B and mark the new position of C. Repeat several times and describe the locus of the point C which moves so that angle ACB is always 90°.

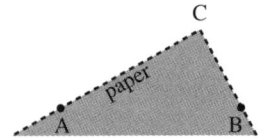

1.4 Symmetry

(a) Line symmetry

The letter M has one line of symmetry, shown dotted.

(b) Rotational symmetry

The shape may be turned about O into three identical positions. It has rotational symmetry of order three.

Exercise 10

For each shape state:
(a) the number of lines of symmetry
(b) the order of rotational symmetry.

1.
2.
3.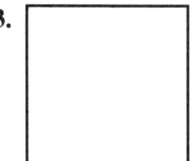
4.

5.
6.
7.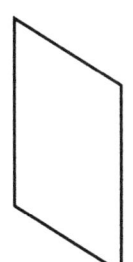
8.

9.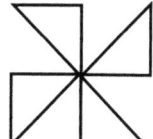
10.
11.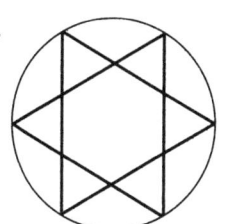
12.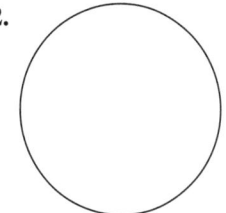

16 Shape and space 1

Exercise 11

In Questions 1 to 8, the broken lines are axes of symmetry. In each question only *part of the shape* is given. Copy what is given onto squared paper and then carefully complete the shape.

1.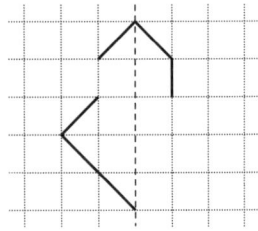
2.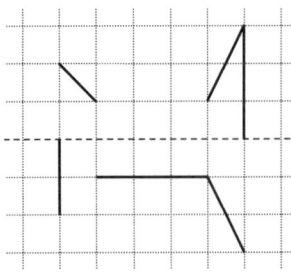
3.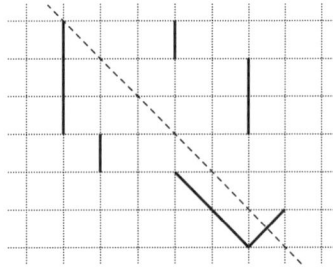
4.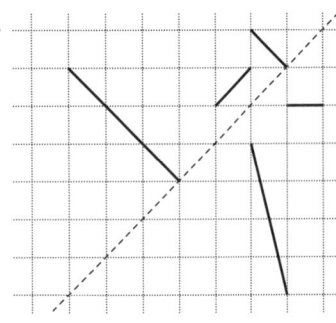
5.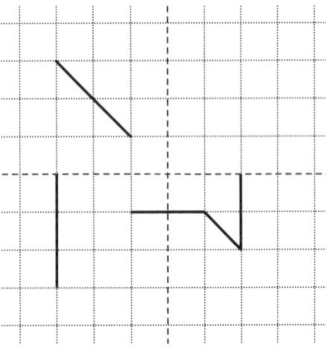
6.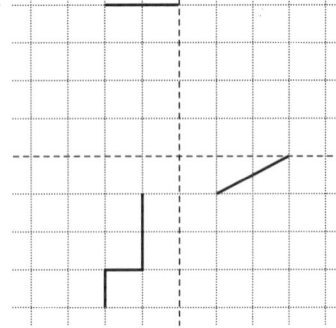
7.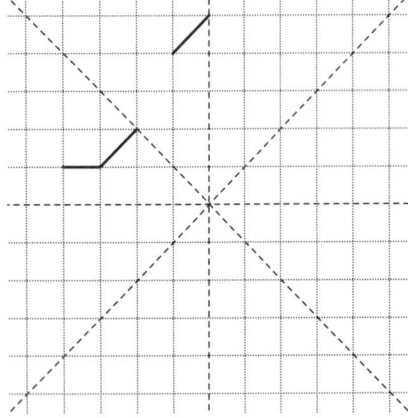
8.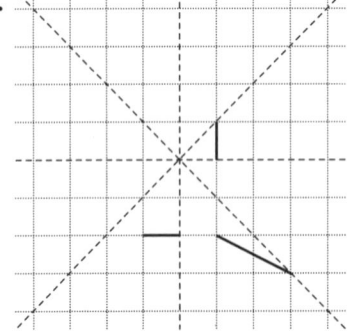

9. Fold a piece of paper twice and cut out any shape from the corner. Stick the cut-out into your book stating the number of lines of symmetry and the order of rotational symmetry.

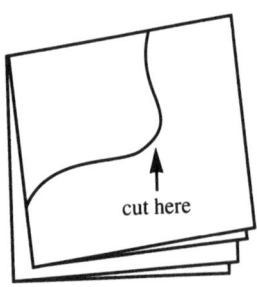
cut here

1.5 Circle calculations

Circumference of a circle

The circumference of a circle is given by $C = \pi d$

Example

Find the circumference of this circle.

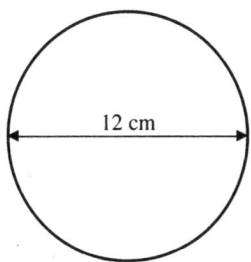

$C = \pi \times 12$ cm
$C = 37 \cdot 7$ cm (to 3 s.f.)
We have used the π button on a calculator. The value of π (pi) is $3 \cdot 142$ approximately.

Exercise 12

Find the circumference. Use the π button on a calculator or take $\pi = 3 \cdot 142$. Give the answers correct to 3 significant figures.

1.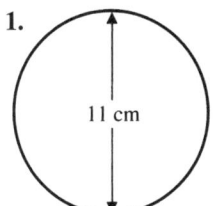
2.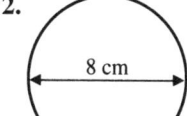
3.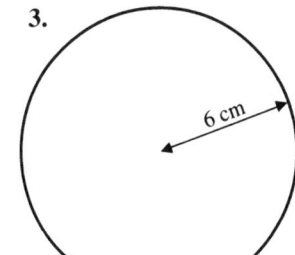
4.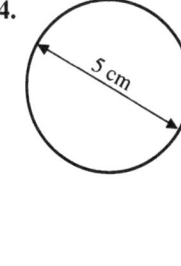

5.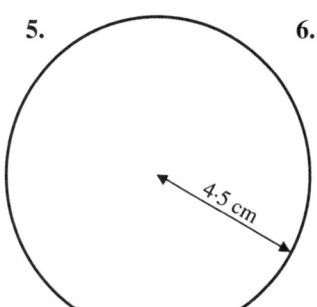
6.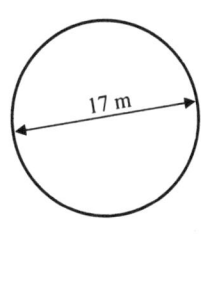
7.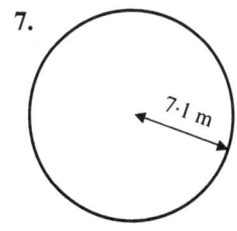
8.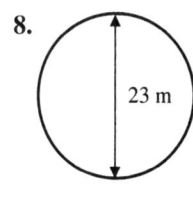

9. In the U.K. the new 10p coin has a diameter of 2·4 cm while the old 10p coin has a diameter of 2·8 cm.

   How much longer, to the nearest mm, was circumference of the old coin?

18 Shape and space 1

10. A circular pond has a diameter of 2·7 m. Calculate the length of the perimeter of the pond.

11. How many complete revolutions does a cycle wheel of diameter 60 cm make in travelling 400 m?

12. A running track has two semicircular ends of radius 34 m and two straights of 93·2 m as shown.

    Calculate the total distance around the track to the nearest metre.

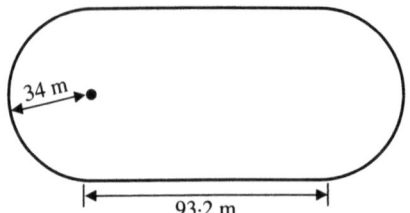

13. A fly, perched on the tip of the minute hand of a grandfather clock, is 14·4 cm from the centre of the clock face.
    How far does the fly move between 12:00 and 12:15?

14. A penny-farthing bicycle is shown. In a journey the front wheel rotates completely 156 times.
    (a) How far does the bicycle travel?
    (b) How many complete turns does the rear wheel make?

15. The diagram shows a framework for a target, consisting of 2 circles of wire and 6 straight pieces of wire. The radius of the outer circle is 30 cm and the radius of the inner circle is 15 cm.
    Calculate the total length of wire needed for the whole framework.

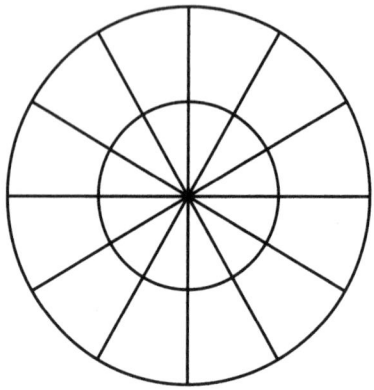

Circle calculations   19

16. For a meeting, chairs are arranged in a large circle. The width of each chair is 40 cm.

   How many chairs are needed to form a circle of diameter 3 m?

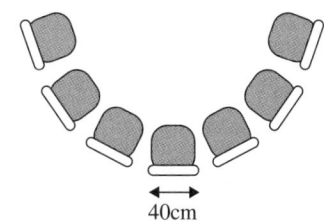
40cm

17. Lord Gibson decides to build a circular wall of radius 200 m around his stately home.

   The diagram shows a section of the wall. Estimate, to the nearest thousand, the number of bricks required for the complete wall.

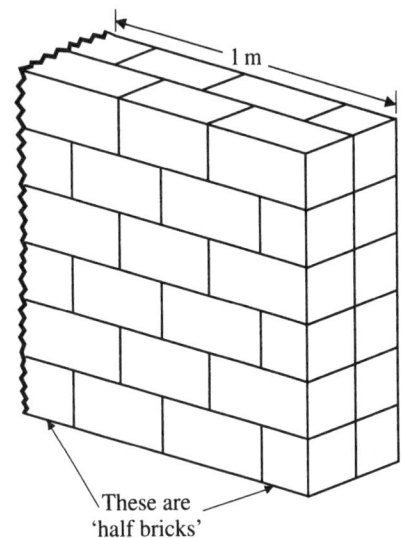

These are 'half bricks'

Area of a circle

The area of a circle of radius r is given by $A = \pi r^2$

Example

Find the area of this circle.

In this circle $r = 4\cdot5$ cm

∴ Area of circle $= \pi \times 4\cdot5^2$

$= 63\cdot6$ cm^2 (to 3 s.f.)

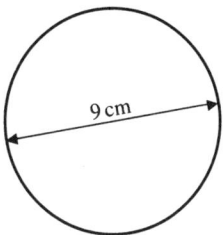

Remember the formula is $\pi(r^2)$ *not* $(\pi r)^2$.

On a calculator, work out the answer like this:

Exercise 13

In Questions 1 to 8 find the area of the circle. Use the π button on a calculator or use π = 3·142. Give the answers correct to three significant figures.

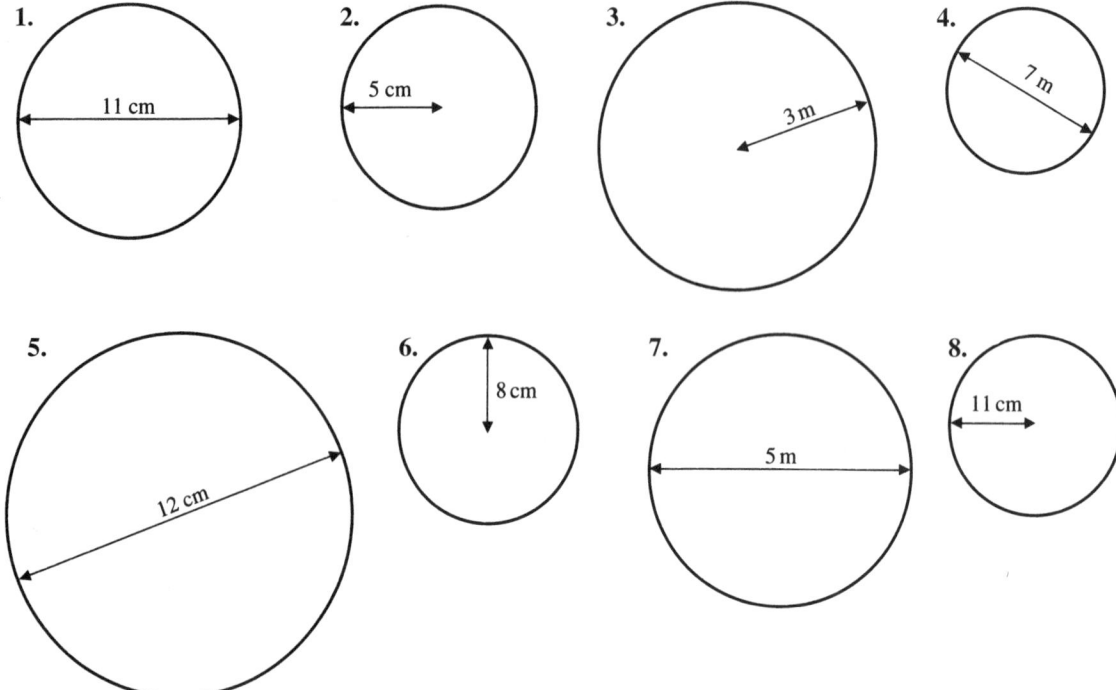

9. A spinner of radius 7·5 cm is divided into six equal sectors. Calculate the area of each sector.

10. A circular swimming pool of diameter 12·6 m is to be covered by a plastic sheet to keep out leaves and insects.
    Work out the surface area it must cover.

11. A circle of radius 5 cm is inscribed inside a square as shown. Find the area shaded.

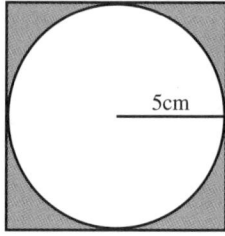

12. A large circular lawn is sprayed with weedkiller. Each square metre of grass requires 2 g of weedkiller. How much weedkiller is needed for a lawn of radius 27 m?

13. Discs of radius 4 cm are cut from a rectangular plastic sheet of length 84 cm and width 24 cm.

How many complete discs can be cut out? Find
(a) the total area of the discs cut
(b) the area of the sheet wasted.

14. A circular pond of radius 6 m is surrounded by a path of width 1 m.
(a) Find the area of the path.
(b) The path is resurfaced with astroturf which is bought in packs each containing enough to cover an area of 7 m². How many containers are required?

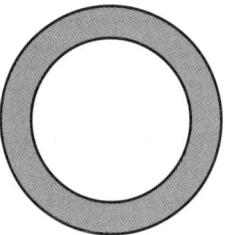

15. The diagram below shows a lawn (unshaded) surrounded by a path of uniform width (shaded). The curved end of the lawn is a semicircle of diameter 10 m.

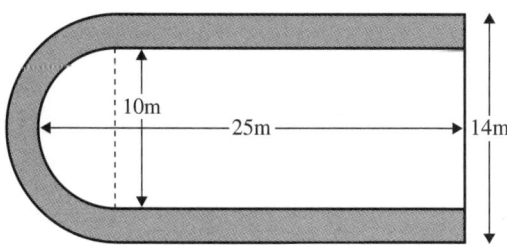

Calculate the total area of the path.

More complicated shapes

Example

For the shape below find:

(a) the perimeter (b) the area.

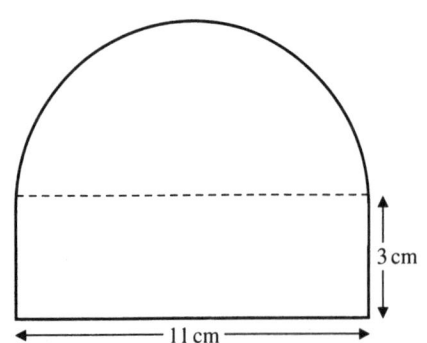

(a) Perimeter $= \left(\dfrac{\pi \times 11}{2}\right) + 11 + 3 + 3$

$= 34{\cdot}3$ cm (3 s.f.)

(b) Area $= \left(\dfrac{\pi \times 5{\cdot}5^2}{2}\right) + (11 \times 3)$

$= 80{\cdot}5\ \text{cm}^2$ (3 s.f.)

Exercise 14

Use the π button on a calculator or take $\pi = 3{\cdot}142$. Give the answers correct to 3 s.f. For each shape find the perimeter.

1.

2.

3.

4.

5.

6.

7.

8.

9.

10.

11.

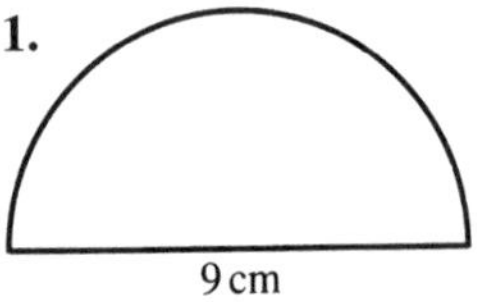

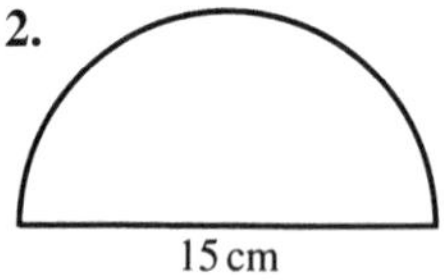

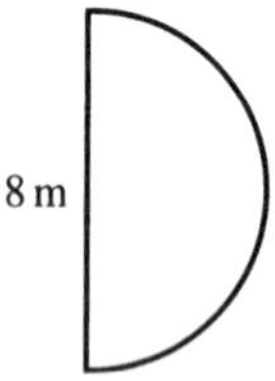

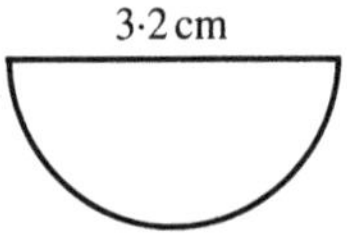

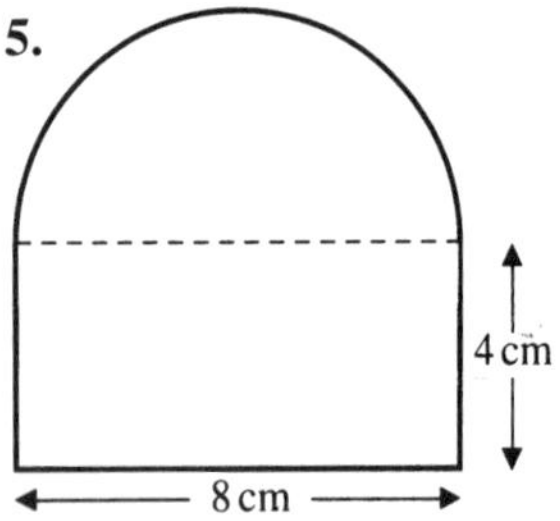

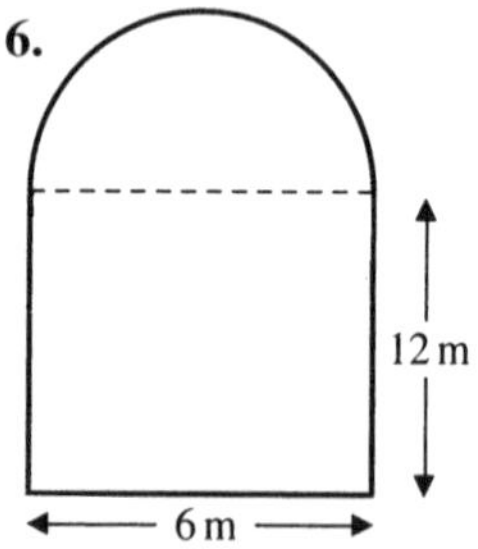

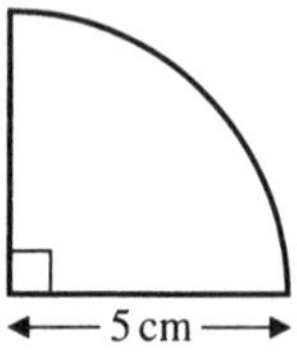

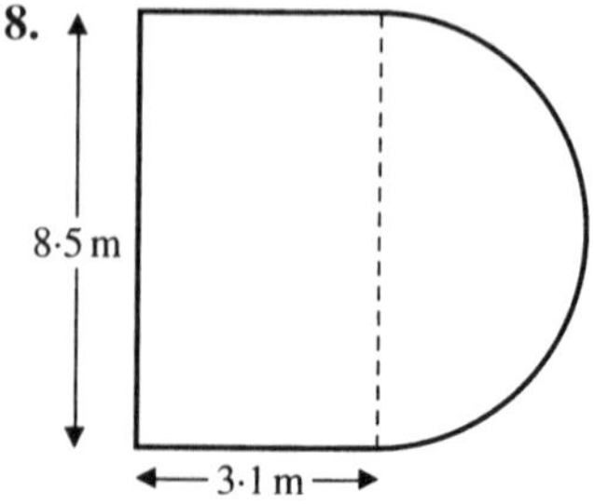

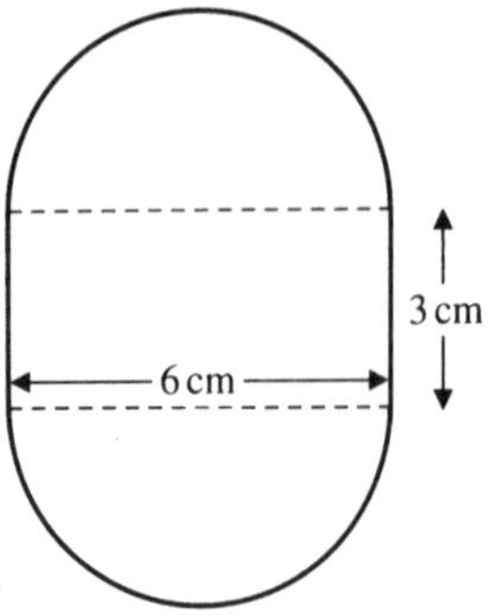

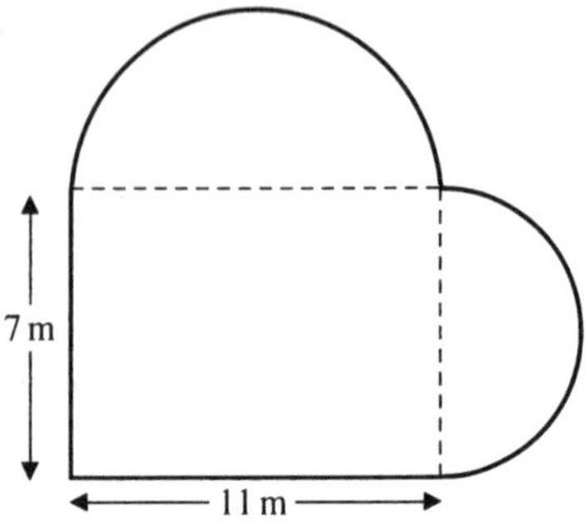

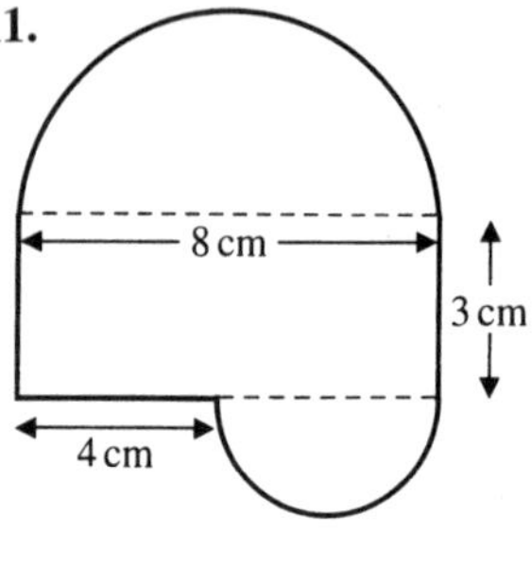

Exercise 15

Find the area of each shape. All lengths are in cm.
In Questions **4, 5, 6** find the shaded area.

1.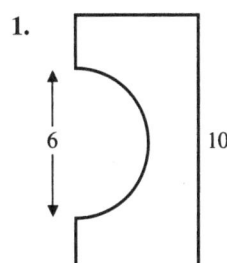

2.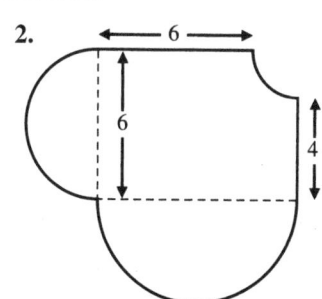

3.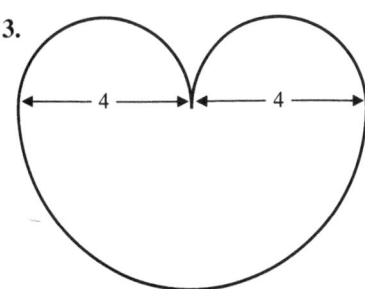

4.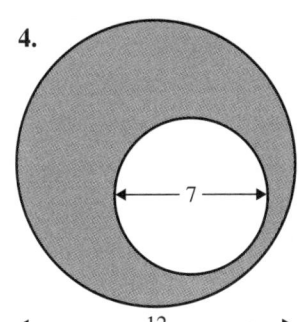

5.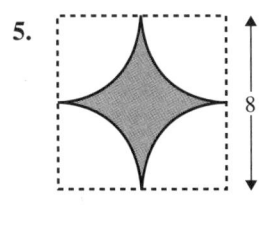

6.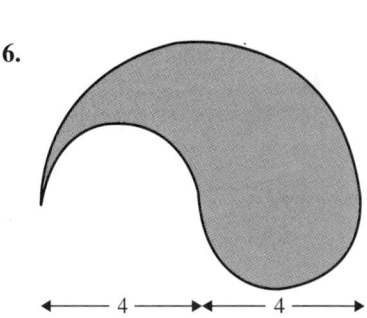

7. (a) Find the area of triangle OAD.
   (b) Hence find the area of the square ABCD.
   (c) Find the area of the circle.
   (d) Hence find the shaded area.

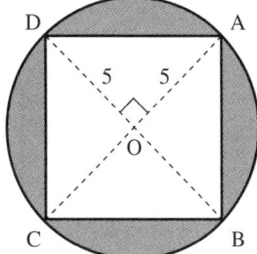

Finding the radius of a circle

Sometimes it is difficult to measure the diameter of a circle but it is fairly easy to measure the circumference.

Example

(a) The circumference of a circle is 60 cm.
Find the radius of the circle.

$$C = \pi d$$
$$\therefore 60 = \pi d$$
$$\therefore \frac{60}{\pi} = d$$
$$\therefore r = \frac{(60/\pi)}{2} = 9.55 \text{ cm (to 3 s.f.)}$$

(b) The area of a circle is 18 m².
Find the radius of the circle.

$$\pi r^2 = 18$$
$$r^2 = \frac{18}{\pi}$$
$$r = \sqrt{\left(\frac{18}{\pi}\right)} = 2.39 \text{ m (to 3 s.f.)}$$

24 Shape and space 1

Exercise 16

In Questions **1** to **10** use the information given to calculate the radius of the circle. Use the π button on a calculator or take π = 3·142.

1. The circumference is 15 cm.
2. The circumference is 28 m.
3. The circumference is 7 m.
4. The area is 54 cm^2.
5. The area is 38 cm^2.
6. The area is 49 m^2.
7. The circumference is 16 m.
8. The area is 60 cm^2.
9. The circumference is 29 cm.
10. The area is 104 cm^2.

11. An odometer is a wheel used for measuring long distances. The circumference of the wheel is exactly one metre.
    Find the radius of the wheel.

12. A sheet of paper is 32 cm by 20 cm. It is made into a hollow cylinder of height 20 cm with no overlap.

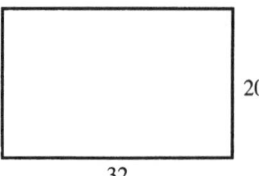 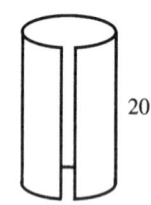

    Find the radius of the cylinder.

13. The area of the centre circle on a football pitch is 265 m^2. Calculate the radius of the circle to the nearest 0·1 m.

14. Eight sections of curved railway track can be joined to make a circular track.
    Each section is 23 cm long.
    Calculate the diameter of the circle.

15. Calculate the radius of a circle whose area is equal to the sum of the areas of three circles of radii 2 cm, 3 cm and 4 cm.

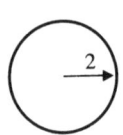 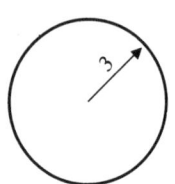 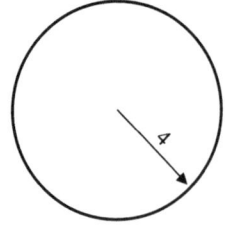

16. The handle of a paint tin is a semicircle of wire which is 28 cm long.
    Calculate the diameter of the tin.

17. A television transmitter is designed so that people living inside a circle of area 120 000 km² can receive pictures.
    What is the radius of this reception circle?
    Give your answer to the nearest km.

18. The circle and the square have the same area.
    Find the radius of the circle.

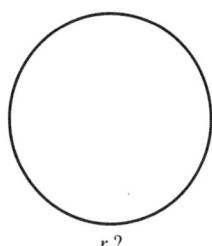 

19. The circumference of this circle is 52 m.
    Find its area.

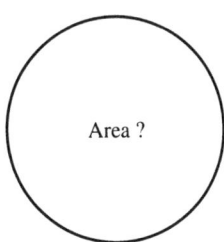

20. The area of a circular target is 1·2 m². Find the circumference of the target.

21. The perimeter of a circular pond is 85 m long. Work out the area of the pond.

22. The sector shown is one quarter of a circle and has an area of 23 cm².
    Find the radius of the circle.

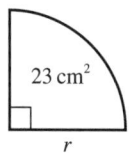

23. 'Muirfield' grass seed is sown at a rate of 40 grams per square metre and one box contains 2·5 kg. The seed is just enough to sow a circular lawn. Calculate the radius of this lawn to the nearest 0·1 metre.

1.6 Area

Rectangle and triangle

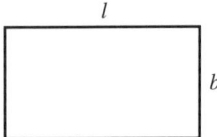
Rectangle:
area = $l \times b$

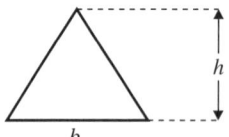
Triangle:
area = $\dfrac{b \times h}{2}$

Exercise 17

Work out the area. All lengths are in cm.

1.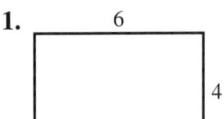

2.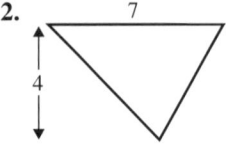

3.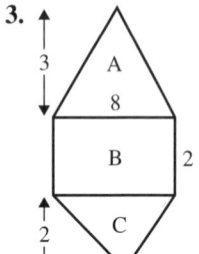

4.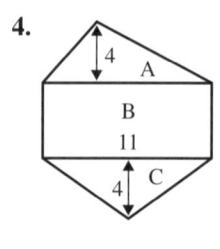

5.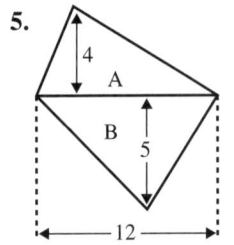

6.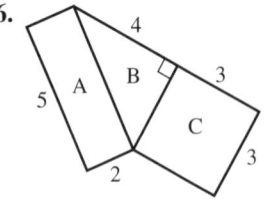

7.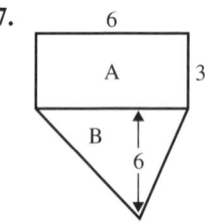

8.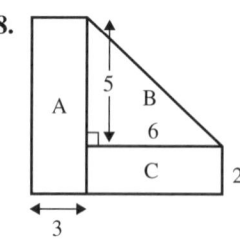

9.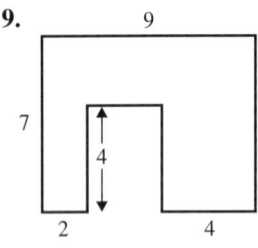

10.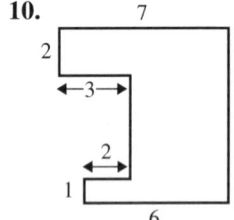

11.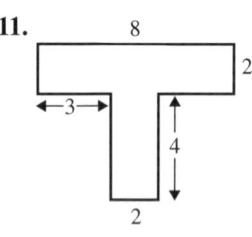

12.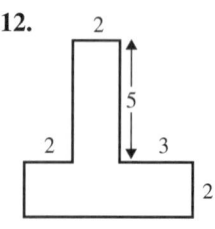

13.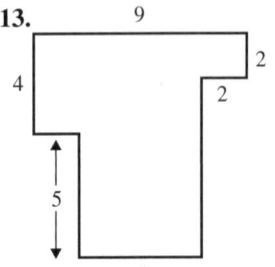

14.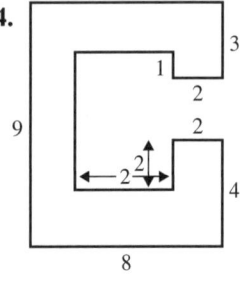

15.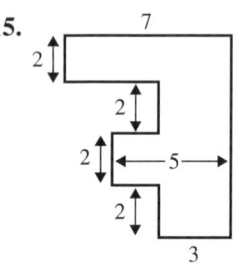

16.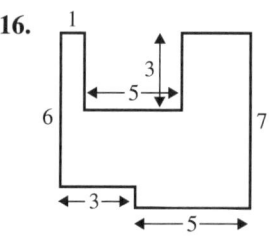

Area 27

Exercise 18

A decorator works out how many rolls of wallpaper he needs for a room from the table below.

Height from skirting	Measurement round walls (including doors and windows) in metres									
	8·6	9·8	11·0	12·2	13·4	14·6	15·8	17·0	18·2	19·4
2·20 m	4	4	5	5	6	6	7	7	8	8
2·35 m	4	4	5	5	6	6	7	8	8	9
2·50 m	4	5	5	6	6	7	7	8	8	9
2·65 m	4	5	5	6	6	7	8	8	9	9
2·80 m	4	5	6	6	7	7	8	9	9	10
2·95 m	5	5	6	7	7	8	9	9	10	10
3·10 m	5	5	6	7	8	8	9	10	10	11

1. A plan of one room is shown.
   Work out:
   (a) the total length round the walls (the perimeter).
   (b) the number of rolls of wallpaper he needs.
   (c) the total cost of the wallpaper if one roll costs $3·20.
   (d) the area of the ceiling of the room.

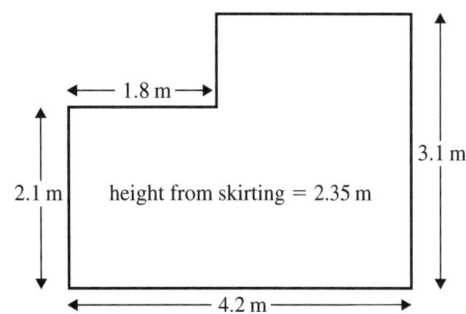

2. Work out the answers to parts (a), (b), (c) and (d) for each of the rooms shown below.

   A.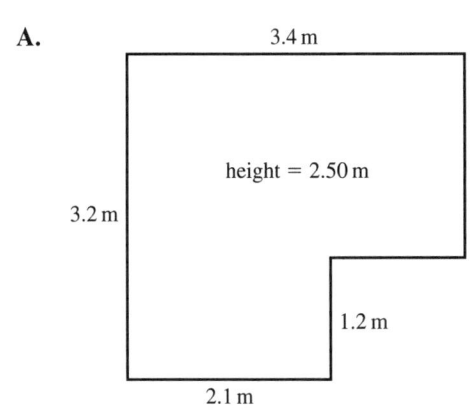

   B.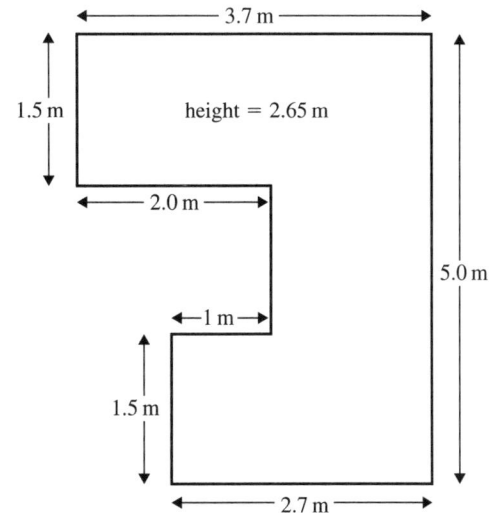

Exercise 19

1. (a) Copy the diagram.
   (b) Work out the areas of triangles A, B and C.
   (c) Work out the area of the square enclosed by the broken lines.
   (d) Hence work out the area of the shaded triangle. Give the answer in square units.

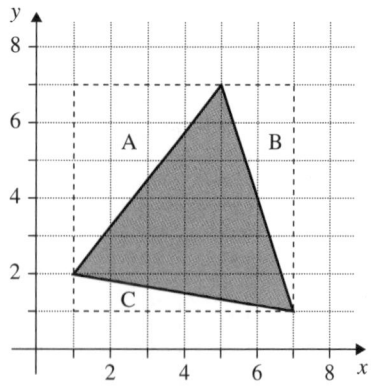

2. (a) Copy the diagram.
   (b) Work out the areas of triangles A, B and C.
   (c) Work out the area of the rectangle enclosed by the broken lines.
   (d) Hence work out the area of the shaded triangle. Give the answer in square units.

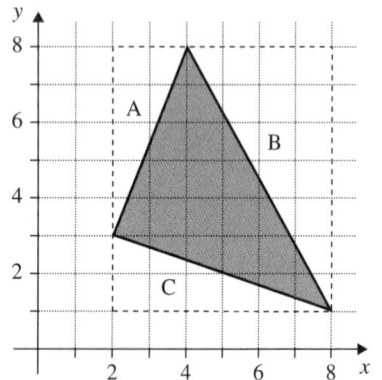

For Questions **3** to **7**, draw a pair of axes similar to those in Questions **1** and **2**. Plot the points in the order given and find the area of the shape enclosed.

3. (1,4), (6,8), (4,1)

4. (1,7), (8,5), (4,2)

5. (2,4), (6,1), (8,7), (4,8), (2,4)

6. (1,4), (5,1), (7,6), (4,8), (1,4)

7. (1,6), (2,2), (8,6), (6,8), (1,6)

8. A wooden cuboid has the dimensions shown.
   (a) Calculate the total surface area.
   (b) The cuboid is painted using paint from a tin sufficient to cover 3 m². How many cuboids can be painted using the paint in one tin?

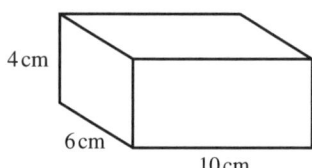

Trapezium and parallelogram

Trapezium (two parallel sides)

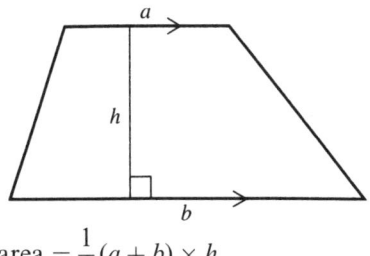

area = $\frac{1}{2}(a+b) \times h$

Parallelogram

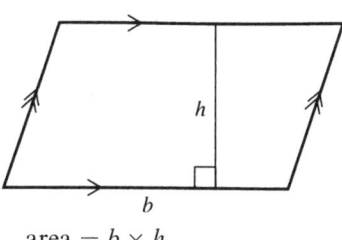

area = $b \times h$

Exercise 20

Find the area of each shape. All lengths are in cm.

1.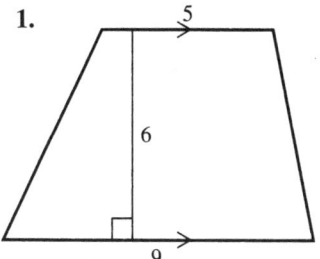

2.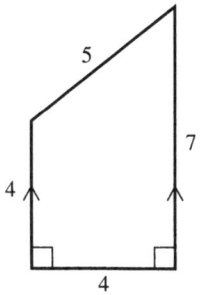

3.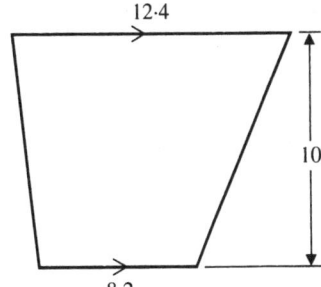

4.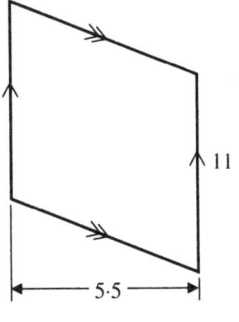

5.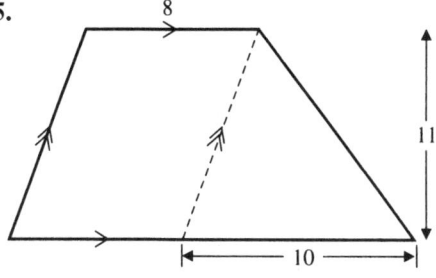

6.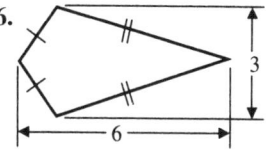

7.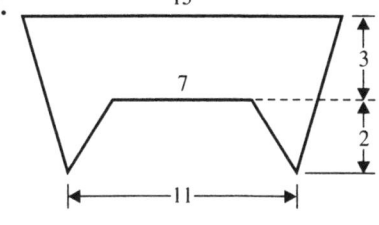

8.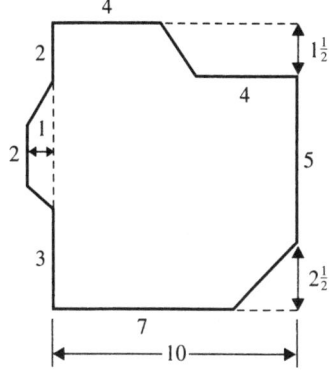

30   Shape and space 1

9. Large areas of land are measured in hectares. One
hectare = 10 000 m². The Imperial unit, used in the past,
is the acre. One hectare is approximately 2.5 acres.
Copy and complete the statements below:

(a)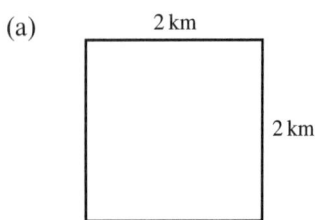

area of square = _____ m²
area of square = _____ hectares

(b)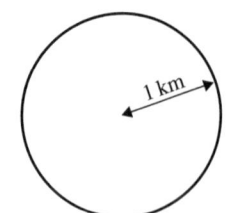

area of circle = _____ hectares
area of circle is
approximately _____ acres

10. The field shown is sprayed at the rate of
2 litres per hectare. The cost of the spray is
$25 for 100 litres.
How much will it cost to spray this field, to
the nearest dollar?

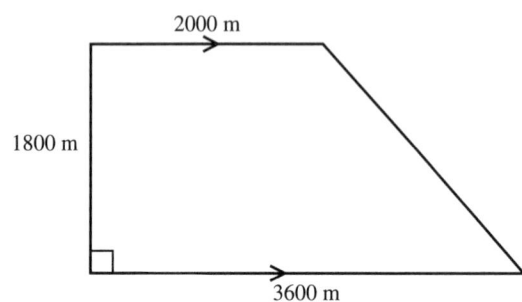

Designing square patterns

The object is to design square patterns of different sizes. The patterns
are all to be made from smaller tiles all of which are themselves square.
Designs for a 4 × 4 square:

(a)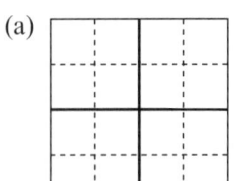

This design consists of four tiles each 2 × 2.
The pattern is rather dull.

(b) Suppose we say that the design must contain at least
one 1 × 1 square.

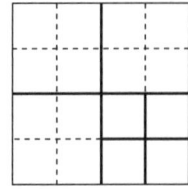

This design is more interesting and consists
of seven tiles.

Exercise 21

1. Try the 5 × 5 square. Design a pattern which divides the 5 × 5 square into eight smaller squares.

2. Try the 6 × 6 square. Here you must include at least one 1 × 1 square. Design a pattern which divides the 6 × 6 square into nine smaller squares. Colour in the final design to make it look interesting.

3. The 7 × 7 square is more difficult. With no restrictions, design a pattern which divides the 7 × 7 square into nine smaller squares.

4. Design a pattern which divides an 8 × 8 square into ten smaller squares. You must not use a 4 × 4 square.

5. Design a pattern which divides a 9 × 9 square into ten smaller squares. You can use only one 3 × 3 square.

6. Design a pattern which divides a 10 × 10 square into eleven smaller squares. You must include a 3 × 3 square.

7. Design a pattern which divides an 11 × 11 square into eleven smaller squares. You must include a 6 × 6 square.

1.7 Volume

Prisms and cuboids

A prism is an object with a uniform cross-section.

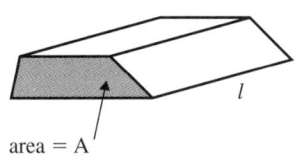

area = A

Volume = $A \times l$

A cuboid is a prism whose cross-section is a rectangle.

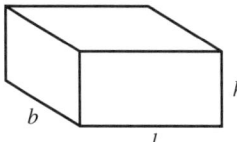

Volume = $l \times b \times h$

Exercise 22

Find the volume of each prism.

1.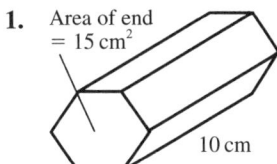
Area of end = 15 cm²
10 cm

2.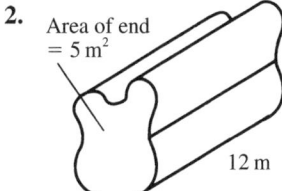
Area of end = 5 m²
12 m

3.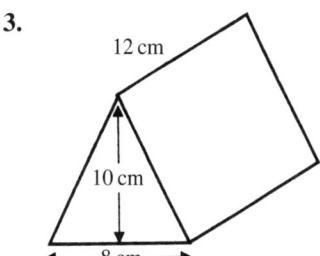
12 cm
10 cm
8 cm

32 Shape and space 1

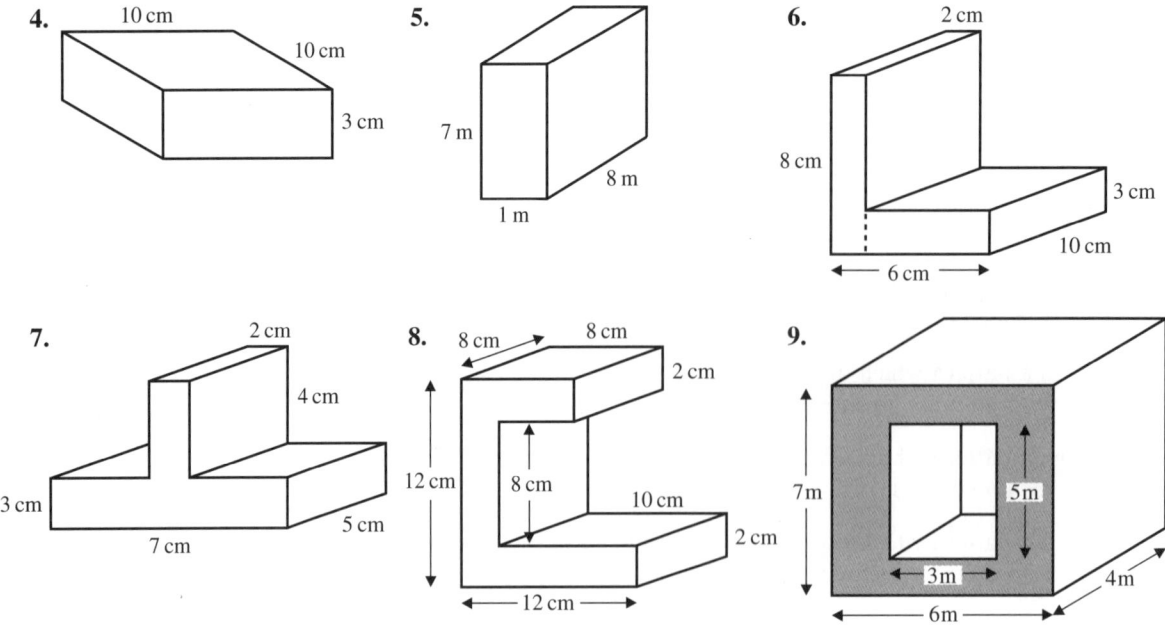

Cylinders

A cylinder is a prism with a circular cross-section

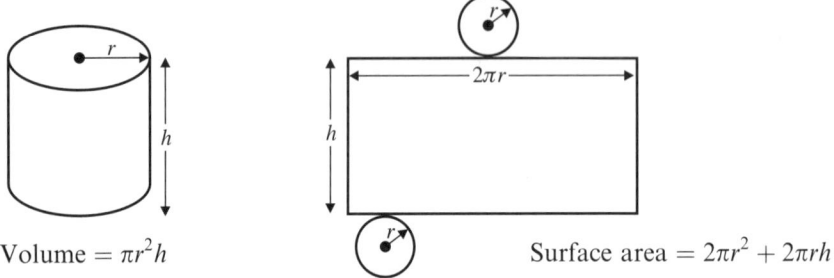

Volume = $\pi r^2 h$ Surface area = $2\pi r^2 + 2\pi rh$

Exercise 23

Find the volume and surface area of each cylinder. Use the π button on a calculator or use $\pi = 3.142$. Give the answers correct to 3 s.f.

1.
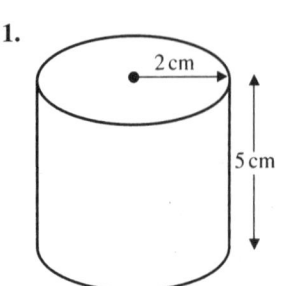

2.
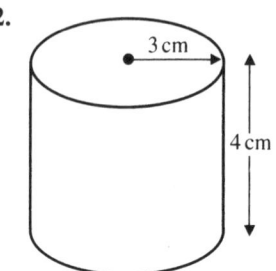

3.
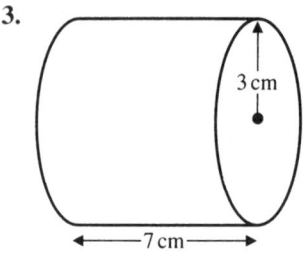

Volume 33

4.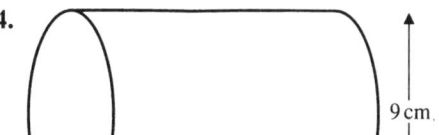
5.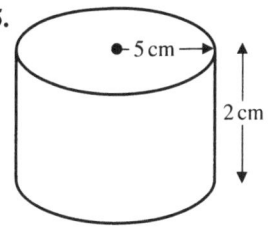
6.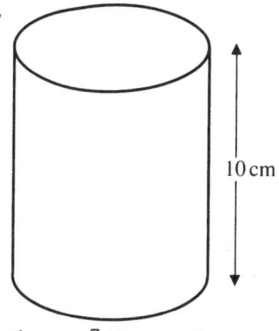

7. radius = 7 cm, height = 5 cm
8. diameter = 8 m, height = 3·5 m
9. diameter = 11 m, height = 2·4 m
10. radius = 3·2 cm, height = 15·1 cm

11. Find the capacity in litres of the oil drum shown below. (1000 cm^3 = 1 litre)

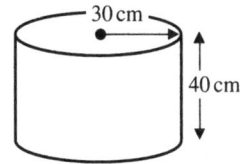

12. Cylinders are cut along the axis of symmetry to form the objects below. Find the volume of each object.

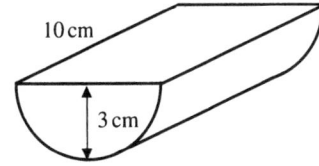 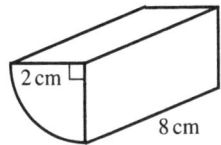

Exercise 24

This exercise contains a mixture of questions involving the volumes of a wide variety of different objects.
Where necessary give answers correct to 3 s.f.

1. A cylindrical bar has a cross-sectional area of 12 cm^2 and a length of two metres. Calculate the volume of the bar in cm^3.

2. The diagram represents a building.
    (a) Calculate the area of the shaded end.
    (b) Calculate the volume of the building.

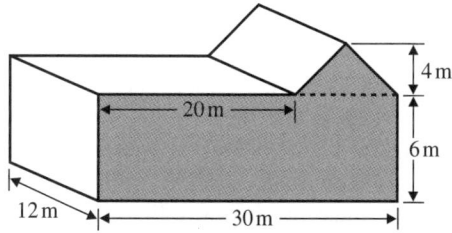

3. A rectangular block has dimensions 20 cm × 7 cm × 7 cm.
   Find the volume of the largest solid cylinder which can be cut from this block.

4. Brass washers are to be made 2 mm thick with a circular cross-section as shown below.

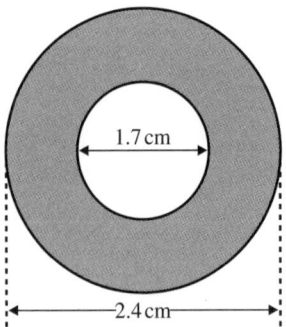

   (a) Find the area of the flat surface of the washer.
   (b) Calculate the volume of the washer.
   (c) Find in cm^3 the volume of brass needed to make 10 000 of these washers.

5. A cylindrical water tank has internal diameter 40 cm and height 50 cm and a cylindrical mug has internal diameter 8 cm and height 10 cm. If the tank is initially full, how many mugs can be filled from the tank?

6. The diagram shows the cross-section of a steel girder which is 4 m long.

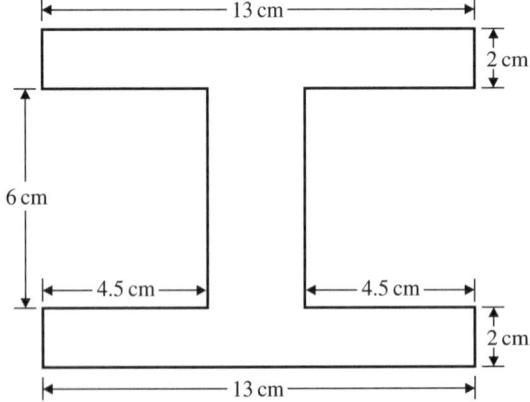

   (a) Calculate the cross-sectional area in cm^2.
   (b) Calculate the volume of the girder in cm^3.
   (c) If 1 cm^3 of steel weighs 7·8 g find the weight of the girder in kg.
   (d) How many girders can be carried on a lorry if its total load must not be more than 8 tonnes? (1 tonne = 1000 kg)

7. In the diagram all the angles are right angles and the lengths are in cm.
Find the volume.

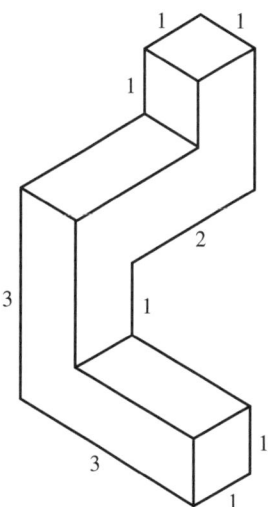

8. Fernando builds a fence at the end of his garden. The planks for the fence measure 1 m by 12 cm by 1 cm. The posts to which the planks are nailed are 10 cm square in cross section and 1·40 m long.

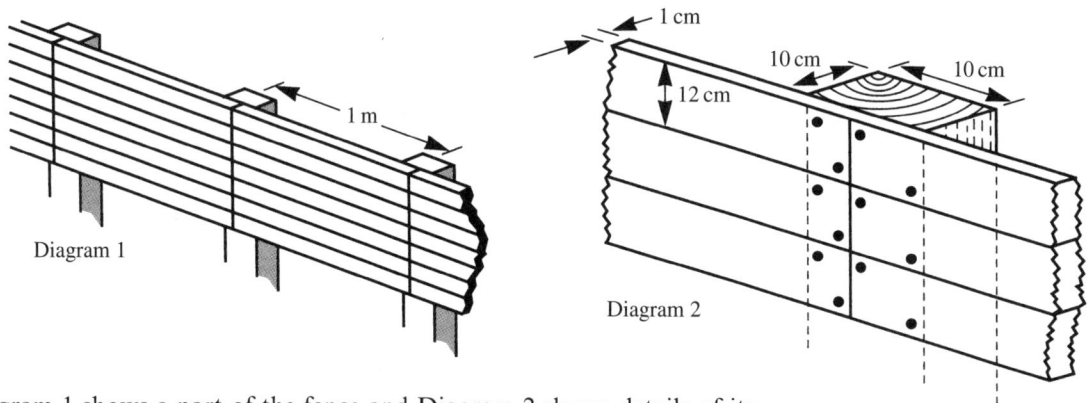

Diagram 1 shows a part of the fence and Diagram 2 shows details of its construction.
(a) How many planks are there between each pair of posts?
(b) If the fence is 5 m long,
    (i) how many planks are needed?
    (ii) how many posts are needed?
        (There is a post at each end of the fence.)
(c) Calculate the volume in cm³ of:
    (i) each plank
    (ii) each post
(d) Wood of the required quality costs 4c per 100 cm³, irrespective of the thickness. Calculate the cost of:
    (i) each plank
    (ii) each post
    (iii) all the wood for the whole fence.
(e) Each end of a plank is nailed to a post with two nails.
How many nails are needed for the whole fence?

36   Shape and space 1

9. Mr Gibson decided to build a garage and began by calculating the number of bricks required. The garage was to be 6 m by 4 m and 2·5 m in height. Each brick measures 22 cm by 10 cm by 7 cm. Mr Gibson estimated that he would need about 40 000 bricks. Is this a reasonable estimate?

10. A cylindrical metal pipe has external diameter of 6 cm and internal diameter of 4 cm. Calculate the volume of metal in a pipe of length 1 m. If 1 cm^3 of the metal weighs 8 g find the weight of the pipe.

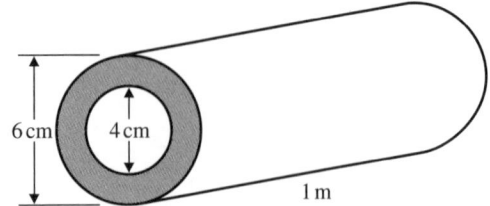

11. A cylindrical tin of height 15 cm and radius 4 cm is filled with sand from a rectangular box. How many times can the tin be filled if the dimensions of the box are 50 cm by 40 cm by 20 cm?

12. Rain which falls onto a flat rectangular surface of length 6 m and width 4 m is collected in a cylinder of internal radius 20 cm. What is the depth of water in the cylinder after a storm in which 1 cm of rain fell?

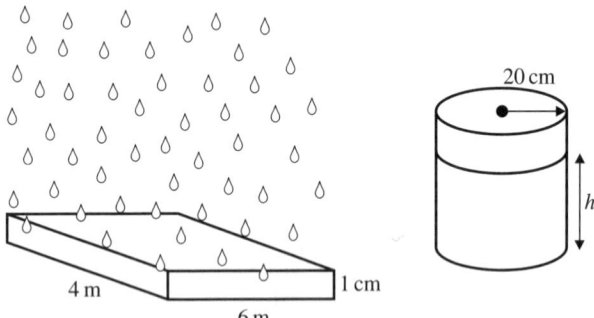

13. Water pours into the trough shown at a rate of 2 litres/min. How long, to the nearest minute, will it take to fill the trough?

14. Water is poured from the cylindrical bottle shown into ice-cube moulds which are then put in a freezer. How many complete ice cubes of side 2·5 cm can be made?

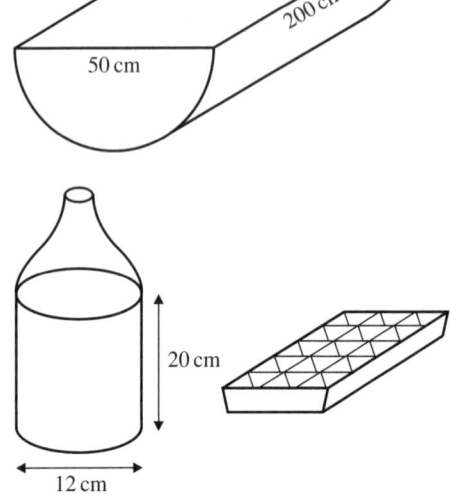

Revision exercise 1A

1. Which of the nets below can be used to make a cube?

   (a) 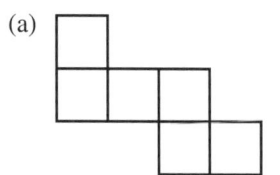 (b)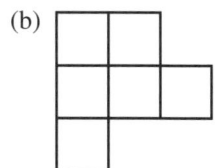

   (c)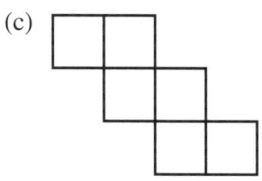

2. Find the area, correct to 3 s.f.

   (a) 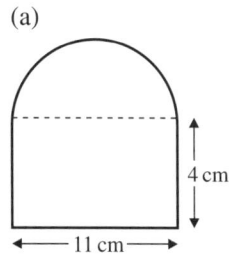 (b)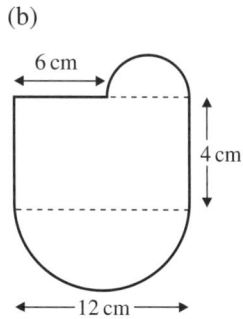

3. The faces of a round and square clock are exactly the same area. If the round clock has a radius of 10 cm, how wide is the square clock?

    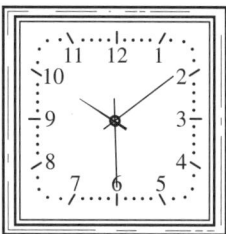

4. A metal ingot is in the form of a solid cylinder of length 7 cm and radius 3 cm.
   (a) Calculate the volume, in cm³, of the ingot.

   The ingot is to be melted down and used to make cylindrical coins of thickness 3 mm and radius 12 mm.
   (b) Calculate the volume, in mm³, of each coin.
   (c) Calculate the number of coins which can be made from the ingot, assuming that there is no wastage of metal.

5. Two girls walk at the same speed from A to B. Aruni takes the large semicircle and Deepa takes the three small semicircles. Who arrives at B first?

6. The diagram shows a lawn in the shape of a rectangle from which two semicircles have been removed. The diameter of each semicircle is 7 metres.

   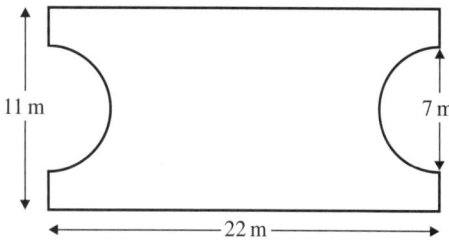

   Taking π as $\frac{22}{7}$, calculate, in metres, the perimeter of the lawn.

7. A swimming pool is of width 10 m and length 25 m. The depth of water in the pool increases uniformly from the shallow end, where the depth is 1·5 m to the deep end, where the depth is 2·5 m.
   (a) Calculate the volume of water in the pool.
   (b) This water is emptied into a cylindrical tank of radius 3·5 m. Calculate the depth of water in the tank.

8. In Figure 1 a circle of radius 4 cm is inscribed in a square. In Figure 2 a square is inscribed in a circle of radius 4 cm.
Calculate the shaded area in each diagram.

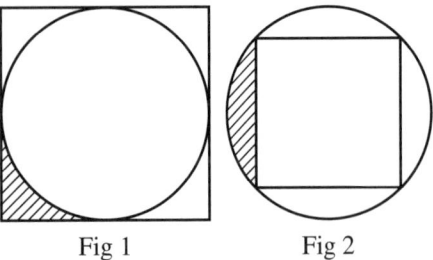

Fig 1   Fig 2

9. A cylinder of radius 8 cm has a volume of 2 litres. Calculate the height of the cylinder.

10. Twenty-seven small wooden cubes fit exactly inside a cubical box without a lid.
How many of the cubes are touching the sides or the bottom of the box?

11. The square has sides of length 3 cm and the arcs have centres at the corners.
Find the shaded area.

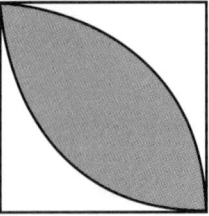

12. In the diagram the area of the smaller square is 10 cm². Find the area of the larger square.

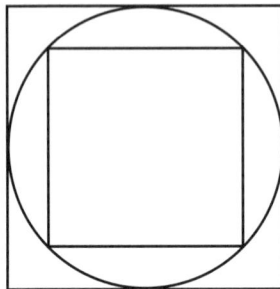

Examination exercise 1B

1. Draw an **accurate** net that could be used to make the square-based pyramid shown in the diagram. All edges are 3 cm long.

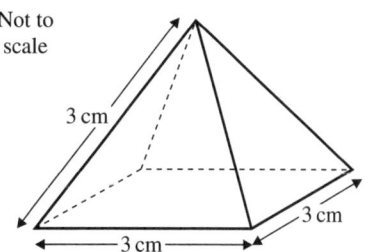

[N 95 1]

2. *ABCDEFGH* is a regular octagon inscribed in a circle, centre *O*.
   (a) Calculate:
       (i) angle *DOC*
       (ii) angle *OCD*
       (iii) angle *BCD*.
   (b) Why is the angle *AHE* a right angle?

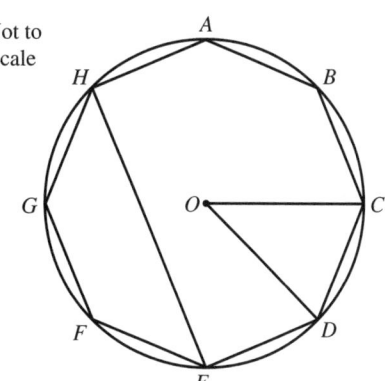

[N 97 1]

3. Describe fully the symmetry of the diagram.

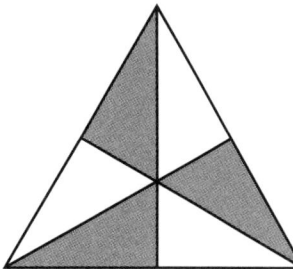

[J 98 1]

4.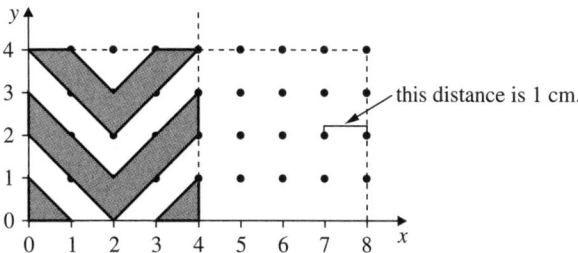

   (a) Consider the square in the diagram whose vertices are (0, 0), (4, 0), (4, 4) and (0, 4).
       (i) What is the ratio: Shaded area : Unshaded area?
       (ii) Given that the horizontal distance between two points is 1 cm, work out the size of the shaded area.
   (b) On a copy of the diagram, continue the pattern by translating it 4 cm to the right.

[N 95 1]

5 *PT* is a tangent to the circle, centre *O*.
The diameter *AOB* is parallel to *PT*.
POQ is a diameter.
QT and *AB* meet at *R*.
Angle *PTQ* = 58°.
Write down the size of:
(a) angle *PQT*
(b) angle *PAQ*
(c) angle *ORT*.

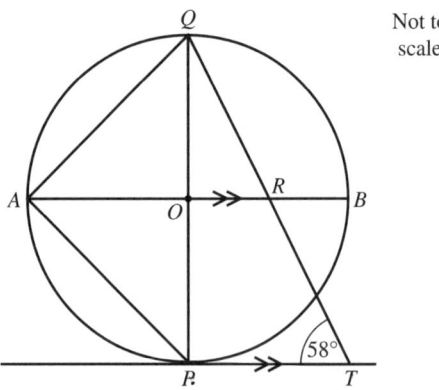

[N 98 1]

6. The diagram shows a design made of four overlapping circle, each of radius 10 cm. Each centre is shown on the diagram.
(a) On a copy of the diagram, draw the lines of symmetry of the design.
(b) Give the order of rotational symmetry of the design.
(c) Calculate the area of one of the circles of radius 10 cm, correct to one decimal place.
(d) The overlapping regions are shaded and each one has an area of 122.8 cm^2. Calculate the area of the design.
(e) Calculate the percentage of the area of the design which is shaded.

[N 96 3]

7. (a) Calculate the area of a circle of radius 3 cm.
   (b) (i) The diagram shows the cross-section of a circular ring, external **diameter** 8 cm and internal **diameter** 6 cm. Calculate the shaded area.

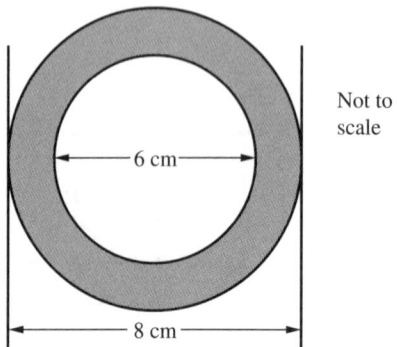

(ii)

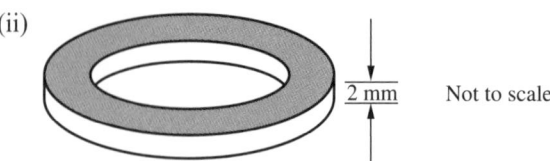

The ring is 2 millimetres thick. Calculate its volume, in cubic centimetres.

[J 97 3]

8.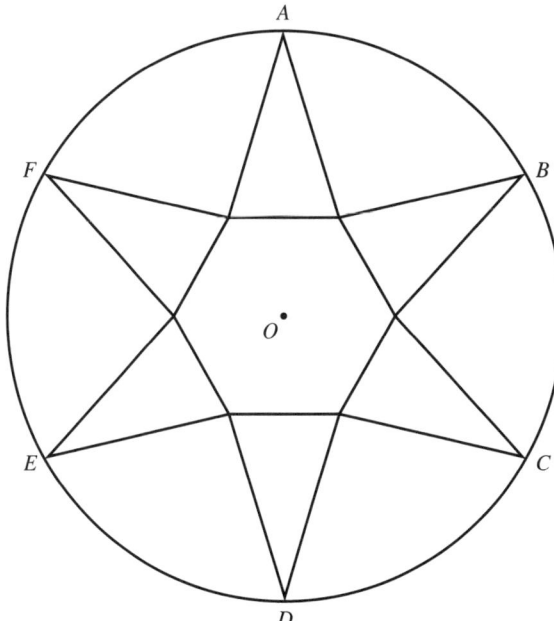

The diagram above is drawn accurately.
(a) The six-sided figure in the centre of the diagram has all its sides and angles equal. Write down its full geometrical name.
(b) What special type are the six triangles in the diagram?
(c) For the whole diagram,
   (i) state the number of lines of symmetry,
   (ii) describe any other symmetry as fully as possible.
(d) (i) Write down the size of angle AOB.
   (ii) If the direction $\overrightarrow{OA}$ is due North, write down the three-figure bearings of the points B, D and F from O.

[N 95 3]

9. [In this question, all pizzas are circular and the same thickness.]
(a) A small pizza has a diameter of 20 cm.
   (i) Write down the radius of a small pizza.
   (ii) Calculate the area of the top surface of a small pizza.
   (iii) If a small pizza costs $4, how many square centimetres of pizza do you get for $1?
(b) A restaurant makes pizzas in three sizes, as follows.

	Small	Medium	Large
Diameter	20 cm	24 cm	50 cm
Price	$4	$5	$25

Which size gives you the most pizza for $1?
You **must** show your working.

[J 95 3]

2 Algebra 1

2.1 Sequences

Exercise 1

1. Find the next number in each sequence.
   (a) 1, 5, 9, 13, ...
   (b) 39, 36, 33, 30, ...
   (c) 3, 6, 12, 24, ...
   (d) 4, 9, 15, 22, ...
   (e) 200, 100, 50, 25, ...
   (f) 88, 99, 110, ...

2. Write down each sequence and find the missing number.
   (a) 1, 6, ☐, 16
   (b) 1, 2, 4, 8, ☐
   (c) ☐, 2, 5, 8, 11
   (d) 2400, 240, 24, ☐
   (e) 1, 2, 4, 7, ☐, 16
   (f) 12, 8, 4, ☐, −4

3. Here is the start of a sequence: 1, 3, 4, ...
   Each new term is found by adding the last two terms.
   For example, $4 = 1 + 3$
   The next term will be 7.
   (a) Write down the next six terms.
   (b) Use the same rule to write down the next four terms of the sequence which starts 2, 5, 7, ...

4. (a) Write down the next two lines of the sequence:
   $3 \times 4 = 3 + 3^2$
   $4 \times 5 = 4 + 4^2$
   $5 \times 6 = 5 + 5^2$
   =
   =
   (b) Complete the lines below:
   $10 \times 11 =$
   $30 \times 31 =$

5. Copy the pattern and write down the next three lines.
   $1 + 9 \times 0 \quad = \quad 1$
   $2 + 9 \times 1 \quad = \quad 11$
   $3 + 9 \times 12 \quad = \quad 111$
   $4 + 9 \times 123 \quad = 1111$
   $5 + 9 \times 1234 =$

6. For the sequence 2, 3, 8, ... each new term is found by squaring the last term and then subtracting one.
   Write down the next two terms.

7. The sequence 3, 3, 5, 4, 4 is obtained by counting the letters in 'one, two, three, four, five, ...'.
Write down the next three terms.

8. The odd numbers 1, 3, 5, 7, 9, ... can be added to give an interesting sequence.

$$\begin{aligned} 1 &= 1 = 1 \times 1 \times 1 \\ 3 + 5 &= 8 = 2 \times 2 \times 2 \\ 7 + 9 + 11 &= 27 = 3 \times 3 \times 3 \\ 13 + 15 + 17 + 19 &= 64 = 4 \times 4 \times 4 \end{aligned}$$

1, 8, 27, 64 are *cube* numbers.
We write $2^3 = 8$ ['two cubed equals eight']
$\quad\quad\quad\quad 4^3 = 64$
Or the other way round:
$\sqrt[3]{8} = 2$ ['the cube root of eight equals two']
$\sqrt[3]{27} = 3$

(a) Continue adding the odd numbers in the same way as before. Do we *always* get a cube number?
(b) Write down:
   (i) $\sqrt[3]{125}$ (ii) $\sqrt[3]{1000}$ (iii) 11^3

9. (a) Write down the next three lines of this pattern.
$$\begin{aligned} 1^3 &= & 1^2 &= 1 \\ 1^3 + 2^3 &= & (1+2)^2 &= 9 \\ 1^3 + 2^3 + 3^3 &= & (1+2+3)^2 &= 36 \end{aligned}$$

(b) Work out as simply as possible:
$1^3 + 2^3 + 3^3 + 4^3 + 5^3 + 6^3 + 7^3 + 8^3 + 9^3 + 10^3$

10. Here is the sequence of the first six odd and even numbers.

	1st	2nd	3rd	4th	5th	6th
odd	1	3	5	7	9	11
even	2	4	6	8	10	12

Find (a) the 8th even number   (b) the 8th odd number
     (c) the 13th even number   (d) the 13th odd number.

You can use a rule to work out the answers.
(e) If the 57th even number is 114, what is the 57th odd number?
(f) Write down:
   (i) the 45th even number   (ii) the 53rd odd number
   (iii) the 100th odd number (iv) the 219th odd number.

44   Algebra 1

11. Here we have written the numbers in three columns.

(a) What number will you get on the right of:
   (i) line 8   (ii) line 12   (iii) line 25?

(b) Write down the number in the middle of:
   (i) line 8   (ii) line 12   (iii) line 20.

(c) What number will you get in:
   (i) line 10 on the left
   (ii) line 13 on the right
   (iii) line 17 in the middle
   (iv) line 30 on the left?

(d) Find the missing number:
   (i) 120 is on the right of line ____.
   (ii) 61 is on the left of line ____.
   (iii) 92 is in the middle of line ____.
   (iv) 148 is on the left of line ____.

Line

1	2	3	1
4	5	6	2
7	8	9	3
10	11	12	4
13	14	15	5
16	17	18	6
19	20	21	7

left ↗   ↑ middle   ↖ right

2.2 Solving equations

We can think of equations as weighing scales which are balanced. The scales stay balanced so long as you add or take away the same weight from both sides.
The same is true of equations.

Exercise 2

The scales are balanced. Work out the weight of the object x in each case. Each small weight □ is 1 kg.

1.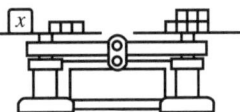

2.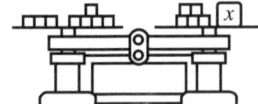

3.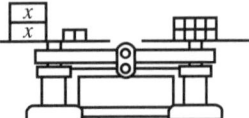

4.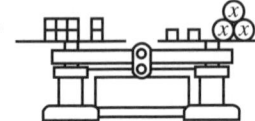

5.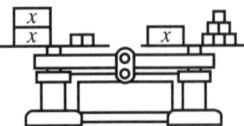

6.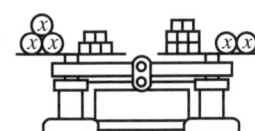

Solving equations

We solve equations by doing the same thing to both sides.

Example

Solve the equations.
(a) $x + 6 = 11$
$x = 11 - 6$ [take away 6]
$x = 5$

(b) $3x + 14 = 16$
$3x = 16 - 14$ [take away 14]
$3x = 2$
$x = \frac{2}{3}$ [divide by 3]

(c) $4x - 5 = -2$
$4x = -2 + 5$ [add 5]
$4x = 3$
$x = \frac{3}{4}$ [divide by 4]

(d) $7 = 2x + 15$
$-15 + 7 = 2x$ [take away 15]
$-8 = 2x$
$-4 = x$ [divide by 2]

Exercise 3

Solve the equations.
1. $x - 7 = 5$
2. $x + 11 = 20$
3. $x + 12 = 30$
4. $x - 6 = -2$
5. $x - 8 = 9$
6. $x + 5 = 0$
7. $x - 13 = -7$
8. $x + 10 = 3$
9. $5 + x = 9$
10. $9 + x = 17$
11. $y - 6 = 11$
12. $y + 8 = 3$
13. $3x + 1 = 16$
14. $4x + 3 = 27$
15. $2x - 3 = 1$
16. $5x - 3 = 1$

17. $3x - 7 = 0$
18. $2x + 5 = 20$
19. $6x - 9 = 2$
20. $7x + 6 = 6$
21. $9x - 4 = 1$
22. $11x - 10 = 1$
23. $15y + 2 = 5$
24. $7y + 8 = 10$
25. $4y - 11 = -8$
26. $3z - 8 = -6$
27. $4p + 25 = 30$
28. $5t - 6 = 0$
29. $9m - 13 = 1$
30. $4 + 3x = 5$
31. $7 + 2x = 8$
32. $5 + 20x = 7$

33. $3 + 8x = 0$
34. $50y - 7 = 2$
35. $200y - 51 = 49$
36. $5u - 13 = -10$
37. $9x - 7 = -11$
38. $11t + 1 = 1$
39. $3 + 8y = 40$
40. $12 + 7x = 2$
41. $6 = 3x - 1$
42. $8 = 4x + 5$
43. $9 = 2x + 7$
44. $11 = 5x - 7$
45. $0 = 3x - 1$
46. $40 = 11 + 14x$
47. $-4 = 5x + 1$
48. $-8 = 6x - 3$
49. $13 = 4x - 20$
50. $-103 = 2x + 7$

Equations with x on both sides

Example

Solve the equations.
(a) $8x - 3 = 3x + 1$
$8x - 3x = 1 + 3$
$5x = 4$
$x = \frac{4}{5}$

(b) $3x + 9 = 18 - 7x$
$3x + 7x = 18 - 9$
$10x = 9$
$x = \frac{9}{10}$

Exercise 4

1. $7x - 3 = 3x + 8$
2. $5x + 4 = 2x + 9$
3. $6x - 2 = x + 8$
4. $8x + 1 = 3x + 2$
5. $7x - 10 = 3x - 8$
6. $5x - 12 = 2x - 6$
7. $4x - 23 = x - 7$
8. $8x - 8 = 3x - 2$
9. $11x + 7 = 6x + 7$
10. $9x + 8 = 10$
11. $5 + 3x = x + 8$
12. $4 + 7x = x + 5$
13. $6x - 8 = 4 - 3x$
14. $5x + 1 = 7 - 2x$
15. $6x - 3 = 1 - x$

16. $3x - 10 = 2x - 3$
17. $5x + 1 = 6 - 3x$
18. $11x - 20 = 10x - 15$
19. $6 + 2x = 8 - 3x$
20. $7 + x = 9 - 5x$
21. $3y - 7 = y + 1$
22. $8y + 9 = 7y + 8$
23. $7y - 5 = 2y$
24. $3z - 1 = 5 - 4z$
25. $8 = 13 - 4x$
26. $10 = 12 - 2x$
27. $13 = 20 - 9x$
28. $8 = 5 - 2x$
29. $5 + x = 7 - 8x$
30. $3x + 11 = 2 - 3x$

Example

Solve the equations.

(a) $3(x - 1) = 2(x + 7)$
$3x - 3 = 2x + 14$
$3x - 2x = 14 + 3$
$x = 17$

(b) $5(2x + 1) = 3(x - 2) + 20$
$10x + 5 = 3x - 6 + 20$
$10x - 3x = -6 + 20 - 5$
$7x = 9$
$x = 1\frac{2}{7}$

Exercise 5

Solve the equations.
1. $2(x + 1) = x + 5$
2. $4(x - 2) = 2(x + 1)$
3. $5(x - 3) = 3(x + 2)$
4. $3(x + 2) = 2(x - 1)$
5. $5(x - 3) = 2(x - 7)$
6. $6(x + 2) = 2(x - 3)$
7. $10(x - 3) = x$
8. $3(2x - 1) = 4(x + 1)$
9. $4(2x + 1) = 5(x + 3)$
10. $3(x - 1) + 7 = 2(x + 1)$
11. $5(x + 1) + 3 = 3(x - 1)$
12. $7(x - 2) - 3 = 2(x + 2)$
13. $5(2x + 1) - 5 = 3(x + 1)$
14. $3(4x - 1) - 3 = x + 1$
15. $2(x - 10) = 4 - 3x$
16. $3x + 2(x + 1) = 3x + 12$
17. $4x - 2(x + 4) = x + 1$
18. $2x - 3(x + 2) = 2x + 1$
19. $5x - 2(x - 2) = 6 - 2x$
20. $3(x + 1) + 2(x + 2) = 10$
21. $4(x + 3) + 2(x - 1) = 4$
22. $3(x - 2) - 2(x + 1) = 5$
23. $5(x - 3) + 3(x + 2) = 7x$
24. $3(2x + 1) - 2(2x + 1) = 10$
25. $4(3x - 1) - 3(3x + 2) = 0$

Equations with fractions

Example

Solve the equations.

(a) $\dfrac{7}{x} = 8$
$7 = 8x$
$\dfrac{7}{8} = x$

(b) $\dfrac{3x}{4} = 2$
$3x = 8$
$x = \dfrac{8}{3}$
$x = 2\frac{2}{3}$

Exercise 6

Solve the equations.

1. $\dfrac{3}{x} = 5$
2. $\dfrac{4}{x} = 7$
3. $\dfrac{11}{x} = 12$
4. $\dfrac{6}{x} = 11$
5. $\dfrac{2}{x} = 3$
6. $\dfrac{5}{y} = 9$
7. $\dfrac{7}{y} = 9$
8. $\dfrac{4}{t} = 3$
9. $\dfrac{3}{a} = 6$
10. $\dfrac{8}{x} = 12$
11. $\dfrac{3}{p} = 1$
12. $\dfrac{15}{q} = 10$
13. $\dfrac{x}{4} = 6$
14. $\dfrac{x}{5} = 3$
15. $\dfrac{y}{5} = -2$

16. $\dfrac{a}{7} = 3$ 17. $\dfrac{t}{3} = 7$ 18. $\dfrac{m}{4} = \dfrac{2}{3}$ 19. $\dfrac{x}{7} = \dfrac{5}{8}$ 20. $\dfrac{2x}{3} = 1$

21. $\dfrac{4x}{5} = 3$ 22. $\dfrac{3y}{2} = 2$ 23. $\dfrac{5t}{6} = 3$ 24. $\dfrac{m}{8} = \dfrac{1}{4}$ 25. $8 = \dfrac{5}{x}$

26. $19 = \dfrac{7}{y}$ 27. $-5 = \dfrac{3}{a}$ 28. $-6 = \dfrac{k}{4}$ 29. $\dfrac{n}{7} = -10$ 30. $4 = \dfrac{33}{q}$

31. $\dfrac{x}{2} = 110$ 32. $\dfrac{500}{y} = -1$ 33. $-99 = \dfrac{98}{f}$ 34. $\dfrac{x}{3} + 5 = 7$ 35. $\dfrac{x}{5} - 2 = 4$

36. $\dfrac{2x}{3} + 4 = 5$ 37. $\dfrac{x}{6} - 10 = 4$ 38. $\dfrac{6}{x} + 1 = 2$ 39. $\dfrac{5}{x} - 7 = 0$ 40. $5 + \dfrac{3}{x} = 10$

Exercise 7

In this exercise □, △, ○ and ∗ represent weights which are always balanced.

1. (a) 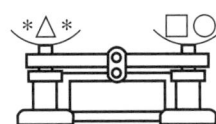   (b) 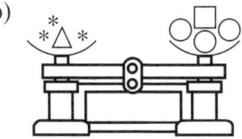   (c)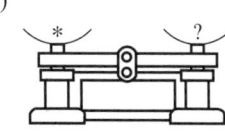

How many ○'s?

2. (a) 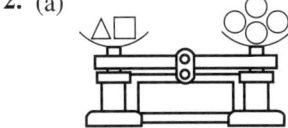   (b) 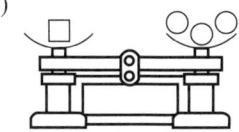   (c)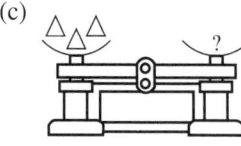

How many ○'s?

3. (a) ○ ○ □ = ∗ ∗
   (b) □ □ ○ = ∗ ∗ ○
   (c) □ = How many ○'s?

4. (a) □ ○ ○ = △ □ □
   (b) □ □ □ ○ = △ △ □
   (c) □ ○ = △ □
   (d) ○ = How many □'s?

5. (a) □ □ = ○ △
   (b) ○ ○ ○ □ = □ △
   (c) ○ □ □ □ = △ △ ○
   (d) □ = How many ○'s?

6. (a) ○ ○ □ = ∗ ○
   (b) ∗ ∗ = ○ ○ ○
   (c) □ ∗ = ○ ○
   (d) ∗ = How many □'s?

7. (a) ○ □ □ = △ ∗
   (b) ∗ ∗ ∗ = △ △
   (c) ○ □ = △
   (d) △ △ △ △ = How many □'s?

8. (a) ○ □ = △
   (b) ○ = □ ∗
   (c) ○ ○ □ = △ ∗ ∗
   (d) □ = How many ∗'s?

Solving problems with equations

Example
If I multiply a 'mystery' number by 2 and then add 3 the answer is 14. Find the 'mystery' number.

Let the mystery number be x.

Then $2x + 3 = 14$
$2x = 11$
$x = 5\frac{1}{2}$

The 'mystery' number is $5\frac{1}{2}$

Exercise 8

Find the 'mystery' number in each question by forming an equation and then solving it.

1. If I multiply the number by 3 and then add 4, the answer is 13.

2. If I multiply the number by 4 and then add 5, the answer is 8.

3. If I multiply the number by 2 and then subtract 5, the answer is 4.

4. If I multiply the number by 10 and then add 19, the answer is 16.

5. If I add 3 to the number and then multiply the result by 4, the answer is 10.

6. If we subtract 11 from the number and then treble the result, the answer is 20.

7. If we double the number, add 4 and then multiply the result by 3, the answer is 13.

8. If we treble the number, take away 6 and then multiply the result by 2, the answer is 18.

9. If we double the number and subtract 7 we get the same answer as when we add 5 to the number.

10. If we multiply the number by 5 and subtract 4, we get the same answer as when we add 3 to the number and then double the result.

11. If we multiply the number by 6 and add 1, we get the same answer as when we add 5 to the number and then treble the result.

12. If I add 5 to the number and then multiply the result by 4, I get the same answer as when I add 1 to the number and then multiply the result by 2.

Example

The length of a rectangle is twice the width.
If the perimeter is 36 cm, find the width.

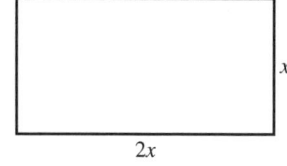

(a) Let the width of the rectangle be x cm.
Then the length of the rectangle is $2x$ cm.

(b) Form an equation.
$x + 2x + x + 2x = 36$

(c) Solve. $\quad 6x = 36$
$\quad\quad\quad\quad x = 6$

The width of the rectangle is 6 cm.

Exercise 9

Answer these questions by forming an equation and then solving it.

1. Find x if the perimeter is 7 cm.

   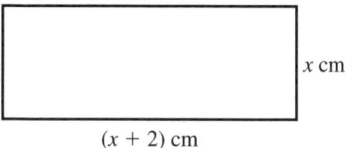

2. Find x if the perimeter is 5 cm.

   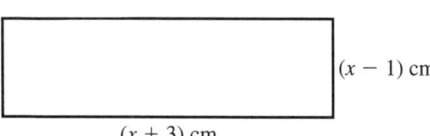

3. The length of a rectangle is 3 times its width. If the perimeter of the rectangle is 11 cm, find its width.
   Hint: Let the width be x cm.

4. The length of a rectangle is 4 cm more than its width. If its perimeter is 13 cm, find its width.

5. The width of a rectangle is 5 cm less than its length. If the perimeter of the rectangle is 18 cm, find its length.

6. Find x in the following rectangles:

   (a) 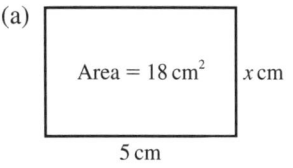   (b)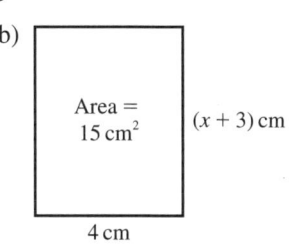

7. Find x in the following triangles:

(a)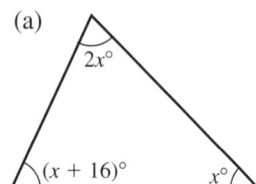

(b)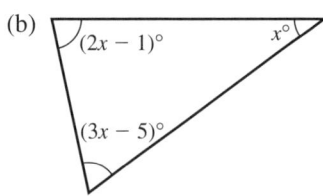

8. The angles of a triangle are 32°, x° and (4x + 3)°. Find the value of x.

9. Find a in the diagrams below

(a)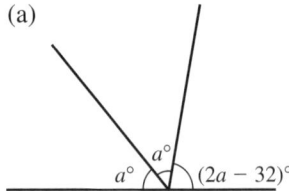

(b)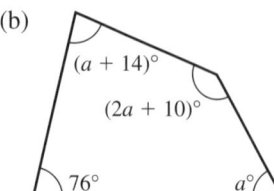

10. The sum of three consecutive whole numbers is 168. Let the first number be x. Form an equation and hence find the three numbers.

11. The sum of four consecutive whole numbers is 170. Find the numbers.

12. In this triangle AB = x cm.
BC is 3 cm shorter than AB.
AC is twice as long as BC.
(a) Write down, in terms of x, the lengths of:
   (i) BC
   (ii) AC
The perimeter of the triangle is 41 cm.
(b) Write down an equation in x and solve it to find x.

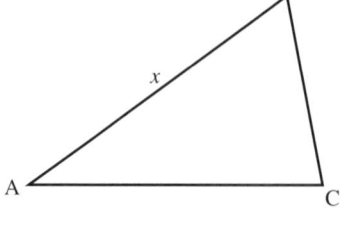

13. This is a rectangle. Work out x and hence find the perimeter of the rectangle.

14. Find the length of the sides of this equilateral triangle.

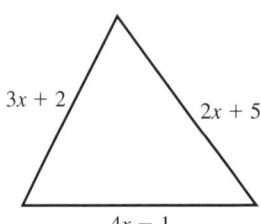

15. Petra has £12 and Suki has nothing. They both receive the same money for doing a delivery job.
Now Petra has three times as much as Suki.
How much did they get for the job?

16. The area of rectangle A is twice the area of rectangle B. Find x.

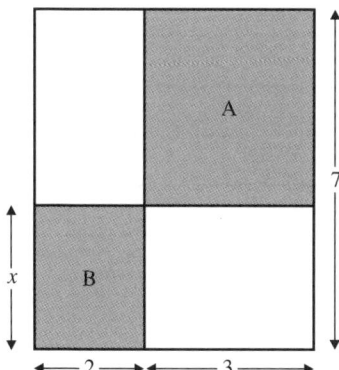

17. Pupils and teachers from Gibson College went on an outing to London in 4 full coaches. Two teachers had to go by train.

Unfortunately 3 of the coaches were parked illegally in London and their wheels were clamped. For the return journey there was one full coach and the other 143 pupils and teachers had to go back by train.

Use x to stand for the number of people in one full coach.
Make an equation involving x and solve it to find the number of people on a coach.

18. Cory has nine soft toys and she decides they each need a new ribbon.

She buys two long pieces of material to cut into nine equal ribbons.
From the first piece of material she cuts 7 ribbons and has 11 cm left over.
From the second piece of material she cuts 2 ribbons and has 146 cm left over.
How long is each ribbon?

2.3 Drawing graphs

Example
Draw the graph of $y = 4 - 2x$ for values of x from -2 to $+3$.

(a)

x	-2	-1	0	1	2	3
4	4	4	4	4	4	4
$-2x$	4	2	0	-2	-4	-6
y	8	6	4	2	0	-2

(b) Plot the values of x and y from the table.

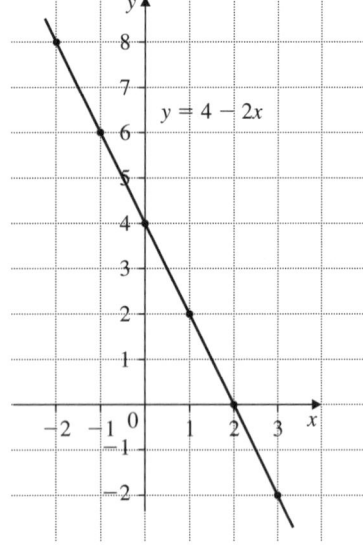

Exercise 10
For each question make a table of values and then draw the graph.
Suggested scales: 1 cm to 1 unit on both axes, unless otherwise stated.

1. $y = 2x + 1$; x from -3 to $+3$.

x	-3	-2	-1	0	1	2	3
$2x$	-6	-4					
$+1$	1	1	1				
y	-5	-3					

2. $y = 3x - 5$; x from -2 to $+3$.

3. $y = x + 2$; x from -4 to $+4$.

4. $y = 2x - 7$; x from -2 to $+5$.

5. $y = 4x + 1$; x from -3 to $+3$.
   (Use scales of 1 cm to 1 unit on the x-axis and 1 cm to 2 units on the y-axis.)

6. $y = x - 3$; x from -2 to $+5$.

7. $y = 2x + 4$; x from -4 to $+2$.

8. $y = 3x + 2$; x from -3 to $+3$.

9. $y = x + 7$; x from -5 to $+3$.

10. $y = 4x - 3$; x from -3 to $+3$.
    (Use scales of 1 cm to 1 unit on the x-axis and 1 cm to 2 units on the y-axis.)

11. $y = 4 - 2x$; x from -3 to $+3$.

x	-3	-2	-1	0	1	2	3
4	4	4	4	4			3
$-2x$	6	4					-6
y	10	8					-2

12. $y = 8 - 2x$; x from -2 to $+4$.

Curved graphs

Example

Draw the graph of $y = x^2 + x - 2$ for values of x from -3 to $+3$.

(a)

x	-3	-2	-1	0	1	2	3
x^2	9	4	1	0	1	4	9
$+x$	-3	-2	-1	0	1	2	3
-2	-2	-2	-2	-2	-2	-2	-2
y	4	0	-2	-2	0	4	10

(b) Plot the x and y values from the table.

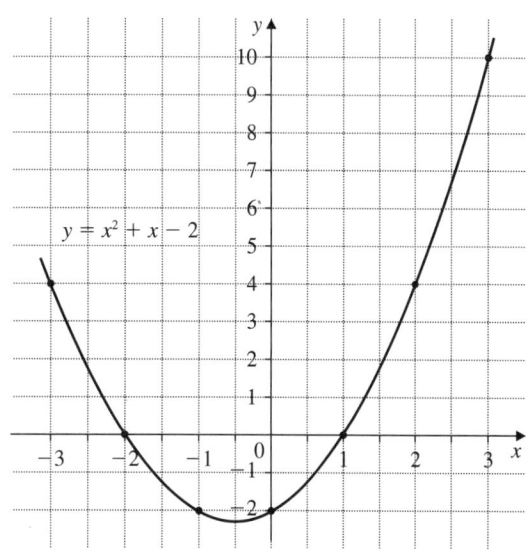

Exercise 11

For each question make a table of values and then draw the graph. Suggested scales: 2 cm to 1 unit on the x-axis and 1 cm to 1 unit on the y-axis.

1. $y = x^2 + 2$; x from -3 to $+3$.

x	-3	-2	-1	0	1	2	3
x^2	9	4	1	0	1		
$+2x$	2	2	2				
y	11	6	3				

2. $y = x^2 + 5$; x from -3 to $+3$.

3. $y = x^2 - 4$; x from -3 to $+3$.

4. $y = x^2 - 8$; x from -3 to $+3$.

5. $y = x^2 + 2x$; x from -4 to $+2$.

x	-4	-3	-2	-1	0	1	2
x^2	16	9					4
$+2x$	-8	-6					4
y	8	3					8

6. $y = x^2 + 4x$; x from -5 to $+1$.

7. $y = x^2 + 4x - 1$; x from -2 to $+4$.

8. $y = x^2 + 2x - 5$; x from -4 to $+2$.

9. $y = x^2 + 3x + 1$; x from -4 to $+2$.

These graphs are more difficult.

10. $y = x^3 + 1$; x from -3 to $+3$.
    Scales: 2 cm to 1 unit for x;
            1 cm to 5 units for y.

11. $y = \dfrac{12}{x}$; x from 1 to 12.

12. $y = 2x^2 + 3x - 1$; x from -4 to $+2$.
    Scales: 2 cm to 1 unit for x;
            1 cm to 1 unit for y.
    (Remember $2x^2 = 2(x^2)$. Work out x^2 and then multiply by 2.)

13. $y = \dfrac{16}{x}$; x from 1 to 10.
    Scales: 1 cm to 1 unit for x;
            1 cm to 1 unit for y.

14. A rectangle has a perimeter of 14 cm and length x cm. Show that the width of the rectangle is $(7 - x)$ cm and hence that the area A of the rectangle is given by the formula $A = x(7 - x)$.
    Draw the graph, plotting x on the horizontal axis with a scale of 2 cm to 1 unit, and A on the vertical axis with a scale of 1 cm to 1 unit. Take x from 0 to 7. From the graph find,
    (a) the area of the rectangle when $x = 2.25$ cm,
    (b) the dimensions of the rectangle when its area is 9 cm^2,
    (c) the maximum area of the rectangle,
    (d) the length and width of the rectangle corresponding to the maximum area.

Graphical solution of equations

Accurately drawn graphs enable approximate solutions to be found for a wide range of equations, many of which are impossible to solve exactly by other methods.

Example

Draw the graph of the function $y = 2x^2 - x - 3$ for $-2 \leqslant x \leqslant 3$ and use it to solve the equations:

$2x^2 - x - 3 = 6$ and $2x^2 - x - 3 = 0$

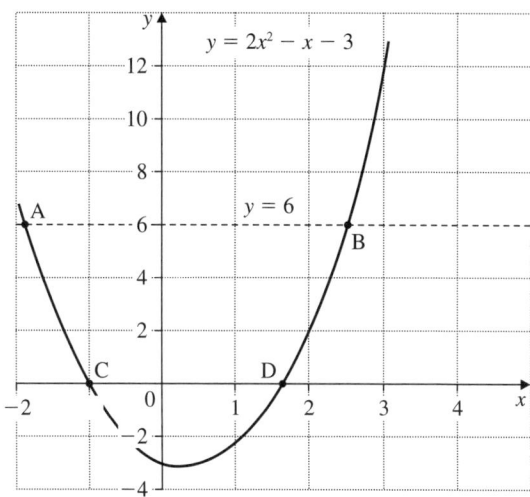

(a) To solve the equation

$2x^2 - x - 3 = 6$,

the line $y = 6$ is drawn.

At the points of intersection (A and B), y simultaneously equals both 6 and $(2x^2 - x - 3)$.

So we may write

$2x^2 - x - 3 = 6$

The solutions are the x-values of the points A and B, i.e. $x = -1{\cdot}9$ and $x = 2{\cdot}4$ approx.

(b) To solve the equation $2x^2 - x - 3 = 0$,

the line $y = 0$ is drawn.

[The line $y = 0$ is the x-axis.]

The solutions of the equation are given by the x-values of C and D where the curve cuts the x-axis,

i.e. $x = -1$ and $x = 1{\cdot}5$ approximately.

Exercise 12

1. In the diagram shown, the graphs of $y = x^2 - 2x - 3$, $y = 3$ and $y = -2$ have been drawn.

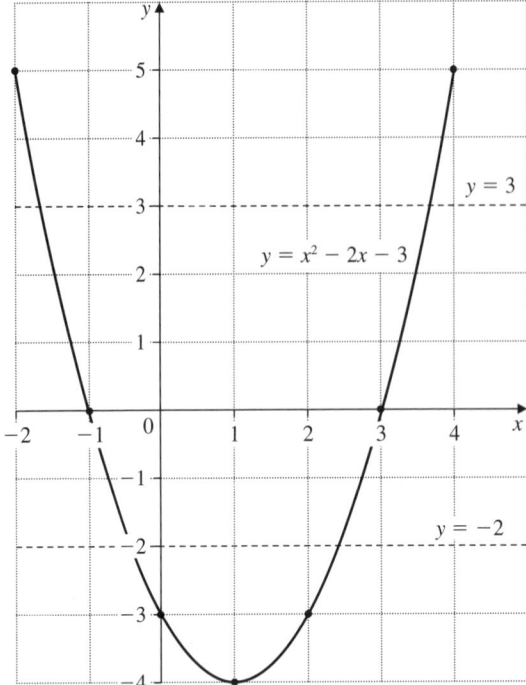

Use the graphs to find approximate solutions to the following equations:
(a) $x^2 - 2x - 3 = 3$ (b) $x^2 - 2x - 3 = -2$ (c) $x^2 - 2x - 3 = 0$

In Questions **2** to **5** use a scale of 2 cm to 1 unit for x and 1 cm to 1 unit for y.

2. Draw the graph of the function $y = x^2 - 2x$ for $-1 \leqslant x \leqslant 4$. Hence find approximate solutions of the equations
   (a) $x^2 - 2x = 1$
   (b) $x^2 - 2x = 0$

3. Draw the graph of the function $y = x^2 - 3x + 5$ for $-1 \leqslant x \leqslant 5$. Hence find approximate solutions of the equations
   (a) $x^2 - 3x + 5 = 5$
   (b) $x^2 - 3x + 5 = 8$

4. Draw the graph of $y = x^2 - 2x + 2$ for $-2 \leqslant x \leqslant 4$. By drawing other graphs, solve the equations
   (a) $x^2 - 2x + 2 = 8$
   (b) $x^2 - 2x + 2 = 3$

5. Draw the graph of $y = x^2 - 7x$ for $0 \leqslant x \leqslant 7$.
   (a) Use the graph to find approximate solutions of the equation $x^2 - 7x = -3$
   (b) Explain why the equation $x^2 - 7x = -14$ does not have a solution.

Revision exercise 2A

1. Write down each sequence and find the next two numbers.
   (a) 2, 9, 16, 23,
   (b) 20, 18, 16, 14,
   (c) −5, −2, 1, 4,
   (d) 128, 64, 32, 16,
   (e) 8, 11, 15, 20,

2. Solve the equations
   (a) $x - 6 = 3$
   (b) $x + 9 = 20$
   (c) $x - 5 = -2$
   (d) $3x + 1 = 22$

3. Solve the equations
   (a) $3x - 1 = 20$
   (b) $4x + 3 = 4$
   (c) $5x - 7 = -3$

4. Look at the number pattern below.
   $(2 \times 1) - 1 = 2 - 1$
   $(3 \times 3) - 2 = 8 - 1$
   $(4 \times 5) - 3 = 18 - 1$
   $(5 \times 7) - 4 = 32 - 1$
   $(6 \times a) - 5 = b - 1$
   (a) What number does the letter a stand for?
   (b) What number does the letter b stand for?
   (c) Write down the next line in the pattern.

5. $1 + 3 = 2^2$. $1 + 3 + 5 = 3^2$.
   (a) $1 + 3 + 5 + 7 = x^2$.
   Calculate x.
   (b) $1 + 3 + 5 + \ldots + n = 100$.
   Calculate n.

6. Here is a sequence:
   $$1 + 2 + 1 = 2^2$$
   $$1 + 2 + 3 + 2 + 1 = 3^2$$
   $$1 + 2 + 3 + 4 + 3 + 2 + 1 = 4^2$$
   (a) Write down the next two lines of the sequence.
   (b) Complete the line below:
   $$1 + 2 + 3 + \ldots + 1 = 9^2$$

7. In the diagram, the equations of the lines are $y = 3x$, $y = 6$, $y = 10 - x$ and $y = \frac{1}{2}x - 3$.

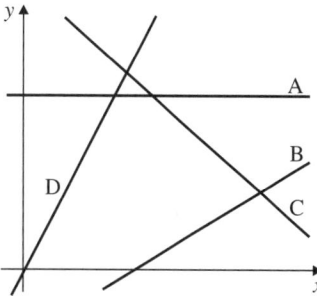

   Find the equation corresponding to each line.

8. The shaded region A is formed by the lines $y = 2$, $y = 3x$ and $x + y = 6$.
   Draw the three lines on a graph and then work out the area of the region A.

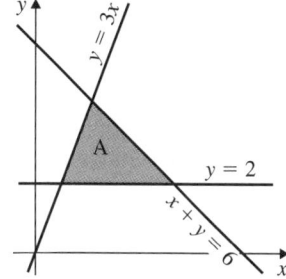

9. The shaded triangle B is formed by the lines $x = 0$, $y = x - 2$ and $x + y = 7$.

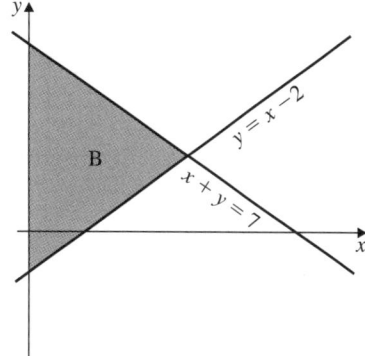

   Draw a graph and use it to find the coordinates of the vertices of triangle B.

10. Nadia said: 'I thought of a number, multiplied it by 6, then added 15. My answer was less than 200'.
    (a) Write down Nadia's statement in symbols, using x as the starting number.
    (b) Nadia actually thought of a prime number. What was the largest prime number she could have thought of?

Examination exercise 2B

1. (a) Show that $44 - 4 \times 7 = 4^2$.
   (b) Continue the pattern below for three more lines.
   $$11 - 1 \times 10 = 1^2$$
   $$22 - 2 \times 9 = 2^2$$
   $$33 - 3 \times 8 = 3^2$$
   $$44 - 4 \times 7 = 4^2$$
   (c) Write down the eleventh line in the pattern.
   (d) $143 - 13 \times (-2) = x^2$. Write down the value of x. [J 98 3]

2. Solve the equation $2x - 1 = \dfrac{x}{2}$. [N 96 3]

3. Solve the equation $3 - 2g = 2g + 6$. [N 97 1]

4. Solve the equation $x = \dfrac{3x + 4}{5}$. [J 95 1]

5. (a) (i) Work out
   $$3 \div 3 = \ldots\ldots\ldots$$
   $$(5 + 7) \div 3 = \ldots\ldots\ldots$$
   $$(7 + 9 + 11) \div 3 = \ldots\ldots\ldots$$
   $$(9 + 11 + 13 + 15) \div 3 = \ldots\ldots\ldots$$
   (ii) What special name is given to the answers in part (i)?
   (iii) Write down the next line of the sequence in part (i).
   (b) (i) Work out 6^2, 7^2, 8^2 and 9^2
   (ii) Find x if $x^2 = 1^2 + 4^2 + 8^2$.
   (iii) Find another set of four positive integers p, q, r and s, all different and all less than 10, such that $p^2 + q^2 + r^2 = s^2$. [J 95 3]

6. (a) Complete the table of values for the function
   $$y = 4 - 2x - x^2$$

x	-4	-3.5	-3	-2	-1	0	1	1.5	2
y		-1.25	1	4		4	1		

   (b) Plot these points on a grid with x from -4 to 2 and y from -5 to 6, and then draw the graph of $y = 4 - 2x - x^2$ for values of x from -4 to 2.
   (c) Use your graph to solve the equation $4 - 2x - x^2 = 0$.
   (d) On the grid above, draw the graph of $y = x$.
   (e) Use the two graphs to solve the equation $4 - 2x - x^2 = x$. [J 98 3]

7. (a) Complete the table of values for the equation $y = 10 + 2x - x^2$.

x	-3	-2	-1	0	1	2	3	4	5
y	-5		7	10		10	7		-5

   (b) On a grid with values of x from -3 to 5 and y from -6 to 12, draw the graph of $y = 10 + 2x - x^2$ for $-3 \leqslant x \leqslant 5$.
   (c) Use your graph to solve the equation $10 + 2x - x^2 = 0$.
   (d) On the same grid, draw the graph of $y = x - 1$.
   (e) Write down the coordinates of the points of intersection of the two graphs. [N 96 3]

3 Number 1

3.1 Place value

Whole numbers are made up from units, tens, hundred, thousands and so on.

thousands	hundreds	tens	units
3	2	6	4

In the number 3264:

the digit 3 means 3 thousands
the digit 2 means 2 hundreds
the digit 6 means 6 tens
the digit 4 means 4 units (ones)

In the words we write 'three thousand, two hundred and sixty-four'.

Exercise 1

In Questions **1** to **8** state the value of the figure underlined.

1. 2<u>7</u>
2. <u>4</u>16
3. 238<u>2</u>
4. 51<u>6</u>
5. <u>6</u>008
6. 26 1<u>0</u>4
7. <u>5</u> 250 000
8. <u>8</u>26 111

In Questions **9** to **16** write down the number which goes in each box.

9. 293 = ☐ + 90 + 3
10. 574 = 500 + ☐ + 4
11. 816 = 800 + ☐ + 6
12. 899 = ☐ + 90 + 9
13. 6217 = ☐ + 200 + 10 + 7
14. 5065 = 5000 + ☐ + 5
15. 63 410 = 60 000 + 3000 + ☐ + 10
16. 75 678 = ☐ + 5000 + 600 + ☐ + 8

17. Write these numbers in figures:
    (a) Seven hundred and twenty
    (b) Five thousand, two hundred and six
    (c) Sixteen thousand, four hundred and thirty
    (d) Half a million
    (e) Three hundred thousand and ninety
    (f) Eight and a half thousand.

18. Here are four number cards:

(a) Use all the cards to make the largest possible number.
(b) Use all the cards to make the smallest possible number.

19. Write these numbers in words:
(a) 4620   (b) 607   (c) 25 400
(d) 6 800 000   (e) 21 425

20. Here are five numbers cards:

(a) Use all the cards to make the largest possible *odd* number.
(b) Use all the cards to make the smallest possible *even* number.

21. Write down the number that is ten more than:
(a) 247   (b) 3 211   (c) 694

22. Write down the number that is one thousand more than:
(a) 392   (b) 25 611   (c) 256 900

23. (a) Prini puts a 2-digit whole number into her calculator.
She multiplies the number by 10.

Fill in *one* other digit which you know must now be on the calculator.

(b) Prini starts again with the same 2-digit number and this time she multiplies it by 1000.
Fill in all five digits on the calculator this time.

24. Write these numbers in order, from the smallest to the largest:
(a)   2142,   2290,   2058,   2136
(b)   5329,   5029,   5299,   5330
(c) 25 117,   25 200,   25 171,   25 000,   25 500

25. Find a number n so that $5n + 7 = 507$.

26. Find a number x so that $6x + 8 = 68$.

27. Find a pair of numbers a and b for which $8a + b = 807$.

28. Find a pair of numbers p and q for which $7p + 5q = 7050$.

3.2 Arithmetic without a calculator

Here are examples to remind you of non-calculator methods.

(a)
```
   4 2 7
 +5 1 8 6
 -------
  5 6 1 3
    1 1
```

(b)
```
  2 7⁷8¹4
 -   6 3 5
 --------
    2 1 4 9
```

(c) $57 \times 100 = 5700$
[add two zeros]

(d)
```
    3 7 4
  ×     6
  -------
    2 2 4 4
      4 2
```

(e)
```
         5 4 2
      _____
    7)3 7²9¹4
```

(f)
```
       1 3 8 r 4    or   138 4/5
      _____
    5)6¹9⁴4
```

Exercise 2

Work out, without a calculator:

1. $653 + 2844$
2. $2106 + 329$
3. $64 + 214 + 507$
4. $65\,941 + 2580$
5. $387 - 175$
6. $527 - 486$
7. $927 - 68$
8. $1024 - 816$
9. 27×10
10. 5×1000
11. 73×5
12. 214×4
13. 316×8
14. 9224×7
15. $340 \div 4$
16. $1944 \div 6$
17. $3195 \div 5$
18. $2600 \div 8$
19. $364 \div 7$
20. $520 \div 10$
21. $289 + 15 + 1714$
22. $9704 - 5135$
23. $6001 - 5994$
24. 54×20
25. $2906 - 1414$
26. $4716 \div 9$
27. 725×8
28. $1504 \div 8$
29. $7 + 1609 + 25$
30. $289 + 154 - 78$
31. $7 + 295 - 48$
32. 53×400

Speed tests

These questions can be done either:
- with books open, or
- read out by the teacher with books closed.

In either case write down the *answer only*. Be as quick as possible.

Test 1	Test 2	Test 3	Test 4
1. $30 - 8$	1. $6 + 16$	1. 8×5	1. 5×7
2. 9×5	2. $32 - 5$	2. $17 + 23$	2. $36 - 18$
3. $40 \div 5$	3. 9×6	3. $60 \div 6$	3. $103 - 20$
4. $24 + 34$	4. $90 \div 2$	4. $101 - 20$	4. $56 \div 7$
5. 11×7	5. $98 + 45$	5. 49×2	5. 8×4
6. $60 - 12$	6. $16 - 7$	6. $52 + 38$	6. $53 + 36$
7. 9×4	7. $45 \div 9$	7. $66 \div 11$	7. $51 - 22$
8. $27 \div 3$	8. 13×100	8. $105 - 70$	8. $36 \div 3$
9. $55 + 55$	9. $99 + 99$	9. 13×4	9. 20×5
10. $60 - 18$	10. $67 - 17$	10. $220 - 30$	10. $99 + 55$
11. 8×6	11. $570 \div 10$	11. $100 \div 20$	11. $200 - 145$

12. $49 \div 7$	**12.** 7×3	**12.** $2 \times 2 \times 2$	**12.** $88 \div 8$
13. $99 + 17$	**13.** $55 - 6$	**13.** $91 + 19$	**13.** 50×100
14. $80 - 59$	**14.** $19 + 18$	**14.** $200 - 5$	**14.** $199 + 26$
15. 9×100	**15.** $60 \div 5$	**15.** 16×2	**15.** $80 - 17$

3.3 Inverse operations

The word inverse means 'opposite'.
- The inverse of adding is subtracting: $5 + 19 = 24$, $5 = 24 - 19$
- The inverse of subtracting is adding: $31 - 6 = 25$, $31 = 25 + 6$
- The inverse of multiplying is dividing: $7 \times 6 = 42$, $7 = 42 \div 6$
- The inverse of dividing is multiplying: $30 \div 3 = 10$, $30 = 10 \times 3$

Example

Find the missing digits.

(a) $\square 4 \div 6 = 14$ Work out 14×6 because multiplying is the inverse of dividing.
Since $14 \times 6 = 84$, the missing digit is 8.

(b) $2\square 8 \times 5 = 1340$ Work out $1340 \div 5$ because dividing is the inverse of multiplying.
Since $1340 \div 5 = 268$, the missing digit is 6.

(c)   3 $\square$ 7
   + 2 5 $\square$
   $\square$ 3 9

Start from the right: $7 + 2 = 9$
Middle column: $8 + 5 = 13$
Check   387
     + 252
     639 ✓
        1

Exercise 3

Find the missing digits.

1. (a)   2 8 5
   +$\square$ 1 4
   7 $\square$ $\square$

(b)   6 3 $\square$
   +$\square$ 5 2
   8 $\square$ 9

(c) $\square$ 3 5
   + 3 4 $\square$
   9 $\square$ 9

2. (a)   3 5 6
   + 5 $\square$ 6
   $\square$ 8 $\square$

(b)   2 $\square$ 4
   + 5 3 7
   $\square$ 6 1

(c)   3 8 8
   +$\square$ 2 $\square$
   8 $\square$ 3

3. (a)   4 $\square$
   ×   3
   1 4 4

(b)   3 $\square$
   ×   7
   2 3 1

(c) $\square$ $\square$ 1
   ×   5
   1 6 0 5

4. (a) ☐☐☐ ÷ 3 = 50   (b) ☐☐ × 4 = 60
   (c) 9 × ☐ = 81   (d) ☐☐☐ ÷ 6 = 92

5. (a) 4 ☐ 5   (b) 4 ☐ 7   (c) ☐ 3 ☐
      + 2 8 ☐   + ☐ 7 ☐   + 2 ☐ 4
      ─────   ─────   ─────
        ☐ 3 0   6 0 4   7 9 9

6. (a) ☐ 5 × 7 = 245   (b) ☐☐ × 10 = 580
   (c) 32 ÷ ☐ = 8   (d) ☐☐☐ ÷ 5 = 190

7. (a) ☐☐ + 29 = 101   (b) ☐☐☐ − 17 = 91
   (c) ☐ 8 9   (d) 3 3 5
      − 3 ☐ 6   − 2 1 ☐
      ─────   ─────
        5 4 ☐   ☐ ☐ 7

8. There is more than one correct answer for each of these questions.
   Ask a friend to check your solutions.
   (a) 2 3 + ☐☐ − ☐☐ = 23
   (b) 8 5 − ☐☐ + ☐☐ = 86
   (c) 2 5 × ☐ ÷ ☐ = 25
   (d) 4 0 × ☐☐ ÷ ☐ = 80

9. In each calculation the same number is missing from all three boxes.
   Find the missing number in each case.
   (a) ☐ × ☐ − ☐ = 12
   (b) ☐ ÷ ☐ + ☐ = 9
   (c) ☐ × ☐ + ☐ = 72

10. In the circle write +, −, × or ÷ to make the calculation correct.
    (a) 7 × 4 ◯ 3 = 25   (b) 8 × 5 ◯ 2 = 20
    (c) 7 ◯ 3 − 9 = 12   (d) 12 ◯ 2 + 4 = 10
    (e) 75 ÷ 5 ◯ 5 = 20

11. Write the following with the correct signs.
    (a) 5 × 4 × 3 ◯ 3 = 63
    (b) 5 + 4 ◯ 3 ◯ 2 = 4
    (a) 5 × 2 × 3 ◯ 1 = 31

3.4 Decimals

Look at these numbers.

tens	units	.	$\frac{1}{10}$	$\frac{1}{100}$	$\frac{1}{1000}$
5	3	.	6	2	
	0	.	8	7	3

Notice that $53.62 = 50 + 3 + \frac{6}{10} + \frac{2}{100}$
$0.873 = \frac{8}{10} + \frac{7}{10} + \frac{3}{100}$

When writing decimals in order of size it is helpful to write them with the same number of figures after the decimal point.

Example

Write these three numbers in order: 0·08, 0·107, 0·1

$$0·08 \longrightarrow 0·080$$
$$0·107 \longrightarrow 0·107$$
$$0·1 \longrightarrow 0·100$$

Now we can see that the correct order from lowest to highest is 0·08, 0·1, 0·107.

Exercise 4

In Questions **1** to **8** write down each statement and decide whether it is true (T) or false (F).

1. 0·3 is less than 0·31.
2. 0·82 is more than 0·825.
3. 0·7 is equal to 0·70.
4. 0·17 is less than 0·71.
5. 0·02 is more than 0·002.
6. 0·6 is less than 0·06.
7. 0·1 is equal to $\frac{1}{10}$.
8. 5 is equal to 5·00.

9. The number 43·6 can be written $40 + 3 + \frac{6}{10}$.
   Write the number 57·2 in this way.

10. Write the decimal numbers for these additions
    (a) $200 + 30 + 5 + \frac{1}{10}$
    (b) $60 + 7 + \frac{2}{10} + \frac{3}{100}$
    (c) $90 + 8 + \frac{3}{10} + \frac{2}{100}$
    (d) $3 + \frac{1}{10} + \frac{6}{100} + \frac{7}{1000}$

In Questions **11** to **18** arrange the numbers in order of size, smallest first.

11. 0·41, 0·31, 0·2
12. 0·75, 0·58, 0·702
13. 0·43, 0·432, 0·41
14. 0·609, 0·61, 0·6
15. 0·04, 0·15, 0·2, 0·35
16. 1·8, 0·18, 0·81, 1·18
17. 0·7, 0·061, 0·07, 0·1
18. 0·2, 0·025, 0·03, 0·009

19. Here are numbers with letters.
    Put the numbers in order and then write down the letters to make a word.

20. Increase these numbers by $\frac{1}{10}$:
  (a) 32·41 (b) 0·753 (c) 1·06

21. Increase these numbers by $\frac{1}{100}$:
  (a) 5·68 (b) 0·542 (c) 1·29

22. Write the following amounts in dollars:
  (a) 350 cents (b) 15 cents (c) 3 cents
  (d) 10 cents (e) 1260 cents (f) 8 cents

23. Copy each statement and say whether it is true or false.
  (a) $5·4 = $5 + 40c (b) $0·6 = 6c
  (c) 5c = $0·05 (d) 50c is more than $0·42

Scale readings

Exercise 5

Work out the value indicated by the arrow.

1.    **2.**

3.    **4.**

5. 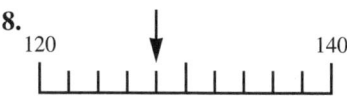   **6.**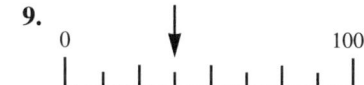

7. 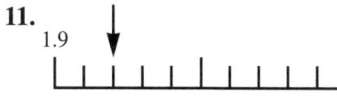   **8.**

9. 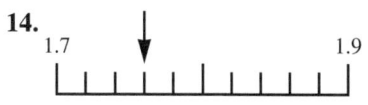   **10.**

11. 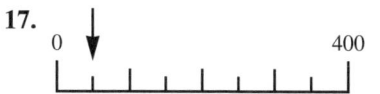   **12.**

Multiplying and dividing decimals by 10, 100, 1000

To *multiply*, move the decimal point to the *right*.

$3 \cdot 24 \times 10 = 32 \cdot 4$
$10 \cdot 61 \times 10 = 106 \cdot 1$
$4 \cdot 134 \times 100 = 413 \cdot 4$
$8 \cdot 2 \times 100 = 820$

$15 \cdot 2 \div 10 = 1 \cdot 52$
$624 \cdot 9 \div 100 = 6 \cdot 249$

To *divide*, move the decimal point to the *left*.

$509 \div 1000 = 0 \cdot 509$

Exercise 6
Work out:

1. $0 \cdot 634 \times 10$
2. $0 \cdot 838 \times 10$
3. $0 \cdot 815 \times 100$
4. $0 \cdot 074 \times 100$
5. $7 \cdot 245 \times 1000$
6. $0 \cdot 032 \times 1000$
7. $0 \cdot 63 \times 10$
8. $1 \cdot 42 \times 100$
9. $0 \cdot 041 \times 100$
10. $0 \cdot 3 \times 100$
11. $0 \cdot 71 \times 1000$
12. $3 \cdot 95 \times 10$

13. $6 \cdot 24 \div 10$
14. $8 \cdot 97 \div 10$
15. $17 \cdot 5 \div 100$
16. $23 \cdot 6 \div 100$
17. $127 \div 1000$
18. $705 \div 1000$
19. $13 \div 10$
20. $0 \cdot 8 \div 10$
21. $0 \cdot 7 \div 100$
22. $218 \div 10$
23. $35 \div 1000$
24. $8 \cdot 6 \div 1000$

25. $0 \cdot 95 \times 100$
26. $11 \cdot 11 \times 10$
27. $3 \cdot 2 \div 10$
28. $0 \cdot 07 \times 1000$
29. $57 \cdot 6 \div 10$
30. $999 \div 100$
31. 66×10
32. $100 \div 100$
33. $42 \div 1000$
34. $0 \cdot 62 \times 10\,000$
35. $0 \cdot 9 \div 100$
36. $555 \div 10\,000$

37. Here are some number cards

   (a) Jason picks the cards  and to make the number 314.

   What extra card could he take to make a number ten times as big as 314?
   (b) Mel chose three cards to make 5·2.
   (i) What cards could she take to make a number ten times as big as 5·2?
   (ii) What cards could she take to make a number 100 times as big as 5·2?
   (iii) What cards could she take to make a number which is $\frac{1}{100}$ of 5·2?

Adding and subtracting decimals
Remember: Line up the decimal points.

(a) $4 \cdot 2 + 1 \cdot 76$

$\quad \begin{array}{r} 4 \cdot 20 \\ +1 \cdot 76 \\ \hline 5 \cdot 96 \end{array}$ ← Put a zero

(b) $26 - 1 \cdot 7$

$\quad \begin{array}{r} 2\overset{5}{\cancel{6}} \cdot \overset{1}{0} \\ -\;\;\; 1 \cdot 7 \\ \hline 24 \cdot 3 \end{array}$

(c) $0 \cdot 24 + 5 + 12 \cdot 7$

$\quad \begin{array}{r} 0 \cdot 24 \\ 5 \cdot 00 \\ +12 \cdot 70 \\ \hline 17 \cdot 94 \end{array}$ ← extra zeros

Exercise 7

Work out, without a calculator:

1. $2 \cdot 84 + 7 \cdot 3$	2. $18 \cdot 6 + 2 \cdot 34$	3. $25 \cdot 96 + 0 \cdot 75$	4. $212 \cdot 7 + 4 \cdot 25$
5. $3 \cdot 6 + 6$	6. $7 + 16 \cdot 1$	7. $8 + 0 \cdot 34 + 0 \cdot 8$	8. $12 + 5 \cdot 32$
9. $0 \cdot 004 + 0 \cdot 058$	10. $4 \cdot 81 - 3 \cdot 7$	11. $6 \cdot 92 - 2 \cdot 56$	12. $8 \cdot 27 - 5 \cdot 86$
13. $3 \cdot 6 - 2 \cdot 24$	14. $8 \cdot 4 - 2 \cdot 17$	15. $8 \cdot 24 - 5 \cdot 78$	16. $15 \cdot 4 - 7$
17. $8 - 5 \cdot 2$	18. $13 - 2 \cdot 7$	19. $0 \cdot 5 - 0 \cdot 32$	20. $5 - 0 \cdot 99$
21. $6 + 0 \cdot 06 + 0 \cdot 6$	22. $12 \cdot 4 + 28 \cdot 71$	23. $11 - 7 \cdot 4$	24. $8 \cdot 2 + 9 \cdot 54 - 11 \cdot 3$

Multiplying decimals

Count up the number of figures to the right of the decimal points in the question. Put the same number of figures to the right of the decimal point in the answer.

Example

(a) $0 \cdot \underline{2} \times 0 \cdot \underline{8}$
     2 figures after the decimal points
     $[2 \times 8 = 16]$
     So $0 \cdot 2 \times 0 \cdot 8 = 0 \cdot \underline{1 \, 6}$

(b) $0 \cdot \underline{4} \times 0 \cdot \underline{07}$
     3 figures after the decimal points
     $[4 \times 7 = 28]$
     So $0 \cdot 4 \times 0 \cdot 07 = 0 \cdot \underline{0 \, 2 \, 8}$

Exercise 8

Work out, without a calculator:

1. $0 \cdot 2 \times 0 \cdot 3$	2. $0 \cdot 5 \times 0 \cdot 3$	3. $0 \cdot 4 \times 0 \cdot 3$	4. $0 \cdot 2 \times 0 \cdot 03$
5. $0 \cdot 6 \times 3$	6. $0 \cdot 7 \times 5$	7. $0 \cdot 9 \times 2$	8. $8 \times 0 \cdot 1$
9. $0 \cdot 4 \times 0 \cdot 9$	10. $0 \cdot 02 \times 0 \cdot 7$	11. $2 \cdot 1 \times 0 \cdot 6$	12. $4 \cdot 7 \times 0 \cdot 5$
13. $21 \cdot 3 \times 0 \cdot 4$	14. $5 \cdot 2 \times 0 \cdot 6$	15. $4 \cdot 2 \times 0 \cdot 03$	16. $212 \times 0 \cdot 6$
17. $0 \cdot 85 \times 0 \cdot 2$	18. $3 \cdot 27 \times 0 \cdot 1$	19. $12 \cdot 6 \times 0 \cdot 01$	20. $0 \cdot 02 \times 17$
21. $0 \cdot 05 \times 1 \cdot 1$	22. $52 \times 0 \cdot 01$	23. $65 \times 0 \cdot 02$	24. $0 \cdot 5 \times 0 \cdot 002$

Dividing by a decimal

Example

(a) $9 \cdot 36 \div 0 \cdot 4$ Multiply both numbers by 10 so that you can divide by a *whole number*.
                                       [Move the decimal points to the right.]
                                       So work out $93 \cdot 6 \div 4$

$$\begin{array}{r} 23 \cdot 4 \\ 4 \overline{)9\,{}^{1}3 \cdot {}^{1}6} \end{array}$$

(b) $0 \cdot 0378 \div 0 \cdot 07$ Multiply both numbers by 100 so that you can divide by a whole number.
                                         [Move the decimal points to the right.]
                                         So work out $3 \cdot 78 \div 7$

$$\begin{array}{r} 0 \cdot 54 \\ 7 \overline{)3 \cdot 7\,{}^{2}8} \end{array}$$

Exercise 9

Work out, without a calculator:

1. $0.84 \div 0.4$
2. $0.93 \div 0.3$
3. $0.872 \div 0.2$
4. $0.8 \div 0.2$
5. $2.8 \div 0.7$
6. $1.25 \div 0.5$
7. $8 \div 0.5$
8. $40 \div 0.2$
9. $7 \div 0.1$
10. $0.368 \div 0.4$
11. $0.915 \div 0.03$
12. $0.248 \div 0.04$
13. $0.625 \div 0.05$
14. $8.54 \div 0.07$
15. $1.272 \div 0.006$
16. $4.48 \div 0.08$
17. $0.12 \div 0.002$
18. $7.5 \div 0.005$
19. $0.09 \div 0.3$
20. $0.77 \div 1.1$
21. $0.055 \div 0.11$
22. $21.28 \div 7$
23. $22.48 \div 4$
24. $3.12 \div 4$
25. $0.7 \div 5$
26. $3 \div 0.8$
27. $0.3 \div 4$
28. $1.2 \div 8$
29. $0.732 \div 0.6$
30. $0.1638 \div 0.001$
31. $1.05 \div 0.6$
32. $7.52 \div 0.4$

33. A cake weighing 7·2 kg is cut into several pieces each weighing 0·6 kg. How many pieces are there?

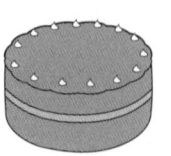

34. A phone call costs $0·04. How many calls can I make if I have $3·52?

35. A sheet of paper is 0·01 cm thick. How many sheets are there in a pile of paper 5·8 cm thick?

Cross-numbers

Make three copies of the crossnumber and then fill in the numbers using the clues given.

A

Across
1. 13×7
2. $0.214 \times 10\,000$
4. $265 - 248$
5. $2 \times 2 \times 2 \times 2 \times 2 \times 2$
7. $90 - (9 \times 9)$
8. 14×5
9. $2226 \div 7$
11. $216 \div (18 \div 3)$
12. $800 - 363$
14. $93 - (6 \times 2)$
15. 0.23×100
16. $8 \times 8 - 1$

Down
1. $101 - 7$
2. $2.7 \div 0.1$
3. $44.1 + 0.9$
4. $(2 \times 9) - (8 \div 2)$
6. 9^2
8. $6523 + 917$
9. $418 \div 11$
10. $216 + (81 \times 100)$
13. $2 \times 2 \times 2 \times 3 \times 3$

B

Across
1. 2.4×40
2. $1600 - 27$
4. $913 - 857$
5. $2 + (9 \times 9)$
7. $0.4 \div 0.05$
8. $27 \times 5 - 69$
9. $4158 \div 7$
11. $2^6 + 6$
12. $5.22 \div 0.03$
14. $201 - 112$
15. 7 million $\div 100\,000$
16. $\frac{1}{4}$ of 372

Down
1. $558 \div 6$
2. $6.4 \div 0.4$
3. 0.071×1000
4. $11.61 + 4.2 + 37.19$
6. $(7 - 3.1) \times 10$
8. $8 \times 8 \times 100 - 82$
9. 0.08×700
10. $40 \times 30 \times 4 - 1$
13. $\frac{1}{5}$ of 235

C

Across
1. 2.6×10
2. 6.314×1000
4. $600 - 563$
5. 0.25×100
7. $3 \div 0.5$
8. 0.08×1000
9. $3.15 \div 0.01$
11. 1.1×70
12. $499 + 103$
14. $1 \div 0.1$
15. 0.01×5700
16. $1000 - 936$

Down
1. 0.2×100
2. $6.7 \div 0.1$
3. $1800 \div 100$
4. $21 \div 0.6$
6. 420×0.05
8. $0.8463 \times 10\,000$
9. 0.032×1000
10. $5.706 \div 0.001$
13. 5^2

3.5 Flow diagrams

Find the operation

Exercise 10

In the flow charts, the boxes A, B, C and D each contain a single mathematical operation (like +5, ×4, −15, ÷2).

Look at flow charts (i) and (ii) together and work out what is the same operation which will replace A. Complete the flow chart by replacing B, C and D.

Now copy and complete each flow chart on the right, using the same operations.

1. (i) 1 → A → 8 → B → 16 → C → 5 → D → 15
(ii) 3 → A → 10 → B → 20 → C → 9 → D → 27

(a) 4 → A → ? → B → ? → C → ? → D → ?
(b) 5 → A → ? → B → ? → C → ? → D → ?
(c) ? → A → ? → B → 28 → C → ? → D → ?
(d) ? → A → 16 → B → ? → C → ? → D → ?
(e) ? → A → ? → B → ? → C → 25 → D → ?
(f) ? → A → ? → B → ? → C → ? → D → 87

2. (i) 2 → A → 4 → B → 19 → C → 12 → D → 3
(ii) 4 → A → 8 → B → 23 → C → 16 → D → 4

(a) 6 → A → ? → B → ? → C → ? → D → ?
(b) 3 → A → ? → B → ? → C → ? → D → ?
(c) ? → A → 16 → B → ? → C → ? → D → ?
(d) ? → A → ? → B → 35 → C → ? → D → ?
(e) ? → A → ? → B → ? → C → ? → D → $2\frac{1}{2}$
(f) ? → A → ? → B → ? → C → ? → D → 8

70 Number 1

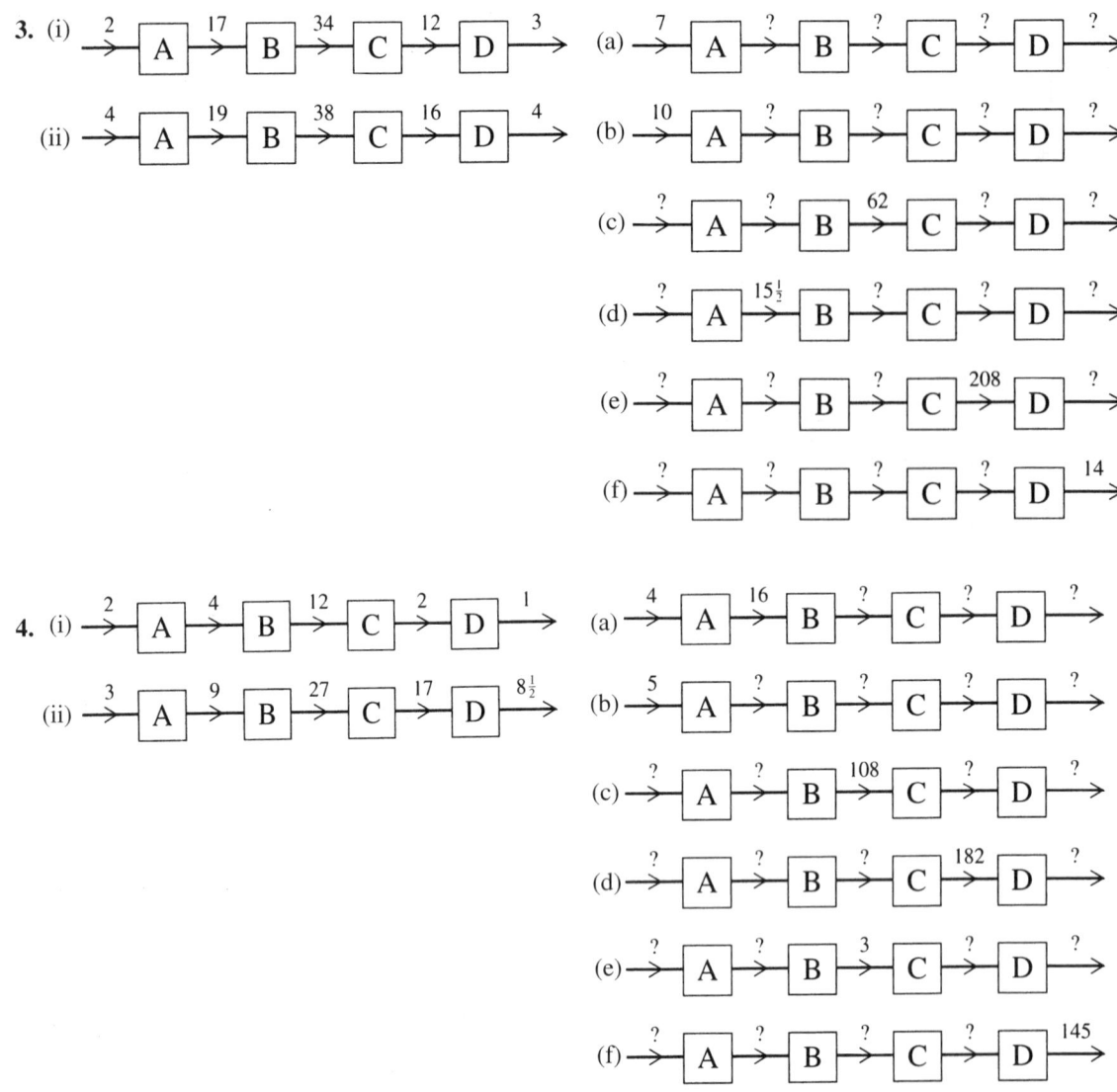

In Questions **5**, **6**, **7** find the operations A,B,C,D.

3.6 Properties of numbers

- **Factors** Any number which divides exactly into 8 is a **factor** of 8.
  The factors of 8 are 1, 2, 4, 8.
- **Multiples** Any number in the 8-times table is a **multiple** of 8.
  The first five multiples of 8 are 8, 16, 24, 32, 40.
- **Prime** A **prime** number has just two different factors: 1 and itself.
  The number 1 is **not** prime. [It does not have two different factors.]
  The first five prime numbers are 2, 3, 5, 7, 11.
- **Prime factor** The factors of 8 are 1, 2, 4, 8. The only **prime factor** of 8 is 2. It is the only prime number which is a factor of 8.

Exercise 11

1. Write down all the factors of the following numbers:
   (a) 6   (b) 15   (c) 18   (d) 21   (e) 40

2. Write down all the prime numbers less than 20.

3. Write down two prime numbers which add up to another prime number. Do this in two different ways.

4. Use a calculator to find which of the following are prime numbers:
   (a) 91   (b) 101   (c) 143   (d) 151   (e) 293
   [Hint: Divide by the prime numbers 2, 3, 5, 7, 11 and so on.]

5. Prime factors can be found using a 'factor tree'.

   - Here is a factor tree for 140.
   - Here is a factor tree for 40.

   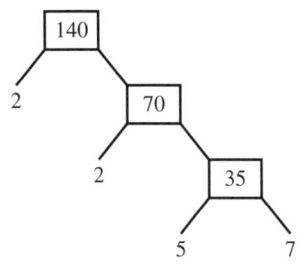
   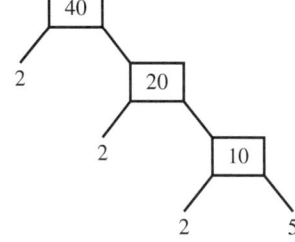

   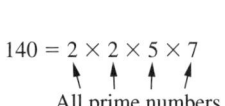
   All prime numbers

   $40 = 2 \times 2 \times 2 \times 5$

   Draw a factor tree for each of these numbers:
   (a) 36   (b) 60   (c) 216   (d) 200   (e) 1500

6. Here is the number 600 written as the product of its prime factors.
   $$600 = 2 \times 2 \times 2 \times 3 \times 5 \times 5$$
   Use this information to write 1200 as a product of its prime factors.

7. Write down the first four multiples of:
   (a) 3   (b) 4   (c) 10   (d) 11   (e) 20

8. Find the 'odd one out'.
   (a) multiples of 6 : 12, 18, 24, 32, 48
   (b) multiples of 9 : 18, 27, 45, 56, 72

9. Write down two numbers that are multiples of both 3 and 4.

10. Copy and complete each sentence:
    (a) An [odd/even] number is exactly divisible by 2.
    (b) An [_____] number leaves a remainder of 1 when divided by 2.
    (c) All [_____] numbers are multiples of 2.

11. Copy the table and then write the numbers 1 to 9, *one in each box*, so that all the numbers satisfy the conditions for both the row and the column.

	Prime number	Multiple of 3	Factor of 16
Number greater than 5			
Odd number			
Even number			

12. Find each of the mystery numbers below.
    (a) I am an odd number and a prime number. I am a factor of 14.
    (b) I am a two-digit multiple of 50.
    (c) I am one less than a prime number which is even.
    (d) I am odd, greater than one and a factor of both 20 and 30.

3.7 Long multiplication and division

To work out 327×53 we will use the fact that $327 \times 53 = (327 \times 50) + (327 \times 3)$
Set out the working like this.

```
    327
     53 ×
  16350  → This is 327 × 50
    981  → This is 327 × 3
  17331  → This is 327 × 53
```

Here is another example.

```
    541
     84 ×
  43280  → This is 541 × 80
   2164  → This is 541 × 4
  45444  → This is 541 × 84
```

Exercise 12

Work out, without a calculator.

1. 35 × 23
2. 27 × 17
3. 26 × 25
4. 31 × 43
5. 45 × 61
6. 52 × 24
7. 323 × 14
8. 416 × 73
9. 504 × 56
10. 306 × 28
11. 624 × 75
12. 839 × 79
13. 694 × 83
14. 973 × 92
15. 415 × 235

With ordinary 'short' division, we divide and find remainders. The method for 'long' division is really the same but we set it out so that the remainders are easier to find.

Example

Work out 736 ÷ 32

```
      23
32 ) 736
     64 ↓
     96
     96
      0
```

(a) 32 into 73 goes 2 times
(b) 2 × 32 = 64
(c) 73 − 64 = 9
(d) 'bring down' 6
(e) 32 into 96 goes 3 times

Exercise 13

Work out, without a calculator:

1. 672 ÷ 21
2. 425 ÷ 17
3. 576 ÷ 32
4. 247 ÷ 19
5. 875 ÷ 25
6. 574 ÷ 26
7. 806 ÷ 34
8. 748 ÷ 41
9. 666 ÷ 24
10. 707 ÷ 52
11. 951 ÷ 27
12. 806 ÷ 34
13. 2917 ÷ 45
14. 2735 ÷ 18
15. 56 274 ÷ 19

Exercise 14

Solve each problem without a calculator.

1. A shop owner buys 56 tins of paint at 84c each. How much does he spend altogether?

2. Eggs are packed eighteen to a box.

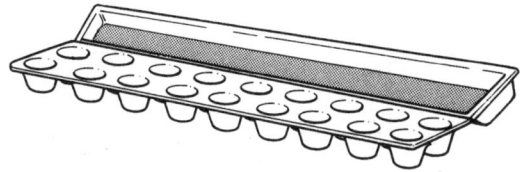 

How many boxes are needed for 828 eggs?

3. On average a man smokes 146 cigarettes a week. How many does he smoke in a year?

4. Sally wants to buy as many 23c stamps as possible. She has $5 to buy them. How many can she buy and how much change is left?

5. How many 49-seater coaches will be needed for a school trip for a party of 366?

6. An office building has 24 windows on each of 8 floors. A window cleaner charges 42c for each window. How much is he paid for the whole building?

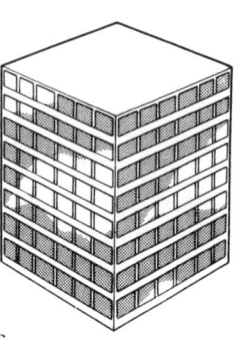

7. A lottery prize of $238 million was won by a syndicate of 17 people who shared the prize equally between them. How much did each person receive?

8. It costs $7905 to hire a plane for a day. A trip is organised for 93 people. How much does each person pay?

9. The headmaster of a school discovers an oil well in the school playground. As is the custom in such cases, he receives all the money from the oil. The oil comes out of the well at a rate of $15 for every minute of the day and night. How much does the headmaster receive in a 24-hour day?

Exercise 15

Each empty square contains either a number or a mathematical symbol (+, −, ×, ÷). Copy each square and fill in the details.

1.

5			→	60
×		÷		
		24	→	44
↓		↓		
	×	$\frac{1}{2}$	→	50

2.

	×	6	→	42
÷		÷		
14	−		→	
↓		↓		
		2	→	1

3.

	×	2	→	38
−		÷		
			→	48
↓		↓		
7	−		→	$6\frac{1}{2}$

Long multiplication and division

4.

17	×		→	170
−		÷		
	÷		→	
↓		↓		
8	−	0.1	→	

5.

0.3	×	20	→	
		−		
11	÷		→	
↓		↓		
11.3	−		→	2.3

6.

	×	50	→	25
−		÷		
		$\frac{1}{2}$	→	0.6
↓		↓		
0.4	×		→	

7.

7	×		→	0.7
÷		×		
	÷		→	
↓		↓		
1.75	+	0.02	→	

8.

	+	8	→	9.4
−				
	×	0.1	→	
↓		↓		
1.3		0.8	→	2.1

9.

	×		→	30
−				
	÷	10	→	0.25
↓		↓		
97.5	+	3	→	

10.

3	÷	2	→	
÷		÷		
8	÷		→	
↓		↓		
	+	$\frac{1}{8}$	→	

11.

	−	$\frac{1}{16}$	→	$\frac{3}{16}$
×				
	÷	4	→	
↓		↓		
$\frac{1}{8}$		$\frac{1}{4}$	→	$\frac{3}{8}$

12.

0.5	−	0.01	→	
		×		
	×		→	35
↓		↓		
4	÷	0.1	→	

13.

	−	1.8	→	3.4
−		÷		
	×		→	
↓		↓		
	+	0.36	→	1

14.

	×	30	→	21
×		−		
	−		→	35
↓		↓		
	−	49	→	

15.

	×	−6	→	72
÷		+		
4	+		→	
↓		↓		
	+	1	→	−2

3.8 Percentages

Example

(a) Work out 22% of $40.

$$\frac{22}{100} \times \frac{40}{1} = \frac{880}{100}$$

Answer: $8·80

(b) Work out 16% of $85.
[Alternative method]

Since $16\% = \frac{16}{100}$ we can replace 16% by 0·16

So 16% of $85 = 0·16 \times 85$
$= \$13·60$

Exercise 16

Work out:

1. 20% of $60
2. 10% of $80
3. 5% of $200
4. 6% of $50
5. 4% of $60
6. 30% of $80
7. 9% of $500
8. 18% of $400
9. 61% of $400
10. 12% of $80
11. 6% of $700
12. 11% of $800
13. 5% of 160 kg
14. 20% of 60 kg
15. 68% of 400 g
16. 15% of 300 m
17. 2% of 2000 km
18. 71% of $1000
19. 26% of 19 kg
20. 1% of 6000 g
21. 8·5% of $2400

Example

Work out 6·5% of $17·50 correct to the nearest cent.

$$\frac{6·5}{100} \times \frac{17·5}{1} = \frac{113·75}{100}$$

$$= \$1·1375$$

Answer: $1·14 to the nearest cent.

Exercise 17

Give the answers to the nearest cent where necessary.

1. 4·5% of $6·22
2. 17% of $6·84
3. 15% of $8·11
4. 17% of $17·07
5. 37% of $9·64
6. 3·5% of $12·90
7. 8% of $11·64
8. 68% of $54·45
9. 73% of $23·24
10. 2·5% of $15·20
11. 6·3% of $12·50
12. 8·2% of $19·50
13. 87% of $15·40
14. 80% of $62·50
15. 12% of $24·50
16. $12\frac{1}{2}$% of $88·50
17. $7\frac{1}{2}$% of $16·40
18. $5\frac{1}{2}$% of $80
19. $12\frac{1}{2}$% of $90
20. 19% of $119·50
21. 8·35% of $110

Example 1

A coat originally cost $24. Calculate the new price after a 5% reduction.

$$\text{Price reduction} = 5\% \text{ of } \$24$$
$$= \frac{5}{100} \times \frac{24}{1} = \$1 \cdot 20$$
$$\text{New price of coat} = \$24 - \$1 \cdot 20$$
$$= \$22 \cdot 80$$

Example 2

A CD originally cost $11·60. Calculate the new price after a 7% increase.
We could work out 7% of $11·60 as in the example above.
There is, however, a *quicker* way which many people prefer.
If we increase the price by 7% the final price is 107% of the old price.

$$\therefore \text{new price} = 107\% \text{ of } \$11 \cdot 60$$
$$= 1 \cdot 07 \times 11 \cdot 6$$
$$= \$12 \cdot 41 \text{ to the nearest cent.}$$

For a 5% *reduction* as in Example 1 we would multiply by 0·95.

Exercise 18

1. Increase a price of $60 by 5%
2. Reduce a price of $800 by 8%
3. Reduce a price of $82·50 by 6%
4. Increase a price of $65 by 60%
5. Reduce a price of $2000 by 2%
6. Increase a price of $440 by 80%
7. Increase a price of $66 by 100%
8. Reduce a price of $91·50 by 50%
9. Increase a price of $88·24 by 25%
10. Reduce a price of $63 by $33\frac{1}{3}$%

In the remaining questions give the answers to the nearest cent.

11. Increase a price of $8·24 by 46%
12. Increase a price of $7·65 by 24%
13. Increase a price of $5·61 by 31%
14. Reduce a price of $8·99 by 22%
15. Increase a price of $11·12 by 11%
16. Reduce a price of $17·62 by 4%
17. Increase a price of $28·20 by 13%
18. Increase a price of $8·55 by $5\frac{1}{2}$%
19. Reduce a price of $9·60 by $7\frac{1}{2}$%
20. Increase a price of $12·80 by $10\frac{1}{2}$%

Exercise 19

1. In a closing-down sale a shop reduces all its prices by 20%. Find the sale price of a coat which previously cost $44.

2. The price of a car was $5400 but it is increased by 6%. What is the new price?

3. The price of a sideboard was $245 but, because the sideboard is scratched, the price is reduced by 30%. What is the new price?

4. A hi-fi shop offers a 7% discount for cash. How much does a cash-paying customer pay for an amplifier advertised at $95?

5. A rabbit weighs 2·8 kg. After being shot, its weight is increased by 1%. How much does it weigh now?

6. The insurance premium for a car is normally $90. With a 'no-claim bonus' the premium is reduced by 35%. What is the reduced premium?

7. Myxomatosis kills 92% of a colony of 300 rabbits. How many rabbits survive?

8. The population of a town increased by 32% between 1945 and 1985. If there were 45 000 people in 1945, what was the 1985 population?

9. A restaurant adds a 12% 'service charge' onto the basic price of meals. How much do I pay for a meal with a basic price of $8·50?

10. A new-born baby weighs 3·1 kg. Her weight increases by 8% over the next fortnight. What does she weigh then?

11. A large snake normally weighs 12·2 kg. After swallowing a rat, the weight of the snake is increased by 7%. How much does it weigh after dinner?

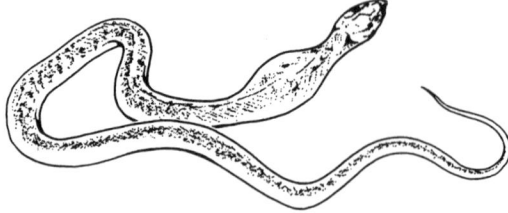

12. At the beginning of the year a car is valued at $3250. During the year its value falls by 15%. How much is it worth at the end of the year?

Exercise 20

In Questions **1** to **4** find the total bill.

1. 2 hammers at $5·30 each
   50 screws at 25c for 10
   5 bulbs at 38c each
   1 tape measure at $1·15
   VAT at 17·5% is added to the total cost.

2. 5 litres of oil at 85c per litre
   3 spanners at $1·25 each
   2 manuals at $4·30 each
   200 bolts at 90c for 10
   VAT at 17·5% is added to the total cost.

3. 12 rolls of wallpaper at $3·70 per roll
   3 packets of paste at $0·55 per packet
   2 brushes at $2·40 each
   1 step ladder at $15·50
   VAT at 17·5% is added to the total cost.

4. 5 golf clubs at $12·45 each
   48 golf balls at $15 per dozen
   100 tees at 1p each
   1 bag at $21·50
   1 umbrella at $12·99
   VAT at 17·5% is added to the total cost.

5. In a sale a dress priced at $35 is reduced by 20%. At the end of the week the *sale price* is reduced by a further 25%.
   Calculate:
   (a) the price in the original sale
   (b) the final price.

6. (a) In 2000 a club has 40 members who each pay $120 annual subscription.
   What is the total income from subscriptions?
   (b) In 2001 the subscription is increased by 35% and the membership increases to 65.
   (i) What is the 2001 subscription?
   (ii) What is the total income from subscriptions in 2001?

Simple interest

When a sum of money $P is invested for T years at $R\%$ interest per annum (each year), then the interest gained I is given by:

$$I = \frac{P \times R \times T}{100}$$

This is known as simple interest.

Example

Joel invests $400 for 6 months at 5%.
Work out the simple interest gained.

$P = \$400 \qquad R = 5 \qquad T = 0·5 \qquad$ (6 months is half a year)

so $\quad I = \dfrac{400 \times 5 \times 0·5}{100}$

$\quad I = \$10$

Exercise 21

1. Calculate:
   (a) the simple interest on $1200 for 3 years at 6% per annum
   (b) the simple interest on $700 at 8·25% per annum for 2 years
   (c) the length of time for $5000 to earn $1000 if invested at 10% per annum
   (d) the length of time for $400 to earn $160 if invested at 8% per annum.

2. Khalid invests $6750 at 8·5% per annum. How much interest has he earned and what is the total amount in his account after 4 years?

3. Shareen invests $10 800. After 4 years she has earned $3240 in interest. At what annual rate of interest did she invest her money?

3.9 Map scales and ratio

The map below is drawn to a scale of 1 : 50 000. In other words 1 cm on the map represents 50 000 cm on the land.

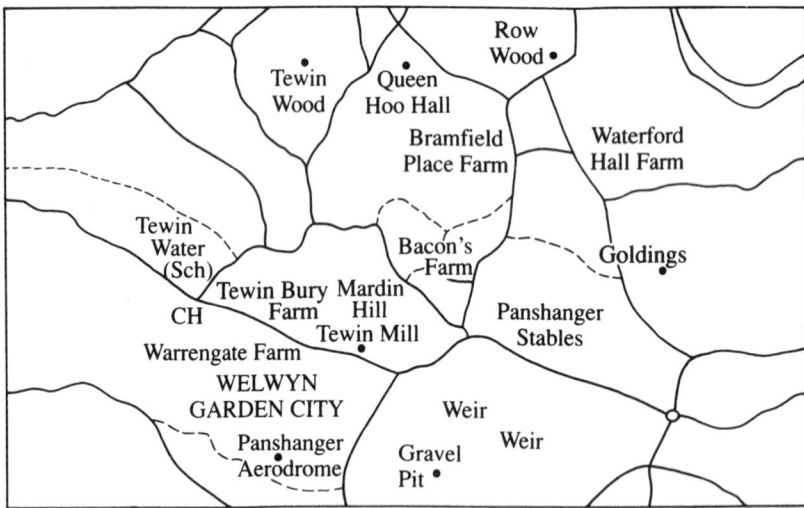

Example

On a map of scale 1 : 25 000 two towns appear 10 cm apart. What is the actual distance between the towns in km?

$$\begin{aligned}
1 \text{ cm on map} &= 25\,000 \text{ cm on land} \\
10 \text{ cm on map} &= 250\,000 \text{ cm on land} \\
250\,000 \text{ cm} &= 2500 \text{ m} \\
&= 2\cdot 5 \text{ km}
\end{aligned}$$

The towns are 2·5 km apart.

Exercise 22

1. The scale of a map is 1 : 1000. Find the actual length in metres represented on the map by 20 cm.

2. The scale of a map is 1 : 10 000. Find the actual length in metres represented on the map by 5 cm.

3. Copy and complete the table.

Map scale	Length on map	Actual length on land
(a) 1 : 10 000	10 cm	1 km
(b) 1 : 2000	10 cm	m
(c) 1 : 25 000	4 cm	km
(d) 1 : 10 000	6 cm	km

4. Find the actual distance in metres between two points which are 6·3 cm apart on a map whose scale is 1 : 1000.

5. On a map of scale 1 : 300 000 the distance between Paris and Bonnieres is 8 cm. What is the actual distance in km?

6. A builder's plan is drawn to a scale of 1 cm to 10 m. How long is a road which is 12 cm on the plan?

7. The map on page 80 is drawn to a scale of 1 : 50 000. Make your own measurements to find the actual distance in km between:
   (a) Goldings and Tewin Wood (marked •).
   (b) Panshanger Aerodrome and Row Wood.
   (c) Gravel Pit and Queen Hoo Hall.

Example

The distance between two towns is 18 km.
How far apart will they be on a map of scale 1 : 50 000?

18 km = 1 800 000 cm
1 800 000 cm on land = $\frac{1}{50\,000}$ × 1 800 000 cm on map

Distance between towns on map = 36 cm

Exercise 23

1. The distance between two towns is 15 km. How far apart will they be on a map of scale 1 : 10 000?

2. The distance between two points is 25 km. How far apart will they be on a map of scale 1 : 20 000?

3. The length of a road is 2·8 km. How long will the road be on a map of scale 1 : 10 000?

4. The length of a reservoir is 5·9 km. How long will it be on a map of scale 1 : 100 000?

5. Copy and complete the table.

Map scale	Actual length on land	Length on map
(a) 1 : 20 000	12 km	cm
(b) 1 : 10 000	8·4 km	cm
(c) 1 : 50 000	28 km	cm
(d) 1 : 40 000	56 km	cm
(e) 1 : 5000	5 km	cm

6. The scale of a drawing is 1 cm to 10 m.
The length of a wall is 25 m. What length will the wall be on the drawing?

Ratio

Example

Share $60 in the ratio 2 : 3.

Total number of shares $= 2 + 3 = 5$
$\therefore$ One share $= \$60 \div 5 = \$12$
$\therefore$ The two amounts are $24 and $36.

Exercise 24

1. Share $30 in the ratio 1 : 2.

2. Share $60 in the ratio 3 : 1.

3. Divide 880 g of food between the cat and the dog in the ratio 3 : 5.

4. Divide $1080 between Isobel and Carlota in the ratio 4 : 5.

5. Share 126 litres of petrol between Maya and Tashu in the ratio 2 : 5.

6. Share $60 in the ratio 1 : 2 : 3.

7. Anwar, Belusa and Nabila divided $560 between them in the ratio 2 : 1 : 5. How much did Belusa receive?

8. A sum of $120 is divided in the ratio 3 : 4 : 5. What is the largest share?

9. At an election 7800 people voted Democrats, Socialists or Republicans in the ratio 4 : 3 : 5. How many people voted Republicans?

Example

In a class, the ratio of boys to girls is 3 : 4.
If there are 9 boys, how many girls are there?

      Boys : Girls = 3 : 4
Multiply both parts by 3.
      Boys : Girls = 9 : 12
So there are 9 boys and 12 girls.

Exercise 25

1. In a room, the ratio of boys to girls is 3 : 2.
   If there are 12 boys, how many girls are there?

2. In a room, the ratio of men to women is 4 : 1.
   If there are 20 men, how many women are there?

3. In a box, the ratio of nails to screws is 5 : 3.
   If there are 15 nails, how many screws are there?

4. An alloy consists of copper, zinc and tin in the ratios 1 : 3 : 4.
   If there is 10 g of copper in the alloy, find the weights of zinc and tin.

5. In a shop the ratio of oranges to apples is 2 : 5.
   If there are 60 apples, how many oranges are there?

6. A recipe for 5 people calls for 1·5 kg of meat. How much meat is required if the recipe is adapted to feed 8 people?

7. A cake for 6 people requires 4 eggs. How many eggs are needed to make a cake big enough for 9 people?

8. A photocopier enlarges the original in the ratio 2 : 3.
   The height of a tree is 12 cm on the original.
   How tall is the tree on the enlarged copy?

original   enlarged copy

9. A photocopier enlarges copies in the ratio 4 : 5. The length of the headline 'BRIDGE COLLAPSES' is 18 cm on the original.
   How long is the headline on the enlarged copy?

10. A photocopier *reduces* in the ratio 5 : 3. The height of a church spire is 12 cm on the original. How tall is the church spire on the reduced copy?

11. A cake weighing 550 g has three ingredients: flour, sugar and raisins. There is twice as much flour as sugar and one and a half times as much sugar as raisins. How much flour is there?

12. If $\frac{5}{8}$ of the children in a school are boys, what is the ratio of boys to girls?

13. A man and a woman share a bingo prize of $1000 between them in the ratio 1 : 4. The woman shares her part between herself, her mother and her daughter in the ratio 2 : 1 : 1.
    How much does her daughter receive?

14. The number of pages in a newspaper is increased from 36 to 54.
    The price is increased in the same ratio. If the old price was 28c, what will the new price be?

15. Two friends bought a house for $220 000. Sam paid $140 000 and Joe paid the rest. Three years later they sold the house for $275 000.
    How much should Sam receive from the sale?

16. Concrete is made from 1 part cement, 2 parts sand and 5 parts aggregate (by volume). How much cement is needed to make 2 m³ of concrete?

3.10 Proportion

Example 1
If 11 litres of petrol costs £5·72, find the cost of 27 litres.

The cost of petrol is *directly* proportional to the quantity bought.

    11 litres costs £5·72
∴ 1 litre costs £5·72 ÷ 11 = £0·52
∴ 27 litres costs £0·52 × 27
                 = £14·04

Example 2
A farmer has enough hay to feed 5 horses for 6 days. How long would the hay last for 3 horses?

The length of time for which the horses can be fed is *inversely* proportional to the number of horses to be fed.

    5 horses can be fed for 6 days
∴ 1 horse can be fed for 30 days
∴ 3 horses can be fed for 10 days.

In the first example above it was helpful to work out the cost of *one* litre of petrol.
In the second example we found the time for which *one* horse could be fed.
To do these questions you need to think logically.

- If five men can paint a tower in 10 days, how long would it take one man?
- If 33 books cost £280·50, how much will one book cost?

Exercise 26

The first seven questions involve *direct* proportion.
The last seven questions involve *inverse* proportion.

1. If 5 hammers cost $20, find the cost of 7 hammers.

2. Magazines cost $16 for 8. Find the cost of 3 magazines.

3. Find the cost of 2 cakes if 7 cakes cost $10·50.

4. A machine fills 1000 bottles in 5 minutes. How many bottles will it fill in 2 minutes?

5. A train travels 100 km in 20 minutes. How long will it take to travel 50 km?

6. Eleven discs cost $13·20. Find the cost of 4 discs.

7. Fishing line costs $1·40 for 50 m. Find the cost of 300 m.

8. If 12 men can build a house in 6 days, how long will it take 6 men?

9. Six women can dig a hole in 4 hours. How long would it take 2 women to dig the same hole?

10. A farmer has enough hay to feed 20 horses for 3 days. How long would the hay last for 60 horses?

11. Twelve people can clean an office building in 3 hours. How long would it take 4 people?

12. Usually it takes 12 hours for 8 men to do a job. How many men are needed to do the same job in 4 hours?

13. Five teachers can mark 60 exam papers in 4 hours. How long would it take one teacher to mark all 60 papers?

14. 10 ladybirds eat 400 greenflies in 3 hours.
    Copy and complete the following:
    (a) 20 ladybirds eat * greenflies in 3 hours.
    (b) 20 ladybirds eat * greenflies in 9 hours.
    (c) 10 ladybirds eat 200 greenflies in * hours.
    (d) * ladybirds eat 4000 greenflies in 3 hours.

Exercise 27

1. If 7 packets of coffee costs $8·54, find the cost of 3 packets.

2. Find the cost of 8 bottles of wine, given that 5 bottles cost $11·90.

3. If 7 cartons of milk hold 14 litres, find how much milk there is in 6 cartons.

4. On an army exercise, 5 soldiers took 6 hours to dig a trench. How long would it have taken 3 soldiers to dig an identical trench?

5. A party of 10 people exploring a desert took enough water to last 5 days. How long would the water have lasted if there had been only 5 people in the party?

6. A worker takes 8 minutes to make 2 circuit boards. How long would it take to make 7 circuit boards?

7. On a rose bush there are enough greenflies to last 9 ladybirds 4 hours. How long would the greenflies last if there were only 6 ladybirds?

8. The total weight of 8 tiles is 1720 g. How much do 17 tiles weigh?

9. A machine can fill 3000 bottles in 15 minutes. How many bottles will it fill in 2 minutes?

10. A train travels 40 km in 120 minutes. How long will it take to travel 55 km at the same speed?

11. If 4 grapefruit can be bought for $2·96, how many can be bought for $8·14?

12. £15 can be exchanged for 126 francs. How many francs can be exchanged for £37·50?

13. Usually it takes 10 hours for 4 men to build a wall. How many men are needed to build the same wall in 8 hours?

14. A car travels 280 km on 35 litres of petrol. How much petrol is needed for a journey of 440 km?

15. Ten bags of corn will feed 60 hens for 3 days. Copy and complete the following:
    (a) 30 bags of corn will feed * hens for 3 days.
    (b) 10 bags of corn will feed 20 hens for * days.
    (c) 10 bags of corn will feed * hens for 18 days.
    (d) 30 bags of corn will feed 90 hens for * days.

16. Four machines produce 5000 batteries in 10 hours. How many batteries would 6 machines produce in 10 hours?

17. Newtonian spiders can spin webs in straight lines. If 15 spiders can spin a web of length 1 metre in 30 minutes, how long will it take 6 spiders to spin a web of the same length?

18. In the army all holes are dug 4 feet deep. It takes 8 soldiers 36 minutes to dig a hole 18 feet long by 10 feet wide. How long will it take 5 soldiers to dig a hole 36 feet by 10 feet?

19. It takes b beavers n hours to build a dam. How long will it take half the beavers to build the same size dam?

3.11 Speed, distance and time

Calculations involving these three quantities are simpler when the speed is *constant*. The formulae connecting the quantities are as follows:

(a) distance = speed × time

(b) speed = $\dfrac{\text{distance}}{\text{time}}$

(c) time = $\dfrac{\text{distance}}{\text{speed}}$

A helpful way of remembering these formulae is to write the letters D, S and T in a triangle, thus:

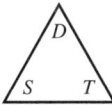

to find D, cover D and we have ST

to find S, cover S and we have $\dfrac{D}{T}$

to find T, cover T and we have $\dfrac{D}{S}$

Great care must be taken with the units in these questions.

Example 1
A man is running at a speed of 8 km/h for a distance of 5200 metres. Find the time taken in minutes.

$$5200 \text{ metres} = 5 \cdot 2 \text{ km}$$

$$\text{time taken in hours} = \left(\frac{D}{S}\right) = \frac{5 \cdot 2}{8}$$

$$= 0 \cdot 65 \text{ hours}$$

$$\text{time taken in minutes} = 0 \cdot 65 \times 60$$

$$= 39 \text{ minutes}$$

Example 2
Change the units of a speed of 54 km/h into metres per second.

$$54 \text{ km/hour} = 54\,000 \text{ metres/hour}$$

$$= \frac{54\,000}{60} \text{ metres/minute}$$

$$= \frac{54\,000}{60 \times 60} \text{ metres/second}$$

$$= 15 \text{ m/s}$$

Exercise 28

1. Find the time taken for the following journeys:
   (a) 100 km at a speed of 40 km/h
   (b) 250 miles at a speed of 80 miles per hour
   (c) 15 metres at a speed of 20 cm/s (answer in seconds)
   (d) 10^4 metres at a speed of 2·5 km/h

2. Change the units of the following speeds as indicated:
   (a) 72 km/h into m/s
   (b) 108 km/h into m/s
   (c) 300 km/h into m/s
   (d) 30 m/s into km/h
   (e) 22 m/s into km/h
   (f) 0·012 m/s into cm/s
   (g) 9000 cm/s into m/s
   (h) 600 miles/day into miles per hour
   (i) 2592 miles/day into miles per second

3. Find the speeds of the bodies which move as follows:
   (a) a distance of 600 km in 8 hours
   (b) a distance of 31·64 km in 7 hours
   (c) a distance of 136·8 m in 18 seconds
   (d) a distance of 4×10^4 m in 10^{-2} seconds
   (e) a distance of 5×10^5 cm in 2×10^{-3} seconds
   (f) a distance of 10^8 mm in 30 minutes (in km/h)
   (g) a distance of 500 m in 10 minutes (in km/h)

4. Find the distance travelled (in metres) in the following:
   (a) at a speed of 55 km/h for 2 hours
   (b) at a speed of 40 km/h for $\frac{1}{4}$ hour
   (c) at a speed of 338·4 km/h for 10 minutes
   (d) at a speed of 15 m/s for 5 minutes
   (e) at a speed of 14 m/s for 1 hour
   (f) at a speed of 4×10^3 m/s for 2×10^{-2} seconds
   (g) at a speed of 8×10^5 cm/s for 2 minutes

5. A car travels 60 km at 30 km/h and then a further 180 km at 160 km/h. Find:
   (a) the total time taken
   (b) the average speed for the whole journey.

6. A cyclist travels 25 kilometres at 20 km/h and then a further 80 kilometres at 25 km/h. Find:
   (a) the total time taken
   (b) the average speed for the whole journey.

7. A swallow flies at a speed of 50 km/h for 3 hours and then at a speed of 40 km/h for a further 2 hours. Find the average speed for the whole journey.

3.12 Approximations

A car travels a distance of 158 km in $3\frac{1}{2}$ hours. What is the average speed?

$$\text{Speed} = \frac{\text{Distance}}{\text{Time}} = \frac{158}{3 \cdot 5}$$

On a calculator the answer is 45·142 857 14 km/h.
It is not sensible to give all these figures in the answer. We have used a distance and a time which may not be all that accurate. It would be reasonable to give the answer as '45 km/h'.

We can approximate in two ways:
   (a) we can give *significant figures* (s.f.)
   (b) we can give *decimal places* (d.p.)

Each type of approximation is described below.

Significant figures

Example
Write the following numbers correct to three significant figures (3 s.f.).

(a) 2·6582 = 2·66 (to 3 s.f.)
      ↑

(b) 0·5142 = 0·514 (to 3 s.f.)
       ↑

(c) 84 660 = 84 700 (to 3 s.f.)
      ↑

(d) 0·04031 = 0·0403 (to 3 s.f.)
        ↑

In each case we look at the number marked with an arrow to see if it is 'five or more'.

Exercise 29

In Questions **1** to **8** write the numbers correct to three significant figures.

1. 2·3462	**2.** 0·814 38	**3.** 26·241	**4.** 35·55
5. 112·74	**6.** 210·82	**7.** 0·8254	**8.** 0·031 162

In Questions **9** to **16** write the numbers correct to two significant figures.

9. 5·894	**10.** 1·232	**11.** 0·5456	**12.** 0·7163
13. 0·1443	**14.** 1·831	**15.** 24·83	**16.** 31·37

In Questions **17** to **24** write the numbers correct to four significant figures.

17. 486·72	**18.** 500·36	**19.** 2·8888	**20.** 3·1125
21. 0·071 542	**22.** 3·0405	**23.** 2463·5	**24.** 488 852

In Questions **25** to **36** write the numbers to the degree of accuracy indicated.

25. 0·5126 (3 s.f.)	**26.** 5·821 (2 s.f.)	**27.** 65·89 (2 s.f.)	**28.** 587·55 (4 s.f.)
29. 0·581 (1 s.f.)	**30.** 0·0713 (1 s.f.)	**31.** 5·8354 (3 s.f.)	**32.** 87·84 (2 s.f.)
33. 2482 (2 s.f.)	**34.** 52 666 (3 s.f.)	**35.** 0·0058 (1 s.f.)	**36.** 6568 (1 s.f.)

Decimal places

Example
Write the following numbers correct to two decimal places (2 d.p.).

(a) 8·358 = 8·36 (to 2 d.p.)
       ↑

(b) 0·0328 = 0·03 (to 2 d.p.)
        ↑

(c) 74·355 = 74·36 (to 2 d.p.)
        ↑

In each case we look at the number marked with an arrow to see if its is 'five or more'.
Here we count figures after the decimal point.

Exercise 30

In Questions **1** to **8** write the numbers correct to two decimal places (2 d.p.).

1. 5·381	**2.** 11·0482	**3.** 0·414	**4.** 0·3666
5. 8·015	**6.** 87·044	**7.** 9·0062	**8.** 0·0724

In Questions **9** to **16** write the numbers correct to one decimal place.

9. 8·424	**10.** 0·7413	**11.** 0·382	**12.** 0·095
13. 6·083	**14.** 19·53	**15.** 8·111	**16.** 7·071

In Questions **17** to **28** write the numbers to the degree of accuracy indicated.

17. 8·155 (2 d.p.)   **18.** 3·042 (1 d.p.)   **19.** 0·5454 (3 d.p.)   **20.** 0·005 55 (4 d.p.)

21. 0·7071 (2 d.p.)   **22.** 6·8271 (2 d.p.)   **23.** 0·8413 (1 d.p.)   **24.** 19·646 (2 d.p.)

25. 0·071 35 (4 d.p.)   **26.** 60·051 (1 d.p.)   **27.** −7·30 (1 d.p.)   **28.** −5·424 (2 d.p.)

29. Use a ruler to measure the dimensions of the rectangles below.
    (a) Write down the length and width in cm correct to one d.p.
    (b) Work out the area of each rectangle and give the answer in cm² correct to one d.p.

(i)

(ii)

Exercise 31

Write the answers to the degree of accuracy indicated.

1. 0·153 × 3·74 (2 d.p.)   **2.** 18·09 ÷ 5·24 (3 s.f.)

3. 184 × 2·342 (3 s.f.)   **4.** 17·2 ÷ 0·89 (1 d.p.)

5. 58 ÷ 261 (2 s.f.)   **6.** 88·8 × 44·4 (1 d.p.)

7. (8·4 − 1·32) × 7·5 (2 s.f.)   **8.** (121 + 3758) ÷ 211 (3 s.f.)

9. (1·24 − 1·144) × 0·61 (3 d.p.)   **10.** 1 ÷ 0·935 (1 d.p.)

11. 78·3524² (3 s.f.)   **12.** (18·25 − 6·941)² (2 d.p.)

13. 9·245² − 65·2 (1 d.p.)   **14.** (2 − 0·666) ÷ 0·028 (3 s.f.)

15. 8·43³ (1 d.p.)   **16.** 0·924² − 0·835² (2 d.p.)

3.13 Metric units

Length	Mass	Volume
10 mm = 1 cm	1000 g = 1 kg	1000 ml = 1 litre
100 cm = 1 m	1000 kg = 1 t	1000 *l* = 1 m³
1000 m = 1 km	(t for tonne)	Also 1 ml = 1 cm³

Exercise 32

Copy and complete.

1. 85 cm = m
2. 2·4 km = m
3. 0·63 m = cm
4. 25 cm = m
5. 7 mm = cm
6. 2 cm = mm
7. 1·2 km = m
8. 7 m = cm
9. 0·58 km = m
10. 815 mm = m
11. 650 m = km
12. 25 mm = cm
13. 5 kg = g
14. 4·2 kg = g
15. 6·4 kg = g
16. 3 kg = g
17. 0·8 kg = g
18. 400 g = kg
19. 2 t = kg
20. 250 g = kg
21. 0·5 t = kg
22. 0·62 t = kg
23. 7 kg = t
24. 1500 g = kg
25. 800 ml = l
26. 2 l = ml
27. 1000 ml = l
28. 4·5 l = ml
29. 6 l = ml
30. 3 l = cm^3
31. 2 m^3 = l
32. 5·5 m^3 = l

33. 0·9 l = cm^3
34. 600 cm^3 = l
35. 15 m^3 = l
36. 240 ml = l
37. 28 cm = m
38. 5·5 m = cm
39. 305 g = kg
40. 0·046 km = m
41. 16 ml = l
42. 208 mm = m
43. 28 mm = cm
44. 27 cm = m
45. 788 m = km
46. 14 t = kg
47. 1·3 kg = g
48. 90 l = m^3
49. 2·9 t = kg
50. 19 ml = l

51. Write down the most appropriate metric unit for measuring:
    (a) the distance between Madrid and Barcelona
    (b) the capacity of a wine bottle
    (c) the mass of raisins needed for a cake
    (d) the diameter of small drill
    (e) the mass of a car
    (f) the area of a football pitch.

Exercise 33

The school's technology department have a wonderful new computer-controlled machine. It is fed with waste plastic and can be programmed to produce any fairly small object. As a demonstration, Mr Evans shows his class how to make dice. He programs the machine to produce centimetre cubes.

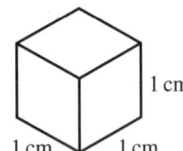
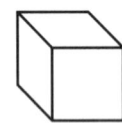
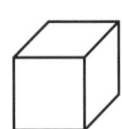

At the end of the afternoon Mr Evans has one million cubes.

1. The million cubes could be stuck together with super glue to make a tower.
   Would the tower be as tall as:
   (a) Nelson's Column?
   (b) The Empire State Building?
   (c) Mount Everest?

2. If the cubes were placed in a single
   layer, would there be enough to cover:
   (a) the floor of your classroom?
   (b) a football pitch?

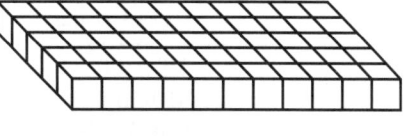

3. If the cubes were in a solid mass,
   would there be enough:
   (a) to fill your classroom?
   (b) to fill a large fridge-freezer?

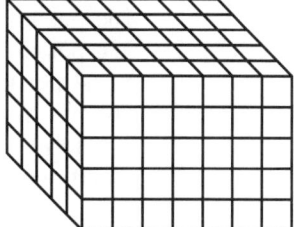

4. Mrs Evans soon realises the potential of the cubes, which by this
   time are rather famous, and she sets out to make not a million
   but a *billion* of the cubes [1,000,000,000].
   (a) Would that be enough to fill your classroom?
   (b) Placed side by side, roughly how many times would they go
       around the London ring road (184 km)?

3.14 Problems 1

Making a profit

Example

A shopkeeper buys potatoes at a wholesale price of $180 per tonne and
sells them at a retail price of 22c per kg.
How much profit does he make on one kilogram of potatoes?

He pays $180 for 1000 kg of potatoes. ∴ he pays $[180 ÷ 1000] for 1 kg of potatoes.
i.e. he pays 18c for 1 kg

He sells at 22c per kg.
∴ profit = 4c per kg

Exercise 34

Find the profit in each case.

Commodity	Retail price	Wholesale price	Profit
1. cans of drink	15c each	$11 per 100	profit per can?
2. rulers	24c each	$130 per 1000	profit per ruler?
3. birthday cards	22c each	$13 per 100	profit per card?
4. soup	27c per can	$8·50 for 50 cans	profit per can?
5. newspapers	22c each	$36 for 200	profit per paper?
6. box of matches	37c each	$15·20 for 80	profit per box?
7. potatoes	22c per kg	$160 per tonne	profit per kg?
8. carrots	38c per kg	$250 per tonne	profit per kg?
9. T-shirts	$4·95 each	$38·40 per dozen	profit per T-shirt?
10. eggs	96c per dozen	$50 per 1000	profit per dozen?

Commodity	Retail price	Wholesale price	Profit
11. oranges	5 for 30c	$14 for 400	profit per orange?
12. car tyres	$19·50 each	$2450 for 200	profit per tyre?
13. wine	55c for 100 ml	$40 for 10 litres	profit per 100 ml?
14. sand	16c per kg	$110 per tonne	profit per kg?
15. wire	23c per m	$700 for 10 km	profit per m?
16. cheese	$2·64 per kg	$87·50 for 50 kg	profit per kg?
17. copper tube	46c per m	$160 for 500 m	profit per m?
18. apples	9c each	$10·08 per gross	profit per apple?
19. carpet	$6·80 per m²	$1600 for 500 m²	profit per m²?
20. tin of soup	33c per tin	$72 for 400 tins	profit per tin?

Exercise 35

1. There are 1128 pupils in a school and there are 36 more girls than boys. How many girls attend the school?

2. A generous, but not very bright, teacher decides to award 1c to the person coming 10th in a test, 2c to the person coming 9th, 4c to the person coming 8th and so on, doubling the amount each time. How much does the teacher award to the person who came top?

3. A tree was planted when James Wilkinson was born. He died in 1920, aged 75. How old was the tree in 1975?

4. Washing-up liquid is sold in 200 ml containers. Each container costs 57c. How much will it cost to buy 10 litres of the liquid?

5. A train is supposed to leave Rome at 11:24 and arrive in Milan at 12:40. The train was delayed and arrived $2\frac{1}{4}$ hours late. At what time did the train arrive?

6. Big Ben was stopped for repairs at 17:15 on Tuesday and restarted at 08:20 on Wednesday. For how long had it been stopped?

7. How much would I pay for nine litres of paint if two litres cost $2·30?

8. A television set was advertised at $282·50 for cash, or by 12 equal instalments of $25·30. How much would be saved by paying cash?

9. Eggs are packed twelve to a box. A farmer has enough eggs to fill 316 boxes with unbroken eggs and he has 62 cracked eggs left over. How many eggs had he to start with?

10. A car travels 9 km on a litre of petrol and petrol costs $0·68 per litre. Over a period of one year the car travels a distance of 9600 km. How much does the petrol cost for the whole year?

Exercise 36

1. Copy and complete the following bill.

   $6\frac{1}{2}$ kg of potatoes at 50c per kg = $

   4 kg of beef at ____ per kg = $7·20

   ____ jars of coffee at 95c per jar = $6·65

   Total = $

2. A hotel manager was able to buy loaves of bread at $4·44 per dozen, whereas the shop price was 43c per loaf. How much did he save on each loaf?

3. John Lowe made darts history in 1984 with the first ever perfect game played in a tournament, 501 scored in just nine darts. He won a special prize of £100 000 from the sponsors of the tournament. His first eight darts were six treble 20s, treble 17 and treble 18.
   (a) What did he score with the ninth dart?
   (b) How much did he win per dart thrown, to the nearest pound?

4. How many 50 ml bottles can be filled from a jar containing 7 litres of liquid?

5. Find two numbers which multiply together to give 60 and which add up to 19.

   ◯ × ◯ = 60, ◯ + ◯ = 19

6. Two numbers m and z are such that z is greater than 10 and m is less than 8. Arrange the numbers 9, z and m in order of size, starting with the smallest.

7. One day a third of the class is absent and 16 children are present. How many children are in the class when no one is away?

8. A train leaves Manchester at 09:00 and travels towards London at 150 km/h. Another train leaves London for Manchester, also at 09:00, and travels at 120 km/h. Which train is nearer to London when they meet?

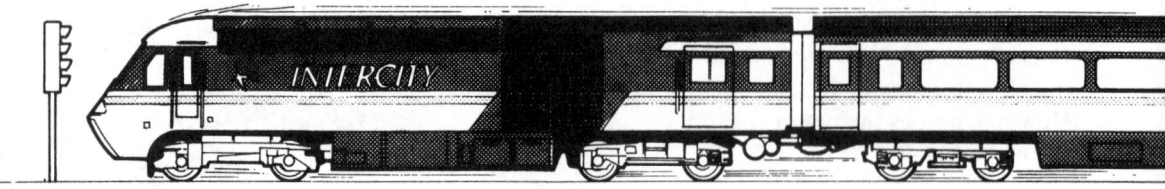

9. A man is 35 cm taller than his daughter, who is 5 cm shorter than her mother. The man was born in 1949 and is 1·80 m tall. How tall is his wife?

10. In a simple code A = 1, B = 2, C = 3, ... Z = 26. Decode the following messages.
   (a) 23, 8, 1, 20
       20, 9, 13, 5
       4, 15
       23, 5
       6, 9, 14, 9, 19, 8.
   (b) 19, 4^2, (3 × 7), 18, (90 − 71)
       1^3, (9 × 2), ($2^2 + 1^2$)
       18, ($\frac{1}{5}$ of 105), 2, (1 ÷ $\frac{1}{2}$), 3^2, 19, 2^3.
   (c) 23, (100 ÷ 20)
       1, (2 × 3 × 3), ($2^2 + 1^2$)
       21, (100 − 86), (100 ÷ 25), 5, ($2^4 + 2$)
       1, (5 × 4), (10 ÷ $\frac{1}{2}$), 1, (27 ÷ 9), (99 ÷ 9).

Exercise 37

1. Twelve calculators cost $102. How many calculators could be bought for $76·50?

2. A car travels 35 m in 0·7 seconds. How far does it travel in
   (a) 0·1 s?   (b) 1 s?   (c) 2 minutes?

3. The outline of a coin is shown below.

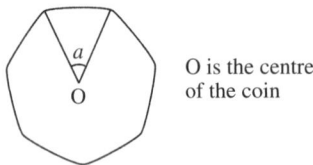

O is the centre of the coin

Calculate the size of the angle, a, to the nearest $\frac{1}{10}$ of a degree.

4. The diagram below shows the map of a farm which grows four different crops in the regions shown.

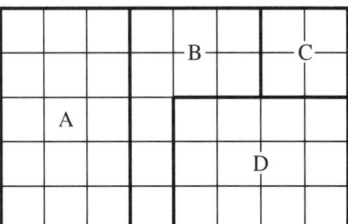

Each square represents one hectare.
(a) What is the total area of the farm?
(b) What area is used for crop A?
(c) What percentage of the farm is used for
    (i) crop C   (ii) crop D
    (iii) crop A   (iv) crop B?

5. An examination is marked out of a total of 120 marks. How many marks did Imran get if he scored 65% of the marks?

6. A man worked 7 hours per day from Monday to Friday and 4 hours overtime on Saturday. The rate of pay from Monday to Friday is $4·50 per hour and the overtime rate is time and a half. How much did he earn during the week?

7. A man smokes 40 cigarettes a day and each packet of 20 cigarettes costs $3·45. How much does he spend on cigarettes in a whole year of 365 days?

8. A shopkeeper buys coffee at $3·65 per kg and sells it at 95c per 100 g. How much profit does he make per kg?

9. Five 2's can make 25: $25 = 22 + 2 + \frac{2}{2}$
    (a) Use four 9's to make 100   (b) Use three 6's to make 7
    (c) Use three 5's to make 60   (d) Use five 5's to make 61
    (e) Use four 7's to make 1   (f) Use three 8's to make 11

10. Find the missing digits.

Exercise 38

1. A special new cheese is on offer at $3·48 per kilogram. Mrs Mann buys half a kilogram. How much change does she receive if she pays with a $5 note?

2. A cup and a saucer together cost $2·80. The cup costs 60c more than the saucer. How much does the cup cost?

3. A garden 9 m by 12 m is to be treated with fertilizer. One cup of fertilizer covers an area of 2 m^2 and one bag of fertilizer is sufficient for 18 cups.
   (a) Find the area of the garden.
   (b) Find the number of bags of fertilizer needed.

4. Copy and complete the pattern below.

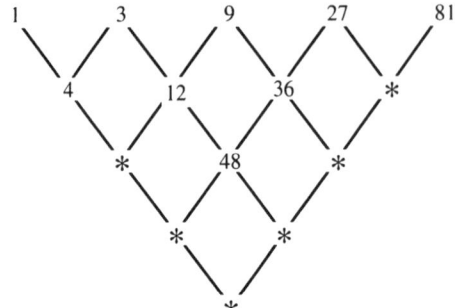

5. Six lamp posts lie at equal distances from each other along a straight road. If the distance between each pair of lamp posts is 20 m, how far is it from the first lamp post to the sixth?

6. An engineering firm offers all of its workers a choice of two pay rises. Workers can choose either an 8% increase on their salaries or they can accept a rise of $3200.
   (a) A fitter earns $20 800 a year. Which pay rise should he choose?
   (b) The personnel manager earns $46 000 a year. Which pay rise should he choose?

7. A ship's voyage started at 20:30 on Tuesday and finished at 07:00 on the next day.
   How long was the journey in hours and minutes?

8. Work out, without using a calculator:
   (a) 0·6 − 0·06
   (b) 0·04 × 1000
   (c) 0·4 ÷ 100
   (d) 7·2 − 5
   (e) 10% of £90
   (f) 25% of £160.

9. In 1984 the population of the United States was 232 million. The population was expected to grow by 12% by the end of the century. Find the expected population at the end of the century, correct to the nearest million.

10. Find two numbers which:
    (a) multiply to give 12 and add up to 7.
    (b) multiply to give 42 and add up to 13.
    (c) multiply to give 32 and add up to 12.
    (d) multiply to give 48 and add up to 26.

Exercise 39

1. In a simple code A = 1, B = 2, C = 3 and so on. When the word 'BAT' is written in code its total score is (2 + 1 + 20) = 23.
   (a) Find the score for the word 'ZOOM'
   (b) Find the score for the word 'ALPHABET'
   (c) Find a word with a score of 40.

2. How many cubes, each of edge 1 cm, are required to fill a box with internal dimensions 5 cm by 8 cm by 3 cm?

3. A swimming pool 20 m by 12 m contains water to a uniform depth of $1\frac{1}{2}$ m and 1 m^3 of water weighs 1000 kg. What is the weight of the water in the pool?

4. Place the following numbers in order of size, smallest first:
   0·12, 0·012, 0·21, 0·021, 0·03.

5. The houses in a street are numbered from 1 to 60.
   How many times does the number '2' appear?

6. Draw a large copy of the square below.

1	2	3	4

   Your task is to fill up all 16 squares using four 1's, four 2's, four 3's and four 4's. Each number may appear only once in any row (↔) or column (↕). The first row has been drawn already.

7. Between the times 11 : 57 and 12 : 27 the odometer of a car changes from 23 793 km to 23 825 km.
   At what average speed is the car travelling?

8. Which of the shapes below can be drawn without going over any line twice and without taking the pencil from the paper? Write 'yes' or 'no' for each shape.

(a) 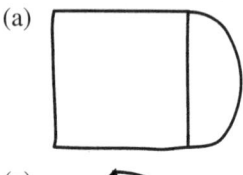 (b) 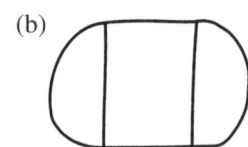 (c) 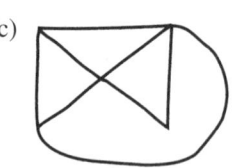 (d)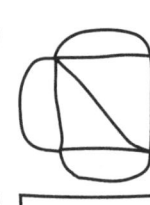

(e)  (f) 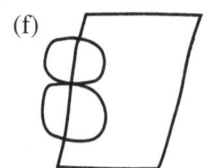 (g) 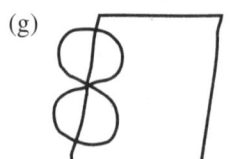 (h)

Revision exercise 3A

1. A supermarket sells their 'own-label' raspberry jam in two sizes.

Which jar represents the better value for money? You are given that 1 kg = 2·20 lb.

2. (a) Calculate the speed (in metres per second) of a slug which moves a distance of 30 cm in 1 minute.
   (b) Calculate the time taken for a bullet to travel 8 km at a speed of 5000 m/s.
   (c) Calculate the distance flown, in a time of four hours, by a pigeon which flies at a speed of 12 m/s.

3. The pump shows the price of petrol in a garage.

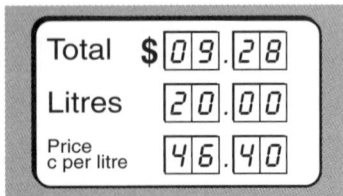

One day I buy $20 worth of petrol: How many litres do I buy?

4. (a) On a map, the distance between two points is 16 cm. Calculate the scale of the map if the actual distance between the points is 8 km.
   (b) On another map, two points appear 1·5 cm apart and are in fact 60 km apart. Calculate the scale of the map.

5. In December 1999, a factory employed 220 people, each person being paid $650 per week.
   (a) Calculate the total weekly wage bill for the factory.
   (b) In January 2000, the work force of 220 was reduced by 10 per cent. Find the number of people employed at the factory after the reduction.
   (c) Also in January 2000, the weekly wage of $650 was increased by 10 per cent. Find the new weekly wage.
   (d) Calculate the total weekly wage bill for the factory in January 2000.
   (e) Calculate the difference between the total weekly wage bills in December 1999 and January 2000.

6. The following are the first six numbers, written in order of size, of a pattern.
   4, 13, 28, 49, 76, 109.
   (a) Which of these numbers are:
      (i) odd numbers,
      (ii) square numbers,
      (iii) prime numbers?

(b) The difference between the first and second numbers, that is 13 − 4, is 9; between the second and the third it is 15, between the third and the fourth it is 21. Work out the difference between
   (i) the fourth and the fifth,
   (ii) the fifth and the sixth.
(c) By considering your answers in (b), find the seventh and eighth numbers of the pattern.
   Explain how you reached this decision.
(d) Use the method you have described to write down the next two terms in the following pattern.
   1, 4, 12, 25, 43, 66, —, —.

7. The sketch of a clock tower is shown.

40 cm

A model of the tower is made using a scale of 1 to 20.
(a) The minute hand on the tower clock is 40 cm long. What is the length of the minute hand on the model?
(b) The height of the model is 40 cm. What is the height h, in metres, of the clock tower?

8. A train travels between Milan and Pina, a distance of 108 km, in 45 minutes, at a steady speed. It passes through Rosta 40 minutes after leaving Milan. How far, in km, is it from Rosta to Pina?

9. A school decides to have a disco from 8 p.m. to midnight. The price of the tickets will be 20c. The costs are as follows:
   Disco and D.J., $25
   Hire of hall, $5 an hour
   200 cans of soft drinks at 15c each
   200 packets of crisps at 10c each
   Printing of tickets, $5
(a) What is the total cost of putting on the disco?
(b) How many tickets must be sold to cover the cost?
(c) If 400 tickets are sold, all the drinks are sold at 20c each and all the packets of crisps at 12c each, calculate the profit or loss the school finally makes.

10. A man buys 500 pencils at 2·4 cents each. What change does he receive from $20?

11. Every day at school Stephen buys a roll for 28c, crisps for 22c and a drink for 42c. How much does he spend in dollars in the whole school year of 200 days?

12. An athlete runs 25 laps of a track in 30 minutes 10 seconds.
    (a) How many seconds does he take to run 25 laps?
    (b) How long does he take to run one lap, if he runs the 25 laps at a constant speed?

13. A pile of 250 tiles is 2 m thick. What is the thickness of one tile in cm?

14. Copy the following bill and complete it by filling in the four blank spaces.

    8 rolls of wallpaper at
    $3·20 each   = $ ...
    3 tins of paint at $ ... each = $ 20·10
    ... brushes at $2·40 each   = $ 9·60
                        Total   = $ ...

15. Work out the difference between one ton and one tonne.

    | 1 tonne | = | 1000 kg |
    | 1 ton | = | 2240 lb |
    | 1 lb | = | 454 g |

Give your answer to the nearest kg.

16. A motorist travelled 200 km in five hours. Her average speed for the first 100 km was 50 km/h. What was her average speed for the second 100 km?

17. Work out
    (a) 20% of $65
    (b) 37% of $400
    (c) 8·5% of $2000.

Examination exercise 3B

1. Copy and complete these statements:

    12 × ☐ = 156

    56 ÷ ☐ = 8

    ☐ − 5 = 4

    42 − ☐ = 19

    [J 97 1]

2. Copy and complete these statements:
   If the number in the answer space is prime, write PRIME next to it.
   If it is not prime, write it as the product of its prime factors.
   The first two have been done for you.

   Answer   39 ... = 3 × 13 ...   43 ....   47 ....

   41 ... PRIME ...   45 ....   49 ....

   [J 96 1]

3. 15 000 people attended a pop concert.
   Half of them paid $30 each, a third of them paid $40 each and the rest paid $50 each.
   Calculate the total amount paid.

   [J 98 1]

4. The woman is standing next to a flood-level marker.
   (a) In what units must the numbers be?
   (b) Estimate the height of the woman, in the same units.
   (c) Write your answer to part (b) in metres.

   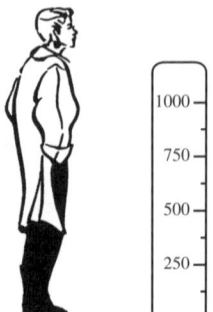

   [J 98 1]

5. 16 500 Europeans were interviewed in a survey on heart disease.

   The results show that
   one in five has high blood pressure,
   seven out of ten have high cholesterol levels,
   one in four is a regular smoker,
   one in five takes no exercise.

   (a) What percentage of the group has high blood pressure?
   (b) How many people in the group have high cholesterol levels?

(c) The population of Europe is 492 million.
Use the survey results to estimate how many people in Europe are regular smokers.

(d) What is the ratio $\dfrac{\text{number of people who take no exercise}}{\text{number of people who take exercise}}$? [J 97 3]

6. (a) Nine dots can be arranged in a square, $\begin{smallmatrix}\cdot&\cdot&\cdot\\\cdot&\cdot&\cdot\\\cdot&\cdot&\cdot\end{smallmatrix}$, so 9 is a square number.
The first three square numbers are 1, 4 and 9.
Write down the next three square numbers.

(b) Six dots can be arranged in a triangle, $\begin{smallmatrix}&\cdot&\\\cdot&\cdot&\cdot\\\cdot&\cdot&\cdot\end{smallmatrix}$, so 6 is a triangle number.
The first four triangle numbers are 1, 3, 6 and 10.
Write down the next two triangle numbers.

(c) (i) Study the sums of odd numbers.
Copy and fill in the two spaces.

$$1 = 1$$
$$1 + 3 = 4$$
$$1 + 3 + 5 = \underline{}$$
$$1 + 3 + 5 + 7 = \underline{}$$

(ii) What do you notice about these answers.
(iii) Work out the sum of the first 10 odd numbers.
(iv) Work out the sum of the first 210 odd numbers.

(d) Study the sums of these triangle numbers.
(i) Copy and fill in the two spaces.

$$1 + 3 = 4$$
$$3 + 6 = \underline{}$$
$$6 + 10 = \underline{}$$

(ii) Write down the next two lines of this pattern.
(iii) What do you notice about these answers? [N 96 3]

4 HANDLING DATA 1

4.1 Displaying data

Raw data in the form of numbers is collected when surveys or experiments are conducted. This sort of information is often much easier to understand when either a pie chart or a frequency diagram is drawn.

Pie charts

Example

The pie chart shows the holiday intentions of 600 people.

(a) Number of people camping $= \frac{60}{360} \times 600$
$= 100$

(b) Number of people touring $= \frac{72}{360} \times 600$
$= 120$

(c) Number of people at seaside $= \frac{102}{360} \times 600$
$= 170$

Exercise 1

1. The total cost of a holiday was $900. The pie chart shows how this cost was made up.

   (a) How much was spent on food?
   (b) How much was spent on travel?
   (c) How much was spent on the hotel?
   (d) How much was spent on other items?

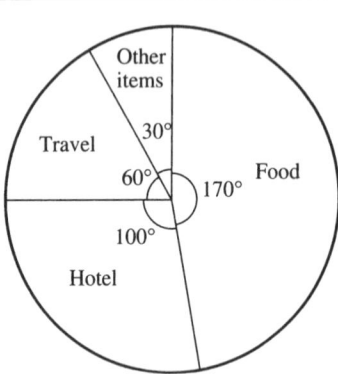

2. Mr Chirac had an income of $60 000. The pie chart shows how he used the money.

   How much did he spend on:
   (a) food,
   (b) rent,
   (c) savings,
   (d) entertainment,
   (e) travel?

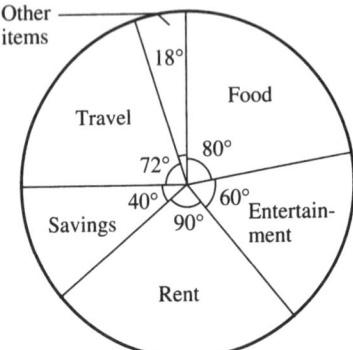

3. The total expenditure of a Council is $36 000 000. The pie chart shows how the money was spent.

   (a) How much was spent on:
       (i) education   (ii) health care?
   (b) What is the angle representing expenditure on highways?
   (c) How much was spent on highways?

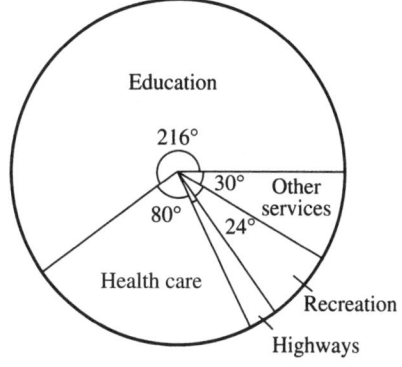

4. The pie chart shows how a pupil spends her time in a maths lesson which lasts 60 minutes.

   (a) How much time does she spend:
       (i) getting ready to work,
       (ii) talking,
       (iii) sharpening a pencil?
   (b) She spends 3 minutes working. What is the angle on the pie chart for the time spent working?

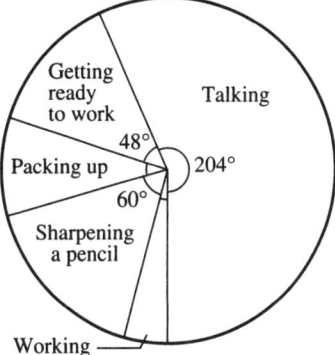

Exercise 2

1. At the semi-final stage of the UEFA Champions' Cup, 72 neutral referees were asked to predict who they thought would win. Their answers were:

   | Bayern Munich | 9 | Real Madrid | 22 |
   | Manchester United | 40 | Milan | 1 |

   (a) Work out
       (i) $\frac{9}{72}$ of 360°   (ii) $\frac{40}{72}$ of 360°   (iii) $\frac{22}{72}$ of 360°   (iv) $\frac{1}{72}$ of 360°
   (b) Draw an accurate pie chart to display the predictions of the 72 referees.

2. A survey was carried out to find what 400 pupils did at the end of the fifth year:

   120 went into the sixth form
   160 went into employment
   80 went to F.E. colleges
   40 were unemployed.

   (a) Simplify the following fractions: $\frac{120}{400}$; $\frac{160}{400}$; $\frac{80}{400}$; $\frac{40}{400}$.
   (b) Draw an accurate pie chart to show the information above.

3. In a survey on washing powder 180 people were asked to state which brand they preferred. 45 chose Brand A.

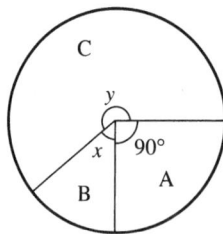

If 30 people chose brand B and 105 chose Brand C, calculate the angles x and y.

4. A packet of breakfast cereal weighing 600 g contains four ingredients as follows:

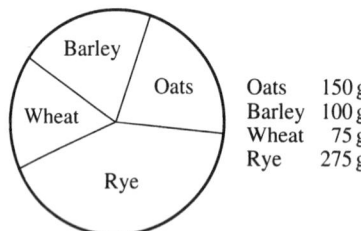

Oats   150 g
Barley   100 g
Wheat   75 g
Rye   275 g

Calculate the angles on the pie chart shown and draw an accurate diagram.

5. The table below shows the share of British car sales achieved by four companies in one year.

Company	A	B	C	D
Share of sales	50%	10%	25%	15%

In a pie chart to show this information, find the angle of the sectors representing:

(a) Company A
(b) Company B
(c) Company C
(d) Company D.

Frequency diagrams and bar charts

Example

The marks obtained by 36 pupils in a test were as follows.

```
1 3 2 3 4 2 1 3 0
5 3 0 1 4 0 4 4 3
3 4 3 1 3 4 3 1 2
1 3 4 0 4 3 2 5 3
```

Show the data:
(a) on a tally chart   (b) on a frequency diagram.

(a)

Mark	Tally	Frequency
0	||||	4
1	⌊卌 |	6
2	||||	4
3	卌 卌 ||	12
4	卌 |||	8
5	||	2

(b)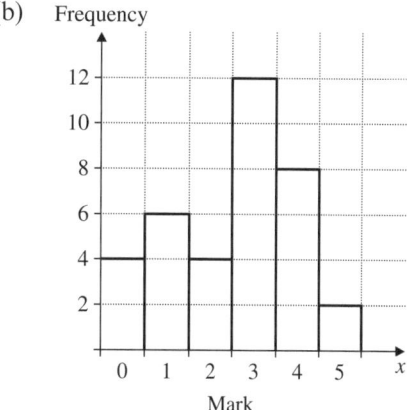

Exercise 3

1. In a survey, the number of occupants in the cars passing a school was recorded.

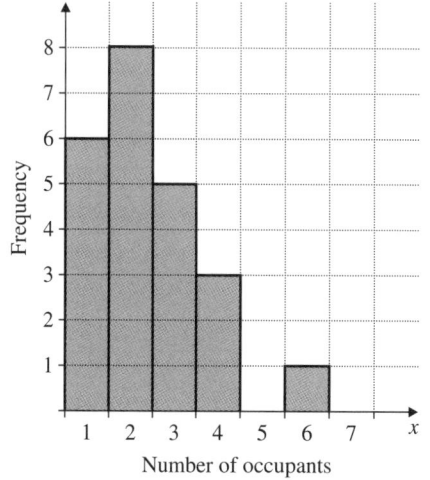

(a) How many cars had 3 occupants?
(b) How many cars had less than 4 occupants?
(c) How many cars were in the survey?
(d) What was the total number of occupants in all the cars in the survey?
(e) What fraction of the cars had only one occupant?

2. In an experiment, two dice were thrown sixty times and the total score showing was recorded.

```
 2   3   5  4   8   6   4   7   5  10
 7   8   7  6  12  11   8  11   7   6
 6   5   7  7   8   6   7   3   6   7
12   3  10  4   3   7   2  11   8   5
 7  10   7  5   7   5  10  11   7  10
 4   8   6  4   6  11   6  12  11   5
```

(a) Draw a tally chart to show the results of the experiment. The tally chart is started below.

Score	Tally marks	Frequency
2	||	2
3	||||	4
4		
.		
.		

(b) Draw a frequency graph to illustrate the results. Plot the frequency on the vertical axis.

3. The bar chart shows the profit/loss made by a toy shop from September 2000 to April 2001.

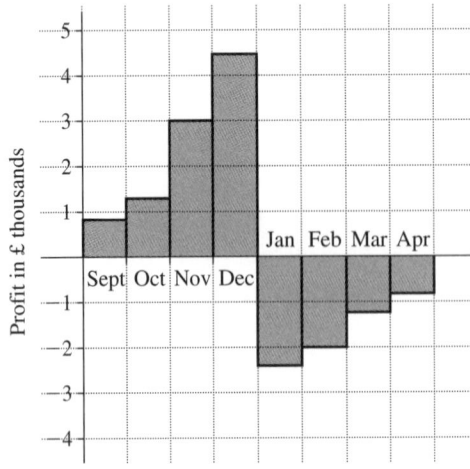

(a) Estimate the total profit in this period.
(b) Describe what is happening to the shop's profits in this period. Try to think of an explanation for the shape of the bar chart.

Grouped data

Sometimes the data to be displayed can take a wide range of values. In such cases, it is convenient to put the data into groups before drawing a tally chart and frequency diagram.

Example

The hand spans  of 21 children were measured as follows:

```
14·8  20·0  16·9  20·7  18·1  17·5  18·7
19·0  19·8  17·8  14·3  19·2  21·7  17·4
16·0  15·9  18·5  19·3  16·6  21·2  18·4
```

Group the data and draw up a tally chart and frequency diagram.

The smallest value is 14·3 cm and the largest is 21·7 cm.
The data can be grouped as follows and the frequency diagram drawn.

Class intervals	Tally
$14 \leqslant s < 16$	|||
$16 \leqslant s < 18$	ⅢⅠ |
$18 \leqslant s < 20$	ⅢⅠ |||
$20 \leqslant s < 22$	||||

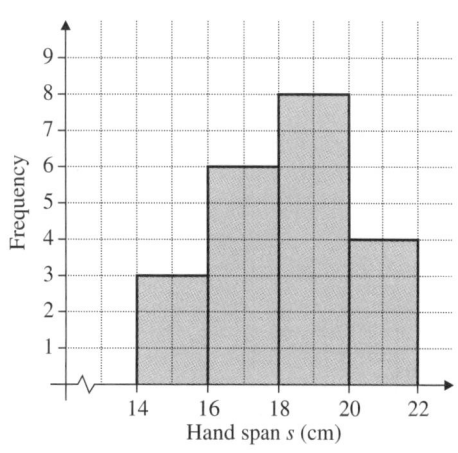

Notice that 20·0 goes into the last group $20 \leqslant s < 22$.

Exercise 4

1. The graph shows the heights of pupils in a class.
   (a) How many pupils were over 150 cm tall?
   (b) How many pupils had a height between 135 cm and 155 cm?
   (c) How many pupils were in the class?
   (d) Would you expect the graph to be this shape or a different shape? Explain why.

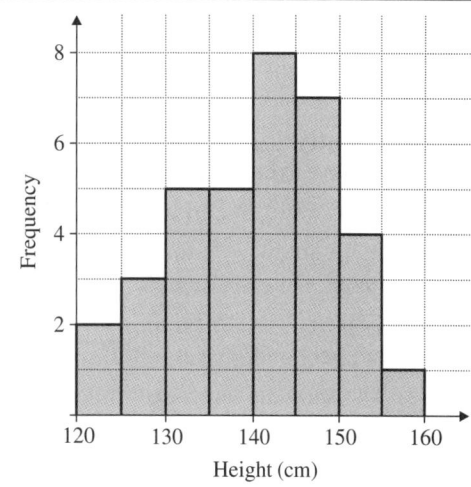

2. In a survey, the heights of children aged 15 were measured in four countries around the world. A random sample of children was chosen by computer, not necessarily the same number from each country.

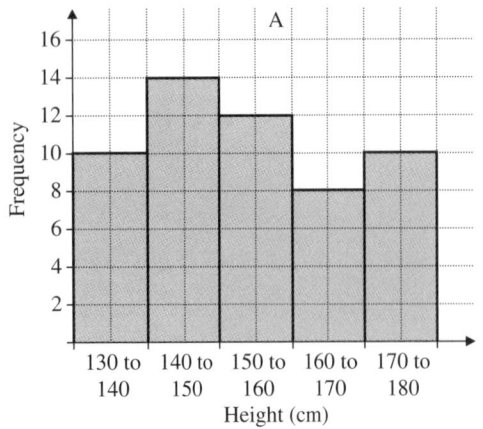
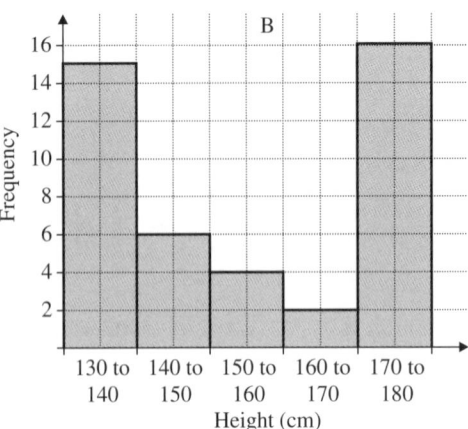
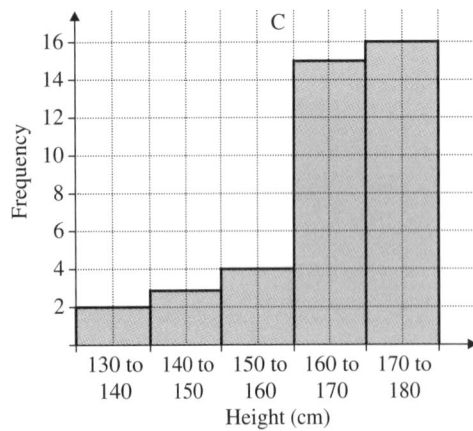
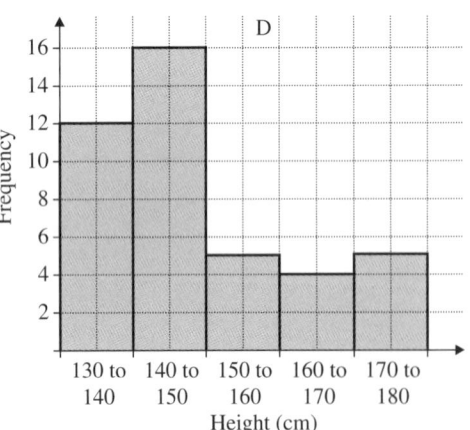

Use the graphs to identify the country in each of the statements below.

(a) Country ____ is poor and the diet of children is not good. Two-thirds of the children were less than 150 cm tall.

(b) There were 54 children in the sample from Country ____.

(c) In Country ____ the heights were spread fairly evenly across the range 130 to 180 cm.

(d) Country ____ is famous for producing lots of good high jumpers and basketball players.

(e) The smallest sample of children came from Country ____.

(f) In Country ____ three-quarters of the children were either tall or short.

3. Scientists have developed a new fertilizer which is supposed to increase the size of carrots. A farmer grew carrots in two adjacent fields A and B and treated one of the fields with the new fertilizer. A random sample of 50 carrots was taken from each field and weighed. Here are the results for Field A (all in grams).

```
118   91   82  105   72   92  103   95   73  109
 63  111  102  116  101  104  107  119  111  108
112   97  100   75   85   94   76   67   93  112
 70  116  118  103   65  107   87   98  105  117
114  106   82   90   77   88   66   99   95  103
```

Make a tally chart using the groups given.

weight	tally	frequency
$60 \leqslant w < 70$		
$70 \leqslant w < 80$		
$80 \leqslant w < 90$		
$90 \leqslant w < 100$		
$100 \leqslant w < 110$		
$110 \leqslant w < 120$		

The frequency graph for Field B is shown below.

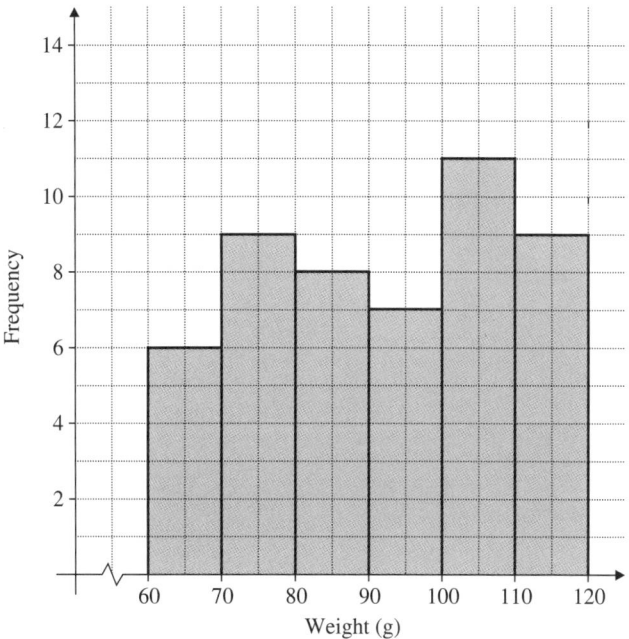

Copy the graph above and, in a different colour, draw the graph for Field A.

Which field do you think was treated with the new fertilizer?

4.

Some people think that childrens' IQs can be increased when they eat extra vitamins.

In an experiment, 52 children took an IQ test before and then after a course of vitamin pills. Here are the results.

Before:

```
 81 107  93 104 103  96 101 102  93 105  82 106  97
108  94 111  92  86 109  95 116  92  94 101 117 102
 95 108 112 107 106 124 125 103 127 118 113  91 113
113 114 109 128 115  86 106  91  85 119 129  99  98
```

After:

```
 93 110  92 125  99 127 114  98 107 128 103  91 104
103  83 125  91 104  99 102 116  98 115  92 117  97
126 100 112 113  85 108  97 101 125  93 102 107 116
 94 117  95 108 117  96 102  87 107  94 103  95  96
```

(a) Put the scores into convenient groups between 80 and 130.
(b) Draw two frequency graphs to display the results.
(c) Write a conclusion. Did the vitamin pills make a significant difference?

Conversion graphs

Exercise 5

Draw the graph and then answer the questions.
1. (a) Convert into dollars:
      (i) £2   (ii) £1.60   (iii) £2.40
   (b) Convert into pounds:
      (i) $1   (ii) $3.50   (iii) $2.50

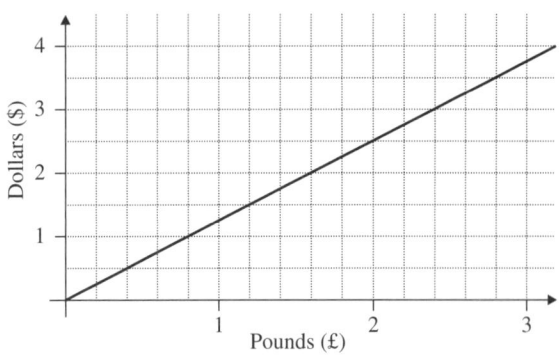

2. Give your answers as accurately as you can.
   [e.g. 3 lb = 1·4 kg approximately]
   (a) Convert into kilograms:
       (i) 5·5 lb   (ii) 8 lb   (iii) 2 lb
   (b) Convert into pounds:
       (i) 2 kg   (ii) 3 kg   (iii) 1·5 kg
   (c) A bag of sugar weighs 1 kg.
       What is its weight in pounds?
   (d) A washing machine has a weight
       limit of 7 lb.
       What is the weight limit in kilograms?

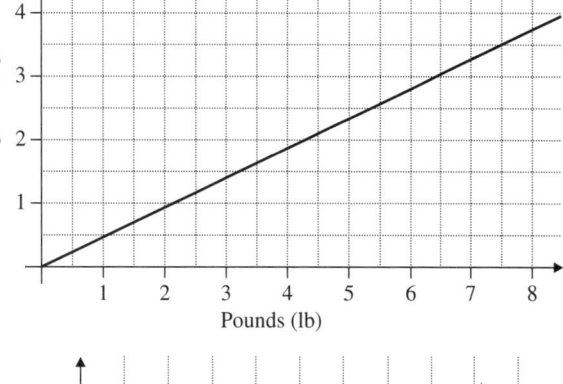

3. Between 1984 and 1994 the value of the
   pound against the German mark changed.
   (a) How much less in DM did you
       receive for £1 in 1994
       compared with 1984?
   (b) Express this change as a
       percentage of the number
       of marks received in 1984.

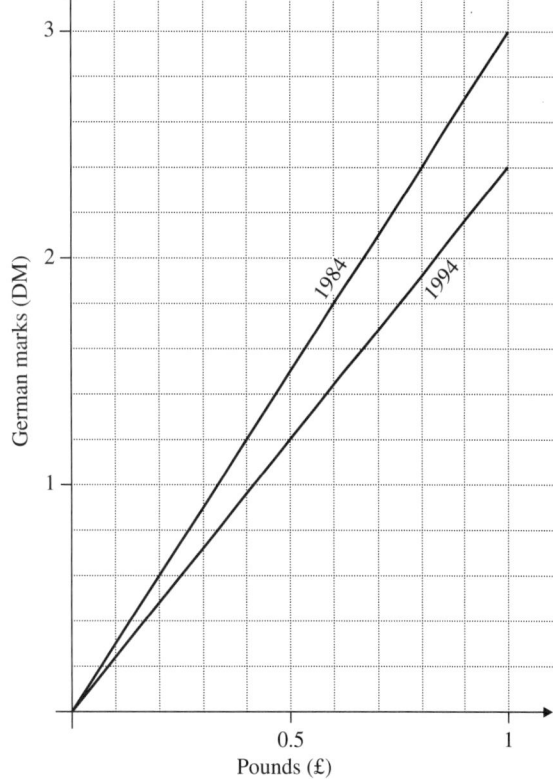

4. Temperature can be measured in °C or in °F.
   A conversion graph can be constructed using
   two points as follows:
   Draw axes with a scale of 1 cm to 5° as shown.

   32° F = 0° C and 95° F = 35° C.

   Draw a line through these two points.
   Use your graph to convert:
   (a) 50° F into °C
   (b) 20° C into °F
   (c) 0° F into °C

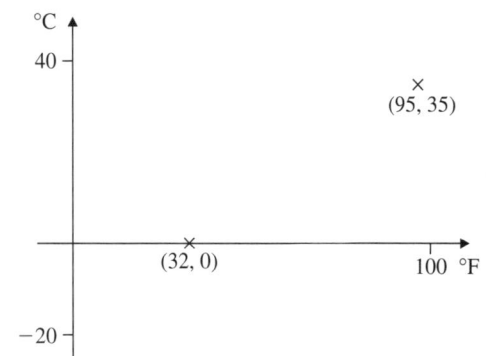

4.2 Questionnaires

Surveys are conducted by organisations for a variety of reasons.

- In the USA newspapers publish opinion polls about the voting intentions of people or the popularity of the President. They provide interesting stories for the newspaper.

- Car makers conduct surveys to find what features most people want to have in their cars such as radios, electric windows, sun roofs and so on. They then use the survey results to help with the design of future models.

- Supermarkets conduct surveys to discover what things are most important to their customers. They might want to find out how people felt about ease of car parking, price of food, quality of food, length of time waiting to pay, etc.

- Surveys are made to find the popularity of various TV programmes. Advertisers are prepared to pay a large sum for a 30 second advertisement in a programme with an audience of 10 million people.

Most surveys are conducted using questionnaires. It is very important to design the questionnaire well so that:
(a) people will cooperate and will answer the questions honestly
(b) the questions are not biased
(c) the answers to the questions can be analysed and presented for ease of understanding.

Here is a checklist of five things to improve your questionnaire design:

1. Provide an introduction to the sheet so that people know the purpose of the questionnaire.

   'Proposed new traffic lights'

2. Make the questions easy to understand and specific to answer.
   Do *not* ask vague questions like this.
   The answers could be:
   'Yes, a lot'
   'Not much'
   'Only the best bits'
   'Once or twice a day'
   You will find it hard to analyse this sort of data.

   ~~Did you see much of the Olympics on TV?~~

   A *better* question is:

   'How much of the Olympic coverage did you watch?' Tick one box

   Not at all ☐
   Up to 1 hour per day ☐
   1 to 2 hours per day ☐
   More than 2 hours per day ☐

3. Make sure that the questions are not *leading* questions. It is human nature not to contradict the questioner. Remember that the survey is to find out opinions of other people, not to support your own.
   Do *not* ask:
   'Do you agree that BBC has the best sports coverage?'
   A better question is:

   'Which of the following has the best sports coverage?'
   BBC   ITV   Channel 4   Satellite TV
   ☐   ☐   ☐   ☐

   You might ask for one tick or possibly numbers 1, 2, 3, 4 to show an order of preference.

4. If you are going to ask sensitive questions (about age or income, for example), design the question with care so as not to offend or embarrass.
   Do *not* ask:
       'How old are you?'
   or 'Give your date of birth'
   A better question is:

   > 'Tick one box for your age group.'
   > 15–17   18–20   21–30   31–50
   > ☐   ☐   ☐   ☐

5. Do not ask more questions than necessary and put the easy questions first.

Exercise 6

Criticise the following questions and suggest a better question which overcomes the problem involved.
Write some questions with 'yes/no' answers and some questions which involve multiple responses.
Remember to word your questions simply.

1. Do you think it is ridiculous to spend money on food 'mountains' in Europe while people in Africa are starving?

2. What do you think of the new head teacher?

3. How dangerous do you think it is to fly in a single-engined aeroplane?

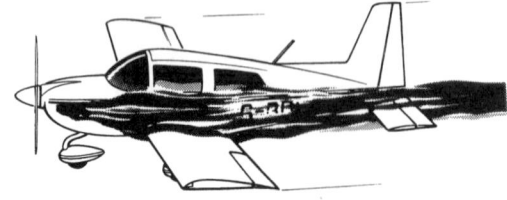

4. How much would you pay to use the new car park?

   ☐ less than £1   ☐ more than £2·50.

5. Do you agree that English and Maths are the most important subjects at school?

6. Do you or your parents often hire videos from a shop?

7. Do you think that we get too much homework?

8. Do you think you would still eat meat if you had been to see the animals killed?

Analysis

Having conducted the survey, you need to display your results clearly. Diagrams like pie charts, frequency diagrams and scatter graphs are a good idea. Do not be afraid to use colours.

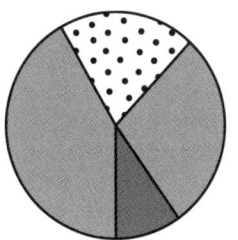 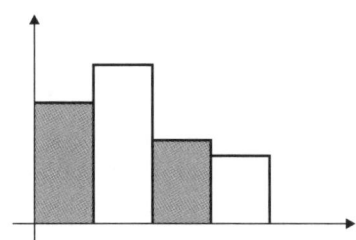 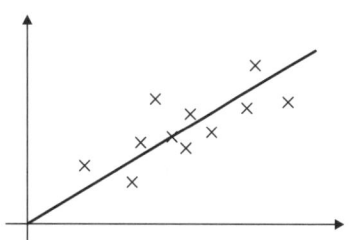

You might want to use a database or spreadsheet program on a computer if you think this would help your work.

Draw *conclusions* from your results but make sure they are justified by the evidence.

The best way to learn about questionnaires is to conduct your own survey on a topic which *you* find interesting.

Hypothesis testing

An hypothesis is defined as 'a statement which may be true, but for which a proof has not been found'. Statisticians are employed to collect and analyse information about a question with the aim of proving or disproving it. Questionnaires are often used for this purpose.
Here are some questions:

A 'Is there too much sport on television?'

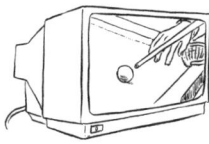

B 'Are people who are good at spelling also good at arithmetic?'

castle √	$51 \times 17 = 867$ √
elefant ×	$0.4 \times 0.2 = 0.08$ √
necessary √	$5.6 - 4 = 5.2$ ×
tomorrow √	$\frac{1}{6} + \frac{1}{2} = \frac{2}{8}$ ×

C 'Does smoking damage your health?'

D 'Do 11-year-old pupils watch more TV than 16-year-old pupils?'

Once you have the question, your first task is to make an hypothesis (make a statement) so that you have something concrete to test. Hypotheses for the above four questions could be:

A   Most people would like TV schedules to contain less coverage of sport.
B   People who are good at spelling are also good at arithmetic.
C   Smokers have a shorter life span than non-smokers.
D   11-year-old pupils watch more television than 16-year-old pupils.

There are several factors which you must consider when making your hypothesis.

1. Can you test it?
   In the smokers problem there are many factors which will affect life span – diet, fitness, stress, heredity etc. How can you eliminate these so that it is *only* the smoking which counts?

2. Can you collect enough data to give a reasonable result? Where will you collect your data?
   For the spelling/arithmetic problem, you could write your own tests and then ask about 30 pupils, preferably of different ages, to do them. You should try to get people with a range of abilities in spelling and arithmetic.

3. How will you know if you have proved or disproved the hypothesis? You need to have some idea of the criteria for proof (or disproof) before you start collecting data.
   In the question about sport on television, what do you mean by 'most'? Do you mean over half of those questioned? What about 'don't knows'?

4. Can you collect the type of data which you can analyse? Consider the techniques at your disposal:
   mean, median, mode, scatter diagrams, pie charts, frequency graphs. The spelling/arithmetic data, for example could be clearly displayed on a scatter diagram.

5. Do you find it interesting?
   If you don't, the whole piece of work will be dull and tedious, both to you and to your teacher.

Your own work
   Almost certainly the best idea for an hypothesis will be an idea which *you* think of because *you* want to know the answer. As a guide, here is a list of questions which some students have looked at. You can use one of these if you find it interesting or if you can't think of a better one yourself.
(a) Young people are more superstitious than older people.
(b) Given a free choice, most girls would hardly ever wear a dress in preference to something else.
(c) More babies are born in the Winter than the Summer.
(d) The age for part-time jobs should be reduced from 16 to 14.
(e) The school day should start at 08:00 and end at 14:00.
(f) Most cars these days use unleaded petrol.

4.3 Averages

If you have a set of data, say exam marks or heights, and are told to find the 'average', just what are you trying to find? The answer is: a single number which can be used to represent the entire set of data. This could be done in three different ways.

(a) The median

The data is arranged in order from the smallest to the largest; the middle number is then selected. This is really the central number of the range and is called the median.
If there are two 'middle' numbers, the median is in the middle of these two numbers.

Median

(b) The mean

All the data is added up and the total divided by the number of items. This is called the mean and is equivalent to sharing out all the data evenly.

(c) The mode

The number of items which occurs most frequently in a frequency table is selected. This is the most popular value and is called the mode (from the french 'a la mode' meaning 'fashionable')

Each 'average' has its purpose and sometimes one is preferable to the others.

The median is fairly easy to find and has an advantage in being hardly affected by untypical values such as very large or very small values that occur at the ends of the distribution.

Consider these exam marks:

20, 21, 21, 22, 23, 23, 25, 27, 27, 27, 29, 98, 98
↑

The median (25) gives a truer picture of the centre of the distribution than the mean (35·5).
The mean takes account of all of the data and is the 'average' which most people readily think of. It does, of course, take a little longer to calculate than either the mode or the median.

The mode of this data is 27. It is easy to calculate and it eliminates some of the effects of extreme values. However it does have disadvantages, particularly in data which has two 'most popular' values, and it is not widely used.

Range

In addition to knowing the centre of a distribution, it is useful to know the range or spread of the data.

range = (largest value) − (smallest value)

For the examination marks, range = 98 − 20 = 78.

Example

Find the median, the mean, the mode and the range of this set of 10 numbers:

5, 4, 10, 3, 3, 4, 7, 4, 6, 5.

(a) Arrange the numbers in order of size to find the median.

3, 3, 4, 4, 4, 5, 5, 6, 7, 10
↑

the median is the 'average' of 4 and 5.
∴ median = 4·5

(b) Mean = $\frac{(5+4+10+3+3+4+7+4+6+5)}{10} = \frac{51}{10} = 5·1$

(c) mode = 4 because there are more 4's then any other number.

(d) range = 10 − 3 = 7

Exercise 7

1. Find the mean, median and mode of the following sets of numbers:
   (a) 3, 12, 4, 6, 8, 5, 4
   (b) 7, 21, 2, 17, 3, 13, 7, 4, 9, 7, 9
   (c) 12, 1, 10, 1, 9, 3, 4, 9, 7, 9
   (d) 8, 0, 3, 3, 1, 7, 4, 1, 4, 4.

2. The temperature in °C on 17 days was:
   1, 0, 2, 2, 0, 4, 1, 3, 2, 1, 2, 3, 4, 5, 4, 5, 5.
   What was the modal temperature?

3. A dice was thrown 14 times as follows:

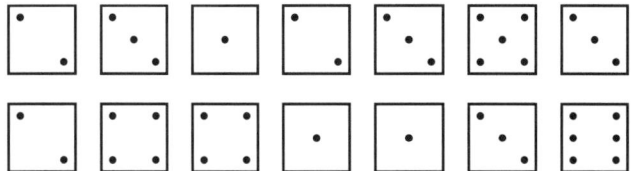

   (a) What was the modal score?
   (b) What was the median score?

4. Write down five numbers so that:
   the mean is 6
   the median is 5
   the mode is 4.

5. Louise claims that she is better at maths than her brother Peter. Louise's last five marks were 63, 72, 58, 84 and 75 and Peter's last four marks were 69, 73, 81 and 70. Find the mean mark for Louise and for Peter. Is Louise better than Peter?

6. The bar chart shows the marks scored in a test. What was the modal mark?

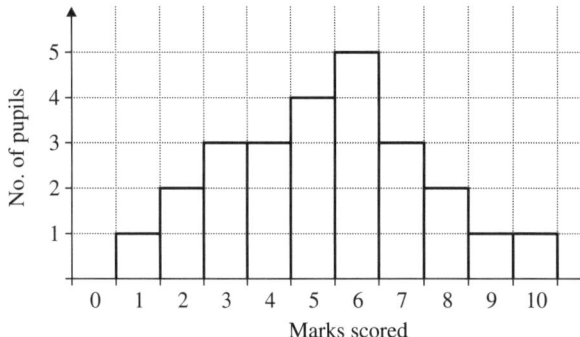

7. Six boys have heights of 1·53 m, 1·49 m, 1·60 m, 1·65 m, 1·90 m and 1·43 m.
   (a) Find the mean height of the six boys.
   (b) Find the mean height of the remaining five boys when the shortest boy leaves.

8. Seven women have weights of 44 kg, 51 kg, 57 kg, 63 kg, 48 kg, 49 kg and 45 kg.
   (a) Find the mean weight of the seven women.
   (b) Find the mean weight of the remaining five women after the lightest and the heaviest women leave.

9. In a maths test the marks for the boys were 9, 7, 8, 7, 5 and the marks for the girls were 6, 3, 9, 8, 2, 2.
   (a) Find the mean mark for the boys.
   (b) Find the mean mark for the girls.
   (c) Find the mean mark for the whole class.

10. The following are the salaries of 5 employees in a small business:
    Mr A: $22,500   Mr B: $17,900   Mr C: $21,400
    Mr D: $22,500   Mr E: $155,300.
    (a) Find the mean and the median of their salaries.
    (b) Which does *not* give a fair 'average'? Explain why in one sentence.

14. A farmer has 32 cattle to sell. The weights of the cattle in kg are:

   81   81   82   82   83   84   84   85
   85   86   86   87   87   88   89   91
   91   92   93   94   96 150 152 153
  154 320 370 375 376 380 381 390

   [Total weight = 5028 kg]

   On the telephone to a potential buyer, the farmer describes the cattle and says the 'average' weight is 'over 157 kg'.
   (a) Find the mean weight and the median weight.
   (b) Which 'average' has the farmer used to describe his animals?
   Does this average describe the cattle fairly?

12. A gardening magazine sells seedlings of a plant through the post and claims that the average height of the plants after one year's growth will be 85 cm. A sample of 24 of the plants was measured after one year with the following results (in cm):

    6   7   7   9 34 56 85 89
   89 90 90 91 91 92 93 93
   93 94 95 95 96 97 97 99

   [The sum of the heights is 1788 cm.]

   (a) Find the mean and the median height of the sample.
   (b) Is the magazine's claim about average height justified?

4.4 Frequency polygons

We have seen earlier on page 107 how a frequency distribution can be shown in the form of a bar chart.

The number of peas in 40 pea pods is shown below. Note: Frequency goes on the vertical axis.

A *frequency polygon* is formed by joining the mid-points of the tops of the bars in a bar chart by straight lines.

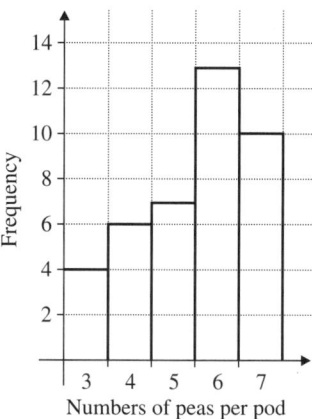

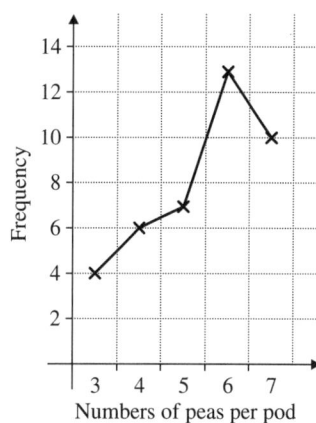

Discrete and continuous data

The data that we record can be either *discrete* or *continuous*. Discrete data can take only certain values:

- the number of peas in a pod
- the number of children in a class
- shoe sizes.

Continuous data comes from measuring and can take any value:

- height of a child
- weight of an apple
- time taken to boil a kettle.

Class boundaries

The lengths of 36 pea pods were measured and rounded to the nearest mm. So a pea pod which is actually 59·2 mm long is rounded off to 59 mm.

```
52  80  65  82  77  60  72  83  63
78  84  75  53  73  70  86  55  88
85  59  76  86  73  89  91  76  92
66  93  84  62  79  90  73  68  71
```

This data can be put into a grouped frequency table.

Length (mm)	Tally	Frequency
$50 \leqslant l < 60$	||||	4
$60 \leqslant l < 70$	卌 |	6
$70 \leqslant l < 80$	卌 卌 ||	12
$80 \leqslant l < 90$	卌 卌	10
$90 \leqslant l < 100$	||||	4

For the class $50 \leqslant l < 60$, the class boundaries are 50 and 60. The bar will go from 50 to 60 mm.

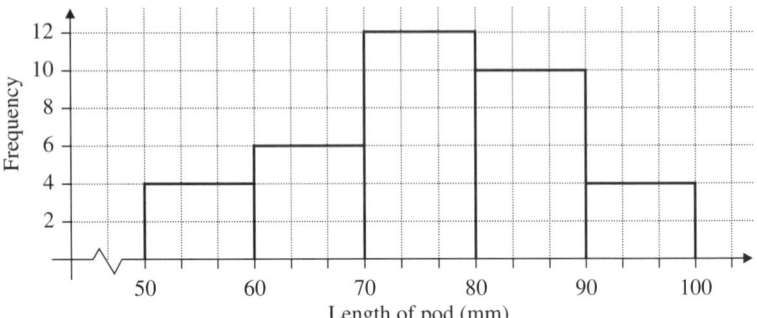

The frequency polygon for this data can be drawn in the same way as with discrete data. Note that you can draw the frequency polygon *without* drawing a bar chart first. You must calculate the mid-points of each group.

For the $50 \leqslant l < 60$ group:

mid-point $= \dfrac{50 + 60}{2} = 55$

Note: This frequency polygon is closed. Lines have been drawn to join the polygon to the horizontal axis.

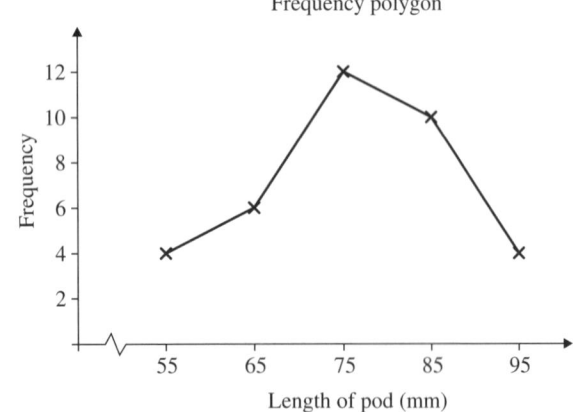

Frequency polygon

Mid-points

The mid-points of other groups can be calculated as follows:

(a)

mark	mid-point
0–9	4·5
10–19	14·5

$\left(\dfrac{0+9}{2}\right)$

$\left(\dfrac{10+19}{2}\right)$

(b)

height	mid-point
$150 \leqslant h < 155$	152·5
$155 \leqslant h < 160$	157·5

$\left(\dfrac{150+155}{2}\right)$

$\left(\dfrac{155+160}{2}\right)$

Exercise 8

1. In a survey the number of people in 100 cars passing a set of traffic lights was counted. Here are the results:

number of people in car	0	1	2	3	4	5	6
frequency	0	10	35	25	20	10	0

(a) Draw a bar chart to illustrate this data.
(b) On the same graph draw the frequency polygon.

   Here we have started the bar chart.
   For frequency, use a scale of 1 cm for 5 units.

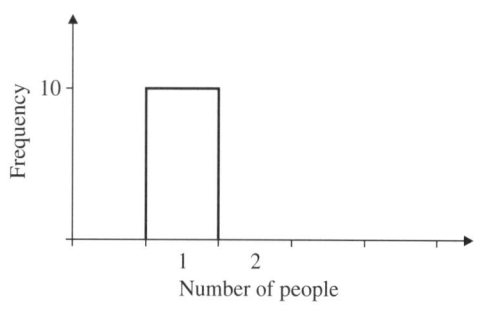

2. The frequency polygon shows the marks obtained by pupils in a maths test.

   (a) How many pupils got 7 marks?
   (b) How many pupils were there altogether?

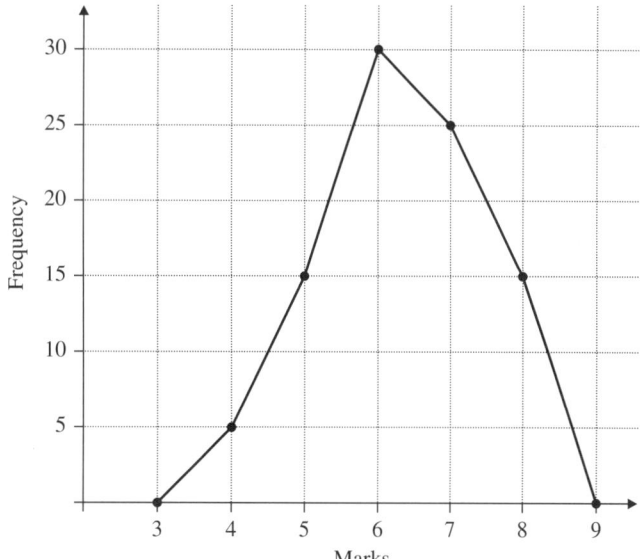

3. The members of several professional basketball teams were measured for their heights. The results were:

height	frequency
$180 \leqslant h < 185$	5
$185 \leqslant h < 190$	8
$190 \leqslant h < 195$	15
$195 \leqslant h < 200$	11
$200 \leqslant h < 205$	6
$205 \leqslant h < 210$	2

Draw a bar chart and a frequency polygon to illustrate this data.

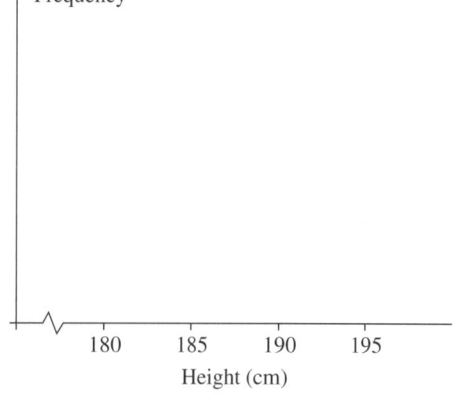

4. Two frequency polygons are shown giving the distribution of the weights of players in two different sports A and B.

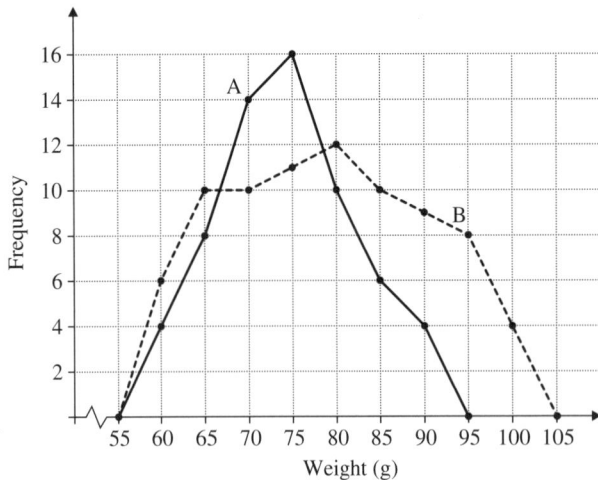

(a) How many people played sport A?

(b) Comment on two differences between the two frequency polygons.

(c) Either for A or for B suggest a sport where you would expect the frequency polygon of weights to have this shape.
Explain in one sentence why you have chosen that sport.

5. A scientist at an agricultural college is studying the effect of a new fertilizer for raspberries. She measures the heights of the plants and also the total weight of fruit collected. She does this for two sets of plants: one with the new fertilizer and one without it. Here are the frequency polygons:

$$\begin{bmatrix} \text{---} & \text{with fertilizer} \\ \text{———} & \text{without fertilizer} \end{bmatrix}$$

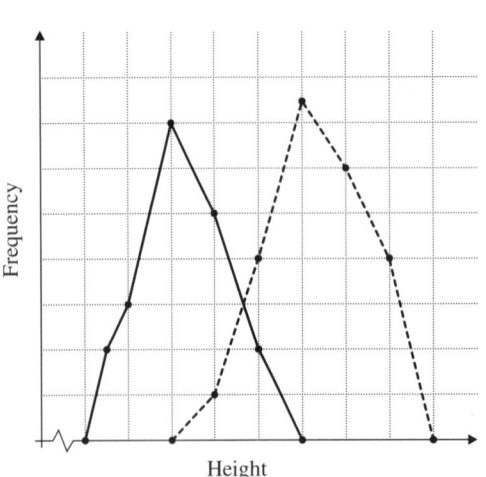

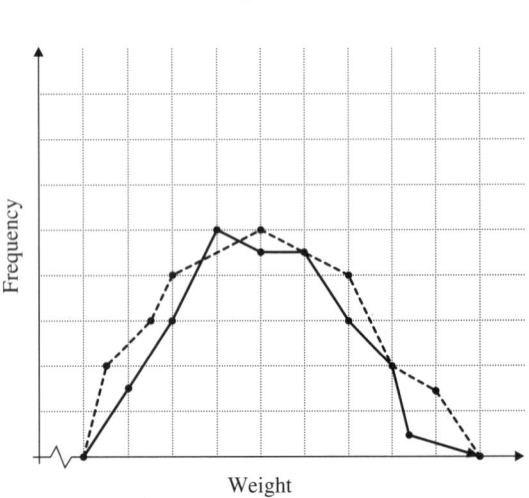

(a) What effect did the fertilizer have on the heights of the plants?
(b) What effect was there on the weights of fruit collected?

Revision exercise 4A

1. In a test, the marks of nine pupils were
   7, 5, 2, 7, 4, 9, 7, 6, 6.
   Find
   (a) the mean mark
   (b) the median mark
   (c) the modal mark.

2. The mean height of 10 boys is 1·60 m and the mean height of 15 girls is 1·52 m. Find the mean height of the 25 boys and girls.

3. (a) The mean mass of 10 boys in a class is 56 kg.
      (i) Calculate the total mass of these 10 boys.
      (ii) Another boy, whose mass is 67 kg, joins the group. Calculate the mean mass of the 11 boys.
   (b) A group of 10 boys whose mean mass is 56 kg joins a group of 20 girls whose mean mass is 47 kg. Calculate the mean mass of the 30 children.

4. The mean of four numbers is 21.
   (a) Calculate the sum of the four numbers.
   Six other numbers have a mean of 18.
   (b) Calculate the mean of the ten numbers.

5. The pie chart shows the after school activities of 200 pupils.

   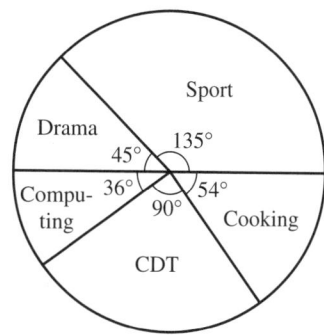

   (a) How many pupils do drama?
   (b) How many pupils do sport?
   (c) How many pupils do computing?

6. Forty teenagers were asked to name their favourite holiday destinations with the following results:

   Spain 12,   France 5,   Greece 10
   Portugal 4,   U.S.A. 9

   Display this information on a pie chart, showing the angles corresponding to each country.

7. The chart shows the rainfall recorded in a village in one month.

   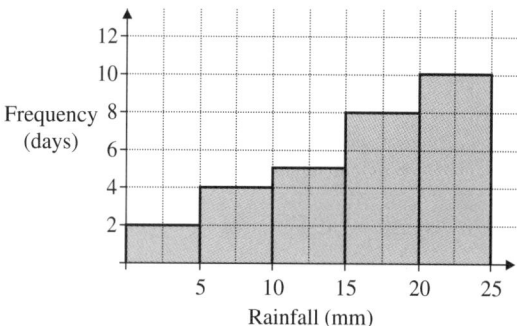

   (a) How many days were there in the month?
   (b) For how many days were there 10 mm or more of rain?
   (c) Chew Ling said 'It rained more at the end of the month'. Explain whether Chew Ling is right or wrong.

8. There were 5 people in a tent. The *median* age of the people was 11 and the range of their ages was 3. Write each sentence below and write near to it whether it is *True*, *Possible* or *False*.
   (a) Every person was either 10 or 11 years old.
   (b) The oldest person in the tent was 14 years old.
   (c) The mean age of the people was less than 11 years.

Examination exercise 4B

1. (a) The bar chart shows the results of a test taken by 24 students.
    (i) How many students scored 7 marks?
    (ii) Use the bar chart to copy and complete the frequency table.

Mark	5	6	7	8	9
Frequency					

    (iii) Write down the mode.
    (iv) Find the median.
    (v) Work out the mean.
    (vi) Ahmed draws a pie chart to show the information in the bar chart above. Calculate the angle he should use to show the number of students who scored 6 marks.

    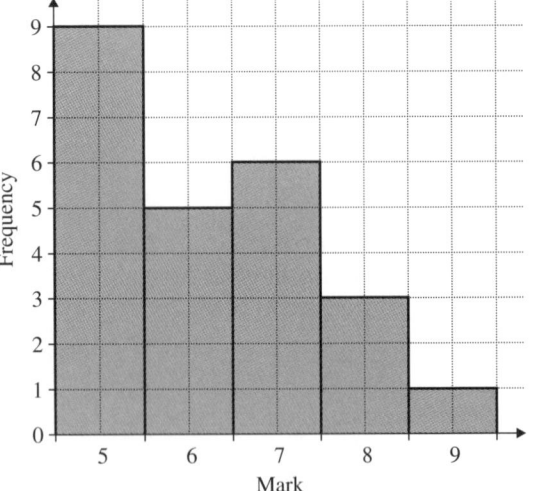

    [N 98 3]

2. The list shows the number of questions attempted by 48 students in a test.

    | 43 | 40 | 41 | 42 | 41 | 44 | 43 | 41 |
    | 39 | 39 | 40 | 42 | 44 | 42 | 41 | 41 |
    | 42 | 40 | 39 | 42 | 43 | 42 | 42 | 39 |
    | 42 | 40 | 44 | 43 | 40 | 42 | 41 | 41 |
    | 41 | 42 | 43 | 41 | 41 | 42 | 42 | 42 |
    | 39 | 40 | 44 | 41 | 41 | 42 | 41 | 40 |

    (a) Copy and complete the frequency table.

Number of questions	Frequency
39	
40	
41	
42	
43	
44	

    (b) (i) Write down the modal number of questions attempted.
        (ii) Find the median number of questions attempted.
        (iii) Calculate the mean number of questions attempted.
    (c) Complete the sentence:
        'The most likely number of questions attempted was ....'
    (d) How many students attempted at least 40 questions?

    [N 97 3]

5 SHAPE AND SPACE 2

5.1 Transforming shapes

Reflection

A′B′C′D′ is the image of ABCD after reflection in the broken line (the mirror line).

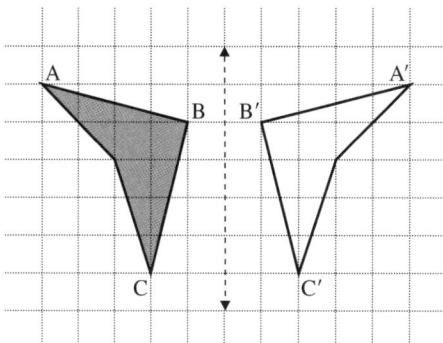

Exercise 1

On squared paper draw the object and its image after reflection in the broken line.

1.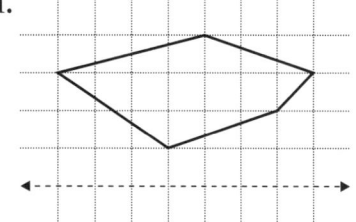

2.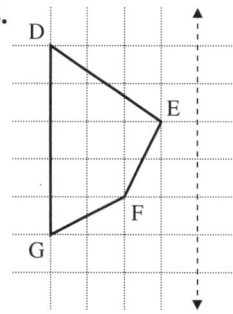

3.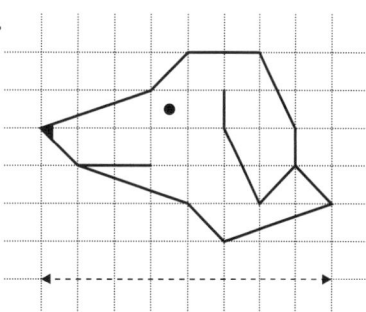

4.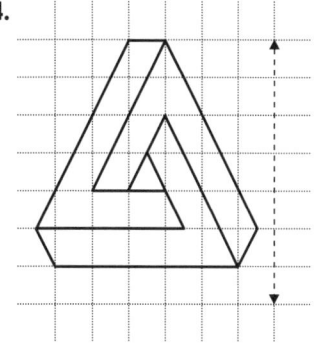

5.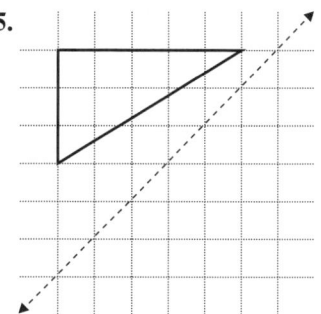

6.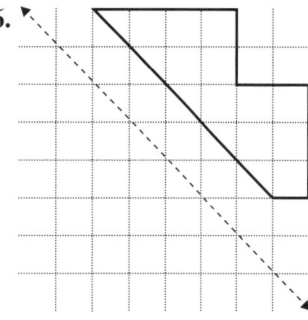

7. 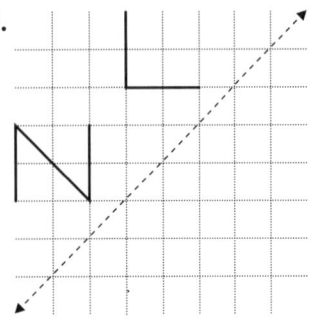   8. 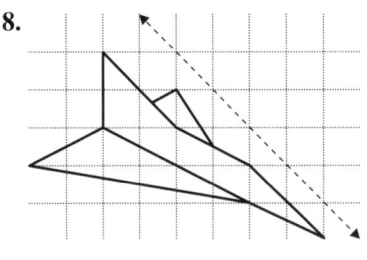   9.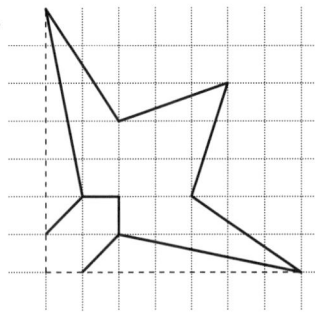

Reflect this shape in *both* of the broken lines

Exercise 2

1. Copy the diagram below.

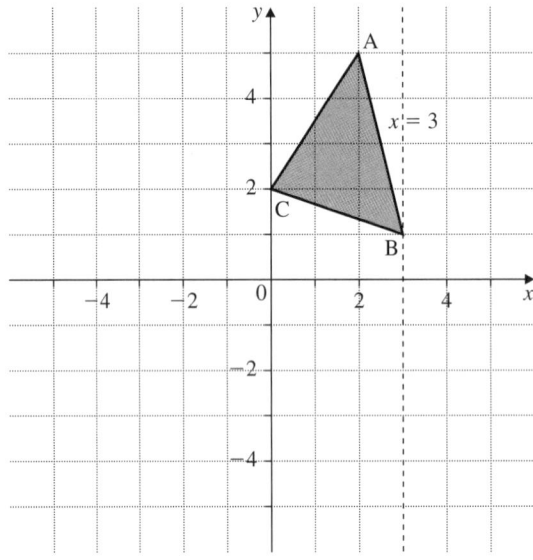

Draw the image of △ABC after reflection in the lines indicated.
(a) the x-axis. Label it △1.
(b) the y-axis. Label it △2.
(c) the line $x = 3$. Label it △3.

For Questions **2** to **5** draw a pair of axes so that both x and y can take values from −7 to +7.

2. (a) Plot and label P(7,5), Q(7,2), R(5,2).
   (b) Draw the lines $y = -1$, $x = 1$ and $y = x$. Use dotted lines.
   (c) Draw the image of △PQR after reflection in:
       (i) the line $y = -1$. Label it △1.
       (ii) the line $x = 1$. Label it △2.
       (iii) the line $y = x$. Label it △3.
   (d) Write down the coordinates of the image of point P in each case.

3. (a) Plot and label L(7,−5), M(7,−1), N(5,−1).
   (b) Draw the lines $y = x$ and $y = -x$. Use dotted lines.
   (c) Draw the image of △LMN after reflection in:
      (i) the x-axis. Label it △1.
      (ii) the line $y = x$. Label it △2.
      (iii) the line $y = -x$. Label it △3.
   (d) Write down the coordinates of the image of point L in each case.

4. (a) Draw the line $x + y = 7$. [It passes through (0,7) and (7,0).]
   (b) Draw △1 at (−3,−1), (−1,−1), (−1,−4).
   (c) Reflect △1 in the y-axis on to △2.
   (d) Reflect △2 in the x-axis on to △3.
   (e) Reflect △3 in the line $x + y = 7$ on to △4.
   (f) Reflect △4 in the y-axis on to △5.
   (g) Write down the coordinates of △5.

5. (a) Draw the lines $y = 2$, $x = -1$ and $y = x$.
   (b) Draw △1 at (1,−3), (−3,−3), (−3,−5).
   (c) Reflect △1 in the line $y = x$ on to △2.
   (d) Reflect △2 in the line $y = 2$ on to △3.
   (e) Reflect △3 in the line $x = -1$ on to △4.
   (f) Reflect △4 in the line $y = x$ on to △5.
   (g) Write down the coordinates of △5.

6. Find the equation of the mirror line for the reflection:

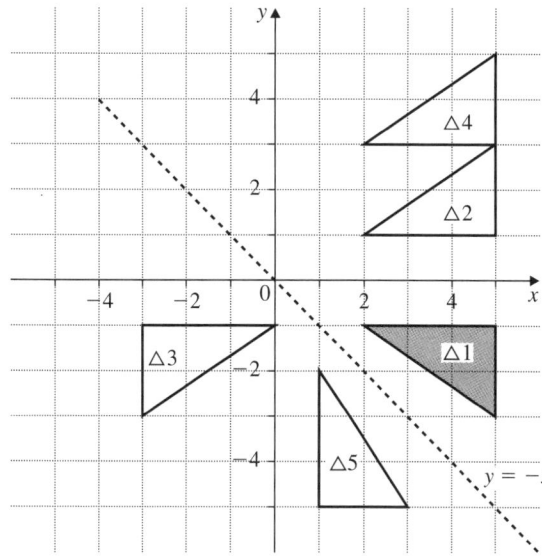

(a) △1 on to △2
(b) △1 on to △3
(c) △1 on to △4
(d) △1 on to △5.

Rotation

△A′B′C′ is the image of △ABC after a 90° clockwise rotation about centre C.

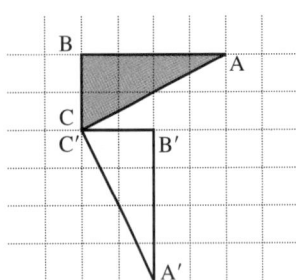

Draw △ABC on tracing paper and then put the tip of your pencil on C. Turn the tracing paper 90° clockwise about C. The tracing paper now shows the position of △A′B′C′.
Notice that you need three things to describe a rotation:
(a) the centre
(b) the angle
(c) the direction (e.g. clockwise)

Exercise 3

Draw the object and its image under the rotation given.
Take O as the centre of rotation in each case.

1.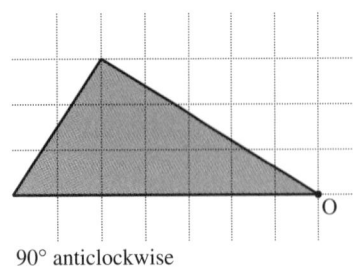

   90° anticlockwise

2.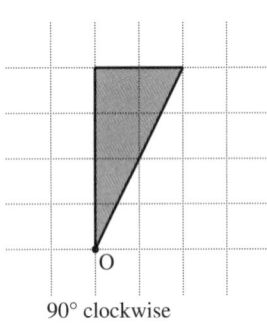

   90° clockwise

3.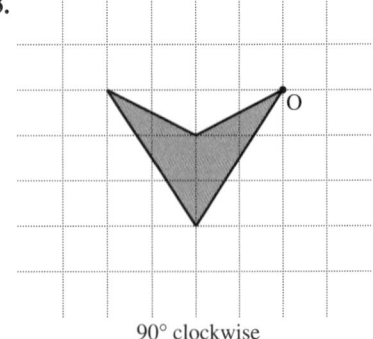

   90° clockwise

4.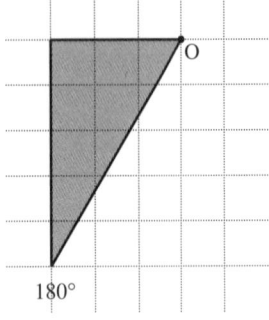

   180°

5.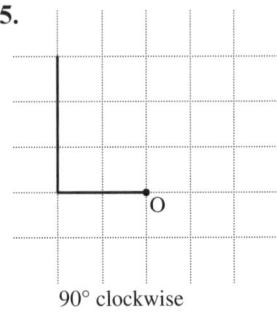

   90° clockwise

6.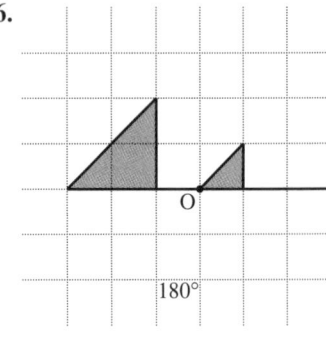

   180°

7. The shape on the right has been rotated about several different centres to form the pattern below.

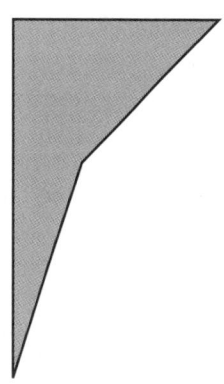

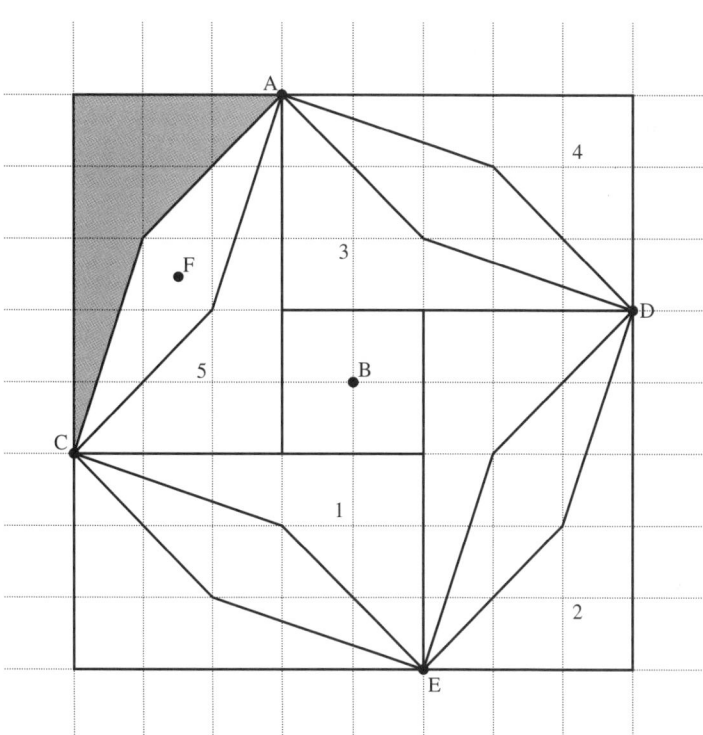

Describe the rotation which takes the shaded shape on to shape 1, shape 2, shape 3, shape 4 and shape 5. For each one, give the centre (A, B, C, D, E or F), the angle and the direction of the rotation.
[e.g. 'centre C, 90°, clockwise']

Exercise 4

1. Copy the diagram on the right.
   (a) Rotate △ABC 90° clockwise about (0,0). Label it △1.
   (b) Rotate △DEF 180° clockwise about (0,0). Label it △2.
   (c) Rotate △GHI 90° clockwise about (0,0). Label it △3.

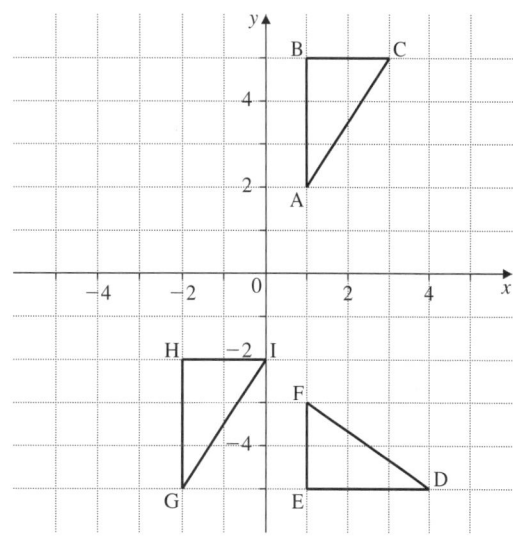

For Questions **2** and **3** draw a pair of axes with values of x and y from -7 to $+7$.

2. (a) Plot △1 at (2,3), (6,3), (3,6).
   (b) Rotate △1 90° clockwise about (2,3) onto △2.
   (c) Rotate △2 180° about (0,0) onto △3.
   (d) Rotate △3 90° anticlockwise about (−2,1) onto △4.
   (e) Write down the coordinates of △4.

3. (a) Plot △1 at (4,4), (6,6), (2,6).
   (b) Rotate △1 90° anticlockwise about (4,4) onto △2.
   (c) Rotate △2 90° anticlockwise about (2,2) onto △3.
   (d) Rotate △3 90° clockwise about (−2,2) onto △4.
   (e) Write down the coordinates of △4.

Finding the centre of a rotation

Exercise 5

In Questions **1** to **3** copy the diagram exactly and then use tracing paper to find the centre of the rotation which takes the shaded shape onto the unshaded shape. Mark the centre of rotation with a cross.

1.
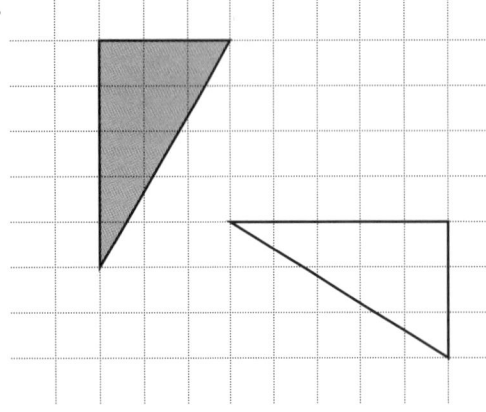

2.
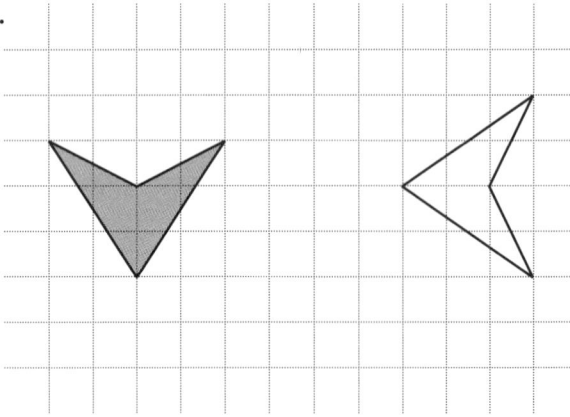

3.
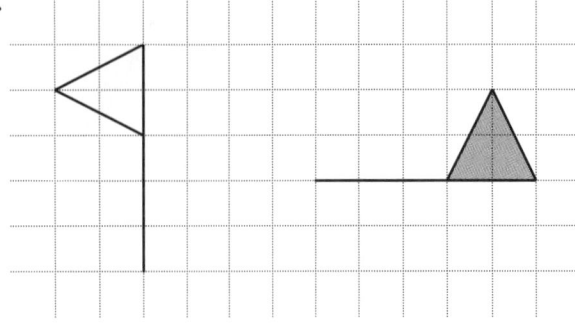

Enlargement

A

B

Photo A has been enlarged to give photos B and C. Notice that the shape of the face is exactly the same in all the pictures.

Photo A measures 22 mm by 27 mm
Photo B measures 44 mm by 54 mm
Photo C measures 66 mm by 81 mm

From A to B both the width and the height have been multiplied by 2.
We say B is an enlargement of A with a *scale factor* of 2.
Similarly C is an enlargement of A with a scale factor of 3.

Also C is an enlargement of B with a scale factor of $1\frac{1}{2}$.

The scale factor of an enlargement can be found by dividing corresponding lengths on two pictures.

In this enlargement the

scale factor is $\frac{21}{14}$ (= 1·5)

C

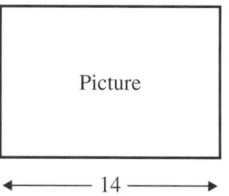

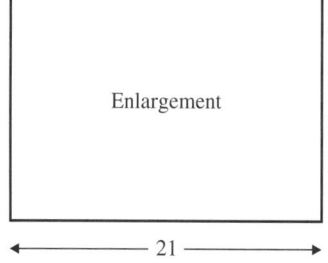

Exercise 6

1. This picture is to be enlarged and we want the enlargement to fit exactly in a frame.
   Which of the following frames will the picture fit? Write 'yes' or 'no'.
   (a) 100 mm by 76 mm
   (b) 110 mm by 76 mm
   (c) 150 mm by 114 mm
   (d) 75 mm by 57 mm.

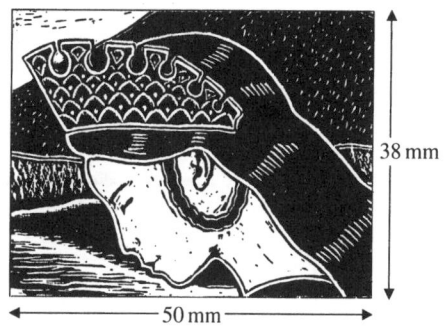

2. This picture is to be enlarged so that it fits exactly into the frame. Find the length x.

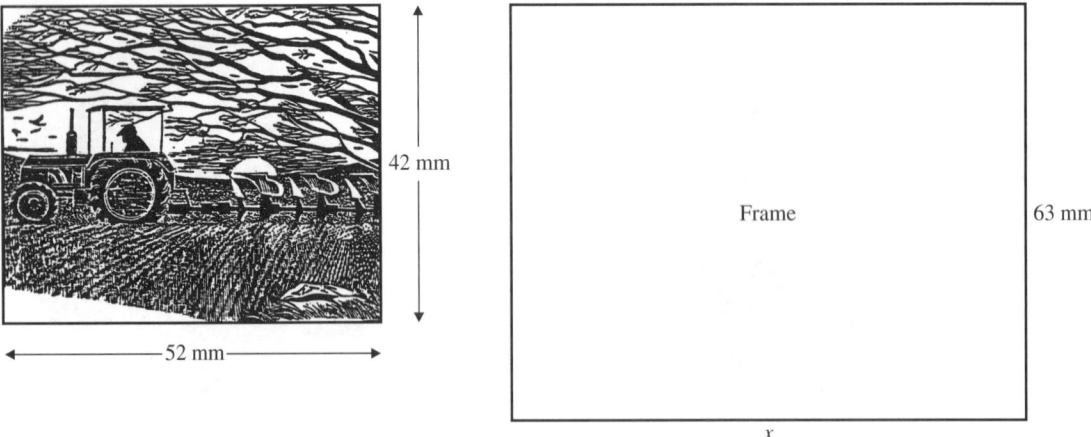

3. This picture is enlarged or reduced to fit into each of the frames shown. Calculate y and z.

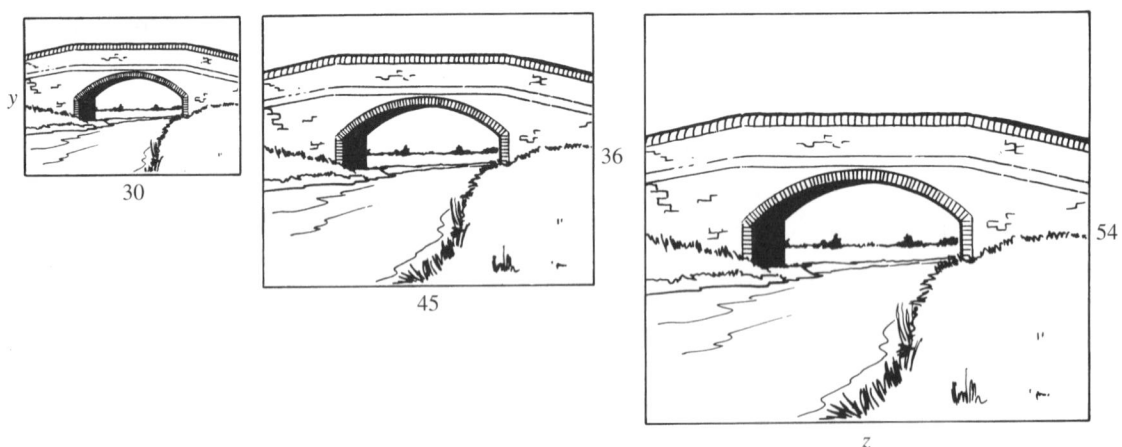

4. Here we have started to draw a two times enlargement of a house using the squares.

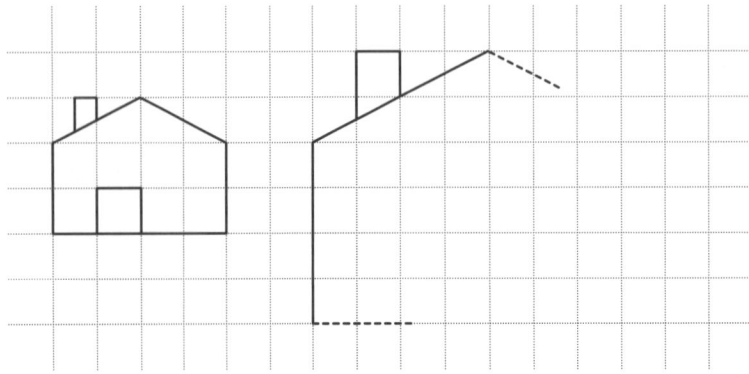

Draw the complete enlargement in your book (use squared paper).

5. Draw a three times enlargement of this figure.

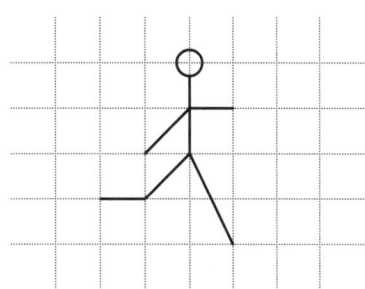

6. Draw a two times and a three times enlargement of this shape. Measure the angles a and b on each enlargement. Write the correct version of this sentence: 'In an enlargement, the angles in a shape are changed/unchanged.'

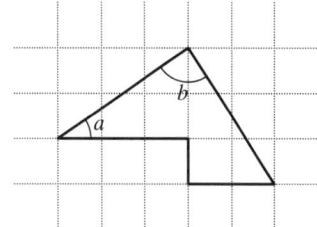

7. This diagram shows an arrowhead and its enlargement. Notice that lines drawn through corresponding points (A, A′ or B, B′) all go through one point O. This point is called the centre of enlargement. Copy and complete:
   OA′ = _____ × OA
   OB′ = _____ × OB.

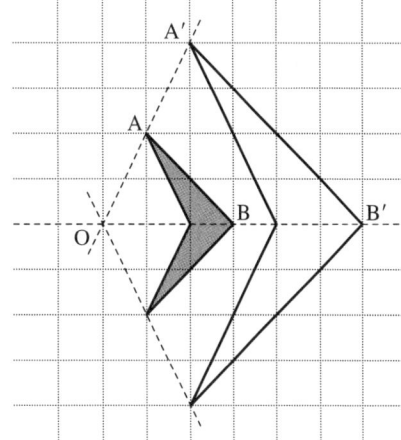

8. Copy this shape and its enlargement. Draw construction lines to find the centre of enlargement.

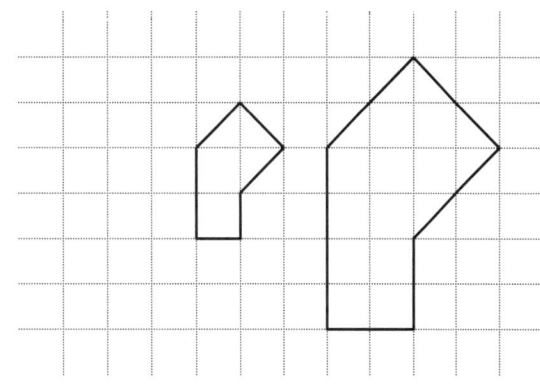

9. In this diagram, △1 is a two times enlargement of the shaded triangle with O_1 as centre of enlargement.
Also △2 is a three times enlargement of the shaded triangle with O_2 as centre of enlargement.

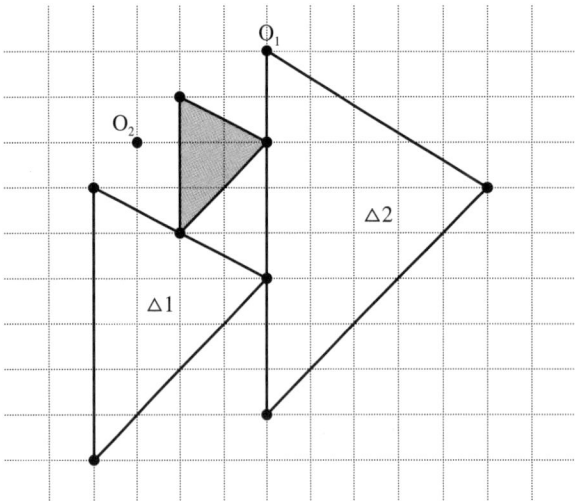

(a) Copy the diagram and draw construction lines to find the centre of enlargement from △1 onto △2.
   [Hint: leave space on the left side of the diagram].
(b) What is the scale factor for the enlargement △1 onto △2?

For a mathematical description of an enlargement we need two things:

(a) the scale factor　　　　(b) the centre of enlargement.

Example

Enlarge triangle ABC onto triangle A′B′C′ with a scale factor of 3 and centre O.

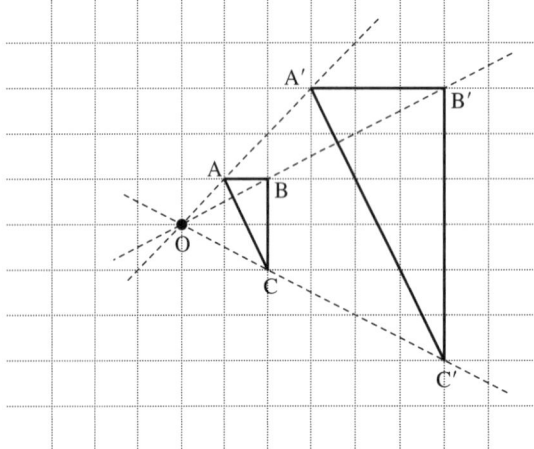

Note: $OA' = 3 \times OA$; $OB' = 3 \times OB$; $OC' = 3 \times OC$.

All lengths are measured from the *centre of enlargement*.

Exercise 7

Copy each diagram and draw an enlargement using the centre O and the scale factor given.

1.
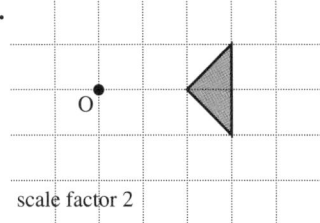
scale factor 2

2.
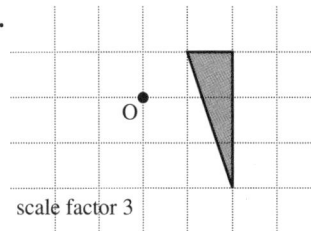
scale factor 3

3.
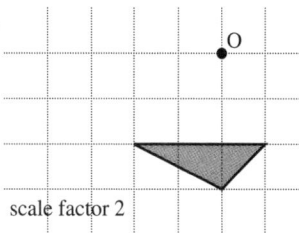
scale factor 2

4.
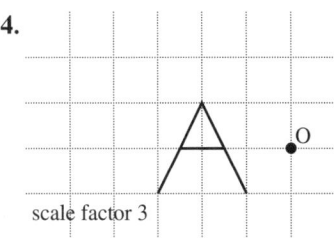
scale factor 3

5.
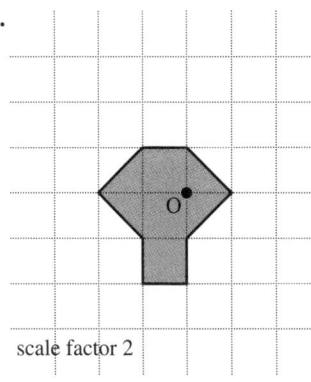
scale factor 2

6.
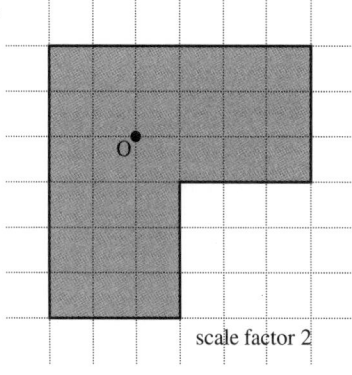
scale factor 2

7. (a) Copy the diagram on the right.
   (b) Draw the image of △1 after enlargement with scale factor 3, centre (0,0).
       Label the image △4.
   (c) Draw the image of △2 after enlargement with scale factor 2, centre (−1,3).
       Label the image △5.
   (d) Draw the image of △3 after enlargement with scale factor 2, centre (−1,−5).
       Label the image △6.
   (e) Write down the coordinates of the 'pointed ends' of △4, △5 and △6.
       [The 'pointed end' is the vertex of the triangle with the smallest angle.]

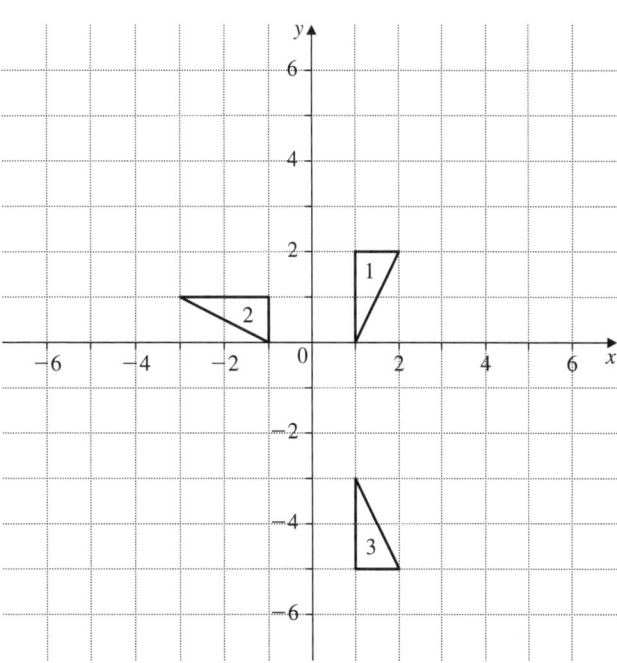

For Questions **8, 9** draw a pair of axes with values from -7 to $+7$.

8. (a) Plot and label the triangles:
   △1: (5,5), (5,7), (4,7)
   △2: (−6,−5), (−3,−5), (−3,−4)
   △3: (1,−4), (1,−6), (2,−6).
   (b) Draw the image of △1 after enlargement with scale factor 2, centre (7,7). Label the image △4.
   (c) Draw the image of △2 after enlargement with scale factor 3, centre (−6,−7). Label the image △5.
   (d) Draw the image of △3 after enlargement with scale factor 2, centre (−1,−5). Label the image △6.
   (e) Write down the coordinates of the 'pointed ends' of △4, △5 and △6.

9. (a) Plot and label the triangles:
   △1: (5,3), (5,6), (4,6)
   △2: (4,−3), (1,−3), (1,−2)
   △3: (−4,−7), (−7,−7), (−7,−6).
   (b) Draw the image of △1 after enlargement with scale factor 2, centre (7,7). Label the image △4.
   (c) Draw the image of △2 after enlargement with scale factor 3, centre (5,−4). Label the image △5.
   (d) Draw the image of △3 after enlargement with scale factor 4, centre (−7,−7). Label the image △6.
   (e) Write down the coordinates of the 'pointed ends' of △4, △5 and △6.

Enlargements with fractional scale factors (reductions)

The unshaded shape is the image of the shaded shape after an enlargement with scale factor $\frac{1}{2}$, centre O.

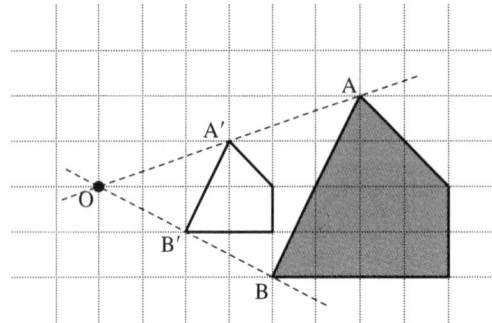

Note that $OA' = \frac{1}{2} \times OA$
$OB' = \frac{1}{2} \times OB$

Even though the shape has undergone a reduction, mathematicians prefer to call it an enlargement with a fractional scale factor.

Exercise 8

Copy each diagram and draw an enlargement using the centre O and the scale factor given.

1.

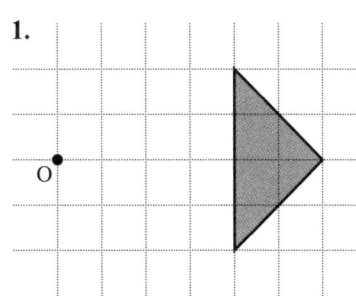

scale factor $\frac{1}{2}$

2.

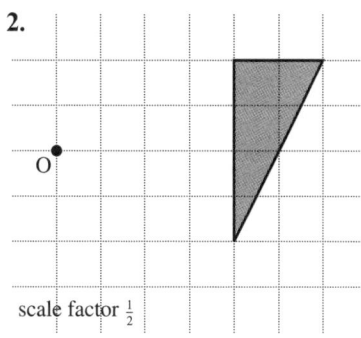

scale factor $\frac{1}{2}$

3.

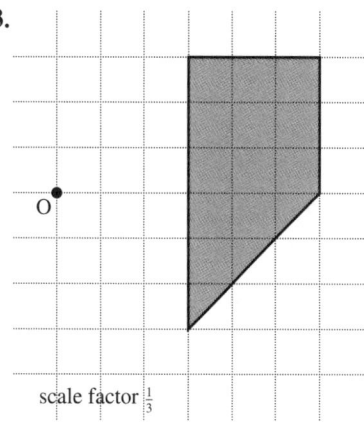

scale factor $\frac{1}{3}$

4. (a) Plot and label the triangles:
   △1: (7,6), (1,6), (1,3)
   △2: (7,−1), (7,−7), (3,−7)
   △3: (−5,7), (−5,1), (−7,1).
   (b) Draw △4, the image of △1 after an enlargement with scale factor $\frac{1}{3}$, centre (−2,0).
   (c) Draw △5, the image of △2 after an enlargement with scale factor $\frac{1}{2}$, centre (−5,−7).
   (d) Draw △6, the image of △3 after an enlargement with scale factor $\frac{1}{2}$, centre (−7,−5).

Translation

A translation is simply a 'shift'. There is no turning or reflection and the object stays the same size.

Example

(a) △1 is mapped on to △2 by the translation with vector $\begin{pmatrix} 4 \\ 2 \end{pmatrix}$

(b) △2 is mapped on to △3 by the translation with vector $\begin{pmatrix} 2 \\ -3 \end{pmatrix}$

(c) △3 is mapped on to △2 by the translation with vector $\begin{pmatrix} -2 \\ 3 \end{pmatrix}$

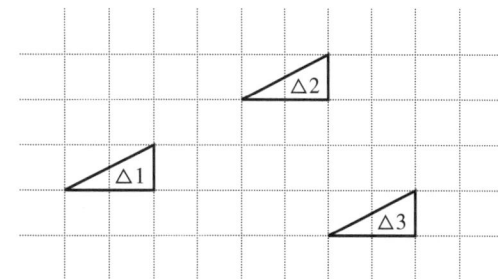

In a vector the top number gives the number of units across (positive to the right) and the bottom number gives the number of units up/down (positive upwards).

So $\begin{pmatrix} 4 \\ 2 \end{pmatrix}$ is 4 across → 2 up ↑ $\begin{pmatrix} -2 \\ 3 \end{pmatrix}$ is 2 across ← 3 up ↑

Exercise 9

1. Look at the diagram shown.

   Write down the vector for each of the following translations:

   (a) △1 → △2   (b) △1 → △3
   (c) △1 → △4   (d) △1 → △5
   (e) △1 → △6   (f) △6 → △5
   (g) △1 → △8   (h) △2 → △3
   (i) △2 → △4   (j) △2 → △5
   (k) △2 → △6   (l) △2 → △8
   (m) △3 → △5   (n) △8 → △2

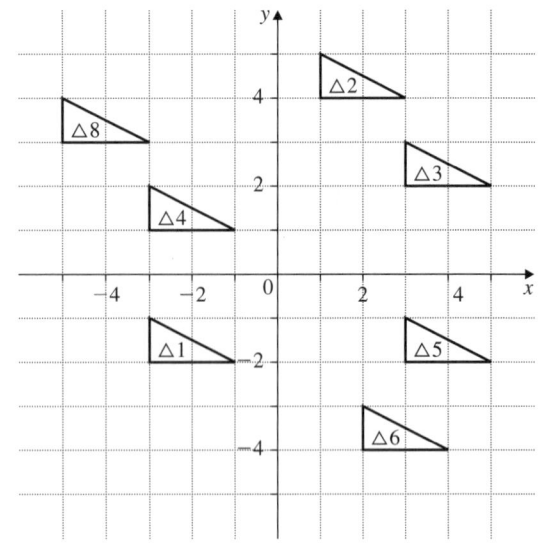

Combined transformations

Exercise 10

1.

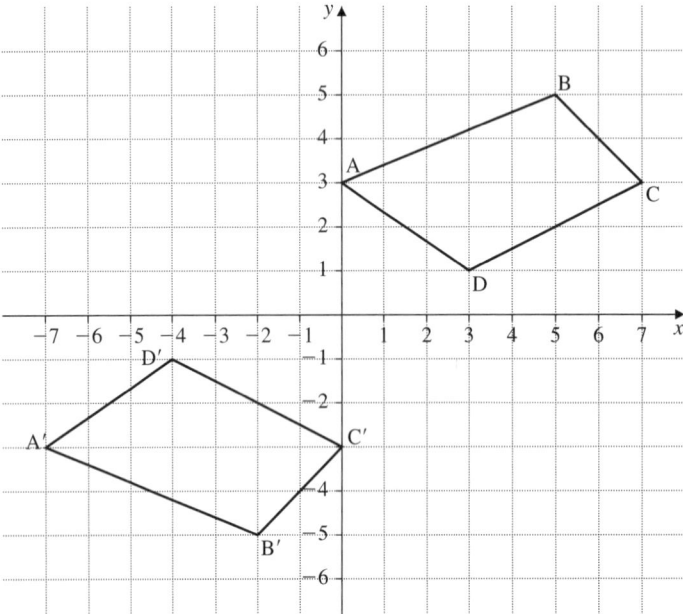

ABCD is mapped onto A'B'C'D' by a reflection followed by a translation parallel to the x axis.

(a) Describe these two transformations as fully as possible
(b) Would the image be the same if the translation was completed before the reflection?

2. Draw axes for both x and y between −8 and +8.
 Plot the points (1, 1), (3, 1) (3, 2), (2, 2), (2, 4) and (1, 4) and join up to make an 'L' shape.
 This is mapped onto the point (−2, −2), (−2, −6), (−4, −6), (−4, −4), (−8, −4), (−8, −2), by *two* transformations; an enlargement with centre (0, 0) followed by a reflection.
 Describe these transformations as fully as possible.

5.2 Quadrilaterals and other polygons

Properties of quadrilaterals

Square:
Four equal sides;
All angles 90°;
Four lines of symmetry.

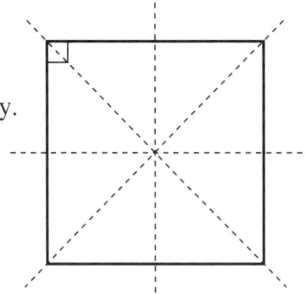

Rectangle (not square):
Two pairs of equal and parallel sides;
All angles 90°;
Two lines of symmetry.

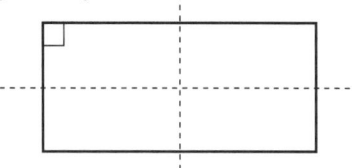

Rhombus:
Four equal sides; Opposite sides parallel;
Diagonals bisect at right angles;
Diagonals bisect angles of rhombus;
Two lines of symmetry.

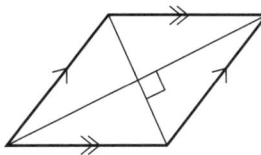

Parallelogram:
Two pairs of equal and parallel sides;
Opposite angles equal;
No lines of symmetry (in general).

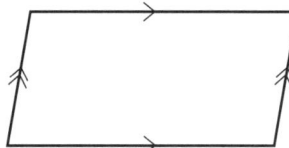

Trapezium: One pair of parallel sides.

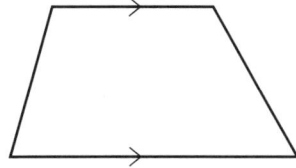

Kite: AB = AD, CB = CD;
Diagonals meet at 90°;
One line of symmetry.

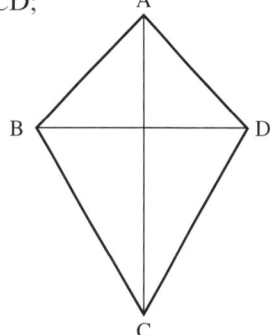

For all quadrilaterals the sum of the interior angles is 360°.

144   Shape and space 2

Exercise 11

1. Find the angle x.

(a) Trapezium, $65°$, x

(b) Rhombus, x

(c) Kite, $150°$, x, $50°$

2. Copy the table and fill all the boxes with either ticks or crosses.

	Diagonals always equal	Diagonals always perpendicular	Diagonals always bisect the angles	Diagonals always bisect each other
Square				
Rectangle				
Parallelogram				
Rhombus				
Kite				

3. ABCD is a rhombus whose diagonals intersect at M. Find the coordinates of C and D.

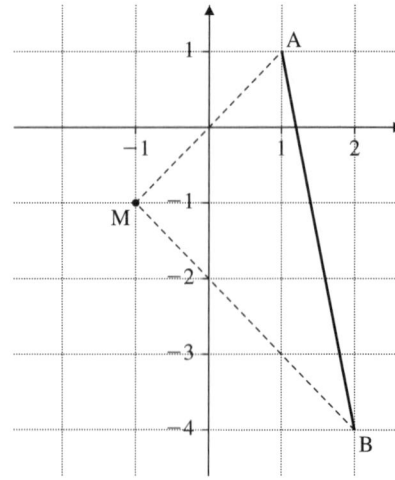

In Questions **4** to **14**, begin by drawing a diagram and remember to put the letters around the shape in alphabetical order.

4. In a rectangle KLMN, $L\hat{N}M = 34°$. Calculate:

(a) $K\hat{L}N$ (b) $K\hat{M}L$

5. In a trapezium ABCD, $A\hat{B}D = 35°$, $B\hat{A}D = 110°$ and AB is parallel to DC. Calculate:

(a) $A\hat{D}B$ (b) $B\hat{D}C$

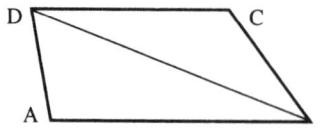

6. In a parallelogram WXYZ, $W\hat{X}Y = 72°$, $Z\hat{W}Y = 80°$.
Calculate:
   (a) $W\hat{Z}Y$ (b) $X\hat{W}Z$ (c) $W\hat{Y}X$

7. In a kite ABCD, AB = AD, BC = CD, $C\hat{A}D = 40°$ and $C\hat{B}D = 60°$. Calculate:
   (a) $B\hat{A}C$ (b) $B\hat{C}A$ (c) $A\hat{D}C$

8. In a rhombus ABCD, $A\hat{B}C = 64°$. Calculate:
   (a) $B\hat{C}D$ (b) $A\hat{D}B$ (c) $B\hat{A}C$

9. In a rectangle WXYZ, M is the mid-point of WX and $Z\hat{M}Y = 70°$. Calculate:
   (a) $M\hat{Z}Y$ (b) $Y\hat{M}X$

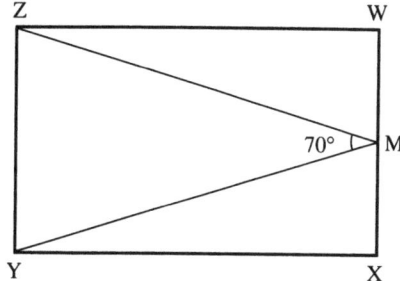

10. In a trapezium ABCD, AB is parallel to DC, AB = AD, BD = DC and $B\hat{A}D = 128°$. Find:
    (a) $A\hat{B}D$ (b) $B\hat{D}C$ (c) $B\hat{C}D$

11. In a parallelogram KLMN, KL = KM and $K\hat{M}L = 64°$. Find:
    (a) $M\hat{K}L$
    (b) $K\hat{N}M$
    (c) $L\hat{M}N$

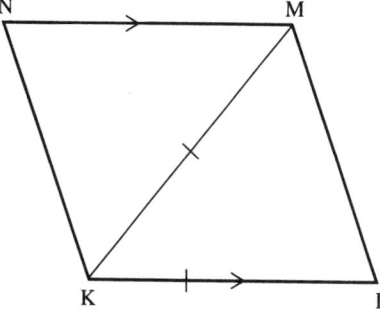

12. In a kite PQRS with PQ = PS and RQ = RS, $Q\hat{R}S = 40°$ and $Q\hat{P}S = 100°$. Find $P\hat{Q}R$.

13. In a rhombus PQRS, $R\hat{P}Q = 54°$. Find:
    (a) $P\hat{R}Q$ (b) $P\hat{S}R$ (c) $R\hat{Q}S$

14. In a kite PQRS, $R\hat{P}S = 2\,P\hat{R}S$, PQ = QS = PS and QR = RS. Find:
    (a) $Q\hat{P}S$ (b) $P\hat{R}S$ (c) $Q\hat{S}R$

5.3 Bearings

Bearings are used where there are no roads to guide the way. Ships, aircraft and mountaineers use bearings to work out where they are.

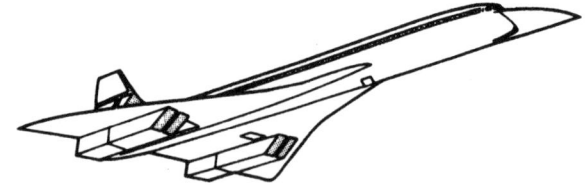

Bearings are measured *clockwise from North*.

Example

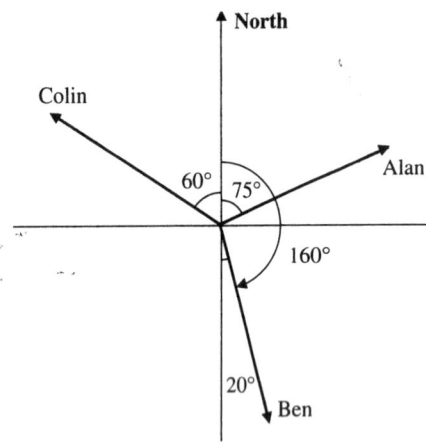

Alan is walking on a bearing of 075°.
Ben is walking on a bearing of 160°.
Colin is walking on a bearing of 300°.

Exercise 12

The diagrams show the directions in which several people are travelling.
Work out the bearing for each person.

1.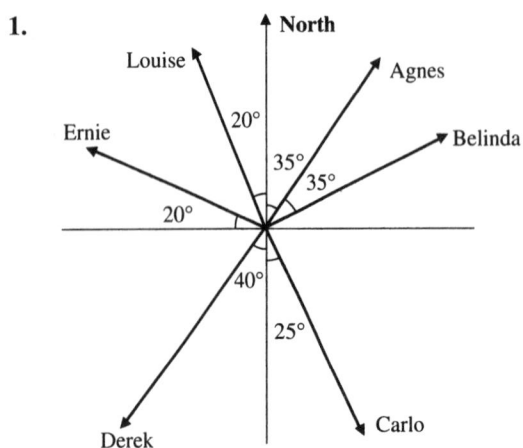

2.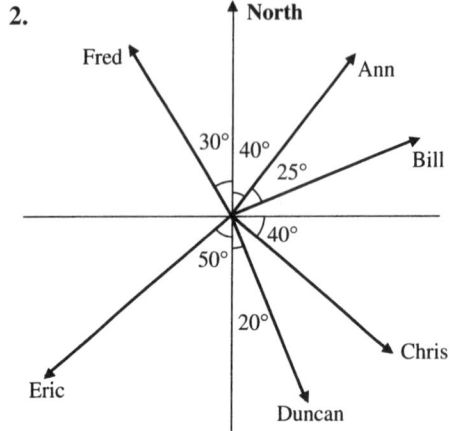

Relative bearings

The bearing of A from B is the direction in which you travel to get to A from B.

It helps to show the journey with an arrow, as in the example below.

Example

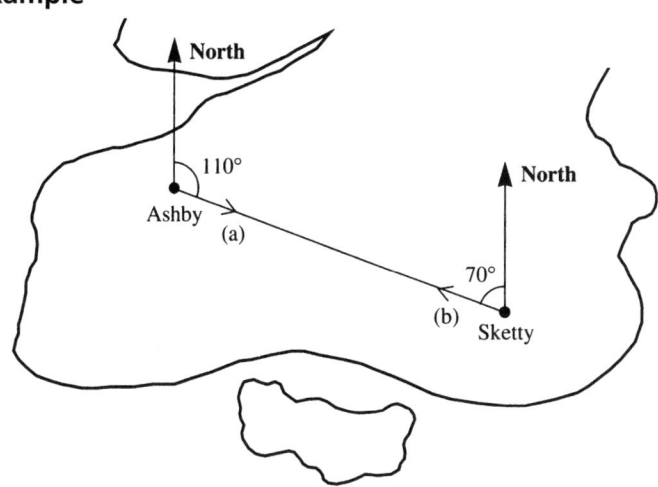

(a) The bearing of Sketty from Ashby is 110°.

(b) The bearing of Ashby from Sketty is 290°.

Exercise 13

The map of North America shows six radar tracking stations, A, B, C, D, E, F.

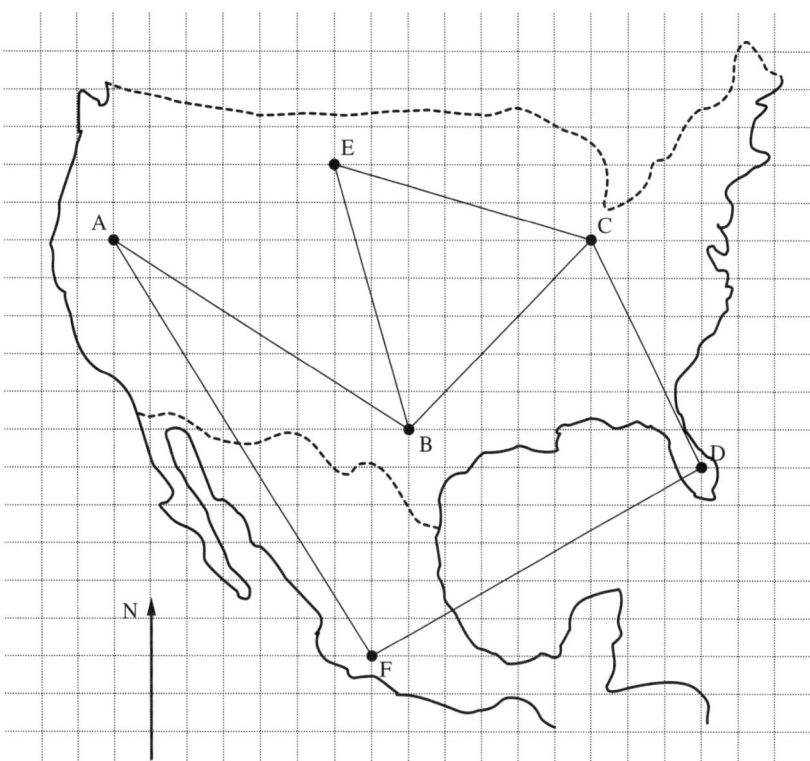

148 Shape and space 2

1. From A, measure the bearing of (a) F (b) B (c) C.

2. From C, measure the bearing of (a) E (b) B (c) D.

3. From F, measure the bearing of (a) D (b) A.

4. From B, measure the bearing of (a) A (b) E (c) C.

Ships or aircraft can be located when their bearings from two places are known.

Example

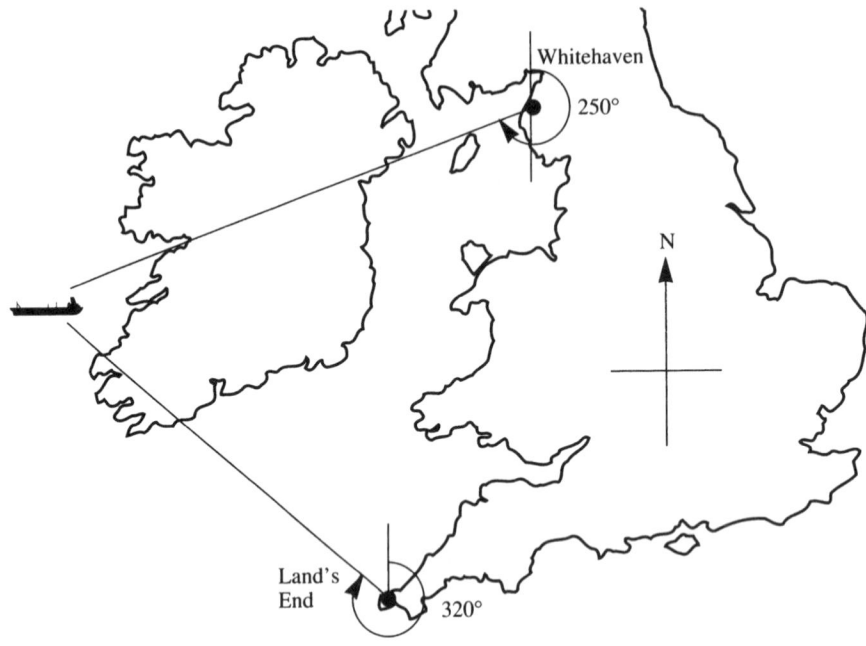

On the map the tanker 'Braer' is on a bearing 320° from Land's End.
From Whitehaven, the Braer is on a bearing of 250°.
There is only one place where the tanker can be.

Exercise 14

Draw the points P and Q below in the middle of a clean page of squared paper. Mark the points A, B, C, D and E accurately, using the information given.

1. A is on a bearing of 040° from P and 015° from Q.

2. B is on a bearing of 076° from P and 067° from Q.

3. C is on a bearing of 114° from P and 127° from Q.

4. D is on a bearing of 325° from P and 308° from Q.

5. E is on a bearing of 180° from P and 208° from Q.

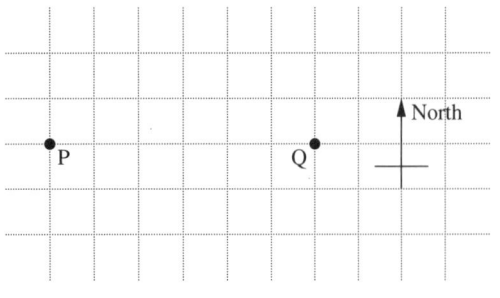

Exercise 15

Draw the points X and Y below in the middle of a clean page of squared paper. Mark the points K, L, M, N and O accurately, using the information given.

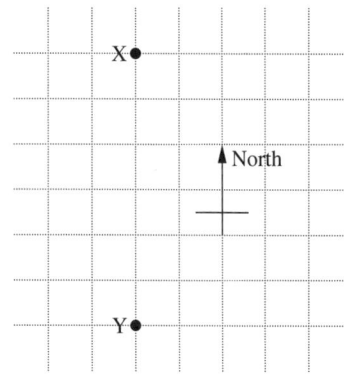

1. K is on a bearing of 041° from X and 025° from Y.
2. L is on a bearing of 090° from X and 058° from Y.
3. M is on a bearing of 123° from X and 090° from Y.
4. N is on a bearing of 203° from X and 215° from Y.
5. O is on a bearing of 288° from X and 319° from Y.

Exercise 16

Make accurate scale drawings with a scale of 1 cm to 1 km, unless told otherwise. Use squared paper and begin each question by drawing a small sketch of the journey.

1. A ship sails 8 km due North and then a further 7 km on a bearing 080°, as in the diagram (which is not drawn to scale).
   How far is the ship now from its starting point?

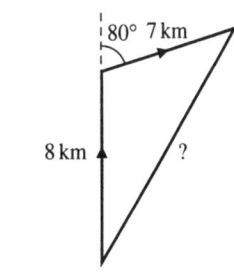

2. A ship sails 9 km on a bearing 090° and then a further 6 km on a bearing 050°, as shown in the diagram.
   How far is the ship now from its starting point?

3. A ship sails 6 km on a bearing 160° and then a further 10 km on a bearing 240°, as shown.
   (a) How far is the ship from its starting point?
   (b) On what bearing must the ship sail so that it returns to its starting point?

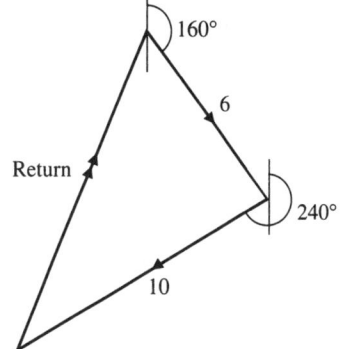

4. A ship sails 5 km on a bearing 030°, then 3 km on a bearing 090° and finally 4 km on a bearing 160°. How far is the ship now from its starting point?

5. Point B is 8 km from A on a bearing 140° from A. Point C is 9 km from A on a bearing 200° from A.
   (a) How far is B from C?
   (b) What is the bearing of B from C?

6. Point Q is 10 km from P on a bearing 052° from P. Point R is 4 km from P on a bearing 107° from P.
   (a) How far is Q from R?
   (b) What is the bearing of Q from R?

7. A laser beam gun L is 120 km from P on a bearing 068°. The laser beam destroys anything on a bearing 270° from L.

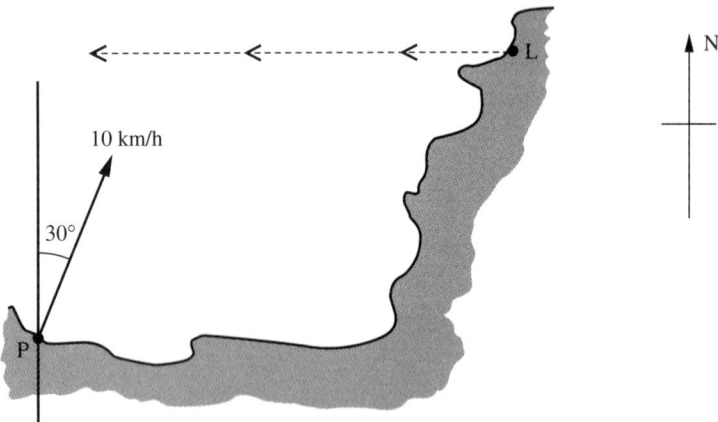

   (a) Draw a diagram, with a scale of 1 cm to 10 km, to show the positions of P and L.
   (b) A ship sails from P at a speed of 10 km/h on a bearing 030°. For how long does the ship sail before being destroyed?

8. Robinson Crusoe is on a tiny island R, dying of starvation. There is an airport at A which is 150 km from R on a bearing 295° from R.

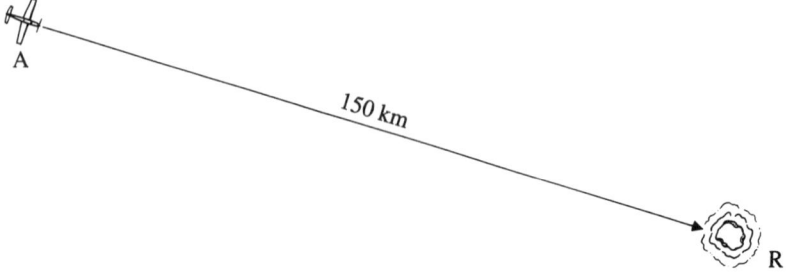

An aircraft flies from A. If the aircraft gets within 40 km of R, the pilot will see Robinson's bonfire and Mr Crusoe will be saved. Will Robinson survive if the plane flies on a bearing of 098°?

5.4 Locus

In mathematics, the word *locus* describes the position of points which obey a certain rule. The locus can be the path traced out by a moving point.

Four important loci

1. The locus of points which are equidistant from a fixed point O is shown. It is a **circle** with centre O.

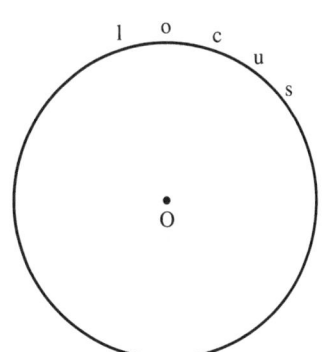

2. The locus of points which are equidistant from two fixed points A and B is shown.

   The locus is the **perpendicular bisector** of the line AB. Use compasses to draw arcs, as shown, or use a ruler and a protractor.

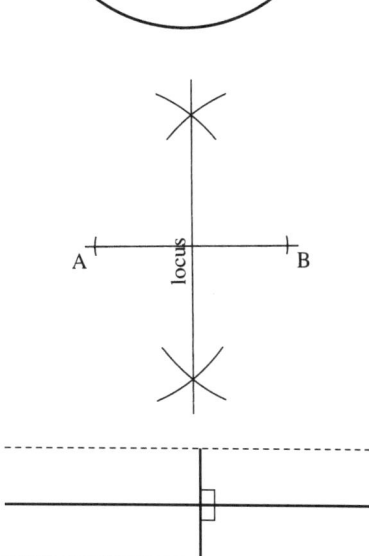

3. The locus of points which are at a given distance from a given straight line is shown.
   In the top diagram the locus of points at a given distance from the line AB is a pair of parallel lines as shown.

   In the lower diagram the locus of points at a given distance from a *line segment* is shown.

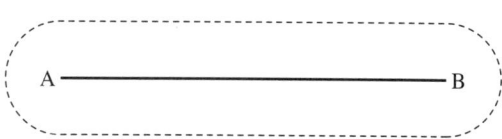

4. The locus of points which are equidistant from two fixed lines AB and AC is shown.

   The locus is the **angle bisector**, the line which bisects the angle BAC. Use compasses to draw arcs or use a protractor to construct the locus.

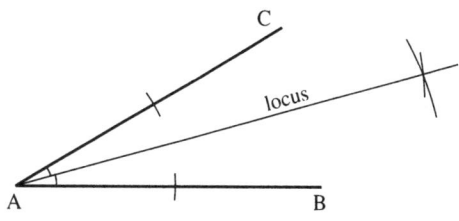

Exercise 17

1. Draw the locus of a point P which moves so that it is always 3 cm from a fixed point X.

   •X

2. Mark two points P and Q which are 10 cm apart. Draw the locus of points which are equidistant from P and Q.

3. Draw two lines AB and AC of length 8 cm, where $B\widehat{A}C = 40°$. Draw the locus of points which are equidistant from AB and AC.

4. A sphere rolls along a surface from A to B. Sketch the locus of the centre of the sphere in each case.

   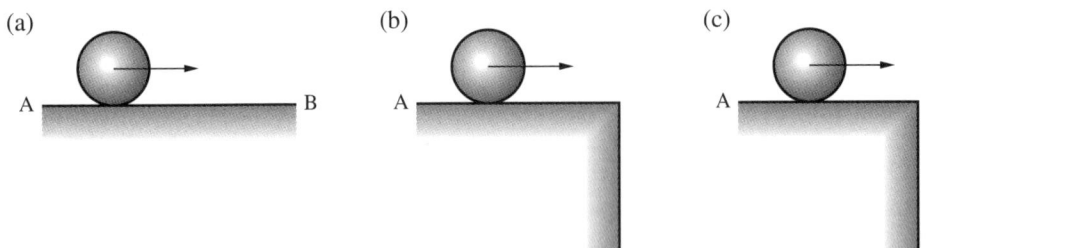

5. A rectangular slab ABCD is rotated around corner B from position 1 to position 2.
   Draw a diagram, on squared paper, to show:
   (a) the locus of corner A
   (b) the locus of corner C.

   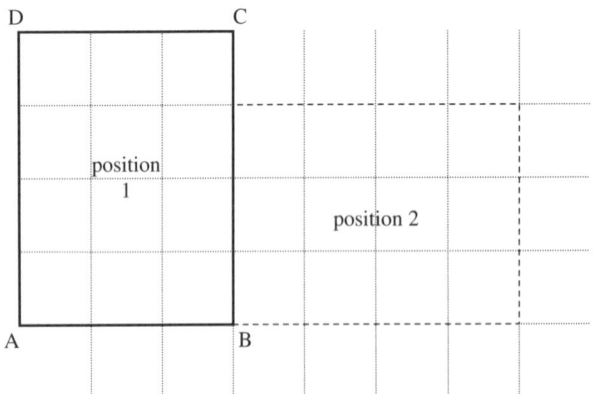

6.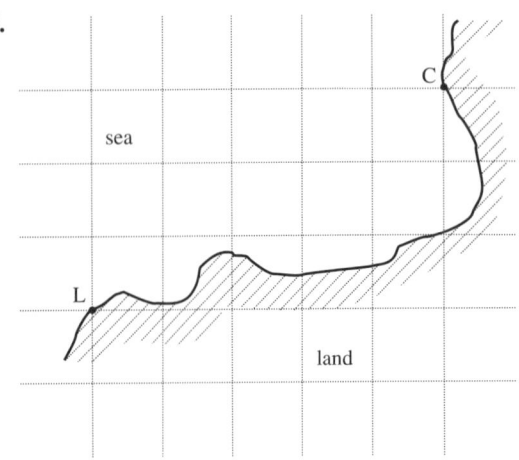

   The diagram shows a section of coastline with a lighthouse L and coastguard C.
   A sinking ship sends a distress signal.
   The ship appears to be up to 40 km from L and up to 30 km from C.
   Copy the diagram and show the region in which the sinking could be.

   Scale 1 cm : 10 km

7. (a) Draw the triangle LMN full size.
   (b) Draw the locus of the points which are:
      (i) equidistant from L and N
      (ii) equidistant from LN and LM
      (iii) 4 cm from M
   [Draw the three loci in different colours].

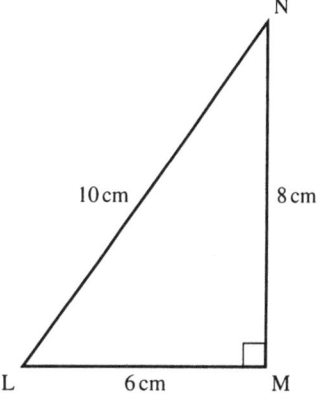

8. Draw a line AB of length 6 cm. Draw the locus of a point P so that angle ABP = 90°.

9. The diagram shows a garden with a fence on two sides and trees at two corners.
   A sand pit is to be placed so that it is:

   (a) equidistant from the two fences,
   (b) equidistant from the two trees.
   Make a scale drawing (1 cm = 1 m) and mark where the sand pit goes.

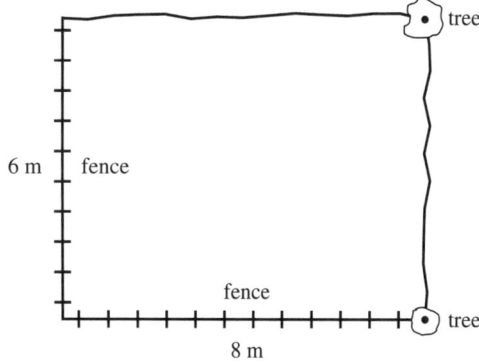

10. Channel 9 in Australia is planning the position of a new TV satellite to send pictures all over the country. The new satellite is to be placed:
    (a) an equal distance from Darwin and Adelaide.
    (b) not more than 2000 km from Perth.
    (c) not more than 1600 km from Brisbane.

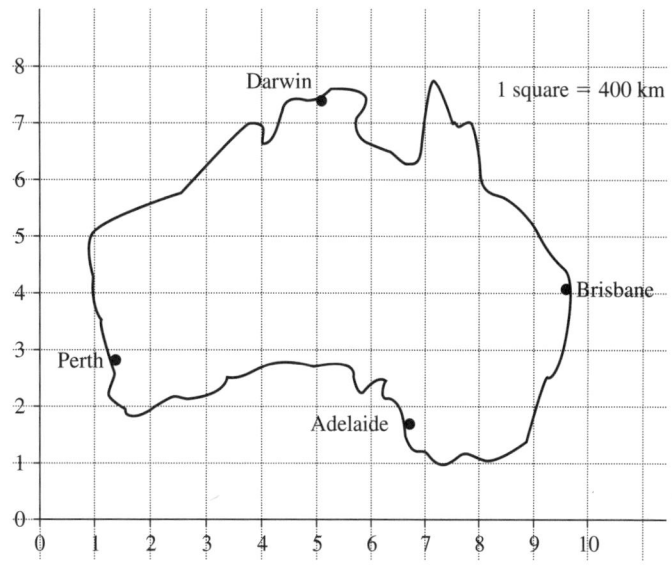

    Make a copy of the map on squared paper using the grid lines as reference.
    Show clearly where the satellite could be placed so that it satisfies the conditions (a), (b), (c) above.

154   Shape and space 2

11. Rod AB rotates about the fixed point A. B is joined to C which slides along a fixed rod. AB = 15 cm and BC = 25 cm.

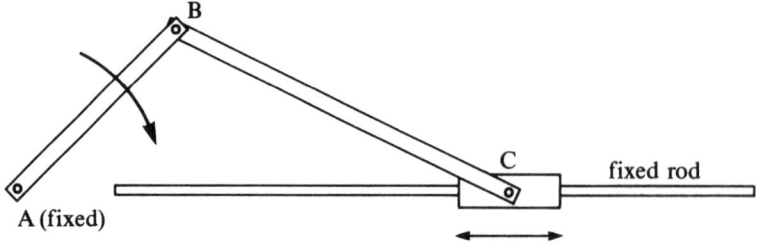

Describe the locus of C as AB rotates clockwise about A.
Find the smallest and the largest distance between C and A.

12. Draw two points M and N 16 cm apart. Draw the locus of a point P which moves so that the area of triangle MNP is 80 cm².

13. Describe the locus of a point which moves in three-dimensional space and is equidistant from two fixed points.

5.5 Pythagoras' theorem

In a right-angled triangle the square on the hypotenuse is equal to the sum of the squares on the other two sides.

$a^2 + b^2 = c^2$

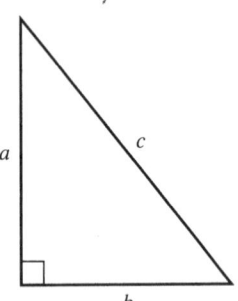

The *converse* is also true:
'If the square on one side of a triangle is equal to the sum of the squares on the other two sides, then the triangle is right-angled.'

Example
Find the side marked d.

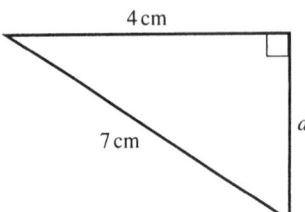

$d^2 + 4^2 = 7^2$
$d^2 = 49 - 16$
$d = \sqrt{33} = 5{\cdot}74$ cm (3 s.f.)

Exercise 18

In Questions **1** to **4**, find x. All the lengths are in cm.

1.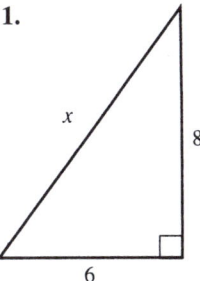
2.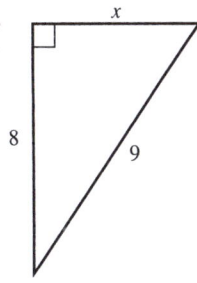
3.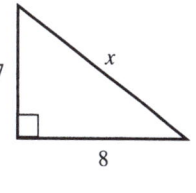
4.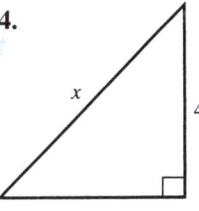

5.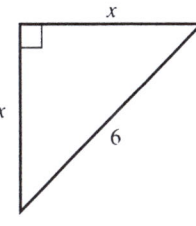
6.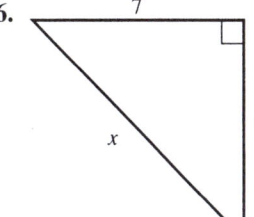
7.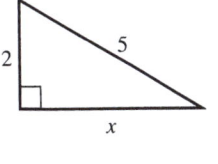
8.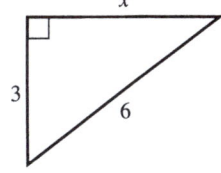

9. Find the length of a diagonal of a rectangle of length 9 cm and width 4 cm.

10. A square has diagonals of length 10 cm. Find the sides of the square.

11. A 4 m ladder rests against a vertical wall with its foot 2 m from the wall. How far up the wall does the ladder reach?

12. A ship sails 20 km due North and then 35 km due East. How far is it from its starting point?

13. A thin wire of length 18 cm is bent in the shape shown.

    Calculate the length from A to B.

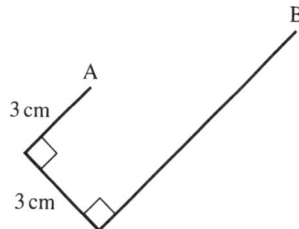

14. A paint tin is a cylinder of radius 12 cm and height 22 cm. Leonardo, the painter, drops his stirring stick into the tin and it disappears.
    Work out the maximum length of the stick.

15. In the diagram A is (1, 2) and B is (6, 4)

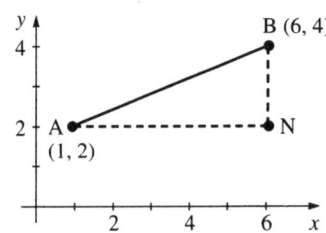

Work out the length AB. [First find the length of AN and BN.]

16. On squared paper plot P(1, 3), Q(6, 0), R(6, 6). Find the lengths of the sides of triangle PQR. Is the triangle isosceles?

In Questions **17** to **22** find x.

17.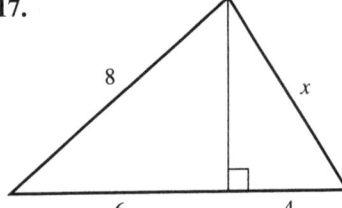

18.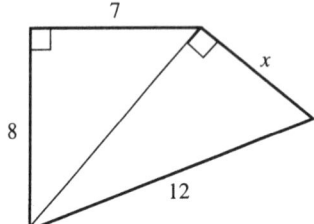

19.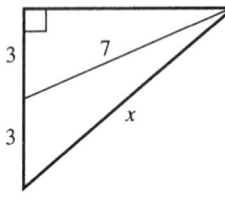

20.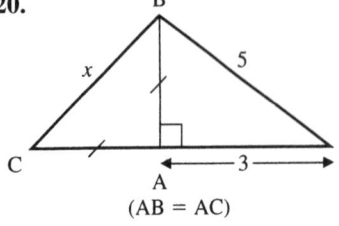

21.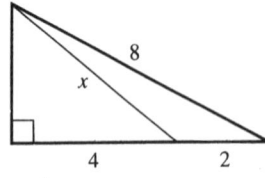

22.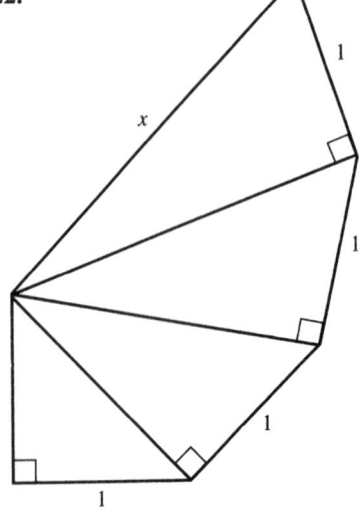

23. The most well known right-angled triangle is the 3, 4, 5 triangle $[3^2 + 4^2 = 5^2]$.
It is interesting to look at other right-angled triangles where all the sides are whole numbers.
  (a) (i) Find c if $a = 5$, $b = 12$
     (ii) Find c if $a = 7$, $b = 24$
     (iii) Find a if $c = 41$, $b = 40$

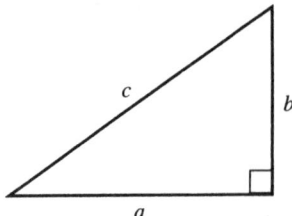

(b) Write the results in a table.

a	b	c
3	4	5
5	12	?
7	24	?
?	40	41

(c) Look at the sequences in the 'a' column and in the 'b' column. Also write down the connection between b and c for each triangle.

(d) Predict the next three sets of values of a, b, c. Check to see if they really do form right-angled triangles.

24. The diagram shows a rectangular block.
    Calculate: (a) AC   (b) AY

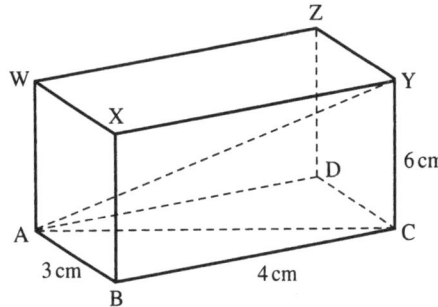

25. The diagram shows a rectangular block.
    Calculate: (a) PQ   (b) PR

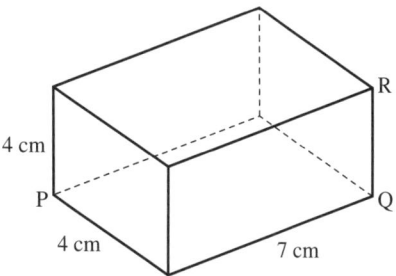

26. Alexis and Philip were arguing about a triangle that had sides 10 cm, 11 cm and 15 cm. Alexis said the triangle had a right angle, and Philip said that it did not. Who was correct?

5.6 Problems in area and volume

Exercise 19

1. Find the capacity in litres of the oil drum shown below. ($1000 \text{ cm}^3 = 1$ litre)

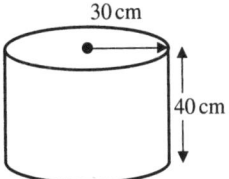

2. Find the volume in litres of a cylinder of height 55 cm and diameter 20 cm.

3. The diagram shows a square ABCD in which DX = XY = YC = AW. The area of the square is 45 cm².

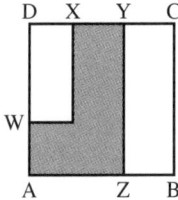

(a) What is the fraction $\dfrac{DX}{DC}$?

(b) What fraction of the square is shaded?

(c) Find the area of the unshaded part.

4. A floor 5 m by 20 m is covered by square tiles of side 20 cm. How many tiles are needed?

5. A rectangular field, 400 m long, has an area of 6 hectares. Calculate the perimeter of the field. [1 hectare = 10 000 m²]

6. Find the shaded area. The lengths are in centimetres.

(a) 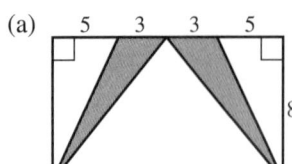   (b)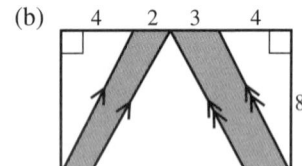

7. Calculate the volume of the object opposite. The lengths are in centimetres.

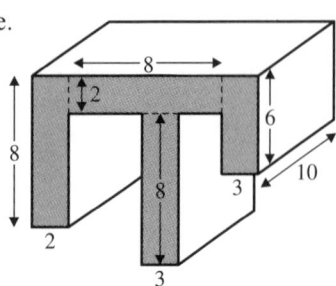

8. The arrowhead has an area of 3·6 cm². Find the length x.

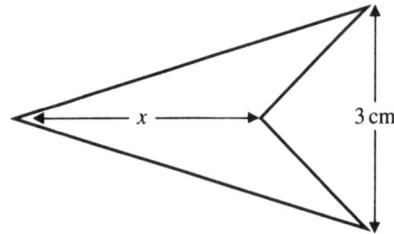

9. Find the length x.

(a)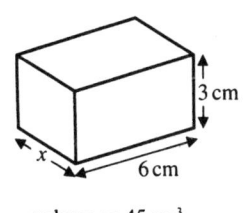
volume = 45 cm³

(b)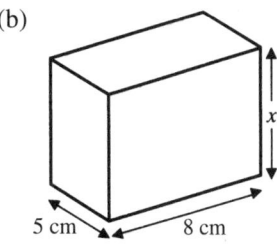
volume = 130 cm³

10. A rectangular block of metal has dimensions 20 cm × 16 cm × 8 cm. It is melted down and recast into cubes of edge length 4 cm. How many cubes will be cast?

11. A freezer makes ice cubes which are rectangular blocks 5 cm × 3 cm × 2 cm. How many ice cubes can be made from 3 litres of water?

12. A wall, 12 m long, 150 cm high and 15 cm thick is constructed using bricks which measure 20 cm × 15 cm × 10 cm. How many bricks are needed (ignoring the cement)?

13. The diagonals of a rhombus measure 24 cm and 32 cm.
    (a) Work out the area of the rhombus.
    (b) Work out the perimeter of the rhombus.

14. The solid object shown is made from 27 small cubes each 1 cm by 1 cm by 1 cm. The small cubes are glued together and then the outside is painted red. Calculate:
    (a) the number of cubes with one face painted
    (b) the number of cubes with two faces painted
    (c) the number of cubes with three faces painted
    (d) the number of cubes with no faces painted
    (Check that the answers to (a), (b), (c) and (d) add up to the correct number.)

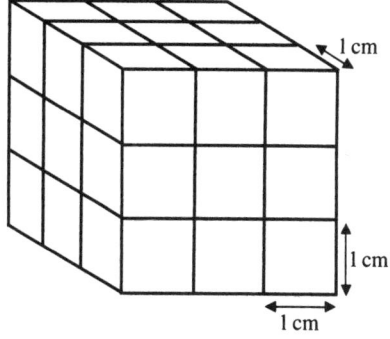

Revision exercise 5A

1. Find x.

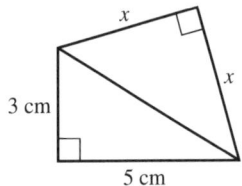

2. In the quadrilateral PQRS, PQ = QS = QR, PS is parallel to QR and QR̂S = 70°.
   Calculate
   (a) RQ̂S
   (b) PQ̂S.

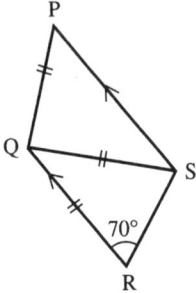

3. A regular octagon of side length 20 cm is to be cut out of a square card.

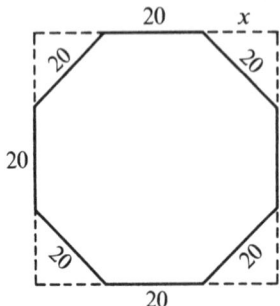

   (a) Find the length x and hence find the size of the smallest square card from which this octagon can be cut.
   (b) Calculate the area of the octagon, correct to 3 s.f.

4. A photo 21 cm by 12 cm is enlarged as shown.

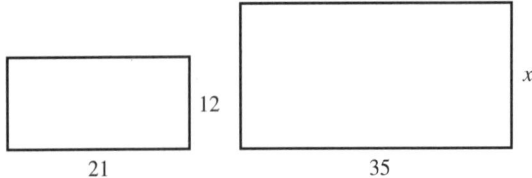

   (a) What is the scale factor of the enlargement?
   (b) Work out the length x.

5. Look at the diagram below

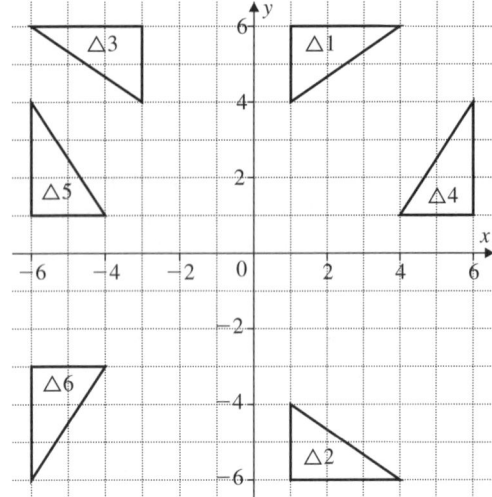

   Describe fully the following transformations.
   (a) △1 → △2   (b) △1 → △3
   (c) △1 → △4   (d) △5 → △1
   (e) △5 → △6   (f) △4 → △6

6. Plot and label the following triangles.
   △1: (−3, −6), (−3, −2), (−5, −2)
   △2: (−5, −1), (−5, −7), (−8, −1)
   △3: (−2, −1), (2, −1), (2, 1)
   △4: (6, 3), (2, 3), (2, 5)
   △5: (8, 4), (8, 8), (6, 8)
   △6: (−3, 1), (−3, 3), (−4, 3)

   Describe fully the following transformations.
   (a) △1 → △2   (b) △1 → △3
   (c) △1 → △4   (d) △1 → △5
   (e) △1 → △6   (f) △3 → △5
   (g) △6 → △2

7. (a) Plot and label
   △1: (−3, 4), (−3, 8), (−1, 8)
   △5: (−8, −2), (−8, −6), (−6, −2)
   (b) Draw the triangles △2, △3, △4, △6 and △7 as follows:
   (i) △1 → △2: translation $\begin{pmatrix} 9 \\ -4 \end{pmatrix}$.
   (ii) △2 → △3: translation $\begin{pmatrix} -4 \\ -8 \end{pmatrix}$.
   (iii) △3 → △4: reflection in the line $y = x$.
   (iv) △5 → △6: rotation 90° anticlockwise, centre (−4, −1).
   (v) △6 → △7: rotation 180°, centre (0, −1).
   (c) Write down the coordinates of the 'pointed ends' of triangles △2, △3, △4, △6, and △7.

8. Point B is on a bearing 120° from point A. The distance from A to B is 110 km.

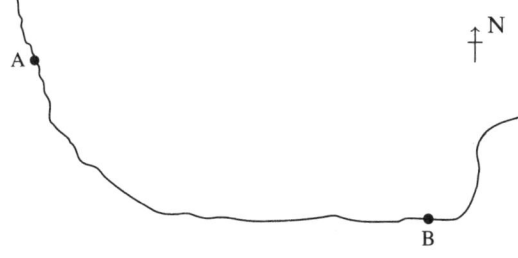

   (a) Draw a diagram showing the positions of A and B. Use a scale of 1 cm to 10 km.
   (b) Ship S is on a bearing 072° from A. Ship S is on a bearing 325° from B. Show S on your diagram and state the distance from S to B.

9. Copy the diagrams and then calculate x, correct to 2 s.f.

   (a) 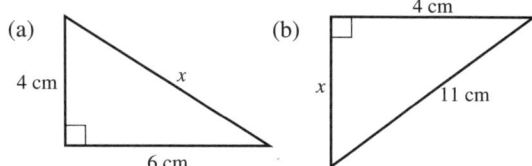 (b)

   (c)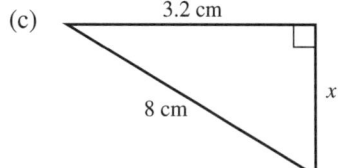

10. (a) A lies on a bearing of 040° from B. Calculate the bearing of B from A.
    (b) The bearing of X from Y is 115°. Calculate the bearing of Y from X.

Examination exercise 5B

1.

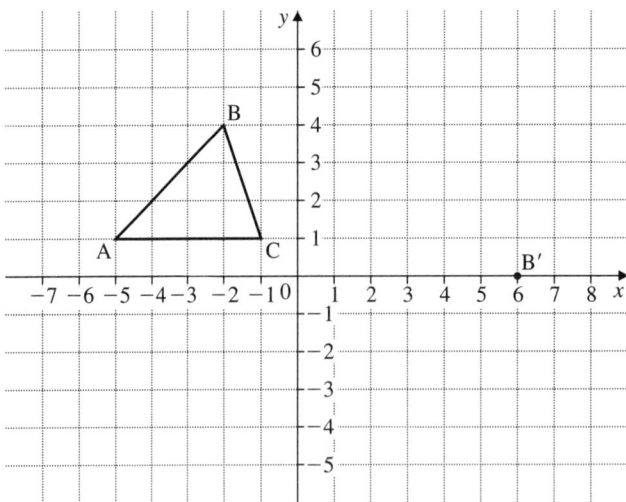

(a) On a copy of the diagram above:
   (i) reflect triangle ABC in the x-axis, labelling your answer P,
   (ii) rotate triangle ABC through 90° clockwise about the origin, labelling your answer Q.
   (iii) draw the locus of the point A during the rotation,
   (iv) translate triangle ABC so that B maps onto B' (6, 0), labelling your answer R.
(b) Write down the column vector for the translation in (a) (iv). [J 96 3]

2. (a) A spider hangs by a thread from a fixed point.
   In the wind, it swings from side to side.
   The length of the thread remains constant.
   Describe, or draw, the locus of the spider.
(b) Another spider crawls along the ground so that it is always an equal distance from two points, A and B. Using ruler and compasses only, construct the spider's path on a copy of the diagram below:
   • A   • B [N 95 1]

3. The village Puylaurens (P) is 14 kilometres north of Revel (R).
Sonal (S) is on a bearing of 040° from Revel.
Angle RPS is 70°.
Calculate:
(a) the bearing of Sonal from Puylaurens,
(b) angle PSR,
(c) the distance from Revel to Sonal.

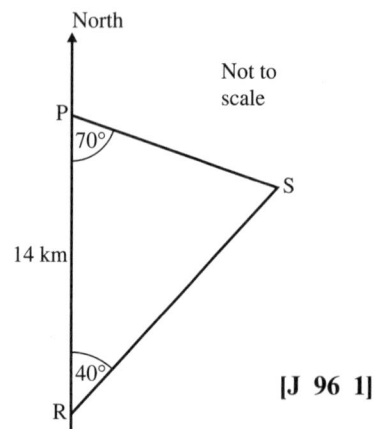

[J 96 1]

4. Calculate the bearing of B from A.

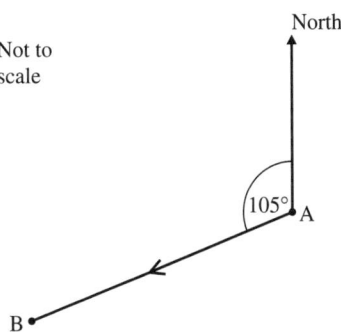

[N 96 1]

5. (a) On a copy of the diagram construct
  (i) the locus of points which are 3 centimetres from A,
  (ii) the locus of points which are equidistant from A and B.

A •   B •

(b) Find the two points on the diagram which are both 3 centimetres from A and 3 centimetres from B. Label them P and Q.

[J 98 1]

6.

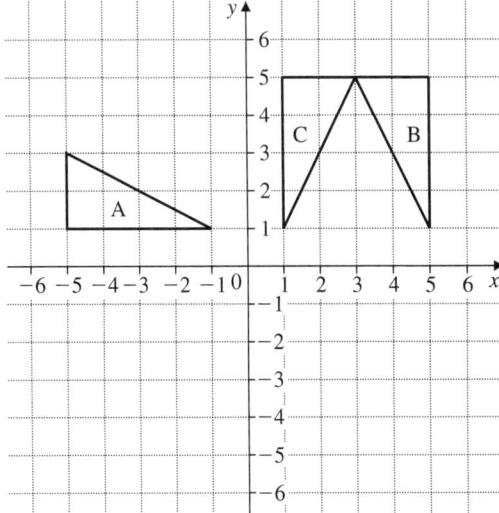

(a) Describe fully the single transformation which maps triangle C onto triangle B.
(b) Describe fully the single transformation which maps triangle C onto triangle A.
(c) Copy the diagram.
  (i) Draw the reflection of triangle A in the x-axis. Label it D.
  (ii) Draw the translation of triangle B by the vector $\begin{pmatrix} -1 \\ -4 \end{pmatrix}$. Label it E.
  (iii) Draw the rotation of triangle C about the point (0, 0) through 180°. Label it F.
  (iv) Draw the enlargement of triangle A, centre (−5, 5) scale factor $\frac{1}{2}$. Label it G.

[N 98 3]

7. The diagram shows a triangular prism on a rectangular base. Angle ABC = 90°, AB = 3 cm, BC = 5 cm and CD = 20 cm.
   (a) (i) Calculate the area of triangle ABC.
       (ii) Calculate the volume of the prism.
       (iii) The prism is made of solid wood and 1 cm³ of this wood has a mass of 0.88 g. Calculate the mass of the prism.
   (b) Calculate the length of AC. [N 98 3]

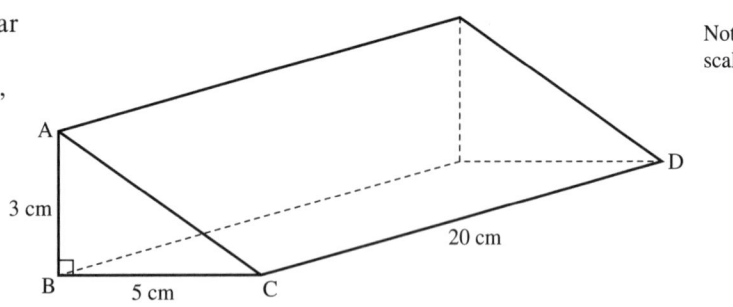

8.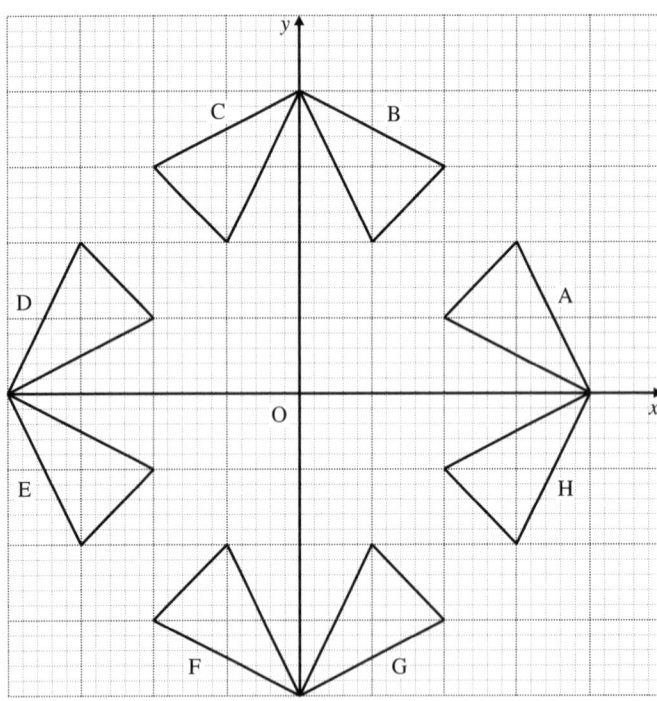

   (a) Look at the diagram.
       (i) How many lines of symmetry does the set of eight triangles have?
       (ii) Triangle A is rotated through 90° anticlockwise about O. Onto which triangle does it map?
   (b) Describe fully a **single** transformation which maps
       (i) triangle C onto triangle F,
       (ii) triangle C onto triangle H,
       (iii) triangle B onto triangle F.
   (c) Enlarge triangle A with centre O and scale factor 2, on a copy of the diagram. [J 95 3]

9.

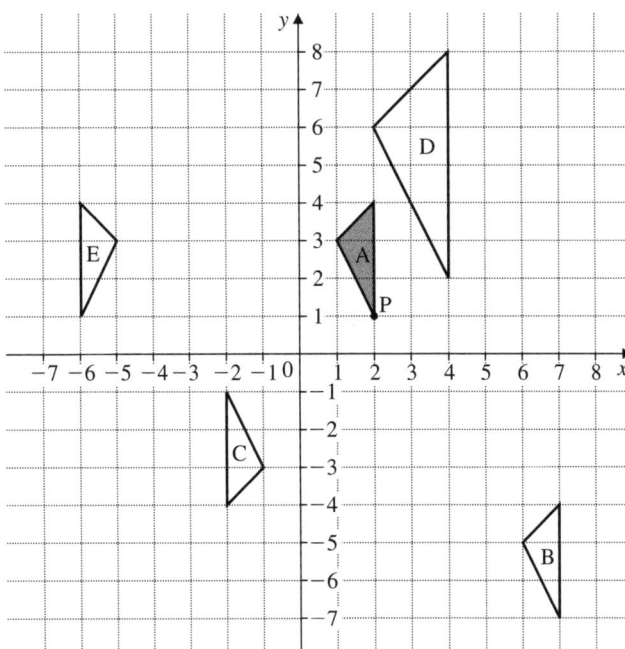

(a) Describe **fully** the single transformation which maps
   (i) triangle A onto triangle B,
   (ii) triangle A onto triangle C,
   (iii) triangle A onto triangle D,
   (iv) triangle A onto triangle E.
(b) On a copy of the grid draw the image of each of the following transformations of **triangle A.**
   (i) Reflection in the y-axis. Label it F.
   (ii) Rotation through 90° clockwise about the point P. Label it G.

[N 98 3]

6 ALGEBRA 2

6.1 Finding a rule

Here is a sequence of 'houses' made from matches.

 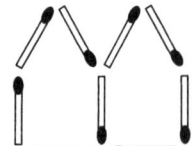  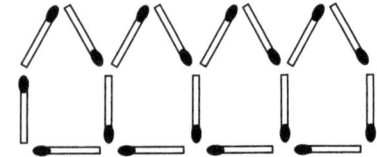

The table on the right records the number of houses h and the number of matches m.

h	m
1	5
2	9
3	13
4	17

If the number in the h column goes up one at a time, look at the number in the m column. If it goes up (or down) by the same number each time, the function connecting m and h is linear. This means that there are no terms in h^2 or anything more complicated.

In this case, the numbers in the m column go up by 4 each time. This suggests that a column for $4h$ might help.

h	m	$4h$
1	5	4
2	9	8
3	13	12
4	17	16

Now it is fairly clear that m is one more than $4h$.

So the formula linking m and h is: $m = 4h + 1$

The table shows how r changes with n.
What is the formula linking r with n?

n	r
2	3
3	8
4	13
5	18

Because r goes up by 5 each time, try writing another column for $5n$.
The table shows that r is always 7 less than $5n$, so the formula linking r with n is: $r = 5n - 7$

n	r	$5n$
2	3	10
3	8	15
4	13	20
5	18	25

Unfortunately if the numbers on the left do not go up by one each time, this method does not work. In that case you have to think of something clever!

Exercise 1

1. Below is a sequence of diagrams showing black tiles b and white tiles w with the related table.

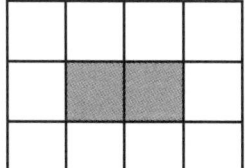 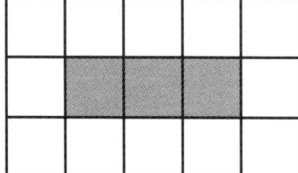 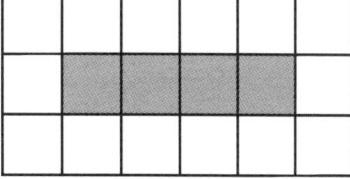

b	w
1	5
2	6
3	7
4	8

What is the formula for w in terms of b? [i.e. write '$w = \ldots\ldots$']

2. This is a different sequence with black tiles b and white tiles w and the related table.

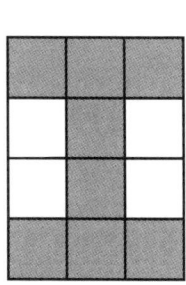 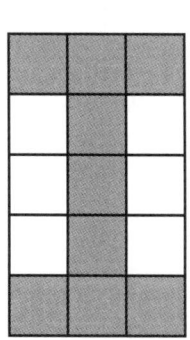 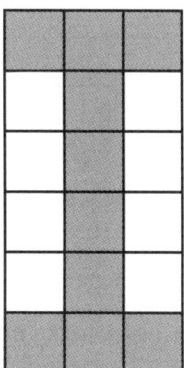

b	w
2	10
3	12
4	14
5	16

What is the formula? Write it as $w = \ldots$

3. Here is a sequence of I's.

Make your own table for black tiles b and white tiles w. What is the formula for w in terms of b?

4. In this sequence we have matches (m) and triangles (t).

   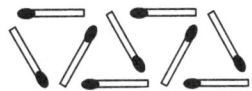

Make a table for t and m. It starts like this:

t	m
1	3
2	5
⋮	⋮

Continue the table and find a formula for m in terms of t. Write '$m = \ldots\ldots$'.

5. Here is a different sequence of matches and triangles.

   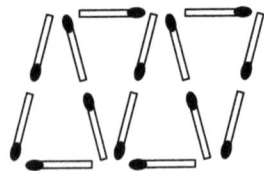

Make a table and find a formula connecting *m* and *t*.

6. In this sequence there are triangles (*t*) and squares (*s*) around the outside.

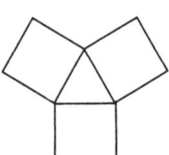 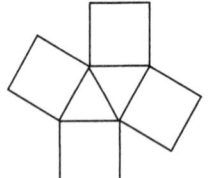 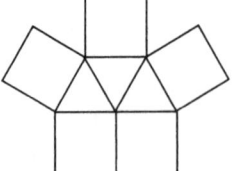 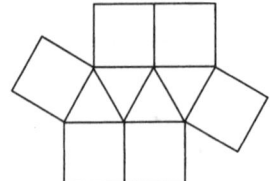

What is the formula connecting *t* and *s*?

7. Look at the tables below. In each case, find a formula connecting the two letters.

(a)

n	p
1	3
2	8
3	13
4	18

write '*p* = ...'

(b)

n	k
2	17
3	24
4	31
5	38

write '*k* = ...'

(c)

n	w
3	17
4	19
5	21
6	23

write '*w* = ...'

8. In these tables it is harder because the numbers on the left do not go up by one each time. Try to find a formula in each case.

(a)

n	y
1	4
3	10
7	22
8	25

(b)

n	h
2	5
3	9
6	21
10	37

(c)

n	k
3	14
7	26
9	32
12	41

9. This is one member of a sequence of cubes (*c*) made from matches (*m*).

Find a formula connecting *m* and *c*.

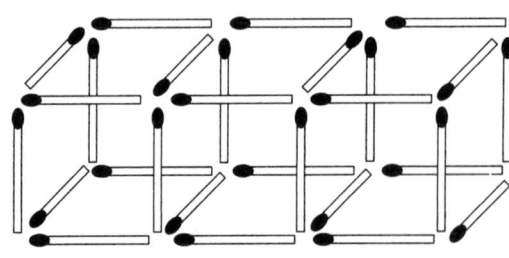

6.2 Simultaneous equations

Graphical solution

Louise and Philip are two children and Louise is 5 years older than Philip.

The sum of their ages is 12 years.
How old is each child?

Let Louise be x years old and Philip be y years old.

We can say $\quad x + y = 12 \quad$ [sum = 12]

and $\quad\quad\quad\quad x - y = 5 \quad$ [difference = 5]

Suppose we draw on the same page the graphs of $\quad x + y = 12$
$$\text{and} \quad x - y = 5$$

$x + y = 12$ goes through (0,12), (2,10), (6,6), (12,0).
$x - y = 5$ goes through (5,0), (7,2), (10,5).

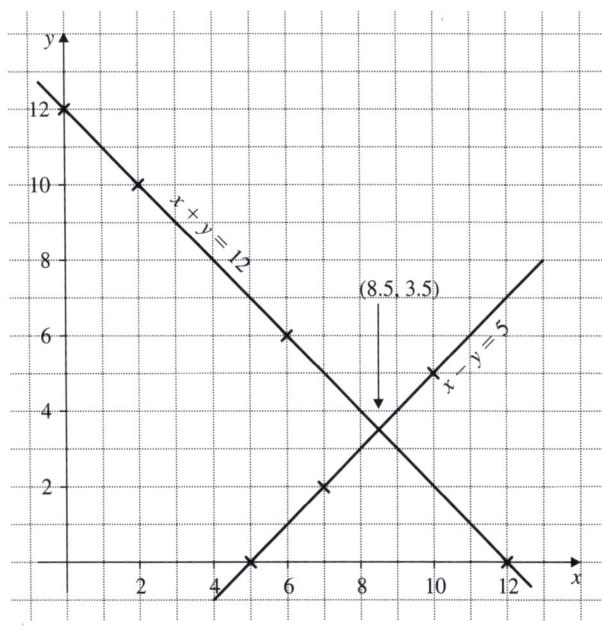

The point (8·5, 3·5) lies on both lines at the same time.

We say that $x = 8·5$, $y = 3·5$ are the solutions of the **simultaneous** equations $\quad x + y = 12, \ x - y = 5$.

So Louise is $8\frac{1}{2}$ years old and Philip is $3\frac{1}{2}$ years old.

Exercise 2

1. Use the graphs to solve these equations.

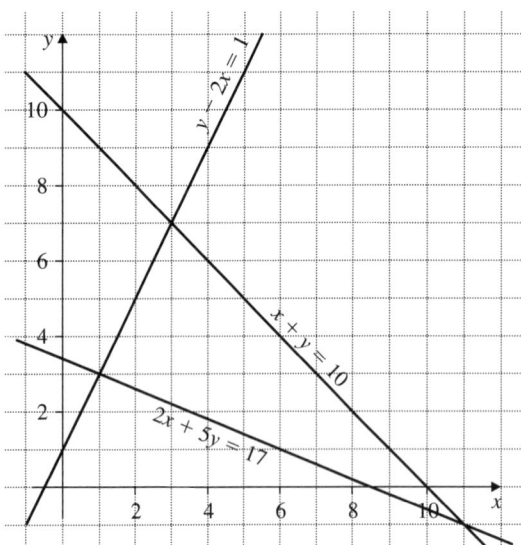

Solve

(a) $x + y = 10$
$y - 2x = 1$

(b) $2x + 5y = 17$
$y - 2x = 1$

(c) $x + y = 10$
$2x + 5y = 17$

In Questions **2** to **6**, solve the simultaneous equations by drawing graphs. Use a scale of 1 cm to 1 unit on both axes.

2. $x + y = 6$
$2x + y = 8$
Draw axes with x and y from 0 to 8.

3. $x + 2y = 8$
$3x + y = 9$
Draw axes with x and y from 0 to 9.

4. $x + 3y = 6$
$x - y = 2$
Draw axes with x from 0 to 8 and y from -2 to 4.

5. $5x + y = 10$
$x - y = -4$
Draw axes with x from -4 to 4 and y from 0 to 10.

6. $a + 2b = 11$
$2a + b = 13$
In this one the unknowns are a and b. Draw the a-axis across the page from 0 to 13 and the b-axis up the page also from 0 to 13.

7. There are four lines drawn here.

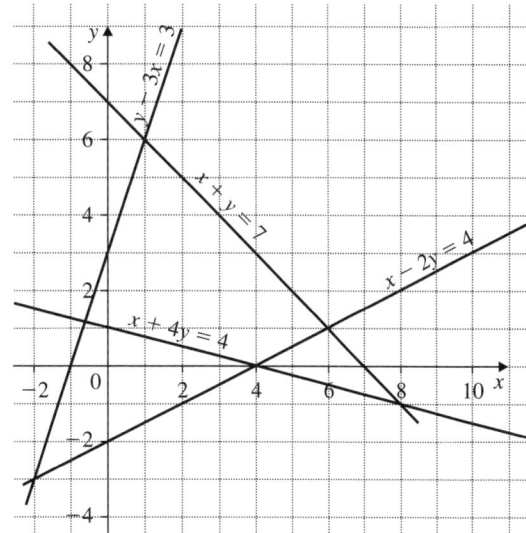

Write down the solutions to the following:

(a) $x - 2y = 4$
$x + 4y = 4$

(b) $x + y = 7$
$y - 3x = 3$

(c) $y - 3x = 3$
$x - 2y = 4$

(d) $x + 4y = 4$
$x + y = 7$

(e) $x + 4y = 4$
$y - 3x = 3$ (For this one give x and y correct to 1 d.p.)

Simultaneous equations: algebraic solution

We can also solve simultaneous equations without drawing graphs.
There are two methods: substitution and elimination.
You can choose for yourself which one to use in any question.

(a) Substitution method

This method is used when one equation contains a single 'x' or 'y', as in equation [2] of the example below.

Example

Solve the simultaneous equations
$3x - 2y = 0$ ... [1]
$2x + y = 7$ ... [2]

From [2] $2x + y = 7$
$y = 7 - 2x$

Substituting in [1]
$3x - 2(7 - 2x) = 0$
$3x - 14 + 4x = 0$
$7x = 14$
$x = 2$

Substituting in [2]
$2 \times 2 + y = 7$
$y = 3$

The solutions are $x = 2$, $y = 3$.
These values of x and y are the only pair which simultaneously satisfy *both* equations.

Exercise 3

Use the substitution method to solve the following:

1. $2x + y = 5$
   $x + 3y = 5$

2. $x + 2y = 8$
   $2x + 3y = 14$

3. $3x + y = 10$
   $x - y = 2$

4. $2x + y = -3$
   $x - y = -3$

5. $4x + y = 14$
   $x + 5y = 13$

6. $x + 2y = 1$
   $2x + 3y = 4$

7. $2x + y = 5$
   $3x - 2y = 4$

8. $2x + y = 13$
   $5x - 4y = 13$

9. $7x + 2y = 19$
   $x - y = 4$

10. $b - a = -5$
    $a + b = -1$

11. $a + 4b = 6$
    $8b - a = -3$

12. $a + b = 4$
    $2a + b = 5$

13. $3m = 2n - 6\frac{1}{2}$
    $4m + n = 6$

14. $2w + 3x - 13 = 0$
    $x + 5w - 13 = 0$

15. $x + 2(y - 6) = 0$
    $3x + 4y = 30$

16. $2x = 4 + z$
    $6x - 5z = 18$

17. $3m - n = 5$
    $2m + 5n = 7$

18. $5c - d - 11 = 0$
    $4d + 3c = -5$

It is useful, at this point to revise the operations of addition and subtraction with negative numbers.

Simplify:

(a) $-7 + -4 = -7 - 4 = -11$
(b) $-3x + (-4x) = -3x - 4x = -7x$
(c) $4y - (-3y) = 4y + 3y = 7y$
(d) $3a + (-3a) = 3a - 3a = 0$

(b) Elimination method

Use this method when the first method is unsuitable (some prefer to use it for every question).

Example

$$2x + 3y = 5 \quad \ldots [1]$$
$$5x - 2y = -16 \quad \ldots [2]$$

$[1] \times 5$ $\quad 10x + 15y = 25 \quad \ldots [3]$
$[2] \times 2$ $\quad 10x - 4y = -32 \quad \ldots [4]$
$[3] - [4]$ $\quad 15y - (-4y) = 25 - (-32)$
$\quad\quad\quad\quad\quad 19y = 57$
$\quad\quad\quad\quad\quad\quad y = 3$

Substitute in [1] $\quad 2x + 3 \times 3 = 5$
$\quad\quad\quad\quad\quad\quad\quad 2x = 5 - 9 = -4$
$\quad\quad\quad\quad\quad\quad\quad\; x = -2$

The solutions are $x = -2$, $y = 3$.

Exercise 4

Use the elimination method to solve the following:

1. $2x + 5y = 24$
   $4x + 3y = 20$

2. $5x + 2y = 13$
   $2x + 6y = 26$

3. $3x + y = 11$
   $9x + 2y = 28$

4. $x + 2y = 17$
   $8x + 3y = 45$

5. $3x + 2y = 19$
   $x + 8y = 21$

6. $2a + 3b = 9$
   $4a + b = 13$

7. $2x + 3y = 11$
   $3x + 4y = 15$

8. $3x + 8y = 27$
   $4x + 3y = 13$

9. $2x + 7y = 17$
   $5x + 3y = -1$

10. $5x + 3y = 23$
    $2x + 4y = 12$

11. $7x + 5y = 32$
    $3x + 4y = 23$

12. $3x + 2y = 4$
    $4x + 5y = 10$

13. $3x + 2y = 11$
    $2x - y = -3$

14. $3x + 2y = 7$
    $2x - 3y = -4$

15. $x - 2y = -4$
    $3x + y = 9$

16. $5x - 7y = 27$
    $3x - 4y = 16$

17. $3x - 2y = 7$
    $4x + y = 13$

18. $x - y = -1$
    $2x - y = 0$

19. $y - x = -1$
    $3x - y = 5$

20. $x - 3y = -5$
    $2y + 3x + 4 = 0$

Problems solved by simultaneous equations

Exercise 5

Solve each problem by forming a pair of simultaneous equations.

1. Find two numbers with a sum of 15 and a difference of 4.
   [Let the numbers be x and y.]

2. Twice one number added to three times another gives 21. Find the numbers, if the difference between them is 3.

3. The average of two numbers is 7, and three times the difference between them is 18. Find the numbers.

4. Here is a puzzle from a newspaper. The ? and * stand for numbers which are to be found. The totals for the rows and columns are given.

   Write down two equations involving ? and * and solve them to find the values of ? and *

?	*	?	*	36
?	*	*	?	36
*	?	*	*	33
?	*	?	*	36
39	33	36	33	

5. The line, with equation $y + ax = c$, passes through the points (1, 5) and (3, 1). Find a and c.
   Hint: For the point (1, 5) put $x = 1$ and $y = 5$ into $y + ax = c$, etc.

6. The line $y = mx + c$ passes through (2, 5) and (4, 13).
   Find m and c.

7. A stone is thrown into the air and its height, h metres above the ground, is given by the equation
   $$h = at - bt^2.$$
   From an experiment we know that $h = 40$ when $t = 2$ and that $h = 45$ when $t = 3$.
   Show that $a - 2b = 20$
   and $a - 3b = 15$.
   Solve these equations to find a and b.

8. A television addict can buy either two televisions and three video-recorders for $1750 or four televisions and one video-recorder for $1250. Find the cost of one of each.

9. A spider can lay either white or brown eggs. Three white eggs and two brown eggs weigh 13 grams, while five white eggs and four brown eggs weigh 24 grams. Find the weight of a brown egg and of a white egg.

10. A bag contains forty coins, all of them either 2c or 5c coins. Let there be x 2c coins and y 5c coins. If the value of the money in the bag is $1·55, find the number of each kind.

11. A slot machine takes only 10c and 50c coins and contains a total of twenty-one coins altogether. If the value of the coins is $4·90, find the number of coins of each value.

6.3 Interpreting graphs

Travel graphs

Exercise 6

1. The graph shows a return journey by car from Grenoble to Sisteron.
   (a) How far is it from Grenoble to Gap?
   (b) How far is it from Gap to Sisteron?
   (c) At which two places does the car stop?
   (d) How long does the car stop at Sisteron?
   (e) When does the car
       (i) arrive in Gap,
       (ii) arrive back in Grenoble?
   (f) What is the speed of the car
       (i) from Grenoble to Gap,
       (ii) from Gap to Sisteron,
       (iii) from Sisteron to Grenoble?

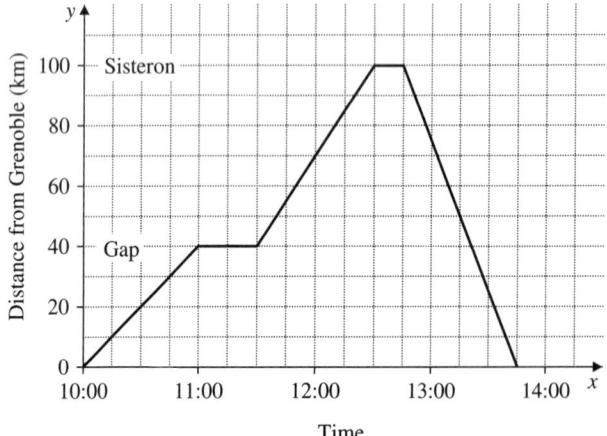

2. Steve cycles to a friend's house but on the way his bike gets a puncture, and he has to walk the remaining distance.
At his friend's house, he repairs the puncture, has a game of snooker and then returns home. On the way back, he stops at a shop to buy a book on how to play snooker.

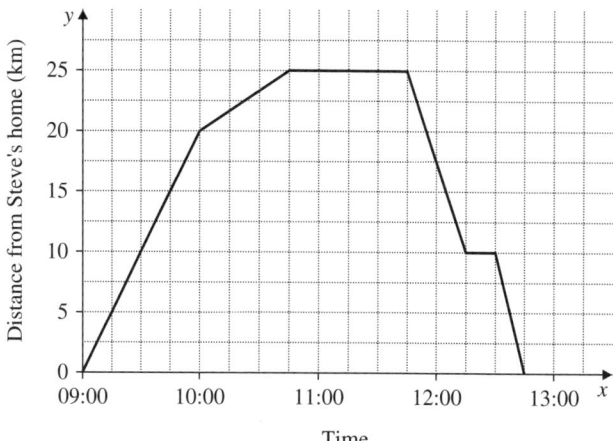

(a) How far is it to his friend's house?
(b) How far is it from his friend's house to the shop?
(c) At what time did his bike get a puncture?
(d) How long did he stay at his friend's house?
(e) At what speed did he travel:
   (i) from home until he had the puncture,
   (ii) after the puncture to his friend's house,
   (iii) from his friend's house to the shop,
   (iv) from the shop back to his own home?

3. Mr Berol and Mr Hale use the same road to travel between Aston and Borton.
   (a) At what time did:
      (i) Mr Berol arrive in Borton,
      (ii) Mr Hale leave Aston?
   (b) (i) When did Mr Berol and Mr Hale pass each other?
      (ii) In which direction was Mr Berol travelling?
   (c) Find the following speeds:
      (i) Mr Hale from Aston to Stanley,
      (ii) Mr Berol from Aston to Borton,
      (iii) Mr Hale from Stanley to Borton,
      (iv) Mr Berol from Borton back to Aston.
   (d) (More difficult) When did Mr Hale arrive in Borton?

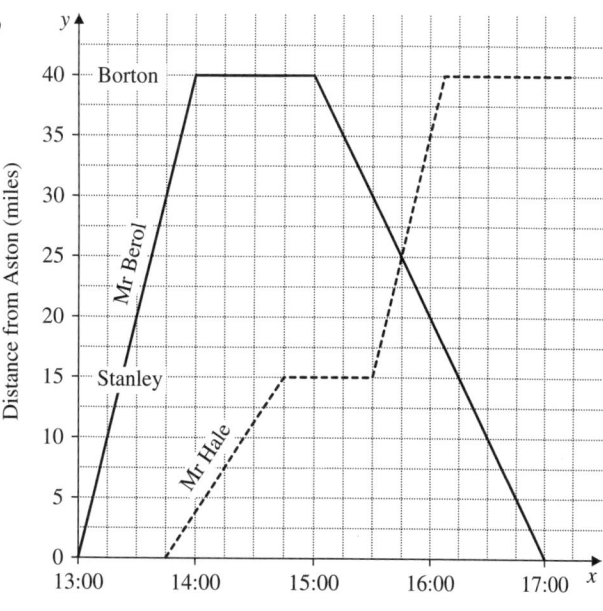

4. The graph shows the journeys made by a van and a car starting at Toledo, travelling to Madrid and returning to Toledo.
   (a) For how long was the van stationary during the journey?
   (b) At what time did the car first overtake the van?
   (c) At what speed was the van travelling between 09:30 and 10:00?
   (d) What was the greatest speed attained by the car during the entire journey?
   (e) What was the average speed of the car over its entire journey?

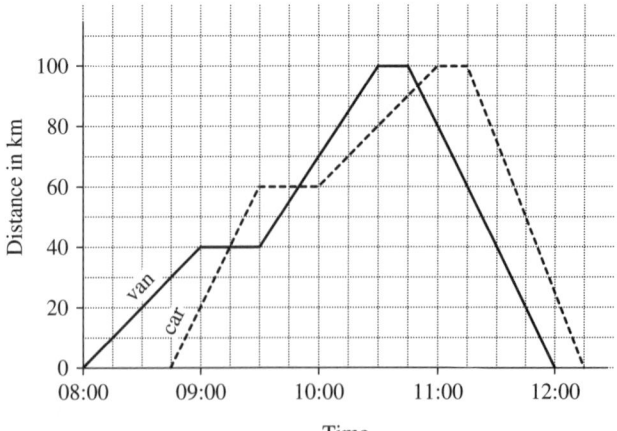

5. The graph shows the journeys of a bus and a car along the same road. The bus goes from Bangkok to Tainan and back to Bangkok. The car goes from Tainan to Bangkok and back to Tainan.

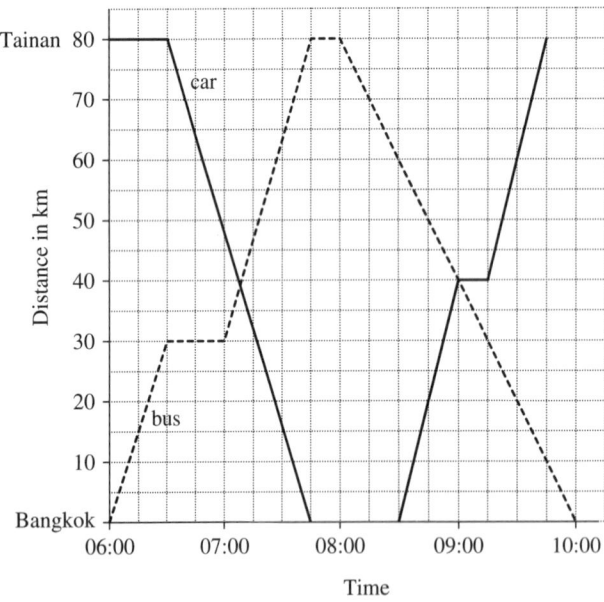

   (a) When did the bus and the car meet for the second time?
   (b) At what speed did the car travel from Tainan to Bangkok?
   (c) What was the average speed of the bus over its entire journey?
   (d) Approximately how far apart were the bus and the car at 09:45?
   (e) What was the greatest speed attained by the car during its entire journey?

In Questions **6, 7, 8**, draw a travel graph to illustrate the journey described. Draw axes with the same scales as in Question **5**.

6. Mrs Chuong leaves home at 08:00 and drives at a speed of 50 km/h. After $\frac{1}{2}$ hour she reduces her speed to 40 km/h and continues at this speed until 09:30. She stops from 09:30 until 10:00 and then returns home at a speed of 60 km/h.
Use a graph to find the approximate time at which she arrives home.

7. Mr Coe leaves home at 09:00 and drives at a speed of 20 km/h. After $\frac{3}{4}$ hour he increases his speed to 45 km/h and continues at this speed until 10:45. He stops from 10:45 until 11:30 and then returns home at a speed of 50 km/h.
Use a graph to find the approximate time at which he arrives home.

8. At 10:00 Akram leaves home and cycles to his grandparents' house which is 70 km away. He cycles at a speed of 20 km/h until 11:15, at which time he stops for $\frac{1}{2}$ hour. He then completes the journey at a speed of 30 km/h. At 11:45 Akram's sister, Hameeda, leaves home and drives her car at 60 km/h. Hameeda also goes to her grandparents' house and uses the same road as Akram.
At approximately what time does Hameeda overtake Akram?

Real life graphs

Exercise 7

1. The graph shows how the share price of the chemical firm ICI varied over a period of weeks. The share price is the price in cents paid for one share in the company.

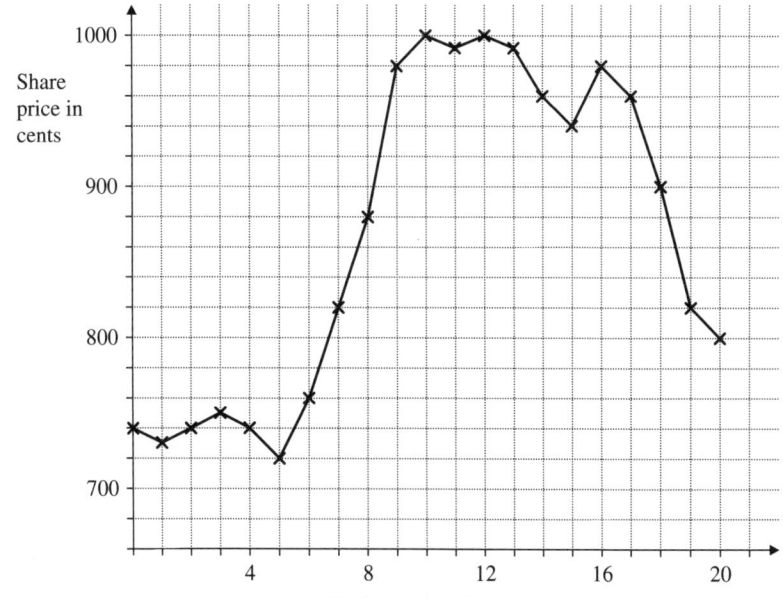

(a) What was the share price in Week 4?
(b) Naomi bought 200 shares in Week 6 and sold them all in week 18. How much profit did she make?
(c) Mr Gibson can buy (and then sell) 5000 shares. He consults a very accurate fortune teller who can predict the share price over coming weeks. What is the maximum profit he could make?
(d) When there is a full moon the fortune teller's predictions can be fairly disastrous. What is the maximum *loss* Mr Gibson could make?

2. The graph shows the number pupils on the premises of a school one day.

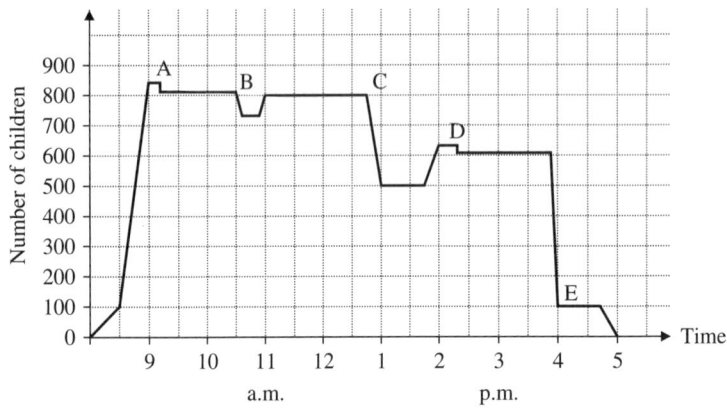

The graph tells you some interesting things. Referring to the points A, B, C, D, E, describe briefly what happened during the day. Give an explanation of what you think might have happened.

3. The graph below shows average television and radio audiences throughout a typical day in 2000.

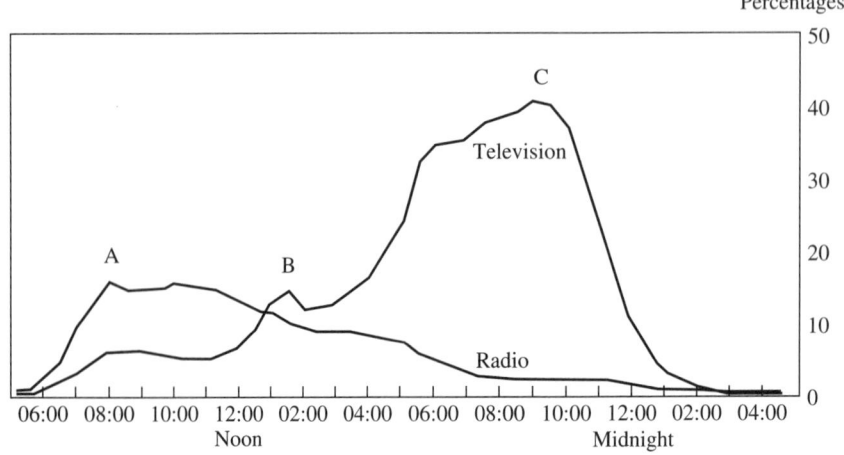

(a) When are the 'peak times' for
   (i) radio audiences   (ii) television audiences?
(b) Give reasons which explain the shapes of the graphs at times A, B and C.

4. A car travels along a motorway and the amount of petrol in its tank is monitored as shown on the graph.
   (a) How much petrol was bought at the first stop?
   (b) What was the petrol consumption in km per litre:
      (i) before the first stop,
      (ii) between the two stops?
   (c) What was the average petrol consumption over the 200 km?

   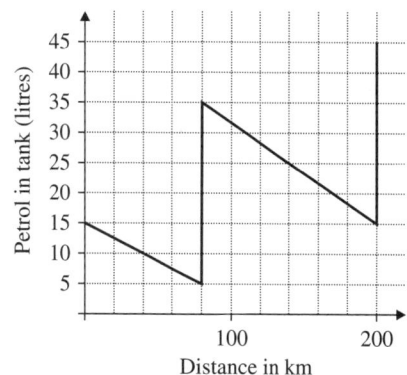

   After it leaves the second service station the car encounters road works and slow traffic for the next 20 km. Its petrol consumption is reduced to 4 km per litre. After that, the road clears and the car travels a further 80 km during which time the consumption is 8 km per litre. Draw the graph above and extend it to show the next 100 km. How much petrol is in the tank at the end of the journey?

5. Kendal Motors hires out vans.

   Copy and complete the table where x is the number of km travelled and C is the total cost in dollars.

x	0	50	100	150	200	250	300
C	35			65			95

   Draw a graph of C against x, using scales of 2 cm for 50 km on the x-axis and 1 cm for $10 on the C-axis.
   Use the graph to find the number of km travelled when the total cost was $71.

6. Jeff sets up his own business as a plumber.

   24hr PLUMBING
   0707 874561   call out $18
   plus $15 per hour   NO VAT!

   Copy and complete the table where C stands for his total charge and h stands for the number of hours he works.

h	0	1	2	3
C		33		

   Draw a graph with h across the page and C up the page. Use scales of 2 cm to 1 hour for h and 2 cm to $10 for C.
   Use your graph to find how long he worked if his charge was $55·50

Sketch graphs

Exercise 8

1. Which of the graphs A to D below best fits the following statement:
   'Unemployment is still rising but by less each month.'

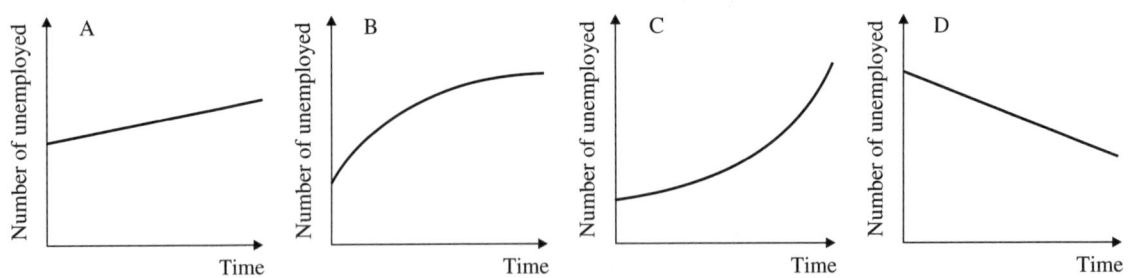

2. Which of the graphs A to D best fits the following statement:
   'The price of oil was rising more rapidly in 1999 than at any time in the previous ten years.'?

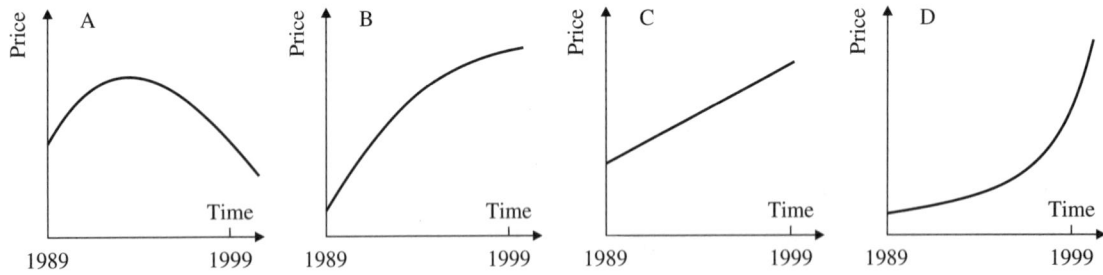

3. Which of the graphs A to D below best fits each of the following statements:
   (a) The birthrate was falling but is now steady.
   (b) Unemployment, which rose slowly until 1999, is now rising rapidly.
   (c) Inflation, which has been rising steadily, is now beginning to fall.
   (d) The price of gold has fallen steadily over the last year.

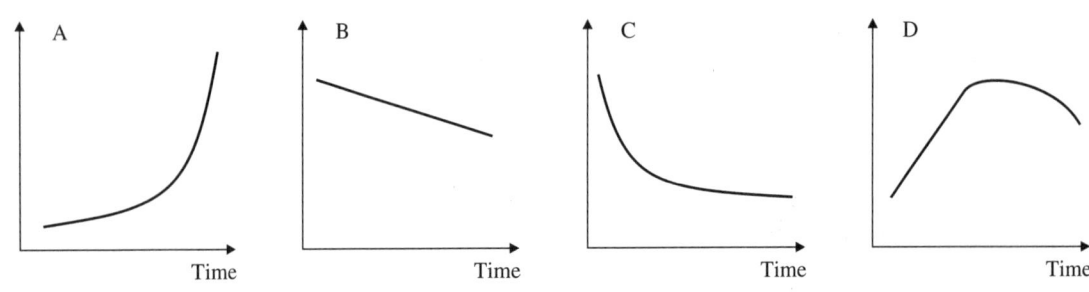

4. The graph shows the motion of three cars A, B and C along the same road.
   Answer the following questions giving estimates where necessary.
   (a) Which car is in front after
       (i) 10 s,   (ii) 20 s?
   (b) When is B in the front?
   (c) When are B and C going at the same speed?
   (d) When are A and C going at the same speed?
   (e) Which car is going fastest after 5 s?
   (f) Which car starts slowly and then goes faster and faster?

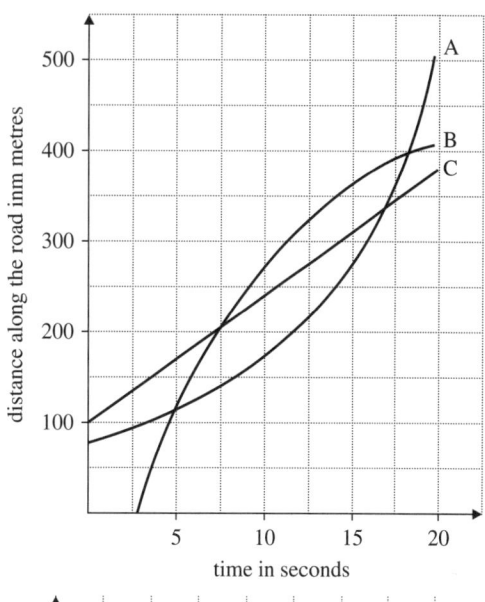

5. Three girls Hanna, Fateema and Carine took part in an egg and spoon race. Describe what happened, giving as many details as possible.

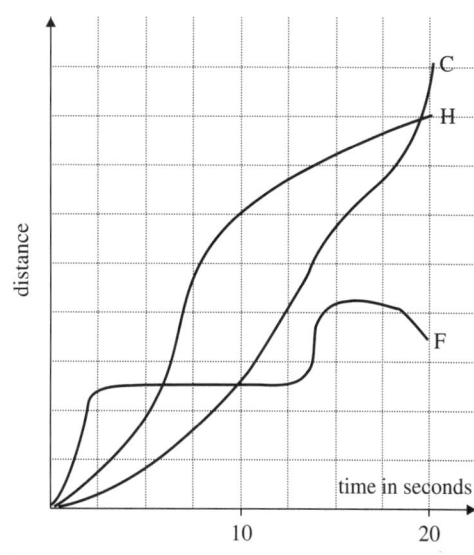

6. The graph shows the speed of the baton during a 4 × 100 m relay race.

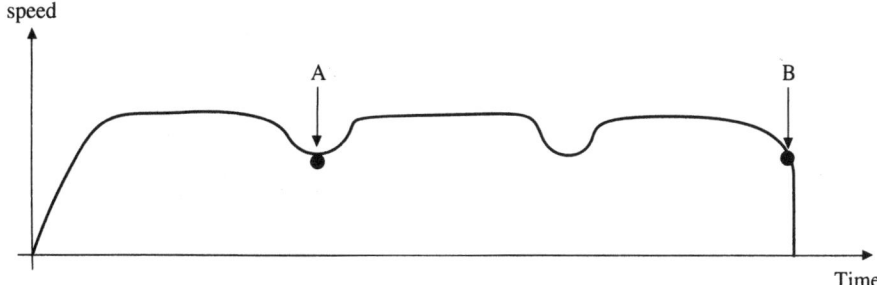

   (a) Describe what is happening at point A.
   (b) Describe what is happening at point B.

6.4 Brackets and factors

Exercise 9

Multiply out the brackets.

1. $3(x+3)$
2. $4(x-2)$
3. $5(2x+1)$
4. $4(a+7)$
5. $6(2x+1)$
6. $10(5-x)$
7. $3(4x+5)$
8. $9(3+x)$
9. $5(y-2)$
10. $7(a-2)$
11. $11(2x-y)$
12. $8(3x+2y)$

Factors

Factorise the following: (a) $12a - 15b$
(b) $3x^2 - 2x$
(c) $2xy + 6y^2$

(a) $12a - 15b = 3(4a - 5b)$
(b) $3x^2 - 2x = x(3x - 2)$
(c) $2xy + 6y^2 = 2y(x + 3y)$

Exercise 10

In Questions **1** to **10** copy and complete the statement.

1. $6x + 4y = 2(3x + \Box)$
2. $9x + 12y = 3(\Box + 4y)$
3. $10a + 4b = 2(5a + \Box)$
4. $4x + 12y = 4(\Box + \Box)$
5. $10a + 15b = 5(\Box + \Box)$
6. $18x - 24y = 6(3x - \Box)$
7. $8u - 28v = \Box(\Box - 7v)$
8. $15s + 25t = \Box(3s + \Box)$
9. $24m + 40n = \Box(3m + \Box)$
10. $27c - 72d = \Box(\Box - 8d)$

In Questions **11** to **31** factorise the expression.

11. $20a + 8b$
12. $30x - 24y$
13. $27c - 33d$
14. $35u + 49v$
15. $12s - 32t$
16. $40x - 16t$
17. $24x + 84y$
18. $12x + 8y + 16z$
19. $12a - 6b + 9c$
20. $10x - 20y + 25z$

21. $20a - 12b - 28c$
22. $48m + 8n - 24x$
23. $42x + 49y - 21z$
24. $6x^2 + 15y^2$
25. $20x^2 - 15y^2$
26. $7a^2 + 28b^2$
27. $27a + 63b - 36c$
28. $12x^2 + 24xy + 18y^2$
29. $64p - 72q - 40r$
30. $36x - 60y + 96z$

6.5 Changing the subject of a formula

Example
Make x the subject in the formulae below.

(a) $ax - p = t$
$ax = t + p$
$x = \dfrac{t + p}{a}$

(b) $y(x + y) = v^2$
$yx + y^2 = v^2$
$yx = v^2 - y^2$
$x = \dfrac{v^2 - y^2}{y}$

Exercise 11
Make x the subject.

1. $x + b = e$
2. $x - t = m$
3. $x - f = a + b$
4. $x + h = A + B$
5. $x + t = y + t$
6. $a + x = b$
7. $k + x = m$
8. $v + x = w + y$
9. $ax = b$
10. $hx = m$
11. $mx = a + b$
12. $kx = c - d$
13. $vx = e + n$
14. $3x = y + z$
15. $xp = r$
16. $xm = h - m$
17. $ax + t = a$
18. $mx - e = k$
19. $ux - h = m$
20. $ex + q = t$
21. $kx - u^2 = v^2$
22. $gx + t^2 = s^2$
23. $xa + k = m^2$
24. $xm - v = m$
25. $a + bx = c$
26. $t + sx = y$
27. $y + cx = z$
28. $a + hx = 2a$
29. $mx - b = b$
30. $kx + ab = cd$
31. $a(x - b) = c$
32. $c(x - d) = e$
33. $m(x + m) = n^2$
34. $k(x - a) = t$
35. $h(x - h) = k$
36. $m(x + b) = n$
37. $a(x - a) = a^2$
38. $c(a + x) = d$
39. $m(b + x) = e$

Formulae involving fractions

Example
Make x the subject in the formulae below.

(a) $\dfrac{x}{a} = p$
$x = ap$

(b) $\dfrac{m}{x} = t$
$m = xt$
$\dfrac{m}{t} = x$

184 Algebra 2

Exercise 12

Make x the subject.

1. $\dfrac{x}{t} = m$
2. $\dfrac{x}{e} = n$
3. $\dfrac{x}{p} = a$
4. $am = \dfrac{x}{t}$
5. $bc = \dfrac{x}{a}$
6. $e = \dfrac{x}{y^2}$
7. $\dfrac{x}{a} = (b+c)$
8. $\dfrac{x}{t} = (c-d)$
9. $\dfrac{x}{m} = s+t$
10. $\dfrac{x}{k} = h+i$
11. $\dfrac{x}{b} = \dfrac{a}{c}$
12. $\dfrac{x}{m} = \dfrac{z}{y}$
13. $\dfrac{x}{h} = \dfrac{c}{d}$
14. $\dfrac{m}{n} = \dfrac{x}{e}$
15. $\dfrac{b}{e} = \dfrac{x}{h}$
16. $\dfrac{x}{(a+b)} = c$
17. $\dfrac{x}{(h+k)} = m$
18. $\dfrac{x}{u} = \dfrac{m}{y}$
19. $\dfrac{x}{(h-k)} = t$
20. $\dfrac{x}{(a+b)} = (z+t)$
21. $t = \dfrac{e}{x}$
22. $a = \dfrac{e}{x}$
23. $m = \dfrac{h}{x}$
24. $\dfrac{a}{b} = \dfrac{c}{x}$
25. $\dfrac{u}{x} = \dfrac{c}{d}$
26. $\dfrac{m}{x} = t^2$
27. $\dfrac{h}{x} = \sin 20°$
28. $\dfrac{e}{x} = \cos 40°$
29. $\dfrac{m}{x} = \tan 46°$
30. $\dfrac{a^2}{b^2} = \dfrac{c^2}{x}$

Mixed questions

Exercise 13

Make the letter in brackets the subject.

1. $ax - d = h$ $[x]$
2. $zy + k = m$ $[y]$
3. $d(y+e) = f$ $[y]$
4. $m(a+k) = d$ $[k]$
5. $a + bm = c$ $[m]$
6. $a + e = b$ $[e]$
7. $yt = z$ $[t]$
8. $x - c = e$ $[x]$
9. $my - n = b$ $[y]$
10. $a(z+a) = b$ $[z]$
11. $\dfrac{a}{x} = d$ $[x]$
12. $\dfrac{k}{m} = t$ $[k]$
13. $\dfrac{u}{m} = n$ $[u]$
14. $\dfrac{y}{x} = d$ $[x]$
15. $\dfrac{a}{m} = t$ $[m]$
16. $\dfrac{d}{g} = n$ $[g]$
17. $\dfrac{t}{k} = (a+b)$ $[t]$
18. $y = \dfrac{v}{e}$ $[e]$
19. $c = \dfrac{m}{y}$ $[y]$
20. $\dfrac{a}{m} = b$ $[a]$
21. $g(m+a) = b$ $[m]$
22. $h + g = x^2$ $[g]$
23. $y - t = z$ $[t]$
24. $2me = c$ $[e]$
25. $a(y+x) = t$ $[x]$
26. $uv - t^2 = y^2$ $[v]$
27. $3k + t = c$ $[k]$
28. $k - w = m$ $[w]$
29. $b + an = c$ $[n]$
30. $m(a+y) = c$ $[y]$
31. $pq - x = ab$ $[x]$
32. $a^2 - k = t$ $[k]$
33. $v^2 z = w$ $[z]$
34. $c = t + u$ $[u]$
35. $xc + t = 2t$ $[c]$
36. $n + w = k$ $[w]$

Revision exercise 6A

1. Here are three diagrams with lines and dots

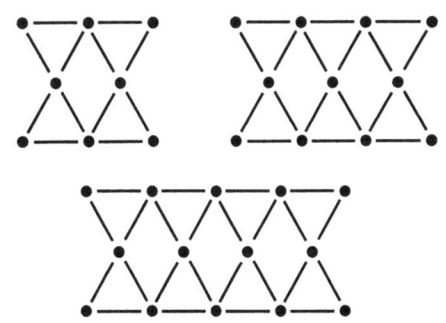

(a) Find a formula connecting the number of lines l and the number of dots d.
(b) How many dots are there in a diagram with 294 lines?

2. A factory cafeteria contains a vending machine which sells drinks. On a typical day:

> the machine starts half full,
> no drinks are sold before 9 a.m. and after 5 p.m.,
> drinks are sold at a slow rate throughout the day, except during the morning and lunch breaks (10.30–11 a.m. and 1–2 p.m.) when there is a greater demand.
> the machine is filled up just before the lunch break. (It takes about 10 minutes to fill.)

Sketch a graph showing how the number of drinks in the machine may vary from 8 a.m. to 6 p.m.

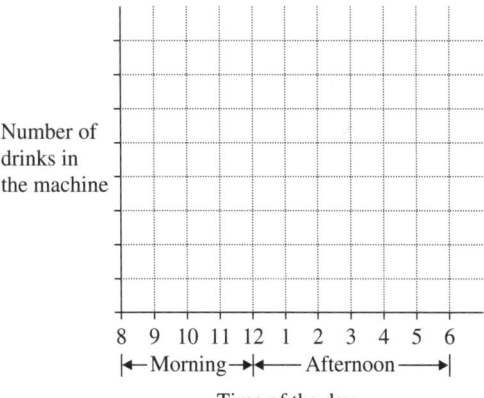

3. The distance-time graphs for several objects are shown. Decide which line represents each of the following:

- hovercraft from Dover
- car ferry from Dover
- cross-channel swimmer
- marker buoy outside harbour
- train from Dover
- car ferry from Calais

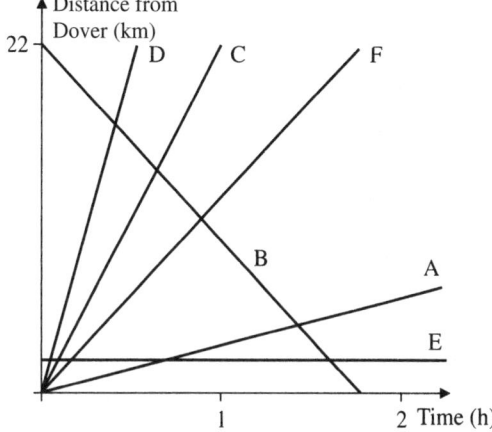

4. Given that $s - 3t = rt$, express:
(a) s in terms of r and t
(b) r in terms of s and t

5.

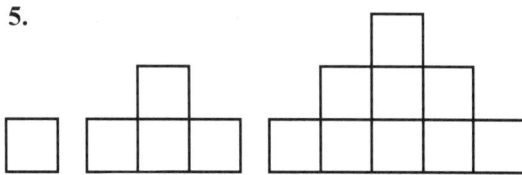

(a) Draw the next diagram in this sequence.
(b) Write down the number of squares in each diagram.
(c) Describe in words the sequence you obtain in part (b).
(d) How many squares will there be in the diagram which has 13 squares on the base?

6. Solve the simultaneous equations:
(a) $7c + 3d = 29$
    $5c - 4d = 33$
(b) $2x - 3y = 7$
    $2y - 3x = -8$

7. This graph shows a car journey from Gateshead to Middlesbrough and back again.

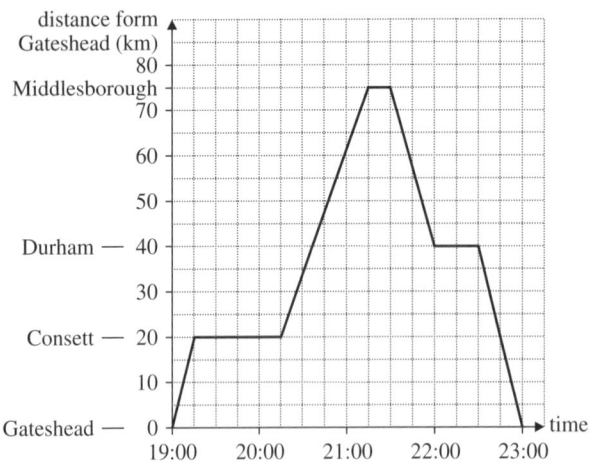

(a) Where is the car
 (i) at 19:15 h
 (ii) at 22:15 h
 (iii) at 22:45 h?
(b) How far is it
 (i) from Consett to Middlesbrough
 (ii) from Durham to Gateshead?
(c) At what speed does the car travel
 (i) from Gateshead to Consett
 (ii) from Consett to Middlesbrough
 (iii) from Middlesbrough to Durham
 (iv) from Durham to Gateshead?
(d) For how long is the car stationary during the journey?

8. Each diagram in the sequence below consists of a number of dots.

Diagram number	1	2	3
	••• •••	•••• • • ••••	••••• • • • • •••••

(a) Draw diagram number 4, diagram number 5 and diagram number 6.
(b) Copy and complete the table below:

Diagram number	Number of dots
1	6
2	10
3	
4	
5	
6	

(c) Without drawing the diagrams, state the number of dots in:
 (i) diagram number 10
 (ii) diagram number 15
(d) If we write x for the diagram number and n for the number of dots, write down a formula involving x and n.

Examination exercise 6B

1.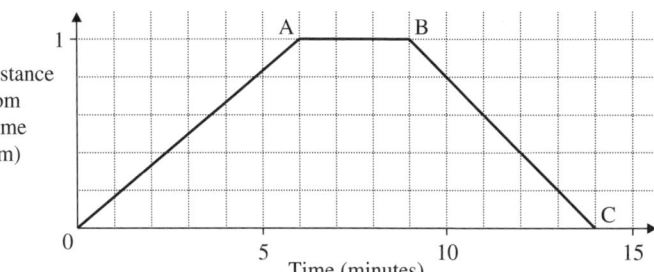

   The travel graph above shows Hassan's daily run. He runs 1 km from home, rests, and then runs back home.
   (a) For how many minutes does he rest?
   (b) (i) How long does it take him to run back home?
   (ii) Calculate the speed, in **km/h**, at which he runs back home. [J 95 1]

2. Simplify: $3(2x + 5) - (7 - x)$ [J 97 1]

3. Make y the subject of the equation: $2x + 5y = 10$ [J 98 1]

4. The diagram shows part of an aircraft's flight record.

Time	Distance travelled (km)
20:55	957
21:07	1083

   (a) How many minutes are there between 20:55 and 21:07?
   (b) How many kilometres did the plane travel between 20:55 and 21:07?
   (c) Calculate the average speed of the aircraft in kilometres **per hour**. [J 96 1]

5. Write one of the symbols $<$, $=$ or $>$ to make each correct statement.
   (a) $0{\cdot}167 \ldots\ldots\ldots \frac{1}{6}$
   (b) $-2\frac{1}{4} \ldots\ldots\ldots -2\frac{1}{2}$ [N 98 1]

6. $$A = bh + c^2$$
   (a) Calculate the exact value of A when $b = 4$, $c = 2\frac{1}{2}$ and $h = 3\frac{1}{4}$.
   (b) Make h the subject of the formula. [N 96 1]

7. (a) List the integer values of p for which $-3 < p \leqslant 3$.
   (b) Simplify: $5(2q - 3) - 4(q - 5)$
   (c) Solve the simultaneous equations:
   $$4m + 3n = 1$$
   $$m + 2n = 4$$ [J 98 3]

8. $$x = 5, \quad y = -6 \quad \text{and} \quad z = xy$$
Insert the correct symbol, $<$ or $>$, in each of the following statements.
(a) $x \ldots y$ (b) $y \ldots z$ (c) $x^2 \ldots y^2$ [N 96 1]

9. (a) Sketch the next diagram in this sequence.

(b) Copy and complete the table.

Number of black squares (x)	1	2	3	4	5
Number of white squares (y)	4	6			

(c) Find the value of
   (i) y when $x = 10$,   (ii) x when $y = 50$.
(d) Write down a formula connecting x and y. [N 95 3]

10.

The graph shows the average world oil price each year from 1979 to 1985.
(a) (i) In which year was the average price of oil greatest?
    (ii) What was that average price?
(b) Between which two consecutive years was there the greatest increase in the average price of oil?

(c) (i) By how many dollars per barrel did the average price of oil decrease between 1984 and 1985?
 (ii) Write your answer to (c) (i) as a percentage of the 1984 price.
(d) Copy and complete the graph, using the figures in the table below.

Year	1986	1987	1988	1989
Average Price ($ per barrel)	18	20	17	19

[N 95 3]

11.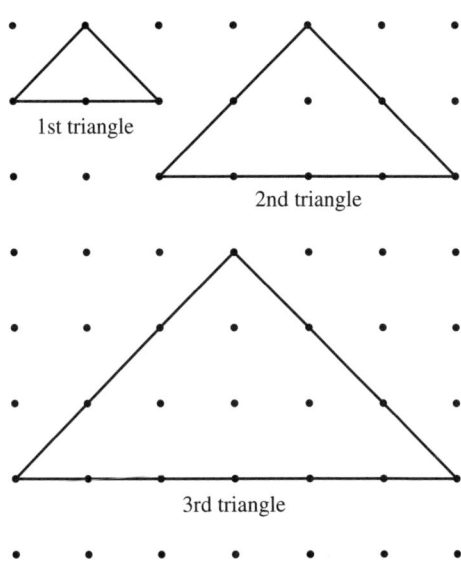

The first three triangles in a set of triangles are drawn on the square grid above.
(a) Draw the 4th triangle in the set on square dotted paper.
(b) Copy and complete the table below for the first six triangles of the set.

Column 1	Column 2	Column 3	Column 4
Triangle	Number of dots on perimeter	Number of dots inside	Column 2 + Column 3
1st	4	0	4
2nd	8	1	9
3rd	12	4	......
4th	......	......	......
5th	......	......	......
6th	......	......	......

(c) Describe the numbers in Column 2.
(d) Describe the numbers in Column 3.
(e) For the 20th triangle, find the numbers in Columns 2, 3 and 4.

[J 96 3]

12. The table shows the air temperature at different heights above the surface of the Earth.

Height (km)	0	1·6	3·4	5	6	7·3	8·4	9·3	10
Temperature (°C)	18	14	7	−2	−9	−18	−27	−35	−43

(a) Show this data by plotting points on a copy of the grid below. Connect the points with a smooth curve.

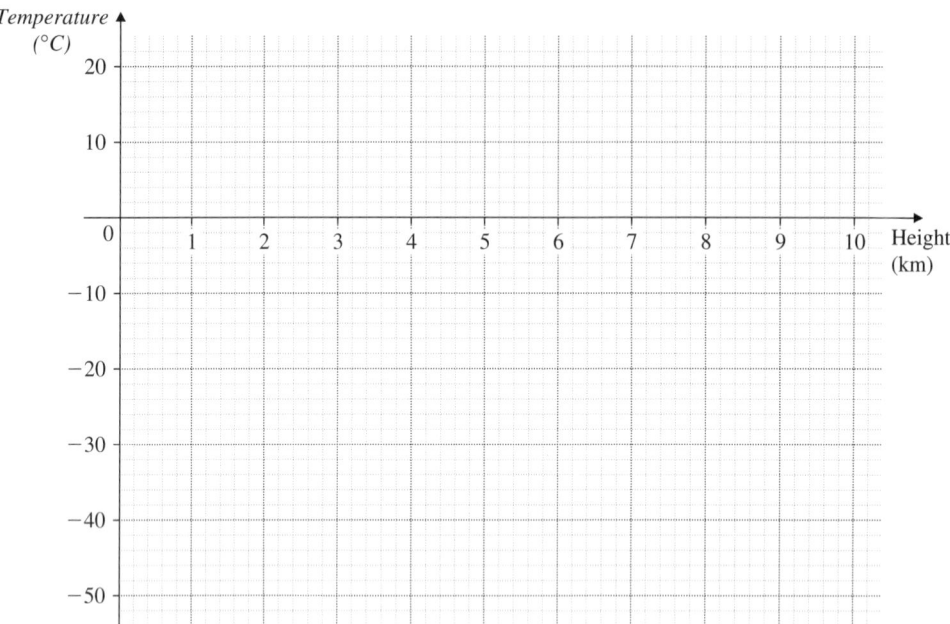

(b) At what height is the temperature 0°C?
(c) What is the temperature at a height of 8 km?
(d) What is the change in temperature between 0 km and 5 km?
(e) What is the change in temperature between 5 km and 10 km?
(f) To the nearest whole number, what is the ratio
Answer (e) : Answer (d)? Give your answer in the form $n : 1$. [J 95 3]

13 (a) Find the next two terms in each of the following sequences.
   (i) 1, 4, 7, 10, 13, ...
   (ii) 2, 6, 18, 54, ...
   (iii) 1, 3, 4, 7, 11, 18, 29, 47, ...

(b) The nth term of a sequence is given by the formula
$$\frac{n^2}{n+1}$$
Find (i) the 9th term, (ii) the 99th term.

(c) Look at the sequence
   1, 4, 9, 16, 25, ...

(i) Write down the next two terms.
(ii) Write down the 15th term.
(iii) Write down the nth term.
(iv) Write down the nth term of the sequence

   2, 5, 10, 17, 26, ... [N 97 3]

7 Number 2

7.1 Percentage change

Price changes are sometimes more significant when expressed as a percentage of the original price. For example if the price of a car goes up from $7000 to $7070, this is only a 1% increase. If the price of a jacket went up from $100 to $170 this would be a 70% increase! In both cases the actual increase is the same: $70.

$$\text{Percentage increase} = \frac{\text{(actual increase)}}{\text{(original value)}} \times \frac{100}{1}$$

Example

The price of a car is increased from $6400 to $6800. Find the percentage increase.

$$\text{Percentage increase} = \frac{400}{6400} \times \frac{100}{1} = 6\tfrac{1}{4}\%$$

For a *decrease*:

$$\text{Percentage decrease} = \frac{\text{actual decrease}}{\text{original value}} \times \frac{100}{1}$$

Exercise 1

In Questions **1** to **10** calculate the percentage increase.

	Original price	Final price
1.	$50	$54
2.	$80	$88
3.	$180	$225
4.	$100	$102
5.	$75	$78
6.	$400	$410
7.	$5000	$6000
8.	$210	$315
9.	$600	$690
10.	$4000	$7200

In Questions **11** to **20** calculate the percentage decrease.

	Original price	Final price
11.	$800	$600
12.	$50	$40
13.	$120	$105
14.	$420	$280
15.	$6000	$1200
16.	$880	$836
17.	$15 000	$14 100
18.	$7·50	$6·00
19.	$8·20	$7·79
20.	$16 000	$15 600

Exercise 2

Find the percentage profit/loss using either the formula:

percentage profit = $\frac{\text{(actual profit)}}{\text{(cost price)}} \times \frac{100}{1}$ or percentage loss = $\frac{\text{(actual loss)}}{\text{(cost price)}} \times \frac{100}{1}$

Give the answers correct to one decimal place.

	Cost price	Selling price		Cost price	Selling price
1.	$11	$15	11.	$20	$18·47
2.	$21	$25	12.	$17	$11
3.	$36	$43	13.	$13	$9
4.	$41	$50	14.	$211	$200
5.	$411	$461	15.	$8·15	$7
6.	$5·32	$5·82	16.	$2·62	$3
7.	$6·14	$7·00	17.	$1·52	$1·81
8.	$2·13	$2·50	18.	$13·50	$13·98
9.	$6·11	$8·11	19.	$3·05	$4·00
10.	$18·15	$20	20.	$1705	$1816

Exercise 3

1. The number of people employed by a firm increased from 250 to 280. Calculate the percentage increase in the workforce.

2. During the first four weeks of her life a baby's weight increases from 3000 g to 3870 g. Calculate the percentage increase in the baby's weight.

3. Before cooking, a joint of meat weighs 2·5 kg. After cooking the same joint of meat weighs only 2·1 kg. Calculate the percentage decrease in the weight of the joint.

4. When cold, an iron rod is 200 cm long. After being heated, the length increases to 200·5 cm. Calculate the percentage increase in the length of the rod.

5. A man buys a car for $4000 and sells it for $4600. Calculate the percentage profit.

6. A shopkeeper buys jumpers for $6·20 and sells them for $9·99. Calculate the percentage profit correct to one decimal place.

7. A grocer buys bananas at 20c per kg but after the fruit are spoiled he has to sell them at only 17c per kg. Calculate the percentage loss.

8. Before a service the petrol consumption of a car was 5·1 km per litre. After the service the consumption improved to 5·8 km per litre. Calculate the percentage improvement in the petrol consumption, correct to one decimal place.

5·1 km per litre   5·8 km per litre

9. After an outbreak of smallpox, the population of a town went down from 22 315 to 21 987. Calculate the percentage reduction, correct to one decimal place.

10. In 1999 a tennis player earned $2 410 200. In 2000 the same player earned $2 985 010. Calculate the percentage increase in her income, correct to one decimal place.

Exercise 4

This exercise is more difficult.

1. A shopkeeper bought 40 articles for $10 and sold them at 32c each. Calculate:
   (a) the cost price of each article
   (b) the total selling price of the 40 articles
   (c) the total profit
   (d) the percentage profit.

2. A shopkeeper bought a crate of 40 tins of pears at 25c per tin.
   (a) Find the total cost of the crate of pears.
   (b) He sold 10 tins at 37c per tin, and the rest of the crate at 35c per tin.
      (i) How much profit did he make?
      (ii) Express this profit as a percentage of his total cost price.

3. ABCD is a square of side 100 cm. Side AB is increased by 20% and side AD is reduced by 25% to form rectangle APQR.
   (a) Calculate: (i) the length of AP
                  (ii) the length of AR
                  (iii) the area of square ABCD
                  (iv) the area of rectangle APQR.
   (b) By what percentage has the area of the square been reduced?

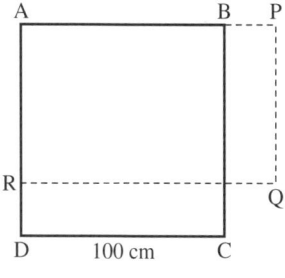

4. When a house was built in 1994 the total cost was made up of the following:
   wages $30 000
   materials $16 000
   overheads $4 000
   (a) Find the total cost of the house in 1994.
   (b) In 1995 the cost of wages increased by 10%, the cost of materials increased by 5% and the overheads remained at their previous cost.
       (i) Find the total cost of the house in 1995.
       (ii) Calculate the percentage increase from 1994 to 1995.

5. Four maths teachers calculate the area of the shape given and they all get different answers,
   As usual Mr Gibson is wrong by 20% but surprisingly Mr Rayner is also wrong, but by only 5%.
   Here are the four answers:
   237·5 m², 250 m², 260 m², 300 m²
   Which is the correct answer?

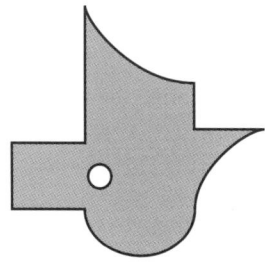

7.2 Fractions, ratio, decimals and percentage

Percentages are simply a convenient way of expressing fractions or decimals. '50% of $60' is the same as '$\frac{1}{2}$ of $60'. You should be able to convert readily from one form to another.

Example
(a) Change $\frac{7}{8}$ to a decimal.

$$\begin{array}{r} 0 \cdot 875 \\ 8\overline{)7 \cdot 000} \end{array}$$

Divide 8 into 7

$\frac{7}{8} = 0 \cdot 875$

(c) Change $\frac{3}{8}$ to a percentage.

$\frac{3}{8} = \frac{3}{8} \times 100\% = 37\frac{1}{2}\%$

(b) Change 0·35 to a fraction.

$0 \cdot 35 = \frac{35}{100} = \frac{7}{20}$

(d) Work out $\frac{1}{6} + 0 \cdot 72$

$\frac{1}{6} = 0 \cdot 1666 \ldots$ [divide 6 into 1]

$\therefore \frac{1}{6} + 0 \cdot 72 = \begin{array}{r} 0 \cdot 1666 \\ 0 \cdot 7200 + \\ \hline 0 \cdot 8866 \end{array}$

$\frac{1}{6} + 0 \cdot 72 = 0 \cdot 89$ (2 d.p.)

Exercise 5

1. Two shops had sale offers on an article which previously cost $69. One shop had '$\frac{1}{3}$ off' and the other had '70% of old price'. Which shop had the lower price?

2. Shareholders in a company can opt for either '$\frac{1}{6}$ of $5000' or '15% of $5000'. Which is the greater amount?

3. A photocopier increases the sides of a square in the ratio 4 : 5. By what percentage are the sides increased?

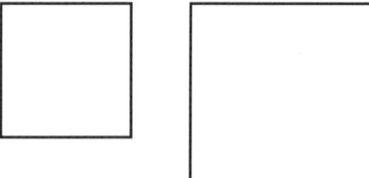

4. In an alloy the ratio of copper to iron to lead is 5 : 7 : 3. What percentage of the alloy is lead?

5. Change the fractions to decimals.
    (a) $\frac{1}{4}$
    (b) $\frac{2}{5}$
    (c) $\frac{3}{8}$
    (d) $\frac{5}{12}$
    (e) $\frac{1}{6}$
    (f) $\frac{2}{7}$

6. Change the decimals to fractions and simplify.
    (a) 0·2
    (b) 0·45
    (c) 0·36
    (d) 0·125
    (e) 1·05
    (f) 0·007

7. Change to percentages.
    (a) $\frac{1}{4}$
    (b) $\frac{1}{10}$
    (c) 0·72
    (d) 0·075
    (e) 0·02
    (f) $\frac{1}{3}$

8. Copy and complete the table:

	Fraction	Decimal	Percentage
(a)	$\frac{1}{4}$		
(b)		0·2	
(c)			80%
(d)	$\frac{1}{100}$		
(e)			30%
(f)	$\frac{1}{3}$		

9. Work out (a) $\frac{3}{4}$ of 65% of 0·3
             (b) 11% of $\frac{3}{5}$ of $240

10. Arrange in order of size (smallest first)
    (a) $\frac{1}{2}$; 45%; 0·6
    (b) 0·38; $\frac{6}{16}$; 4%
    (c) 0·111; 11%; $\frac{1}{9}$

Evaluate, giving the answer to 2 decimal places:

11. $\frac{1}{4} + \frac{1}{3}$
12. $\frac{2}{3} + 0.75$
13. $\frac{8}{9} - 0.24$
14. $\frac{7}{8} + \frac{5}{9} + \frac{2}{11}$
15. $\frac{1}{3} \times 0.2$
16. $\frac{5}{8} \times \frac{1}{4}$
17. $\frac{8}{11} \div 0.2$
18. $(\frac{4}{7} - \frac{1}{3}) \div 0.4$

19. Pure gold is 24 carat gold. What percentage of pure gold is 15 carat gold?

7.3 Estimating

In some circumstances it is unrealistic to work out the exact answer to a problem. It might be quite satisfactory to give an estimate for the answer.

For example a builder does not know *exactly* how many bricks a new garage will require. He may estimate that he needs 2500 bricks and place an order for that number. In practice he may need only 2237.

Exercise 6

Estimate which answer is closest to the actual answer.

1. The height of a double-decker bus:

A	B	C
3 m	6 m	10 m

2. The height of the tallest player in the Olympic basketball competition:

A	B	C
1·8 m	3·0 m	2·2 m

3. The height of the Eiffel Tower:
   - A 30 m
   - B 300 m
   - C 1000 m

4. The weight of half a litre of milk in a cardboard carton:
   - A 500 g
   - B 1000 g
   - C 5000 g

5. The volume of your classroom:
   - A 100 m^3
   - B 1000 m^3
   - C 10 000 m^3

6. The top speed of a Grand Prix racing car:
   - A 600 km/h
   - B 80 km/h
   - C 300 km/h

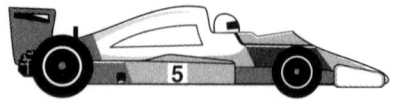

7. The number of times your heart beats in one day (24 h):
   - A 10 000
   - B 100 000
   - C 1 000 000

8. The thickness of one page in this book:
   - A 0·01 cm
   - B 0·001 cm
   - C 0·0001 cm

9. The number of cars in a traffic jam 10 km long on a 3-lane motorway:
   - A 4000
   - B 40 000
   - C 200 000

10. The time it takes to walk 1½ km:
    - A 10 minutes
    - B 20 minutes
    - C 60 minutes

11. The area of an ordinary postcard:
    - A 150 cm^2
    - B 1000 cm^2
    - C 0·1 m^2

12. The weight of an ordinary apple is:
    - A 100 g
    - B 250 g
    - C 400 g

13. The cheap rate telephone charge to Australia is 70c per minute. The number of words you will be able to say in a call costing $4 is:
    - A 120
    - B 500
    - C 1200

14. The speed at which the hair on your head grows in km/h is:
    - A 0·0001
    - B 0·000 01
    - C 0·000 001

15. Mr Gibson, the famous maths teacher, has won the lottery. He decides to give a rather unusual prize for the person who comes top in his next maths test. The prize winner receives his or her own weight in coins and they can choose to have either 1p, 2p, 5p, 10p, 20p, 50p or £1 coins. All the coins must be the same.

Approximate masses	
1p	3·6 g
2p	7·2 g
5p	3·2 g
10p	6·5 g
20p	5·0 g
50p	7·5 g
£1	9·0 g

Shabeza is the winner and she weighs 47 kg.
Use the table on the right to find the highest value of her prize. Give your answer correct to the nearest £100.

16. The largest tree in the world has a diameter of 11 m.

Estimate the number of 'average' 15 year olds required to circle the tree so that they form an unbroken chain.

17. • When you multiply by a number greater than 1 you make it bigger.
    so $5·3 \times 1·03 > 5·3$ and $6·75 \times 0·89 < 6·75$

    • When you divide by a number greater than 1 you make it smaller.
    so $8·92 \div 1·13 < 8·92$ and $11·2 \div 0·73 > 11·2$

State whether true or false:
(a) $3·72 \times 1·3 > 3·72$
(b) $253 \times 0·91 < 253$
(c) $0·92 \times 1·04 > 0·92$
(d) $8·5 \div 1·4 > 8·5$
(e) $113 \div 0·73 < 113$
(f) $17·4 \div 2·2 < 17·4$
(g) $0·73 \times 0·73 < 0·73$
(h) $2511 \div 0·042 < 2511$
(i) $614 \times 0·993 < 614$

Example
Estimate the answers to the following questions:
(a) $9·7 \times 3·1 \approx 10 \times 3$.   About 30.
(b) $81·4 \times 98·2 \approx 80 \times 100$.   About 8000.
(c) $19·2 \times 49·1 \approx 20 \times 50$.   About 1000.
(d) $102·7 \div 19·6 \approx 100 \div 20$.   About 5.

Exercise 7

Write down each question and decide (by estimating) which answer is correct. Do not do the calculations exactly.

	Question	Answer A	Answer B	Answer C
1.	7·79 ÷ 1·9	8·2	4·1	1·9
2.	27·03 ÷ 5·1	5·3	0·5	8·7
3.	59·78 ÷ 9·8	12·2	2·8	6·1
4.	58·4 × 102	600·4	5956·8	2450·4
5.	6·8 × 11·4	19·32	280·14	77·52
6.	97 × 1·08	104·76	55·66	1062·3
7.	972 × 20·2	2112·4	19 634·4	8862·4
8.	7·1 × 103	74·3	731·3	7210·3
9.	18·9 × 21	396·9	58·7	201·9
10.	1·078 ÷ 0·98	6·4	10·4	1·1
11.	1250·5 ÷ 6·1	21·4	205	66·2
12.	20·48 ÷ 3·2	6·4	12·2	2·8
13.	25·11 ÷ 3·1	8·1	15·1	19·3
14.	216 ÷ 0·9	56·3	24·3	240
15.	19·2 + 0·41	23·3	8·41	19·61
16.	207 + 18·34	25·34	225·34	1248
17.	68·2 − 1·38	97·82	48·82	66·82
18.	7 − 0·64	6·36	1·48	0·48
19.	974 × 0·11	9·14	107·14	563·14
20.	551·1 ÷ 11	6·92	50·1	5623
21.	207·1 + 11·65	310·75	23·75	218·75
22.	664 × 0·51	256·2	338·64	828·62
23.	(5·6 − 0·21) × 39	389·21	210·21	20·51
24.	$\dfrac{17·5 \times 42}{2·5}$	294	504	86
25.	(906 + 4·1) × 0·31	473·21	282·131	29·561
26.	$\dfrac{543 + 472}{18·1 + 10·9}$	65	35	85
27.	$\dfrac{112·2 \times 75·9}{6·9 \times 5·1}$	242	20·4	25·2

28. There are about 7000 cinemas in the U.K. and every day about 300 people visit each one. The population of the U.K. is about 60 million.

    Here is a film magazine report.
    Is the magazine report fair?
    Show the working you did to decide.

29. The petrol consumption of a car is 4 km per litre and petrol costs $0·42 per litre.
Jasper estimates that the petrol costs of a round trip of about 1200 km will be $150. Is this a reasonable estimate?

30. The 44 teachers in a rather difficult school decide to buy 190 canes at $2·42 each. They share the cost equally between them.
The headmaster used a calculator to work out the cost per teacher and got an answer of $1·05 to the nearest cent.
Without using a calculator, work out an estimate for the answer to check whether or not he got it right. Show your working.

31. Each year in Britain about 150 million trees are cut down to make paper. One tree is enough to make about 650 kg of paper.

(a) Weigh several newspapers (large and small) and estimate the number of newspapers which can be made from one tree.
(b) Estimate the number of newspapers which could be made from all the trees cut down each year.
(c) Weigh some of the exercise books you use at school. Estimate the number of books your class will use in a whole year and hence estimate the number of trees required to supply the paper for your class for one year.

7.4 Measurement is approximate

(a) If you measure the length of some cloth for a dress you might say the length is 145 cm to the nearest cm. The actual length could be anything from 144·5 cm to 145·49999... cm if we use the normal convention which is to round up a figure of 5 or more. Clearly 145·4999... is effectively 145·5 and we could use this figure.

(b) If you measure the length of a page in a book you might say the length is 437 mm to the nearest mm. In this case the actual length could be anywhere from 436·5 mm to 437·5 mm. We write 'length is between 436·5 mm and 437·5 mm'.

In both cases (a) and (b) the measurement expressed to a given unit is in *possible error* of *half a unit*.

(c) (i) Similarly if you say you weigh 57 kg to the nearest kg you could actually weigh anything from 56·5 kg to 57·5 kg.
 (ii) If your brother was weighed on more sensitive scales and the result was 57·2 kg, his actual weight could be from 57·15 kg to 57·25 kg.
 (iii) The weight of a butterfly might be given as 0·032 g. The actual weight could be from 0·0315 g to 0·0325 g.

Exercise 8

1. In a DIY store the height of a door is given as 195 cm to the nearest cm. Write down the greatest possible height of the door.

2. A vet weighs a sick goat at 37 kg to the nearest kg. What is the least possible weight of the goat?

3. A cook's weighing scales weigh to the nearest 0·1 kg. What is the greatest possible weight of a chicken which she weighs at 3·2 kg?

4. A surveyor using a laser beam device can measure distances to the nearest 0·1 m.

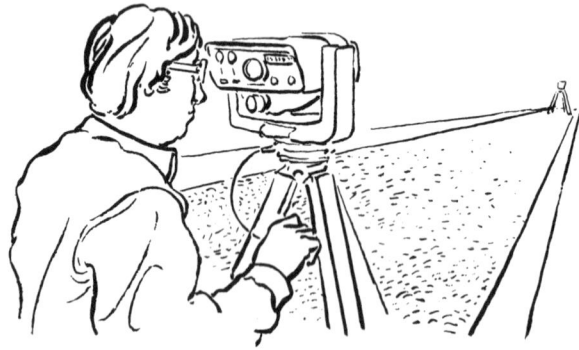

What is the least possible length of a warehouse which he measures at 95·6 m?

5. In the county sports Jill was timed at 28·6 s for the 200 m. What is the greatest time she could have taken?

6. The length of a telephone is measured as 193 mm, to the nearest mm. The length lies between:
    A   B   C
192 and 194 mm   192·5 and 193·5 mm   188 and 198 mm

7. The weight of a labrador is 35 kg, to the nearest kg.
   The weight lies between:

A	B	C
30 and 40 kg	34 and 36 kg	34·5 and 35·5 kg

8. Liz and Julie each measure a different worm and they both say that their worm is 11 cm long to the nearest cm.
   Does this mean that both worms are the same length?

In Questions **9** to **23** you are given a measurement. Write down the upper and lower bounds of the number. For example if you are given a length as 13 cm you can write 'length is between 12·5 cm and 13·5 cm'.

9. mass = 17 kg
10. $d = 256$ km
11. length = 2·4 m
12. $m = 0·34$ grams
13. $v = 2·04$ m/s
14. $x = 12·0$ cm [N.B. not 12 cm!]
15. $T = 81·4°$C
16. $M = 0·3$ kg
17. $d = 4·80$ cm
18. $y = 0·07$ m
19. mass = 0·7 tonne
20. $t = 615$ seconds
21. $d = 7·13$ m
22. $n = 52$ million (nearest million)
23. $x = 85·0$ seconds

In Questions **24** to **31** you are given the answer to a calculation. Write 'Yes' if the answer is sensible and 'No' if the answer is not.

24. Total weight of apples off a large tree = 62 kg.

25. Cost of a school meal in U.S.A. = $35·80.

26. Time taken by an aircraft to fly non-stop from London to Hong Kong = 14·2 h.

27. Ratio of population of China to population of U.K. = 200 : 1.

28. The top speed of a family car = 300 km/h.

29. Number of bricks needed to build an 'average' size house = 3·2 million.

30. Time required for your maths teacher to run 100 m = 11·2 seconds.

31. Weight of a 'typical' saloon car = 384 600 kg.

7.5 Mental arithmetic

Ideally these questions should be read out by a teacher or friend and you should not be looking at them. Each question should be repeated once and then the answer, and only the answer, should be written down. Each test, including the recording of results, should take about 30 minutes.
If you do not have anyone to read out the questions for you, try to do the test without writing down any detailed working.

Test 1

1. Find the cost in dollars of ten books at 35 cents each.
2. Add together $4·20 and 75 cents.
3. What number divided by six gives an answer of eight?
4. I spend $1·60 and pay with $2. My change consists of three coins. What are they?
5. Find the difference between $13\frac{1}{2}$ and 20.
6. Write one centimetre as a fraction of one metre.
7. How many ten cents coins are there in a pile worth $5.60?
8. Ten per cent of the pupils in a school play hockey, 15% play basketball and the rest play football. What percentage play football?
9. In a room of 20 people, three quarters were women. What was the number of women?
10. Four lemons costing eleven cents each are bought with a one dollar note. What is the change?
11. I arrive at the railway station at 5.20 p.m. and my train is due at 6.10 p.m. How long do I have to wait?
12. What number is ten times a big as 0·65?
13. A hockey pitch measures 25 metres by 40 metres. Find the distance around the pitch.
14. Write the number 768 correct to the nearest ten.
15. By how many does a half of 62 exceed 20?
16. How many 2c coins are worth the same as ten 5c coins?
17. What number must be added to $1\frac{1}{4}$ to make $2\frac{1}{2}$?
18. Three books cost six dollars. How much will five books cost?
19. A rubber costs 20 cents. How many can be bought for $2?
20. What number is a hundred times as big as 0·605?
21. How many millimetres are there in $5\frac{1}{2}$ cm?
22. Find the average of 12 and 20.
23. A car travelling at 80 kilometres per hour takes 30 minutes for a journey. How long will the car take at 40 kilometres per hour?
24. A certain number multiplied by itself gives 81 as the answer. What is half of that number?
25. The difference between two numbers is 15. One of the numbers is 90. What is the other?

26. How many half-litre glasses can be filled from a vessel containing ten litres?
27. How much will a dozen oranges cost at 20 cents each?
28. On a coach forty-one out of fifty people are men. What percentage is this?
29. A prize of $400 000 is shared equally between one hundred people. How much does each person receive?
30. If electric cable is 6 pence for 50 cm, how much will 4 metres cost?

Test 2

1. What are 48 twos?
2. How many fives are there in ninety-five?
3. What is 6.30 a.m. on the 24-hour clock?
4. Add together $2·25 and 50 cents.
5. I go shopping with $2·80 and buy a magazine for ninety cents. How much money have I left?
6. Two angles of a triangle are 65° and 20°. What is the third angle?
7. Write in figures the number 'five million, eighteen thousand and one.'
8. How many 20 cent biros can be bought for $3?
9. Work out 1% of $600.
10. A packet of 10 small cakes costs 35 cents. How much does each cake cost?
11. Add eight to 9 fives.
12. A packet of flour weighing 2400 grams is divided into three equal parts. How heavy is each part?
13. Add together 7, 23 and 44.
14. A car does 4 km per litre of petrol. How far does the car travel on seven litres of petrol?
15. How many twenty cents coins are needed to make eight dollars?
16. A certain butterfly lives for just 96 hours. How many days is this?
17. What number is 25 more than 37?
18. Find the average of 2, 5 and 8.
19. Pears cost eleven cents each. How many can I buy for sixty cents?
20. How many minutes are there in eight hours?
21. What number is twice as big as seventy-nine?

22. How many minutes are there between 6.25 p.m. and 8.00 p.m.?
23. Write one-fifth as a decimal.
24. Which is the larger: 0·7, or 0·071?
25. If a woman earns $8·40 per hour, how much does she earn in ten hours?
26. A car costing $2500 is reduced by $45. What is the new price?
27. How many half kilogram packets of sugar can be filled from a large sack containing 32 kilograms?
28. My daily paper costs 15 cents and I buy the paper six days a week. What is my weekly bill?
29. A car journey of 110 km took two hours. What was the average speed of the car?
30. How many days will there be in February 2003?

Test 3

1. What number is fifteen more than fifty-five?
2. What is a tenth of 2400?
3. What is twenty times forty-five?
4. Write in figures the number ten thousand, seven hundred and five.
5. A play lasting $2\frac{1}{4}$ hours starts at half-past eight. When does it finish?
6. What number is fifty-five less than 300?
7. How many twelves are there in 240?
8. A book costs $1·95. How much change do I receive from five dollars?
9. Find the cost of eight biros at 22 cents each.
10. What four coins make 61 cents?
11. Work out $\frac{1}{2}$ plus $\frac{1}{4}$ and give the answer as a decimal.
12. A box holds 16 cans. How many boxes are needed for 80 cans?
13. If the 25th of December is a Tuesday, what day of the week is the first of January?
14. By how much is two kilos more than 500 g?
15. Write down fifteen thousand and fifty cents in dollars and cents.
16. The sides of a square field measure 160 metres. Find the total distance around the field.
17. A three-piece suite costing $970 is reduced by $248. What is the new price?

18. A bingo prize of $150 000 is shared equally between six people. How much does each person receive?
19. Ice creams cost twenty-four cents each. How many can I buy with one dollar?
20. A bag contains 22 five cent coins. How much is in the bag?
21. How many metres are there in twelve kilometres?
22. A wine merchant puts 100 bottles in crates of 12. How many crates does he need?
23. Add together 73 and 18.
24. What is 5% of $120?
25. Peaches cost fourteen cents each. How much do I pay for seven peaches?
26. A toy costs 54 cents. Find the change from five dollars.
27. A boy goes to and from school by bus and a ticket costs 33 cents each way. How much does he spend in a five-day week?
28. In your purse, you have two ten dollar notes, three five dollar notes and seven one dollar notes. How much have you got altogether?
29. What are eighty twelves?
30. True or false: $\frac{1}{10}$ is greater than 0·2?

Test 4

1. What is the change from a $10 note for goods costing $1·95?
2. Add 12 to 7 nines.
3. How many 20 cent coins are needed to make $5?
4. A pile of 100 sheets of paper is 10 cm thick. How thick is each sheet?
5. Lemons cost 7 cents each or 60 cents a dozen. How much is saved by buying a dozen instead of 12 separate lemons?
6. How many weeks are there in two years?
7. What is 1% of $40?
8. How much more than $92 is $180?
9. My watch reads five past 6. It is 15 minutes fast. What is the correct time?
10. If a litre of beer costs 82c, how much does a man pay for 10 litres?
11. A cycle track is 800 metres long. How far do I go in kilometres if I complete 5 laps of the track?

12. A train travels at an average speed of 30 km/h for $1\frac{1}{2}$ hours. How far does it travel?
13. I go shopping with $5 and buy 3 items at 25 cents each. How much money have I left?
14. From one thousand and seven take away nine.
15. If I can cycle 1 km in 3 minutes, how many km can I cycle in one hour?
16. How many millimetres are there in 20 cm?
17. A metal rod 90 cm long is cut into four equal parts. How long is one part?
18. Find the cost of fifteen items at 5 cents each.
19. A 2 cent coin is about 2 mm thick. How many coins are in a pile which is 2 cm high?
20. Add up the first four odd numbers.
21. Add up the first four even numbers.
22. My daily paper costs 18 cents. I pay for it with a $10 note. What change do I receive?
23. A film starts at 8.53 p.m. and finishes at 9.15 p.m. How long is the film?
24. We finish school at twenty to four. What is that on the 24-hour clock?
25. Add together $2·34 and $5·60.
26. What is 10% of $7?
27. How many 2 cent coins are needed to make $4?
28. 35% of a class prefer BBC1 and 30% prefer ITV. What percentage prefer the other two channels?
29. How many minutes is it between 6.20 p.m. and 8.00 p.m.?
30. What is the cost of 1000 books at $2·50 each?

The questions in the next three tests are a little harder.

Test 5

1. A car travels at a speed of 50 km/h for 30 minutes. How far does it travel?
2. I bought two books costing $2·50 and $1·90. How much did I spend altogether?
3. What is the cost of six items at thirty-five cents each?
4. Tickets for a concert cost $6·50 each. What is the cost of four tickets?

5. It takes me 24 minutes to walk to school. I cycle three times as fast as I walk. How long do I take to cycle to school?
6. Work out as a single number, four squared plus three squared.
7. Write down an approximate value for forty-nine times eleven.
8. Write one metre as a fraction of one kilometre.
9. What number is exactly half-way between 2·5 and 2·8?
10. The First World War started in 1914. How long ago was that?
11. Lottery tickets cost $2·50 each. How much is raised from the sale of six thousand tickets?
12. Train fares are increased by ten per cent. If the old fare was $3·50, what is the new fare?
13. If a man earns $5·50 per hour, how much does he earn in five hours?
14. A beer crate holds twelve bottles. How many crates are needed for 90 bottles?
15. When playing darts you score double ten, double twenty and treble eight. What is your total score?
16. How many cm are there in twelve metres?
17. A petrol pump delivered $2\frac{1}{2}$ litres in 5 seconds. How many litres will it deliver in one minute?
18. A square has sides of length 5 cm. How long is a diagonal to the nearest centimetre?
19. How much more than 119 is 272?
20. What is the cube root of 64?
21. Find the average of 4, 8 and 9.
22. A rectangular lawn is 7 m wide and 15 m long. What area does it cover?
23. How many centimetres are there in 20 km?
24. A ship was due at noon on Tuesday, but arrived at 15:00 on Thursday. How many hours late was it?
25. A litre of wine fills 9 glasses. How many litre bottles are needed to fill 50 glasses?
26. Work out 15% of $40.
27. A cake weighs 2·3 kg. How many grams is that?
28. How many seconds are there in $2\frac{1}{2}$ minutes?
29. How many days are there altogether in 19 weeks?
30. If the eighth of May is a Monday, what day of the week is the seventeenth?

Test 6

1. What is the angle between the hands of a clock at two o'clock?
2. What is a half of a half of 0·2?
3. In a test Paul got 16 out of 20. What percentage is that?
4. Work out $2 \times 20 \times 200$.
5. Two friends share a bill for $33·80. How much does each person pay?
6. Work out $\frac{1}{2}$ plus $\frac{1}{5}$ and give the answer as a decimal.
7. How long will it take a car to travel 320 km at an average speed of 60 km/h?
8. What is $\frac{1}{8}$ as a percentage?
9. What is the height of a triangle with base 12 cm and area 36 cm^2?
10. Work out 0·1 cubed.
11. Between which two consecutive whole numbers does the square root of 58 lie?
12. What is eight per cent of $25?
13. A car has a 1795 c.c. engine. What is that approximately in litres?
14. The mean of four numbers is 12·3. What is their sum?
15. Find the cost of smoking 40 cigarettes a day for five days if a packet of 20 costs $1·25.
16. How many minutes are there in $2\frac{3}{4}$ hours?
17. A pie chart has a red sector representing 20% of the whole chart. What is the angle of the sector?
18. How many five cent coins are needed to make $12?
19. I buy three kg of oranges for $1·02. How much do they cost per kg?
20. A rectangular pane of glass is 3 m long and 2 m wide. Glass costs $1·50 per square metre. How much will the pane cost?
21. A car journey of 150 km took $2\frac{1}{2}$ hours. What was the average speed?
22. Add 218 to 84.
23. Pencils cost 5 cents each. How many can I buy with $2·50?
24. Write down the next prime number after 31.
25. A ruler costs 37 cents. What is the total cost of three rulers?
26. A salesman receives commission of $1\frac{1}{2}$% on sales. How much commission does he receive when he sells a computer for $1000?
27. How many edges does a cube have?

28. Between which two consecutive whole numbers does the square root of 80 lie?
29. A coat is marked at a sale price of $60 after a reduction of 25%. What was the original price?
30. Theatre tickets cost $3·45 each. How much will four tickets cost?

Test 7

1. Two angles of a triangle are 42° and 56°. What is the third angle?
2. Telephone charges are increased by 20%. What is the new charge for a call which previously cost 60c?
3. What number is exactly half way between 0·1 and 0·4?
4. A boat sails at a speed of 18 knots for five hours. How far does it go?
5. How many 23p stamps can be bought for $2?
6. The mean age of three girls is 12 years. If two of the girls are aged 9 and 16 years, how old is the third girl?
7. Multiply $3\frac{1}{4}$ by 100.
8. What is a quarter of a third?
9. A prize of five million dollars is shared between 200 people. How much does each person receive?
10. The attendance at an athletics meeting was forty-eight thousand, seven hundred and eleven. Write this number correct to two significant figures.
11. Work out 0·1 multiplied by 63.
12. Find the cost of 6 litres of wine at $1·45 per litre.
13. Three people agree to share a bill equally. The cost comes to $7·20. How much does each person pay?
14. A pump removes water at a rate of 6 litres per minute. How many hours will it take to remove 1800 litres?
15. Work out three-eighths of $100.
16. A metal rod of length 27·1 cm is cut exactly in half. How long is each piece?
17. A square has sides of length 7 cm. How long is a diagonal to the nearest centimetre?
18. The cost of five tins of salmon is $7·50. How much will six tins cost?
19. What number is a thousand times as big as 0·2?
20. Pencils cost five cents each. How much will two dozen pencils cost?
21. How many fours are there in a thousand?

22. Work out the area, in square metres, of a rectangular field of width twenty metres and length twenty-five metres.

23. A packet of peanuts costs 65 cents. I buy two packets and pay with a ten dollar note. Find the change.

24. What is a half of a half of 0·1?

25. I bought three kilograms of flour and I use four hundred and fifty grams of it. How many grams of flour do I have left?

26. A bingo prize of two hundred thousand dollars is shared equally between five people. How much does each person receive?

27. What is the angle between the hands of a clock at 5 o'clock?

28. Five boys and three girls share $240. How much do the boys get altogether?

29. How many 17c stamps can I buy for $2?

30. A milk crate has space for 24 bottles. How many crates are needed for 200 bottles?

Mathematical magic

Here is a trick which you can perform to demonstrate that you can add even quicker than a calculator!

(a) Ask someone to give a five-digit number with the figures all jumbled up to make it more 'difficult'.

(b) Ask for two more five-digit numbers. You may now have:

$$47563 \ldots A$$
$$25608 \ldots B$$
$$87265 \ldots C$$

(c) Pretend to add two more five-digit numbers at random. In fact choose the fourth number so that when added to number B it makes 99999. Similarly the fifth number is chosen so that when added to number C it also makes 99999. We now have:

$$\begin{array}{r} 47563 \\ 25608 \\ 87265 \\ 74391 \\ 12734 \end{array}$$

(d) You now add them together 'in your head' and write down the answer. (Check this on a calculator.)

Answer = 247561

How does it work?

The first digit is always a '2'.
The next five digits are simply 2 less than number A.
i.e. 47563 − 2 = 47561.

Here is another example.

Can you work out why it works?

Now challenge your friends or relatives to an addition race: your brain versus their calculator.

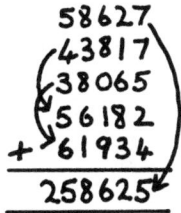

7.6 Using a calculator

Order of operations

Calculators cannot think for themselves. *You* have to decide in which order the buttons have to be pressed.

Always perform operations in the following order:
(a) Brackets
(b) Divide and multiply
(c) Add and subtract.

Example

(a) $\quad 7 + 6 \div 3 = 7 + 2$
$= 9$

(b) $\quad 6 \times 4 - 8 \div 2 = 24 - 4$
$= 20$

(c) $\quad 5 + (28 + 5) \div 3 = 5 + 33 \div 3$
$= 5 + 11$
$= 16$

(d) $\quad \dfrac{4 \cdot 2}{1 \cdot 2 - 0 \cdot 7} = \dfrac{4 \cdot 2}{0 \cdot 5}$
$\phantom{\dfrac{4 \cdot 2}{1 \cdot 2 - 0 \cdot 7} }= 8 \cdot 4$

Notice that the division line ——— acts like a pair of brackets so that we work out $1 \cdot 2 - 0 \cdot 7$ first.

Exercise 9

Work out, without a calculator:

1. $11 + 8 \div 1$
2. $60 - 7 \times 8$
3. $15 - 2 \times 6$
4. $15 \div 5 - 3$
5. $30 + 15 \div 3$
6. $9 \times 5 + 15$
7. $40 - 3 \times 8$
8. $12 - 36 \div 6$
9. $3 + 20 \div 2$
10. $13 + 8 \div 8$
11. $2 \times 4 + 3 \times 5$
12. $6 \times 6 + 7 \times 5$
13. $1 \times 6 + 7 \times 2$
14. $2 \times 8 + 2 \times 10$
15. $3 \times 5 - 12 \div 2$
16. $3 \times 5 - 28 \div 4$
17. $7 \times 4 + 2 \times 2$
18. $30 \div 3 + 5 \times 4$
19. $20 \div 2 - 3 \times 2$
20. $8 \div 8 - 1 \times 1$
21. $\dfrac{27 + 3 \times 3}{(3 \times 2)}$
22. $\dfrac{6 + 8 \times 3}{(8 \times 2 - 10)}$
23. $\dfrac{13 - 12 \div 4}{4 + 3 \times 2}$
24. $\dfrac{11 + 6 \times 6}{5 - 8 \div 2}$
25. $\dfrac{12 + 3 \times 6}{4 + 3 \div 3}$
26. $\dfrac{24 - 18 \div 3}{1 \cdot 5 + 4 \cdot 5}$

27. $(42 - 5 \times 6) \times (8 - 4 \times 2) + (7 + 3 \times 3)$
28. $(10 - 24 \div 3) + (8 + 3 \times 4) \div (8 - 6 \times 1)$
29. $7 + 9 \times (8 - 6 \div 2)$
30. $[(7 - 2) \times 5] - (6 \times 3 - 2 \times 4)$
31. $[(60 - 7 \times 5) \div 5] + (12 + 7 \times 10)$
32. $(15 - 3 \times 4) \times 4 + [60 \div (24 \div 2)]$
33. $[(9 - 7) \times 12] - (7 \times 3 - 5 \times 4)$
34. $(50 - 8 \times 6) \times 2 + [40 \div (5 \times 2)]$
35. $[(12 - 8) \times 4] \div (11 - 3 \times 1)$
36. $(7 \times 2 - 6) + (7 + 16 \div 8) \times (10 - 4 \times 2)$

Exercise 10

This exercise is more difficult. Write down each question and find the missing signs. ($+$, $-$, $\times$, $\div$). There are no brackets.

1. 7 5 4 = 27
2. 3 5 10 = 25
3. 4 2 3 = 5
4. 11 3 3 = 20
5. 31 10 2 = 11
6. 10 6 5 = 40
7. 4 8 7 = 25
8. 12 9 2 = 30
9. 18 4 4 = 2
10. 28 10 2 = 8
11. 21 3 5 = 2
12. 7 3 3 = 16
13. 10 2 3 = 8
14. 10 3 12 = 42
15. 18 3 7 = 13
16. 31 40 5 = 39
17. 15 16 4 = 11
18. 15 8 9 = 87
19. 37 35 5 = 44
20. 11 5 9 = 64
21. 8 3 2 4 = 10
22. 12 3 3 1 = 4
23. 11 4 1 6 = 9
24. 15 5 2 4 = 11
25. 7 2 3 3 = 5
26. 12 2 3 4 = 22
27. 8 9 6 11 = 6
28. 20 20 9 0 = 1
29. 20 30 10 8 = 25
30. 30 6 11 11 = 85

Calculator

Example

(a) Work out $8 \cdot 43 + \dfrac{9 \cdot 72}{3 \cdot 3}$ correct to four significant figures.

| 8·43 | + | 9·72 | ÷ | 3·3 | = |

Answer = 11·38 (to 4 s.f.)

(b) Work out $(5 \cdot 2 - 4 \cdot 737)^2$.

| 5·2 | − | 4·737 | = | x^2 |

Answer = 0·2144 (to 4 s.f.)

Exercise 11

Work out, correct to four significant figures:

1. $85 \cdot 3 \times 21 \cdot 7$
2. $18 \cdot 6 \div 2 \cdot 7$
3. $10 \cdot 074 \div 8 \cdot 3$
4. $0 \cdot 112 \times 3 \cdot 74$
5. $8 - 0 \cdot 111 \, 11$
6. $19 + 0 \cdot 3456$
7. $0 \cdot 841 \div 17$
8. $11 \cdot 02 \times 20 \cdot 1$
9. $18 \cdot 3 \div 0 \cdot 751$

10. $0 \cdot 982 \times 6 \cdot 74$
11. $\dfrac{8 \cdot 3 + 2 \cdot 94}{3 \cdot 4}$
12. $\dfrac{6 \cdot 1 - 4 \cdot 35}{0 \cdot 76}$

13. $\dfrac{19\cdot7+21\cdot4}{0\cdot985}$

14. $7\cdot3+\left(\dfrac{8\cdot2}{9\cdot5}\right)$

15. $\left(\dfrac{6\cdot04}{18\cdot7}\right)-0\cdot214$

16. $\dfrac{2\cdot4\times0\cdot871}{4\cdot18}$

17. $19\cdot3+\left(\dfrac{2\cdot6}{1\cdot95}\right)$

18. $6\cdot41+\dfrac{9\cdot58}{2\cdot6}$

19. $\dfrac{19\cdot3\times0\cdot221}{0\cdot689}$

20. $8\cdot3+\dfrac{0\cdot64}{0\cdot325}$

21. $2\cdot4+(9\cdot7\times0\cdot642)$

22. $11\cdot2+(9\cdot75\times1\cdot11)$

23. $0\cdot325+\dfrac{8\cdot6}{11\cdot2}$

24. $8\cdot35^2-25$

25. $6\cdot71^2+0\cdot64$

26. $3\cdot45^3+11\cdot8$

27. $2\cdot93^3-2\cdot641$

28. $\dfrac{7\cdot2^2-4\cdot5}{8\cdot64}$

29. $\dfrac{13\cdot9+2\cdot97^2}{4\cdot31}$

30. $(3\cdot3-2\cdot84)^2$

Using the memory

Example

(a) Work out $\dfrac{4\cdot2+1\cdot75}{3\cdot63-2\cdot14}$, correct to 4 s.f., using the memory buttons.

Find the bottom line first:

$\boxed{3\cdot63}\ \boxed{-}\ \boxed{2\cdot14}\ \boxed{=}\ \boxed{\text{Min}}\ \boxed{C}\ \boxed{4\cdot2}\ \boxed{+}\ \boxed{1\cdot75}\ \boxed{=}\ \boxed{\div}\ \boxed{\text{MR}}\ \boxed{=}$

It is even quicker to use brackets:
$(4\cdot2+1\cdot75)\div$
$(3\cdot63-2\cdot4)=$

The calculator reads 3·9932886

∴ Answer = 3·993 (to 4 s.f.)

(b) Work out $18\cdot75-2\cdot11^3$.

$\boxed{2\cdot11}\ \boxed{x^y}\ \boxed{3}\ \boxed{=}\ \boxed{\text{Min}}\ \boxed{18\cdot75}\ \boxed{-}\ \boxed{\text{MR}}\ \boxed{=}$

Answer = 9·356 (to 4 s.f.)

Exercise 12

Work out the following, correct to four significant figures. Use the memory buttons where necessary.

1. $\dfrac{7\cdot3+2\cdot14}{3\cdot6-2\cdot95}$

2. $\dfrac{2\cdot3+0\cdot924}{1\cdot3+0\cdot635}$

3. $\dfrac{5\cdot89}{7-3\cdot83}$

4. $\dfrac{102}{58\cdot1+65\cdot32}$

5. $\dfrac{18\cdot8}{3\cdot72\times1\cdot86}$

6. $\dfrac{904}{65\cdot3\times2\cdot86}$

7. $12\cdot2-\left(\dfrac{2\cdot6}{1\cdot95}\right)$

8. $8\cdot047-\left(\dfrac{6\cdot34}{10\cdot2}\right)$

9. $14\cdot2-\left(\dfrac{1\cdot7}{2\cdot4}\right)$

10. $\dfrac{9\cdot75-8\cdot792}{4\cdot31-3\cdot014}$

11. $\dfrac{19\cdot6\times3\cdot01}{2\cdot01-1\cdot958}$

12. $3\cdot7^2-\left(\dfrac{8\cdot59}{24}\right)$

13. $8 \cdot 27 - 1 \cdot 56^2$
14. $111 \cdot 79 - 5 \cdot 04^2$
15. $18 \cdot 3 - 2 \cdot 841^2$
16. $(2 \cdot 93 + 71 \cdot 5)^2$
17. $(8 \cdot 3 - 6 \cdot 34)^4$
18. $54 \cdot 2 - 2 \cdot 6^4$
19. $(8 \cdot 7 - 5 \cdot 95)^4$
20. $\sqrt{68 \cdot 4} + 11 \cdot 63$
21. $9 \cdot 45 - \sqrt{8 \cdot 248}$
22. $3 \cdot 24^2 - \sqrt{1 \cdot 962}$
23. $\dfrac{3 \cdot 54 + 2 \cdot 4}{8 \cdot 47^2}$
24. $2065 - \sqrt{44\,000}$
25. $\sqrt{(5 \cdot 69 - 0 \cdot 0852)}$
26. $\sqrt{(0 \cdot 976 + 1 \cdot 03)}$
27. $\sqrt{\left(\dfrac{17 \cdot 4}{2 \cdot 16 - 1 \cdot 83}\right)}$
28. $\sqrt{\left(\dfrac{28 \cdot 9}{\sqrt{8 \cdot 47}}\right)}$
29. $257 - \dfrac{6 \cdot 32}{0 \cdot 059}$
30. $75\,000 - 5 \cdot 6^4$
31. $\dfrac{11 \cdot 29 \times 2 \cdot 09}{2 \cdot 7 + 0 \cdot 082}$
32. $85 \cdot 5 - \sqrt{105 \cdot 8}$
33. $\dfrac{4 \cdot 45^2}{8 \cdot 2^2 - 51 \cdot 09}$
34. $\left(\dfrac{8 \cdot 53 + 7 \cdot 07}{6 \cdot 04 - 4 \cdot 32}\right)^4$
35. $2 \cdot 75 + \dfrac{5}{8 \cdot 2} + \dfrac{11 \cdot 2}{4 \cdot 3}$
36. $8 \cdot 2 + \dfrac{6 \cdot 3}{0 \cdot 91} + \dfrac{2 \cdot 74}{8 \cdot 4}$
37. $\dfrac{18 \cdot 5}{1 \cdot 6} + \dfrac{7 \cdot 1}{0 \cdot 53} + \dfrac{11 \cdot 9}{25 \cdot 6}$
38. $\dfrac{83 \cdot 6}{105} + \dfrac{2 \cdot 95}{2 \cdot 7} + \dfrac{81}{97}$
39. $\left(\dfrac{98 \cdot 76}{103} + \dfrac{4 \cdot 07}{3 \cdot 6}\right)^2$
40. $\dfrac{(5 \cdot 843 - \sqrt{2 \cdot 07})^2}{88 \cdot 4}$
41. $\left(\dfrac{1}{7 \cdot 6} - \dfrac{1}{18 \cdot 5}\right)^3$
42. $\dfrac{\sqrt{(4 \cdot 79)} + 1 \cdot 6}{9 \cdot 63}$
43. $\dfrac{(0 \cdot 761)^2 - \sqrt{(4 \cdot 22)}}{1 \cdot 96}$
44. $\sqrt[3]{\left(\dfrac{1 \cdot 74 \times 0 \cdot 761}{0 \cdot 0896}\right)}$
45. $\left(\dfrac{8 \cdot 6 \times 1 \cdot 71}{0 \cdot 43}\right)^3$
46. $\dfrac{\sqrt[3]{(86 \cdot 6)}}{\sqrt[4]{(4 \cdot 71)}}$
47. $\dfrac{1}{8 \cdot 2^2} - \dfrac{3}{19^2}$
48. $\dfrac{100}{11^3} + \dfrac{100}{12^3}$

Exercise 13

If we work out $25 \times 503 \times 4 + 37$ on a calculator we should obtain the number 50337. If we turn the calculator upside down (and use a little imagination) we see the word 'LEEDS'.

Find the words given by the clues below.

1. $83 \times 85 + 50$ (Lots of this in the garden)
2. $211 \times 251 + 790$ (Tropical or Scilly)
3. $19 \times 20 \times 14 - 2 \cdot 66$ (Not an upstanding man)
4. $(84 + 17) \times 5$ (Dotty message)
5. $0 \cdot 014\,43 \times 7 \times 4$ (Three times as funny)
6. $79 \times 9 - 0 \cdot 9447$ (Greasy letters)
7. $50 \cdot 19 - (5 \times 0 \cdot 0039)$ (Not much space inside)
8. $2 \div 0 \cdot 5 - 3 \cdot 295$ (Rather lonely)
9. $0 \cdot 034 \times 11 - 0 \cdot 002\,92$; $9^4 - (8 \times 71)$ (two words) (Nice for breakfast)
10. $7420 \times 7422 + 118^2 - 30$ (Big Chief)
11. $(13 \times 3 \times 25 \times 8 \times 5) + 7$ (Dwelling for masons)
12. $71^2 - 11^2 - 5$ (Sad gasp)
13. $904^2 + 89\,621\,818$ (Prickly customer)
14. $(559 \times 6) + (21 \times 55)$ (What a surprise!)
15. $566 \times 711 - 23\,617$ (Bolt it down)

16. $\dfrac{9999 + 319}{8 \cdot 47 + 2 \cdot 53}$ (Sit up and plead)

17. $\dfrac{2601 \times 6}{4^2 + 1^2}$; $(401 - 78) \times 5^2$ (two words) (Not a great man)

18. $0 \cdot 4^2 - 0 \cdot 1^2$ (Little Sidney)

19. $\dfrac{(27 \times 2000 - 2)}{(0 \cdot 63 \div 0 \cdot 09)}$ (Not quite a mountain)

20. $(5^2 - 1^2)^4 - 14\,239$ (Just a name)
21. $48^4 + 102^2 - 4^2$ (Pursuits)
22. $615^2 + (7 \times 242)$ (Almost a goggle)
23. $14^4 - 627 + 29$ (Good book, by God!)
24. $6 \cdot 2 \times 0 \cdot 987 \times 1\,000\,000 - 860^2 + 118$ (Flying ace)
25. $(426 \times 474) + (318 \times 487) + 22\,018$ (Close to a bubble)
26. $\dfrac{36^3}{4} - 1530$ (Swiss girl's name)
27. $(594 \times 571) - (154 \times 132) - 38$ (Female Bobby)
28. $(7^2 \times 100) + (7 \times 2)$ (Lofty)
29. $240^2 + 134$; $241^2 - 7^3$ (two words) (Devil of a chime)
30. $1384 \cdot 5 \times 40 - 1 \cdot 991$ (Say this after sneezing)
31. $(2 \times 2 \times 2 \times 2 \times 3)^4 + 1929$ (Unhappy ending)
32. $141\,918 + 83^3$ (Hot stuff in France)

Mixed questions

Exercise 14

1. Four dozen bags of grain weigh 2016 kg. How much does each bag weigh?

2. An office building has twelve floors and each floor has twenty windows.
A window cleaner charges 50c per window. How much will he charge to clean all the windows in the building?

3. Write the following to the degree of accuracy stated:
   (a) 7·243 (to 1 d.p.)   (b) 11·275 (to 2 d.p.)
   (c) 0·115 (to 1 d.p.)   (d) 0·0255 (to 3 d.p.)
   (e) 28·21 (to 1 d.p.)   (f) 0·0072 (to 2 d.p.))

4. Work out, without using a calculator.
   (a) 0·6 + 2·72   (b) 3·21 − 1·6
   (c) 2·8 − 1·34   (d) 8 − 3·6
   (e) 100 × 0·062   (f) 27·4 ÷ 10

5. A rectangular wheat field is 200 m by 400 m. One hectare is 10 000 m² and each hectare produces 3 tonnes of wheat.
   (a) What is the area of the field in hectares?
   (b) How much wheat is produced in this field?

6. A powerful computer is hired out at a rate of 50c per minute. How much will it cost to hire the computer from 06:30 to 18:00?

7. An old sailor keeps all of his savings in gold. Altogether the gold weighs ten pounds. One day the price of gold goes up by $40 an ounce to $520 an ounce.
   (a) By how much did his gold rise in value?
   (b) How much was it worth after the rise?
      (1 pound = 16 ounces)

8. This packet of sugar cubes costs 60p.   How much would you have to pay for this packet?

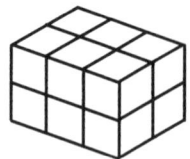
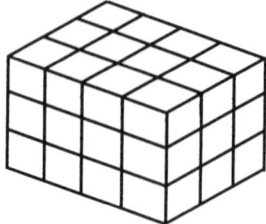

9. A wall measuring 3 m by 2 m is to be covered with square tiles of side 10 cm.
   (a) How many tiles are needed?
   (b) If the tiles cost $3·40 for ten, how much will it cost?

10. Draw the next member of the sequence.

(a)   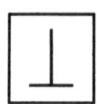   (b)

(c)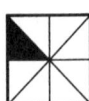

Exercise 15

1. The results of a test given to 50 children are shown below.

Mark	0	1	2	3	4	5
Number of pupils	1	4	10	12	15	8

   (a) How many pupils scored less than 3 marks?
   (b) Find the percentage of the pupils who scored:
      (i) 2 marks
      (ii) 5 marks
      (iii) 3 marks or more
      (iv) no marks.

2. The thirteenth number in the sequence 1, 3, 9, 27, ... is 531 441.
   What is
   (a) the twelfth number
   (b) the fourteenth number?

3. 6 sacks of corn will feed 80 hens for 12 days.
   Copy and complete the following:
   (a) 18 sacks of corn will feed 80 hens for ... days.
   (b) 6 sacks of corn will feed 40 hens for ... days.
   (c) 60 sacks of corn will feed 40 hens for ... days.
   (d) 30 sacks of corn will feed 80 hens for ... days.

4. Calculate the area of the shape below. Take $\pi = 3$.

   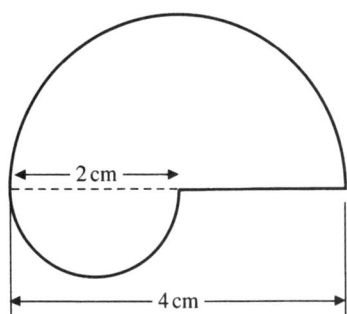

5. The odometer of a car shows a reading of 14 941 km. This number is called 'palindromic' because it reads the same backwards or forwards.
   (a) What will be the reading when the next palindromic number appears?
   (b) How far will the car have travelled by then?

6. Copy and complete the telephone bill shown.

DATE	METER READING	UNITS USED	PRICE PER UNIT	AMOUNT (£)
29/7/99	18714			
30/4/99	17956	A	3.80c	B
			Rental Charges	21.50
			Total Charges (excluding VAT)	C
			Value Added Tax at $17\frac{1}{2}$%	D
			Total Charges (including VAT)	E

7. A salesman is paid a basic salary of $5400 per year, plus commission of 5% on all his sales. Calculate his total salary if his sales totalled $40 000.

8. Petrol costs 54·3 cents per litre. How any litres can be bought for $8? Give your answer to one decimal place.

Exercise 16

1. A slimmer's calorie guide shows how many calories are contained in various foods:

   Bread 1·2 calories per g
   Cheese 2·5 calories per g
   Meat 1·6 calories per g
   Butter 6 calories per g

   Calculate the number of calories in the following meals:
   (a) 50 g bread, 40 g cheese, 100 g meat, 15 g butter.
   (b) 150 g bread, 85 g cheese, 120 g meat, 20 g butter.

2. Write as a single number.
   (a) 8^2 (b) 1^4
   (c) 10^2 (d) 3×10^3
   (e) 2^5 (f) 3^4

3. A cylinder has a volume of 200 cm^3 and a height of 10 cm. Calculate the area of its base.

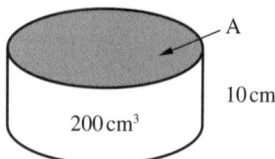

4. The diagram represents a railway siding. Each ● is a junction where a train can turn left or right. A turn to the left has a code 0 and a turn to the right has a code 1.

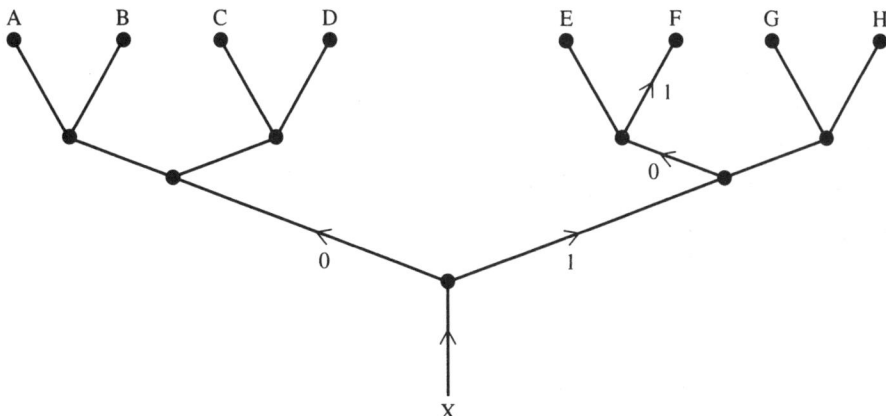

For example, a train starting at X would have code 101 in order to arrive at F.
Copy and complete the table below.

Point	A	B	C	D	E	F	G	H
Code						101		

5. A group of four adults are planning a holiday in France. The ferry costs, for the return journey, are:

Adult	$25
Car	$62

Travel around France is estimated at 2000 km and petrol costs 5 francs per litre. The car travels 10 km on one litre of petrol.
(a) Calculate the total cost of the return journey on the ferry.
(b) Calculate the number of litres of petrol to be used.
(c) Calculate the total cost, in francs, of the petrol.

6. A journey by boat takes 2 hours 47 minutes. How long will it take at half the speed?

7. Copy the following tables and write down the next *two* lines:
(a) $2^2 = 1^2 + 3$
$3^2 = 2^2 + 5$
$4^2 = 3^2 + 7$
$5^2 = 4^2 + 9$

(b) $3^2 = 4 + 1^2 + 2^2$
$5^2 = 12 + 2^2 + 3^2$
$7^2 = 24 + 3^2 + 4^2$
$9^2 = 40 + 4^2 + 5^2$

8. The area of a county is 6000 km². What volume of rain falls on the county during a day when there is 2 cm of rain? Give the answer in m³.

9. Ten posts are equally spaced in a straight line. It is 450 m from the first to the tenth post. What is the distance between successive posts?

10. Find the smallest whole number that is exactly divisible by all the numbers 1 to 10 inclusive.

Exercise 17

1. Seven fig rolls together weigh 560 g. A calorie guide shows that 10 g of fig roll contains 52 calories.
   (a) How much does one fig roll weigh?
   (b) How many calories are there in 1 g of fig roll?
   (c) How many calories are there in one fig roll?

2. Two numbers x and t are such that t is greater than 6 and x is less than 4. Arrange the numbers 5, t and x in order of size, starting with the smallest.

3. To the nearest whole number 5·84, 16·23 and 7·781 are 6, 16 and 8 respectively.
   (a) Use these approximate values to obtain an approximate result for $\dfrac{5\cdot84 \times 16\cdot23}{7\cdot781}$.
   (b) Use the same approach to obtain approximate results for:
   (i) $\dfrac{15\cdot72 \times 9\cdot78}{20\cdot24}$ (ii) $\dfrac{23\cdot85 \times 9\cdot892}{4\cdot867}$

4. King Richard is given three coins which look identical, but in fact one of them is an overweight fake.
   Describe how he could discover the fake using an ordinary balance and only *one* weighing operation.

5. A light aircraft flies 375 km on 150 litres of fuel. How much fuel is needed for a journey of 500 km?

6. A pile of 400 sheets of paper is 2·5 cm thick. What is the thickness in cm of one sheet of paper?

7. A map uses a scale of 1 to 100 000.
  (a) Calculate the actual length, in km, of a canal which is 5·4 cm long on the map.
  (b) A path is 600 m long. Calculate, in cm, the length this would be on the map.

8. Given the circumference C of a circle it is possible to estimate the area A by the following method:

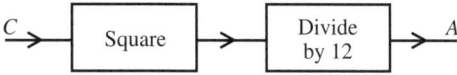

  (a) Find A when $C = 6$ cm.
  (b) Find A when $C = 18$ cm.
  (c) Write down the formula involving A and C.

9. I think of a number. If I subtract 4 and then divide the result by 4 the answer is 3. What number was I thinking of?

10. Try to draw four straight lines which pass through all of the 9 points in the diagram, without taking your pen from the paper and without going over any line twice.

  (Hint: The lines may go outside the pattern of dots).

Revision exercise 7A

1. A motorist travelled 800 km during May, when the cost of petrol was 50 cents per litre. In June the cost of petrol increased by 10% and he travelled 5% less distance.
  (a) What was the cost, in cents per litre, of petrol in June?
  (b) How many km did he travel in June?

2. Work out on a calculator, correct to 4 s.f.
  (a) $3·61 - (1·6 \times 0·951)$
  (b) $\dfrac{(4·65 + 1·09)}{(3·6 - 1·714)}$

3. Evaluate the following and give the answers to 3 significant figures:
  (a) $\sqrt[3]{(9·61 \times 0·0041)}$
  (b) $\left(\dfrac{1}{9·5} - \dfrac{1}{11·2}\right)^3$
  (c) $\dfrac{15·6 \times 0·714}{0·0143 \times 12}$
  (d) $\sqrt[4]{\left(\dfrac{1}{5 \times 10^3}\right)}$

4. Estimate the answer correct to one significant figure. Do not use a calculator.
  (a) $(612 \times 52) \div 49·2$
  (b) $(11·7 + 997·1) \times 9·2$
  (c) $\sqrt{\left(\dfrac{91·3}{10·1}\right)}$
  (d) $\pi\sqrt{(5·2^2 + 18·2^2)}$

5. The mass of the planet Jupiter is about 350 times the mass of the Earth. The mass of the Earth is approximately $6·03 \times 10^{21}$ tonnes. Give an estimate correct to 2 significant figures for the mass of Jupiter.

6. Evaluate the following using a calculator: (answers to 4 sig. fig.)
  (a) $\dfrac{0·74}{0·81 \times 1·631}$
  (b) $\sqrt{\left(\dfrac{9·61}{8·34 - 7·41}\right)}$
  (c) $\left(\dfrac{0·741}{0·8364}\right)^4$
  (d) $\dfrac{8·4 - 7·642}{3·333 - 1·735}$

7. Copy and complete the table.

	Fraction	Decimal	Percentage
(a)	$\frac{3}{5}$		
(b)		0·75	
(c)			5%
(d)	$\frac{1}{8}$		

8. A wedding cake weighing 9·2 kg is cut up and shared between 107 guests. About how much cake, in grams, does each person get? [No calculator!]

9. The total weight of 95 000 marbles is 308 kg. Roughly how many grams does each marble weigh?

10. Here are nine calculations and nine answers. Write down each calculation and choose the correct answer from the list given.

(a) $1·8 \times 10·4$ (b) $9·8 \times 9·1$
(c) $7·9 \times 8·1$ (d) $76·2 \times 1·9$
(e) $3·8 \times 8·2$ (f) $8·15 \times 5·92$
(g) $36·96 \div 4$ (h) $9·6 \div 5$
(i) $0·11 + 3·97$

Answers: 63·99, 18·72, 31·16, 4·08, 1·92, 9·24, 144·78, 89·18, 48·248.

11. (a) Copy this pattern and write down the next two lines.
$3 \times 5 = \quad 15$
$33 \times 5 = \quad 165$
$333 \times 5 = \quad 1\,665$
$3333 \times 5 = 16\,665$
(b) Copy and complete $333\,333\,333 \times 5 =$

12. (a) Copy this pattern and write down the next line.
$1 \times 9 = \quad 9$
$21 \times 9 = \quad 189$
$321 \times 9 = \quad 2\,889$
$4\,321 \times 9 = \quad 38\,889$
$54\,321 \times 9 = 488\,889$
(b) Complete this line $87\,654\,321 \times 9 =$

Examination exercise 7B

1. Copy the statements given below.
Make correct statements by putting two of the four symbols $+$, $-$, $\times$ and $\div$ in the gaps between 8, 7 and 5 below.

Example $8 + 7 \times 5 = 43$

Answer
(a) $8 \quad 7 \quad 5 = 10$ (b) $8 \quad 7 \quad 5 = -27$ (c) $8 \quad 7 \quad 5 = 11·2$ [N 98 3]

2.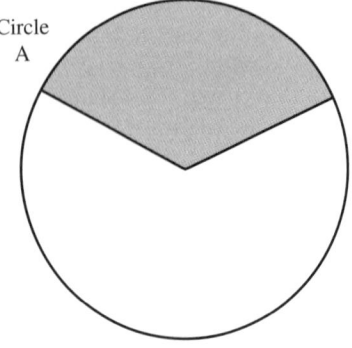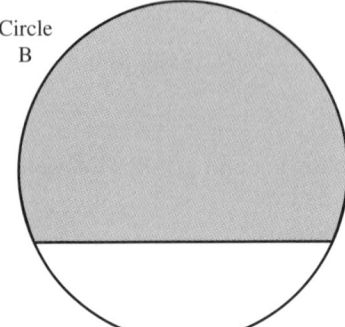

Circle A   Circle B

(a) Estimate what **fraction** of circle A is shaded.
(b) Estimate what **percentage** of circle B is shaded.   [J 97 1]

3. The length (l centimetres) of a rectangle is 70 cm, correct to the nearest 10 cm. The width (w centimetres) of the rectangle is 15 cm, correct to the nearest centimetre. Copy and complete the inequalities to show the limits of l and w.

   .... $\leqslant l <$ ....

   .... $\leqslant w <$ .... [N 98 1]

4. (a) Calculate $(4\cdot74^2 + 6\cdot29^2)^3$, writing down your full calculator display.
   (b) Round your answer to part (a) to 2 significant figures. [N 98 1]

5. 3800 students took an examination.
   19% received Grade A,
   24% received Grade B,
   31% received Grade C,
   10% received Grade D,
   11% received Grade E
   and the rest received Grade U.
   (a) What percentage of the students received Grade U?
   (b) What fraction of the students received Grade B?
   Give your answer in its lowest terms.
   (c) How many students received Grade A?
   (d) Margaret plans to show the information given at the beginning of the question on a pie chart.
   Calculate the angle she should use for Grade D. [J 96 3]

6. The owner of a shop bought 240 blouses for $1392.
   (a) How much did she pay for each blouse?
   (b) She put the blouses on sale at $8·99 each.
   Calculate the percentage profit that she hoped to make.
   (c) She only sold 190 blouses at $8·99 each. The rest were sold at $2·99 each.
   (i) Calculate the total amount received from the sale of blouses.
   (ii) Calculate the percentage that she made on the original cost. [J 97 3]

8 PROBABILITY

8.1 One event

The probability of an event is a measure of how likely it is to occur. This probability can be any number between 0 and 1 (inclusive).

- Events which are very likely to occur have a probability of nearly 1. For example, the probability of failing to select the ace of diamonds at random from an ordinary pack of cards is equal to $\frac{51}{52}$.
- Events which are very unlikely to occur have a probability of nearly 0. e.g. the probability of your maths teacher becoming prime minister one day is 0·000 001 (approximately).
- Events which are certain to occur have a probability of 1.
- Events which cannot occur have a probability of 0. For example,
    the probability that tomorrow is Tuesday if today is Monday is 1;
    the probability that one day a man will run a mile in under ten seconds is 0.

There are four different ways of estimating probabilities.

Method A   Use symmetry.

- The probability of rolling a 3 on a fair dice is $\frac{1}{6}$. This is because all the scores 1, 2, 3, 4, 5, 6 are equally likely.

- Similarly the probability of getting a head when tossing a fair coin is $\frac{1}{2}$.

Method B   Conduct an experiment or survey to collect data.

- Suppose I wanted to estimate the probability of a drawing pin landing point upwards when dropped onto a hard surface. I could not use symmetry for obvious reasons but I could conduct an experiment to see what happened in say 500 trials.

- I might want to know the probability that the next car going past the school gates is driven by a woman.
  I could conduct a survey in which the drivers of cars are recorded over a period of time.

Method C Look at past data.

- If I wanted to estimate the probability of my plane crashing as it lands at Heathrow airport I could look at accident records at Heathrow over the last five years or so.

Method D Make a subjective estimate.

We have to use this method when the event is not repeatable. It is not really a 'method' in the same sense as are methods A, B, C.

- We might want to estimate the probability of England beating France in a soccer match next week. We could look at past results but these could be of little value for all sorts of reasons. We might consult 'experts' but even they are notoriously inaccurate in their predictions.

Exercise 1

In Questions **1** to **12** state which method A, B, C or D you would use to estimate the probability of the event given.

1. The probability that a person chosen at random from a class will be left-handed.

2. The probability that there will be snow in the ski resort to which a school party is going in February next year.

3. The probability of drawing an 'ace' from a pack of playing cards.

4. The probability that you hole a six-foot putt when playing golf.

5. The probability that the world record for running 1500 m will be under 3 min 20 seconds by the year 2020.

6. The probability that a person who smokes will suffer from lung cancer later in life.

7. The probability of rolling a 3 using a dice which is suspected of being biased.

8. The probability that a person selected at random would vote 'Democrat' in an election tomorrow.

9. The probability that a train will arrive within ten minutes of its scheduled arrival time.

10. The probability of winning first prize in a raffle if you have 5 tickets and 1000 are sold.

11. The probability that the current Wimbledon Ladies Champion will successfully defend her title next year.

12. The probability that the next pupil expelled from a certain school will be a girl.

Working out probabilities

The probability of an event occurring can be calculated using symmetry. We argue, for example, that when we toss a coin we have an equal chance of getting a 'head' or a 'tail'. So the probability of spinning a 'head' is a half.

We write 'p (spinning a head) $= \frac{1}{2}$'.

Exercise 2

1. A bag contains 3 white discs and 5 black discs.
   One disc is taken out at random.
   What is the probability that it is:
   (a) white
   (b) black?

   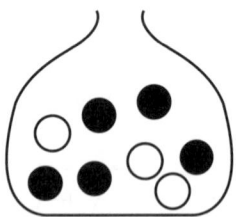

2. Nine counters numbered 1, 2, 3, 4, 5, 6, 7, 8, 9 are placed in a bag.
   One is taken out at random. What is the probability that it is:
   (a) a '5',   (b) divisible by 3,
   (c) less than 5,   (d) divisible by 4?

3. A bag contains 5 green balls, 2 red balls and 4 yellow balls.
   One ball is taken out at random.
   What is the probability that it is:
   (a) green,
   (b) red,
   (c) yellow?

4. A cash bag contains two 20c coins, four 10c coins, five 5c coins, three 2c coins and three 1c coins.
   Find the probability that one coin selected at random is:
   (a) a 10c coin,   (b) a 2c coin.

5. A bag contains 8 orange balls, 5 green balls and 4 silver balls.
   Find the probability that a ball picked out at random is:
   (a) silver,   (b) orange,   (c) green.

6. The numbers of matches in ten boxes is as follows:
   48, 46, 45, 49, 44, 46, 47, 48, 45, 46.
   One box is selected at random.
   Find the probability of the box containing:
   (a) 49 matches,
   (b) 46 matches,
   (c) more than 47 matches.

7. One ball is selected at random from those below.

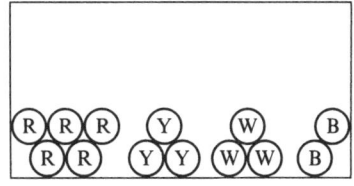

R = red
Y = yellow
W = white
B = black

Find the probability of selecting:
(a) a white ball,
(b) a yellow or a black ball,
(c) a ball which is not red.

8. (a) A bag contains 5 red balls, 6 green balls and 2 black balls. Find the probability of selecting:
    (i) a red ball   (ii) a green ball.
   (b) One black ball is removed from the bag. Find the new probability of selecting:
    (i) a red ball   (ii) a black ball.

9. A bag contains 12 white balls, 12 green balls and 12 purple balls. After 3 white balls, 4 green balls and 9 purple balls have been removed, what is the probability that the next ball to be selected will be white?

10. A large firm employs 3750 people. One person is chosen at random. What is the probability that that person's birthday is on a Monday in the year 2000?

11. The numbering on a set of 28 dominoes is as follows:

6	6	6	6	6	6	6		5	5	5
6	5	4	3	2	1	0		5	4	3

5	5	5		4	4	4	4	4		3	3
2	1	0		4	3	2	1	0		3	2

3	3		2	2	2		1	1		0
1	0		2	1	0		1	0		0

(a) What is the probability of drawing a domino from a full set with:
    (i) at least one six on it?
    (ii) at least one four on it?
    (iii) at least one two on it?
(b) What is the probability of drawing a 'double' from a full set?
(c) If I draw a double five which I do not return to the set, what is the probability of drawing another domino with a five on it?

Example

A fair dice is rolled 240 times. How many times would you expect to roll a number greater than 4?

We can roll a 5 or a 6 out of the six equally likely outcomes.

∴ p(number greater than 4) $= \frac{2}{6} = \frac{1}{3}$.

Expected number of successes = (probability of a success)
×(number of trials)

Expected number of scores greater than 4 $= \frac{1}{3} \times 240$
$= 80$

Exercise 3

1. A fair dice is rolled 300 times. How many times would you expect to roll:
   (a) an even number
   (b) a 'six'?

2. The spinner shown has four equal sectors. How many 3's would you expect in 100 spins?

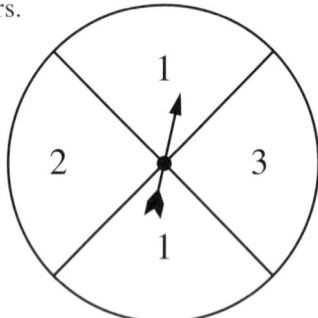

3. About one in eight of the population is left-handed. How many left-handed people would you expect to find in a firm employing 400 people?

4. A bag contains a large number of marbles of which one in five is red. If I randomly select one marble on 200 occasions how many times would I expect to select a red marble?

5. The spinner shown is used for a simple game. A player pays 10c and then spins the pointer, winning the amount indicated.
   (a) What is the probability of winning nothing?
   (b) If the game is played by 200 people how many times would you expect the 50c to be won?

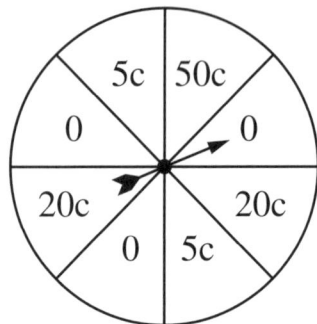

6. The numbered cards are shuffled and put into a pile.

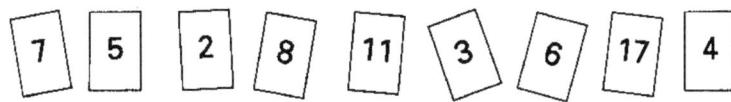

One card is selected at random and not replaced. A second card is then selected.
(a) If the first card was the '11' find the probability of selecting an even number with the second draw.
(b) If the first card was an odd number, find the probability of selecting another odd number.

8.2 Exclusive events

Events are *mutually exclusive* if they cannot occur at the same time.

Examples
- Selecting an ace } from a
  Selecting a ten   } pack of cards

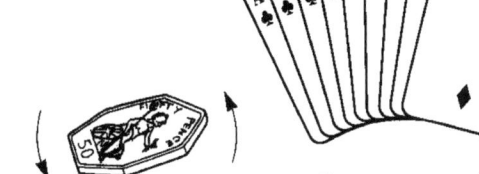

- Tossing a 'head'
  Tossing a 'tail'

- Getting a total of 5 on two dice
  Getting a total of 7 on two dice

The total sum of the probabilities of mutually exclusive events is 1.

The probability of something happening is 1 minus the probability of it not happening.

Example
Every day Anna has the choice of going to work by bus, by train or by taxi.
The probability of choosing to go by bus is 0·5 and the probability of choosing to go by train is 0·3. Find:
(a) the probability of choosing not to go by train
(b) the probability of choosing to go by taxi

The three events 'going by bus', 'going by train' and 'going by taxi' are mutually exclusive.

(a) p(not going by train) $= 1 - p$(going by train)
$= 1 - 0 \cdot 3$
$= 0 \cdot 7$
(b) The sum of the probabilities is 1.
∴ p(going by taxi) $= 1 - (0 \cdot 5 + 0 \cdot 3)$
$= 0 \cdot 2$

Exercise 4

1. A bag contains a large number of balls including some red balls. The probability of selecting a red ball is $\frac{1}{5}$. What is the probability of selecting a ball which is not red?

2. A bag contains 7 white balls, 4 blue balls and 9 yellow balls. Find the probability of selecting:
   (a) a white ball
   (b) a ball which is not white..

3. On a roulette wheel the probability of getting '21' is $\frac{1}{36}$. What is the probability of not getting '21'?

4. A motorist does a survey at some traffic lights on his way to work every day. He finds that the probability that the lights are 'red' when he arrives is 0·24. What is the probability that the lights are not 'red'?

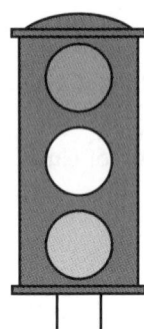

5. Government birth statistics show that the probability of a woman giving birth to a boy is 0·506.
   What is the probability of having a girl?

6. The spinner has 8 equal sectors.
   Find the probability of:
   (a) spinning a 5
   (b) not spinning a 5
   (c) spinning a 2
   (d) not spinning a 2
   (e) spinning a 7
   (f) not spinning a 7.

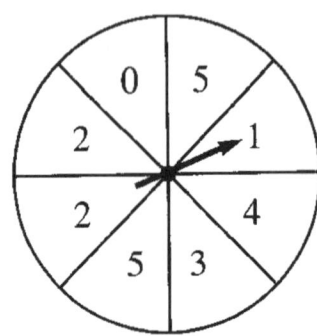

7. A bag contains a large number of balls coloured red, white, black or green. The probabilities of selecting each colour are as follows:

colour	red	white	black	green
probability	0·3	0·1		0·3

Find the probability of selecting a ball:
(a) which is black
(b) which is not white.

8. In a survey the number of people in cars is recorded.
   When a car passes the school gates the probability of having
   1, 2, 3, ... occupants is as follows.

number of people	1	2	3	4	more than 4
probability	0·42	0·23		0·09	0·02

   (a) Find the probability that the next car past the school gates
       contains: (i) three people   (ii) less than 4 people.
   (b) One day 2500 cars passed the gates. How many of the cars
       would you expect to have 2 people inside?

Revision exercise 8A

1. A bag contains 3 red balls and 5 white balls.
   Find the probability of selecting:
   (a) a red ball,   (b) a white ball.

2. A box contains 2 yellow discs, 4 blue discs
   and 5 green discs. Find the probability of
   selecting:
   (a) a yellow disc,   (b) a green disc,
   (c) a blue or a green disc.

3. When two dice are thrown simultaneously,
   what is the probability of obtaining the
   same number on both dice?

4. A coin is tossed four times. What is the
   probability of obtaining at least three
   'heads'?

5. Two dice are thrown. What is the
   probability that the *product* of the numbers
   on top is:
   (a) 12,   (b) 4,   (c) 11?

6. A bag contains a large
   number of discs of which one
   in six is gold. If I randomly
   select one disc on 300
   occasions, how many times
   would I expect to select a
   gold disc?

7. (a) What is the probability of
       getting a 6 with this
       spinner?

   (b) Draw a spinner like this
       with 8 equal sectors. Shade
       some sectors so that the
       chance of getting a shaded
       sector is three times the
       chance of getting a white sector.

   (c) This spinner has some
       1s, 2s and 3s written
       in the sectors. The
       chance of getting a 2
       is twice the chance of
       getting a 3. The
       chance of getting a 1
       is three times the chance of getting a 3.
       Draw the spinner and replace the
       question marks with the correct number
       of 1s, 2s and 3s.

   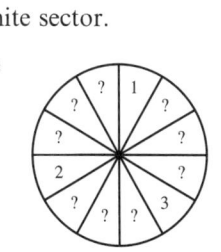

8. Cards with numbers 1, 2, 3, 4, 5, 6, 7, 8, 9,
   10 are shuffled and then placed face down in
   a line. The cards are then turned over one at
   a time from the left. In this example the first
   card is a '4'.

   Find the probability that the next card
   turned over will be:
   (a) 7   (b) a number higher than 4.

9. Suppose the second card is a 1

   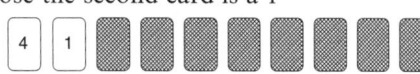

   Find the probability that the next card will be:
   (a) the 6   (b) an even number
   (c) higher than 1.

Examination exercise 8B

1. Sian has three cards, two of them black and one red. She places them side by side, in random order, on a table. One possible arrangement is

    Red,   Black,   Black

    (a) Write down the other possible arrangements.
    (b) Find the probability that the two black cards are next to each other. Give your answer as a fraction. [J 95 1]

2.

    (a) Margaret chooses a card at random from the six cards shown in the diagram.
    What is the probability that the card is:
    (i) an A,
    (ii) an A or a U,
    (iii) an E?
    (b) From the six cards, the card B is removed. Paul chooses a card at random from the five remaining cards.
    What is the probability that the card is an A? [N 95 1]

3. A bag contains 5 black beads, 7 white beads and 4 blue beads.
    (a) Mohini picks a bead at random. What is the probability that it is:
    (i) black
    (ii) not black?
    (b) One of the 16 beads is lost. The probability that Mohini picks a black bead is now $\frac{1}{3}$. What can you say about the colour of the lost bead? [N 98 1]

4. Seat tickets are numbered from 106 to 133 **inclusive**.
    (a) How many tickets are there?
    (b) A ticket is chosen at random.
    What is the probability that the number on the ticket is:
    (i) odd,
    (ii) a multiple of 5,
    (iii) more than 100?
    (c) From another set of tickets numbered from 106 to x **inclusive**, a ticket is chosen at random.
    The probability that it is odd is $\frac{4}{9}$.
    What is the number x? [N 97 1]

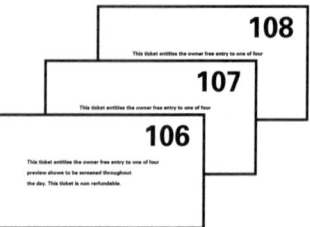

9 SHAPE AND SPACE 3

9.1 Similar shapes

If one shape is an enlargement of another, the two shapes are mathematically *similar*.

The two triangles A and B are similar if they have the same angles.

For other shapes to be similar, not only must corresponding angles be equal, but also corresponding edges must be in the same proportion.

The two quadrilaterals C and D are similar. All the edges of shape D are twice as long as the edges of shape C.

The two rectangles E and F are not similar even though they have the same angles.

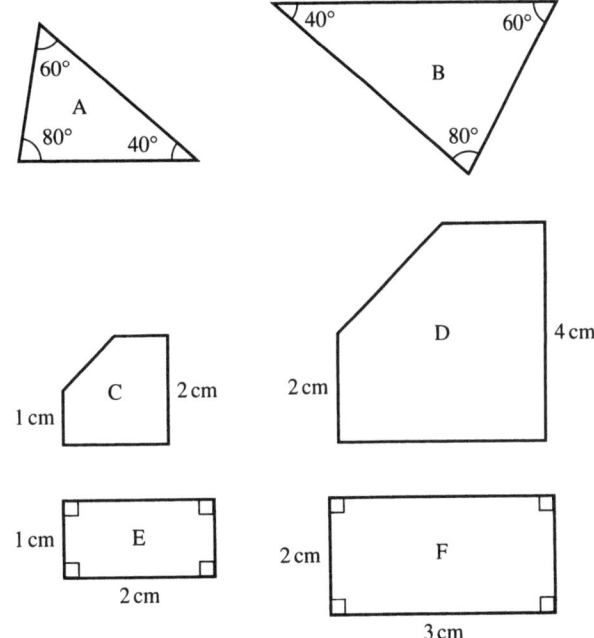

Example

The triangles below are similar.
Find x.

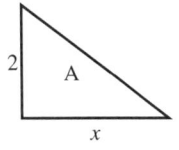 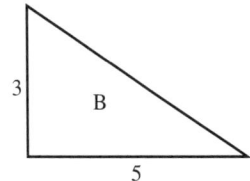

Triangle B is an enlargement of triangle A.

The scale factor of the enlargement is $\frac{3}{2}$.

Corresponding sides are in the same ratio.

$$\therefore \frac{x}{5} = \frac{2}{3}$$

$$x = \frac{2}{3} \times 5$$

$$x = 3\frac{1}{3}$$

Exercise 1

1. Which of the shapes B, C, D is/are similar to shape A?

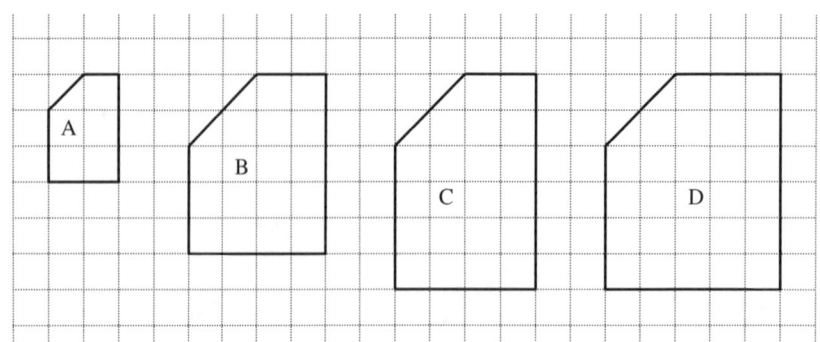

In Questions **2** to **7**, find the sides marked with letters; all lengths are given in cm. The pairs of shapes are similar.

2.
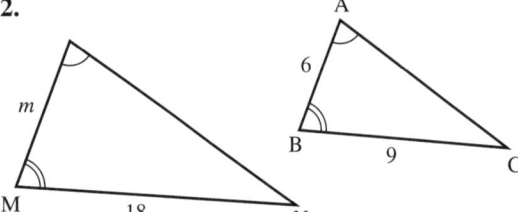

3.
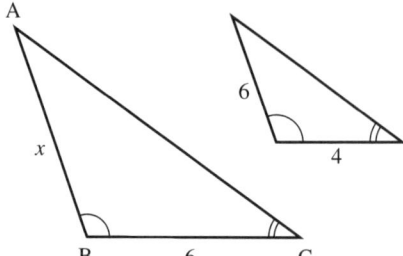

4.
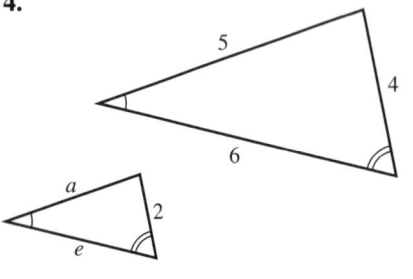

5.
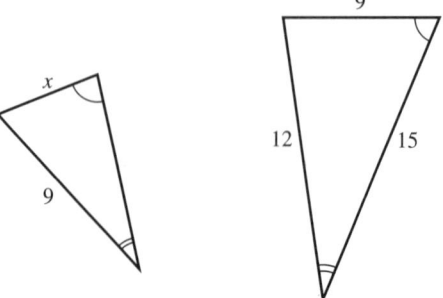

6.
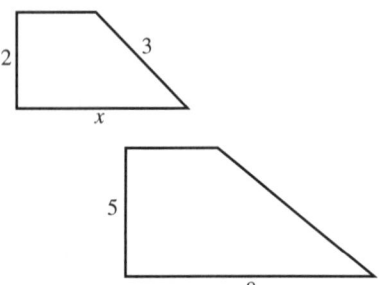

7.
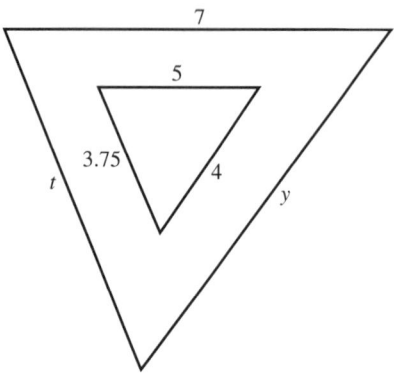

8. Picture B is an enlargement of picture A. Calculate the length x.

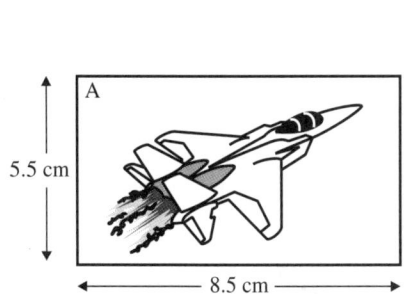

9. The drawing shows a rectangular picture 16 cm × 8 cm surrounded by a border of width 4 cm.
   Are the two rectangles similar?

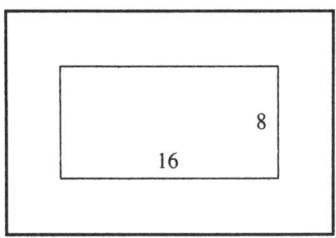

10. Which of the following *must* be similar to each other?
    (a) Two equilateral triangles. (b) Two rectangles. (c) Two isosceles triangles.
    (d) Two squares. (e) Two regular pentagons. (f) Two kites.
    (g) Two rhombuses. (h) Two circles.

11.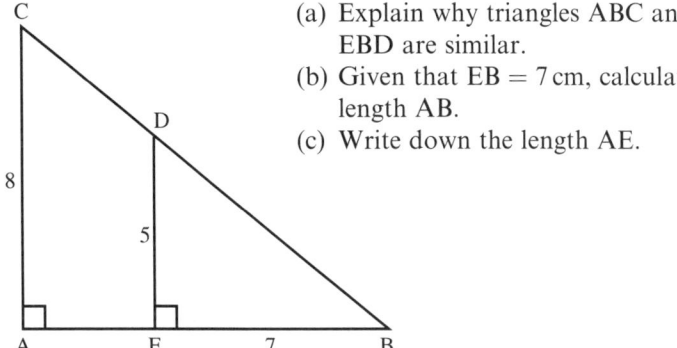
    (a) Explain why triangles ABC and EBD are similar.
    (b) Given that EB = 7 cm, calculate the length AB.
    (c) Write down the length AE.

In Questions 12, 13 and 14 use similar triangles to find the sides marked with letters. All lengths are in cm.

12.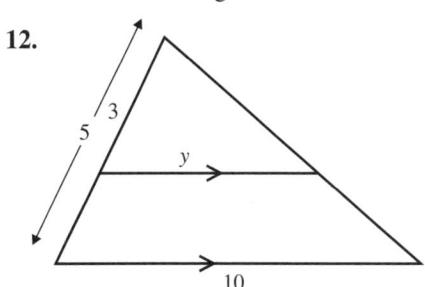

13.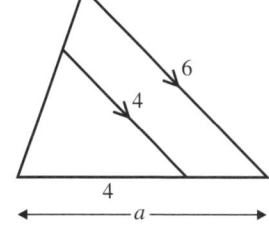

14.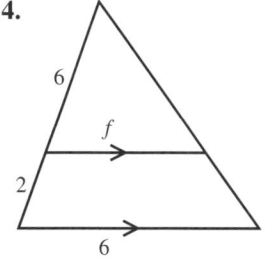

15. A tree of height 4 m casts a shadow of length 6·5 m.
Find the height of a house casting a shadow 26 m long.

16. A small cone is cut from a larger cone.
Find the radius of the smaller cone.

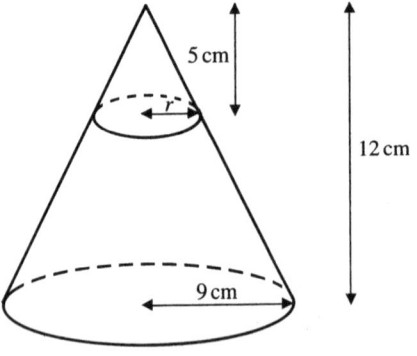

17. The diagram shows the side view of a swimming pool being filled with water. Calculate the length x.

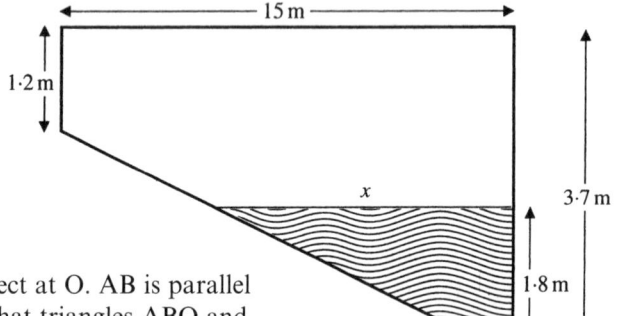

18. The diagonals of a trapezium ABCD intersect at O. AB is parallel to DC, AB = 3 cm and DC = 6 cm. Show that triangles ABO and CDO are similar. If CO = 4 cm and OB = 3 cm, find AO and DO.

9.2 Trigonometry

Trigonometry is used to calculate sides and angles in triangles. The triangle must have a right angle.

The side opposite the right angle is called the *hypotenuse* (H). It is the longest side.

The side opposite the marked angle is called the opposite (O).

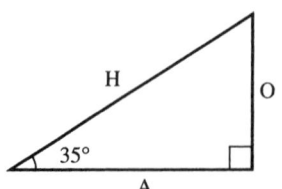

The other side is called the adjacent (A).

Consider two triangles, one of which is an enlargement of the other.
It is clear that, for the angle 30°, the

$$\text{ratio} = \frac{\text{opposite}}{\text{hypotenuse}} = \frac{6}{12} = \frac{2}{4} = \frac{1}{2}$$

This is the same for both triangles.

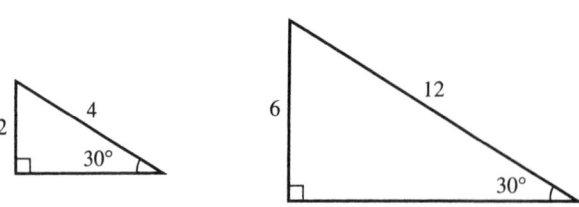

Sine, cosine, tangent

Three important ratios are defined for angle x.

$\sin x = \dfrac{O}{H}$ $\cos x = \dfrac{A}{H}$ $\tan x = \dfrac{O}{A}$

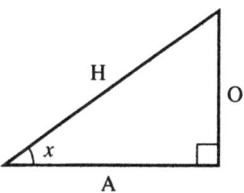

It is important to get the letters in the correct positions.

Some people find a simple sentence helpful where the first letters of each word describe sine, cosine or tangent, Hypotenuse, Opposite or Adjacent. An example is:

Silly Old Harry Caught A Herring Trawling Off Afghanistan

e.g. SOH $\sin = \dfrac{O}{H}$

Finding the length of a side

Example

Find the length of l.

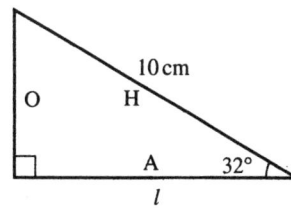

$\cos 32° = \dfrac{A}{H} = \dfrac{l}{10}$

$\therefore\ l = 10 \times \cos 32°$

$l = 8{\cdot}48$ cm (to 3 s.f.)

Exercise 2

Find the lengths marked with letters. All lengths are in cm.
Give answers correct to 3 s.f.

1.
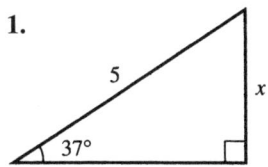

2.
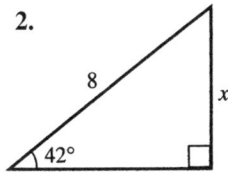

3.
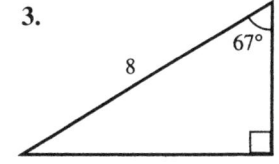

4.
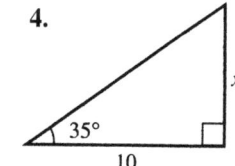

5.
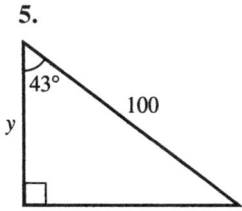

6.
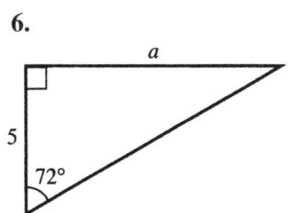

7.
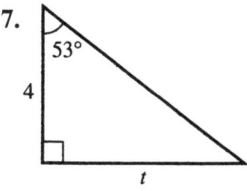

8.
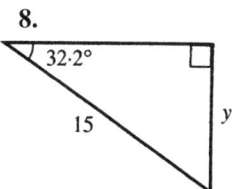

9.
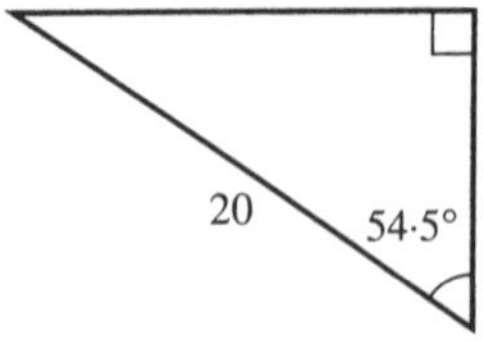

10.
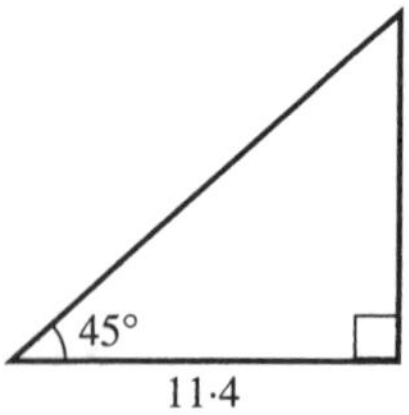

11.
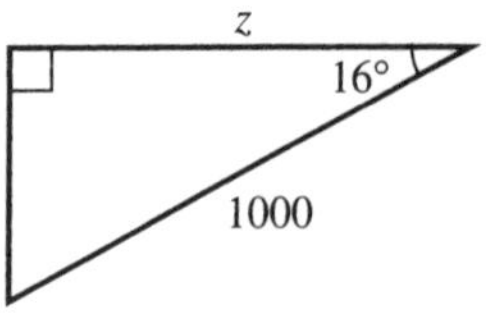

12.
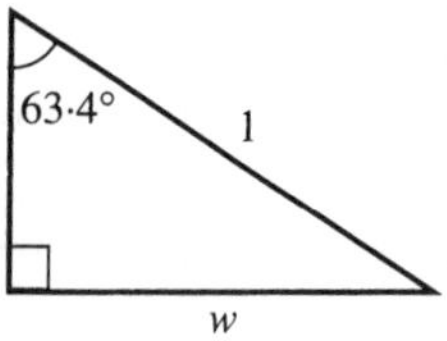

13.
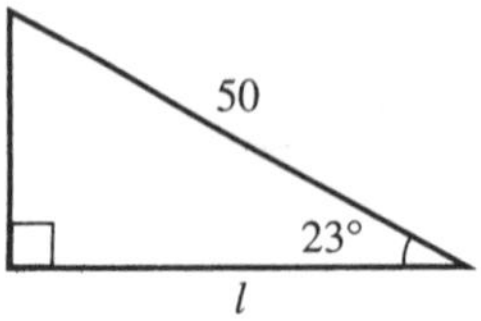

14.
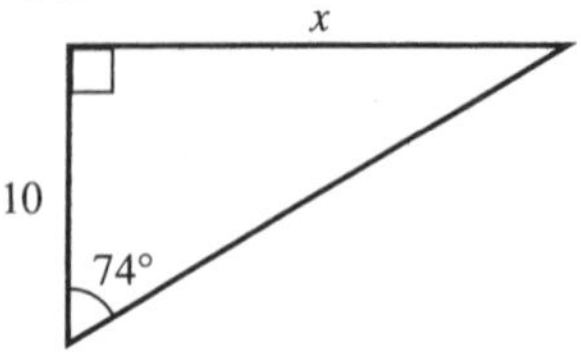

15.
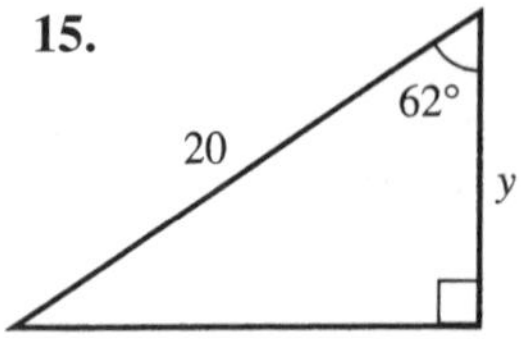

16.
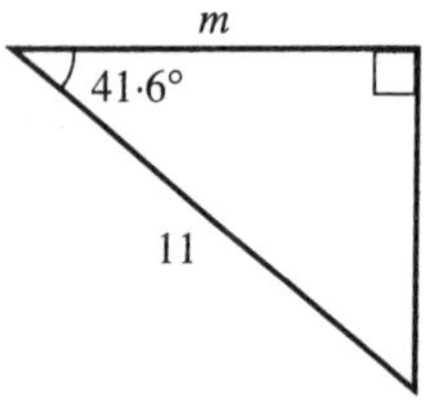

17.
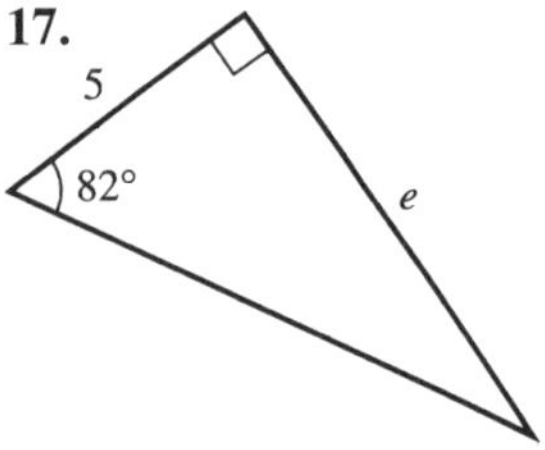

18.
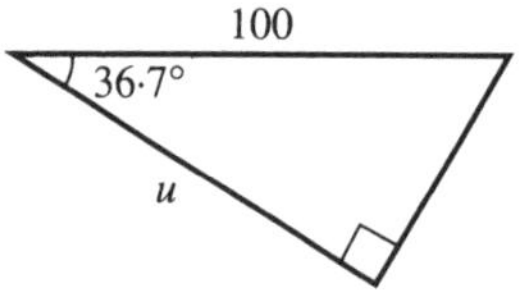

19.
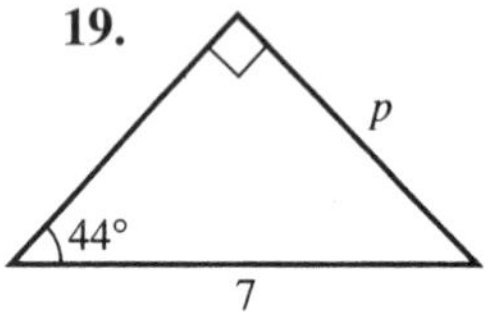

20.
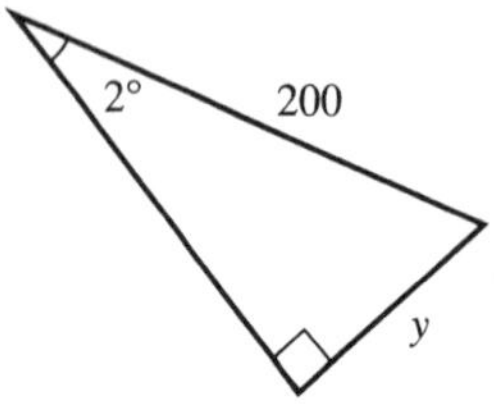

Example

Find the length of x.

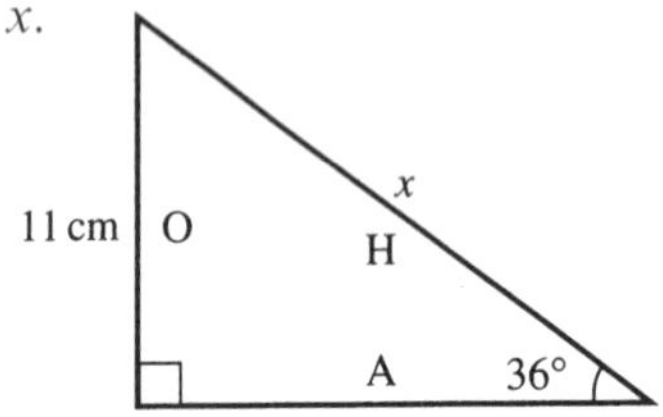

$$\sin 36° = \frac{O}{H} = \frac{11}{x}$$

$$\therefore\ x \sin 36° = 11 \quad \text{[Multiply by } x\text{]}$$

$$x = \frac{11}{\sin 36°} = 18{\cdot}7 \text{ cm (to 3 s.f.)}$$

Exercise 3

This exercise is more difficult. Find the lengths marked with letters.

1.
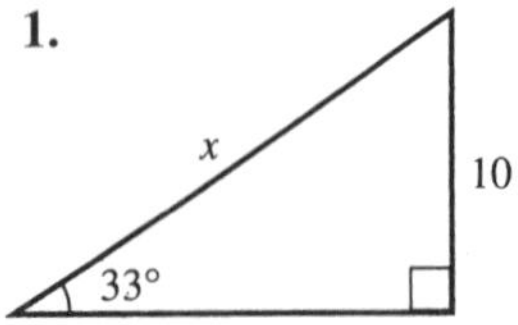

2.
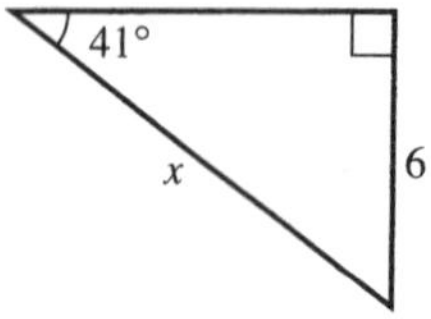

3.
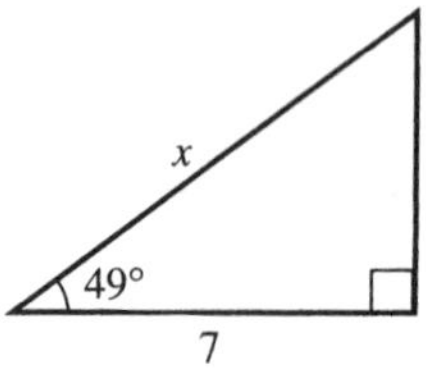

4.
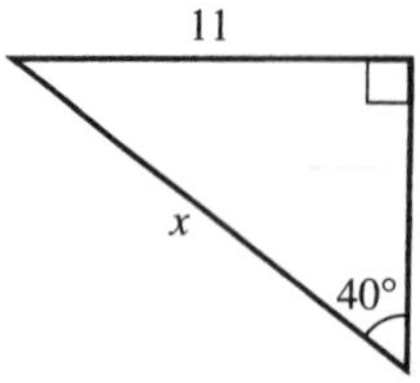

5.
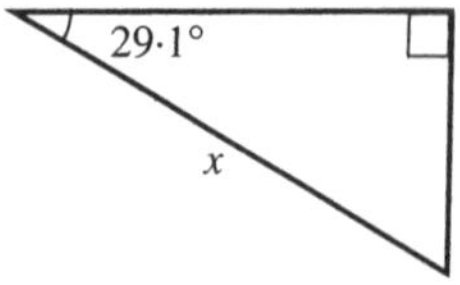

6.
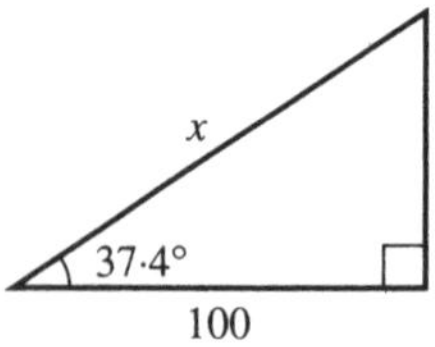

7.
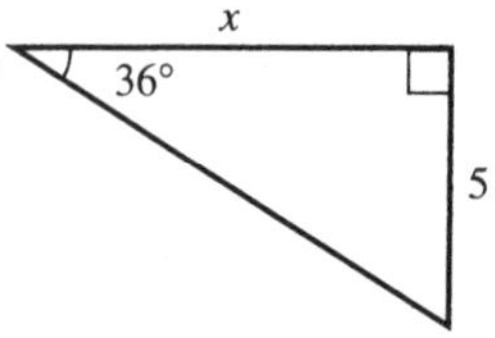

8.
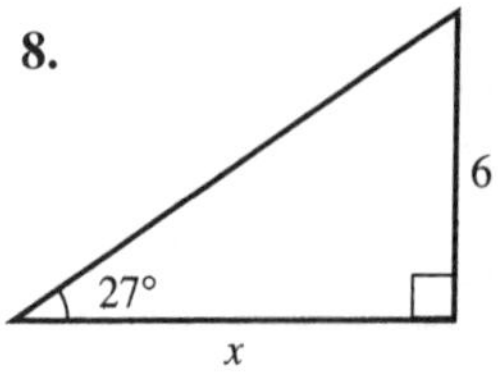

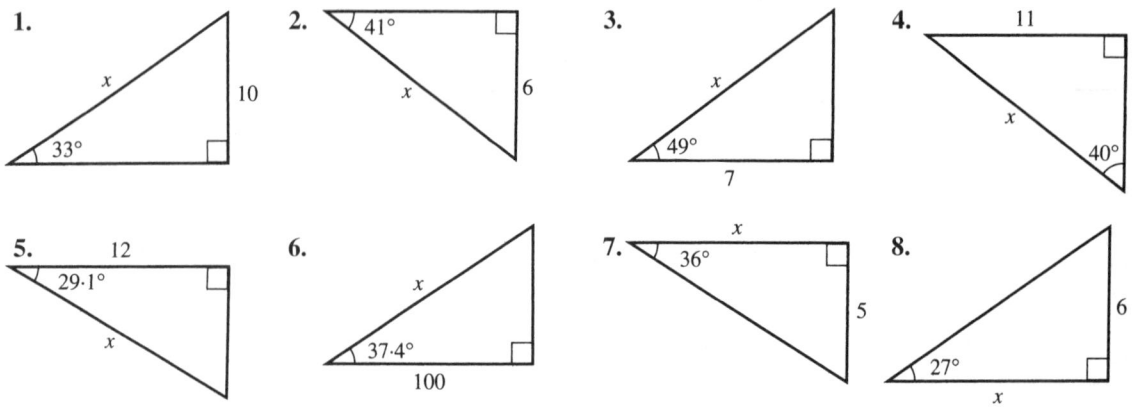

Trigonometry 241

9.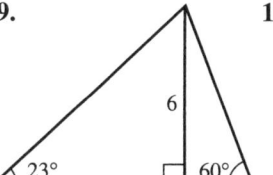
10.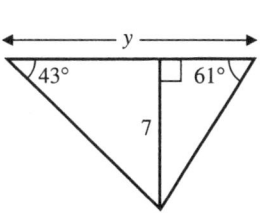
11.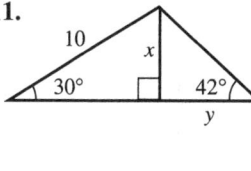
12.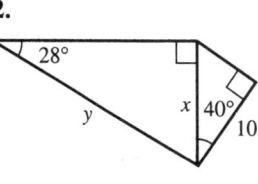

13.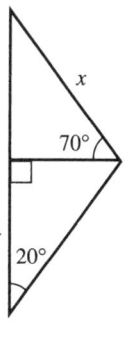
14.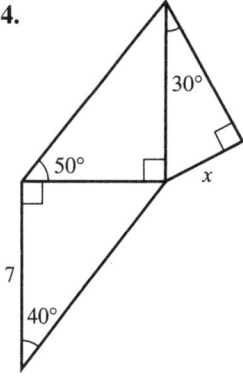
15.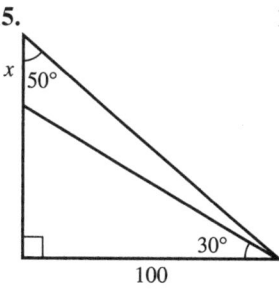
16.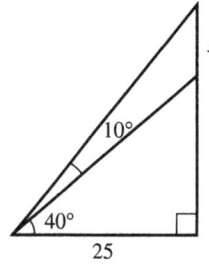

Finding angles

Example
Find the angle x.

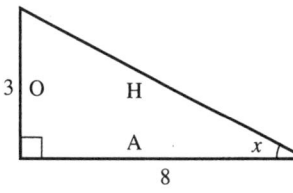

$\tan x = \dfrac{O}{A} = \dfrac{3}{8}$

$\tan x = 0{\cdot}375$

$\quad x = 20{\cdot}6°$ (to 1 d.p.)

On a calculator:

[3] [÷] [8] [=] [INV] [tan]

Exercise 4
Find the angles marked with letters. Give the answers correct to 1 d.p.

1.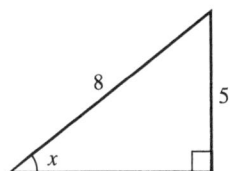
2.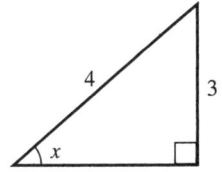
3.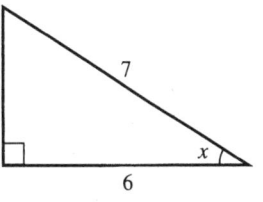
4.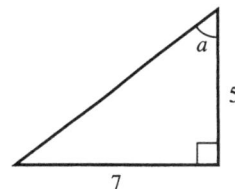

5.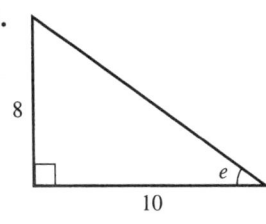
6.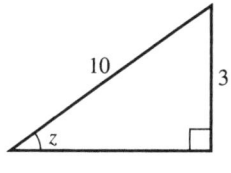
7.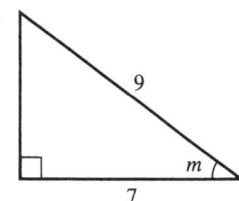
8.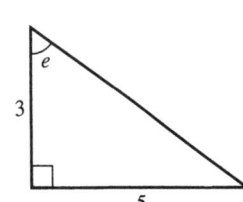

242 Shape and space 3

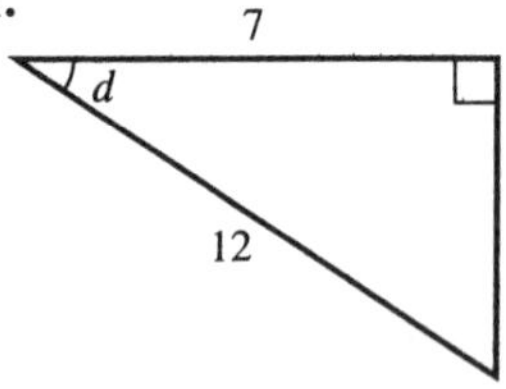

9.
33, 50, y (right angle)

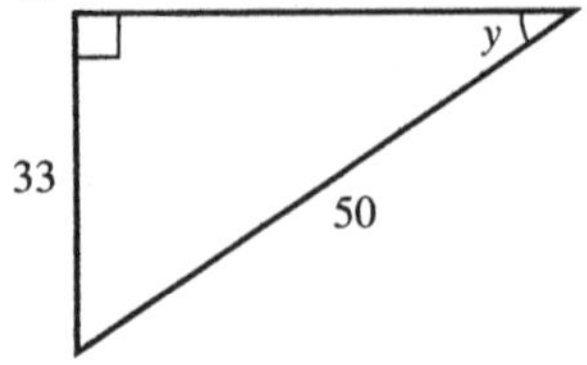

10.
9, 8, c (right angle)

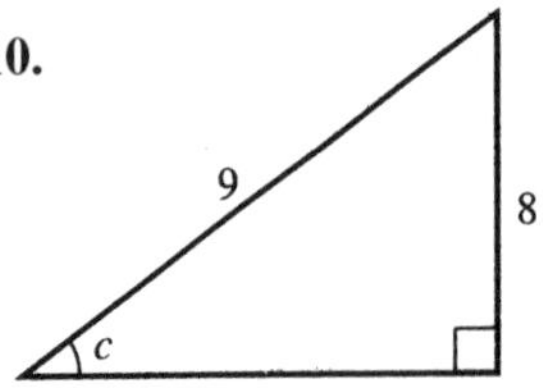

11.
7, 12, d (right angle)

12.
9, 4, w (right angle)

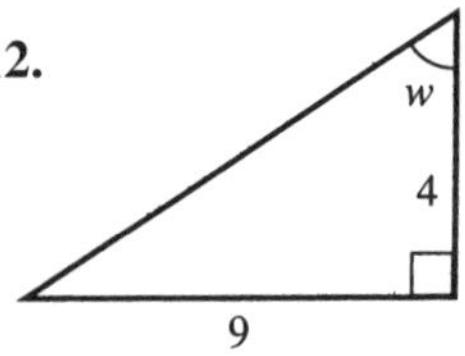

13.
2, 3, k (right angle)

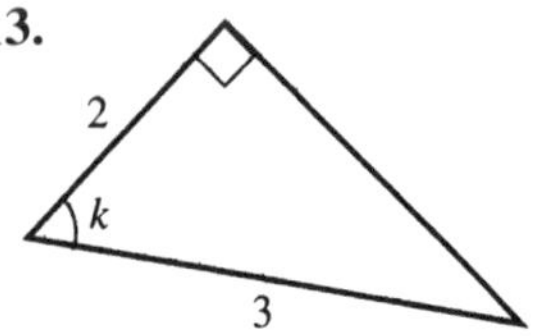

14.
w, 1000, 215 (right angle)

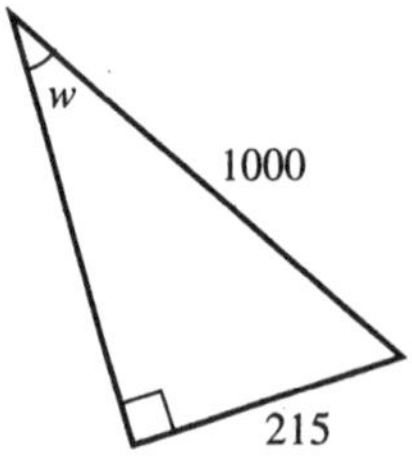

15.
13, 4, e (right angle)

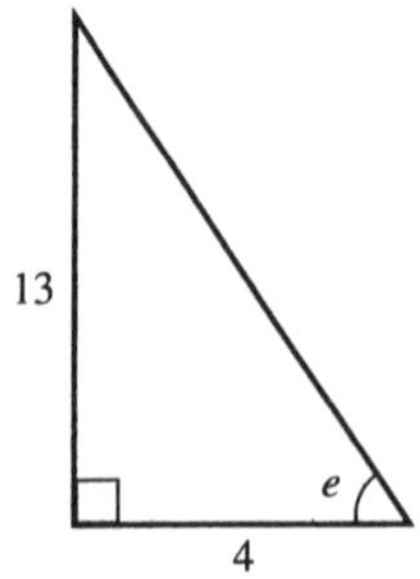

16.
11, 6, z (right angle)

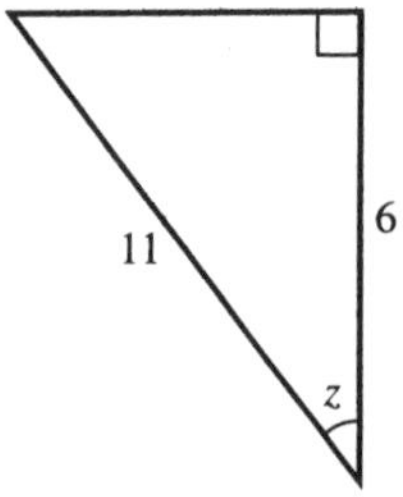

17.
5, 3, 4, x (right angle)

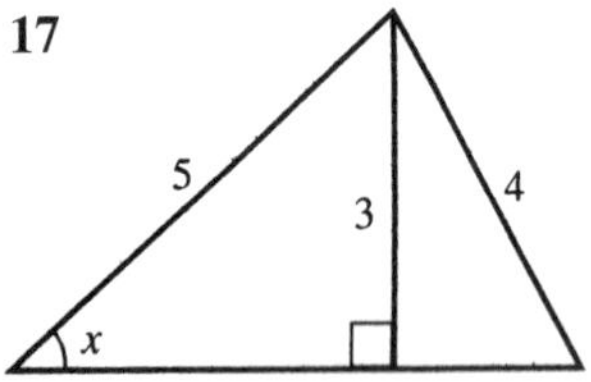

18.
y, 6, 4, 5 (right angle)

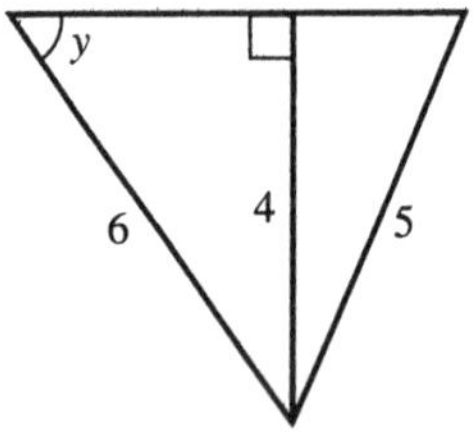

19.
7, 5, 6, x (right angle)

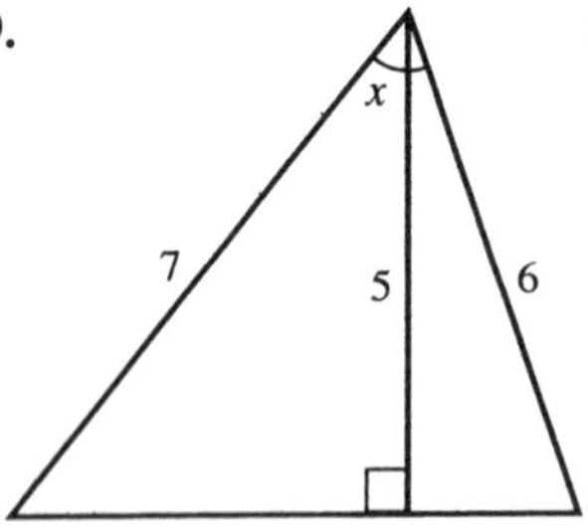

20.
11, 7, 9, a (right angle)

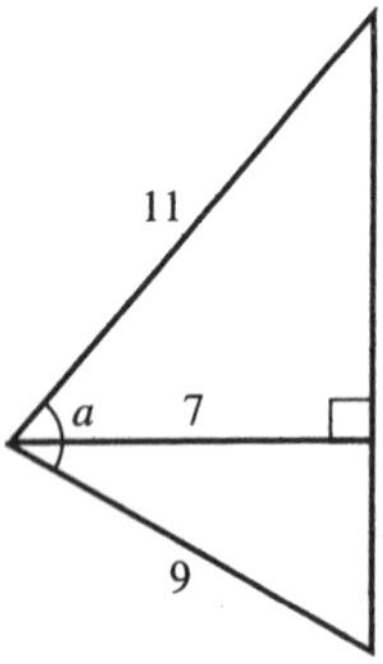

Angles of elevation and depression

(a)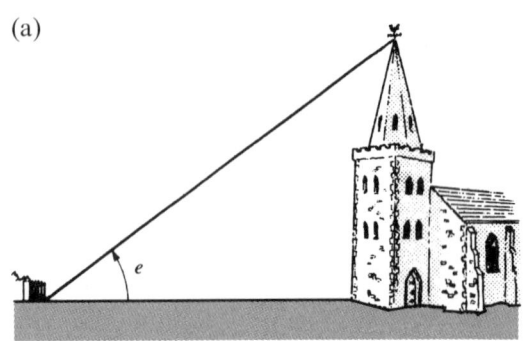

e is the angle of elevation of the Steeple from the Gate.

(b)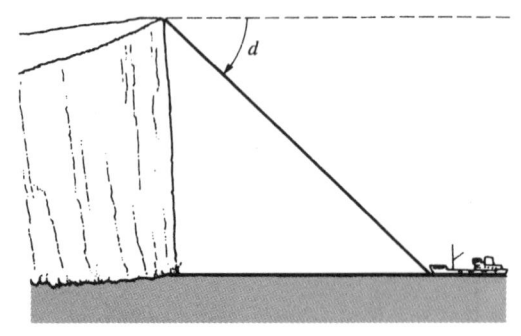

d is the angle of depression of the Boat from the Cliff top.

Exercise 5

Begin each question by drawing a large clear diagram.

1. A ladder of length 4 m rests against a vertical wall so that the base of the ladder is 1·5 m from the wall.
   Calculate the angle between the ladder and the ground.

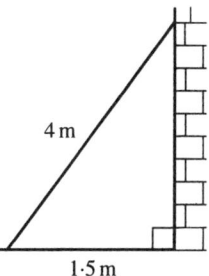

2. A ladder of length 4 m rests against a vertical wall so that the angle between the ladder and the ground is 66°. How far up the wall does the ladder reach?

3. From a distance of 20 m the angle of elevation to the top of a tower is 35°.

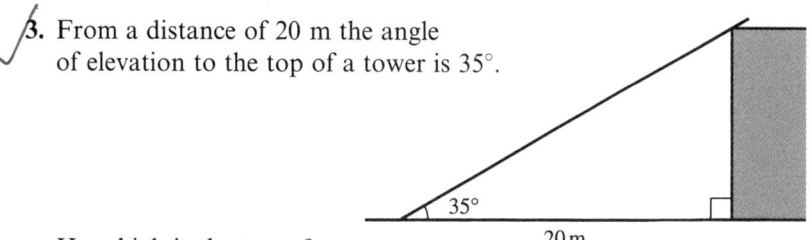

   How high is the tower?

4. A point G is 40 m away from a building, which is 15 m high. What is the angle of elevation to the top of the building from G?

5. A boy is flying a kite from a string of length 60 m. If the string is taut and makes an angle of 71° with the horizontal, what is the height of the kite? Ignore the height of the boy.

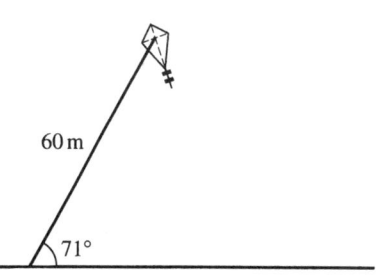

6. A straight tunnel is 80 m long and slopes downwards at an angle of 11° to the horizontal. Find the vertical drop in travelling from the top to the bottom of the tunnel.

7. The frame of a bicycle is shown in the diagram. Find the length of the cross bar.

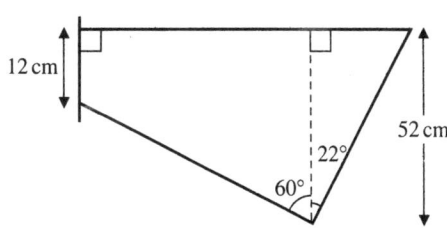

8. Calculate the length x.

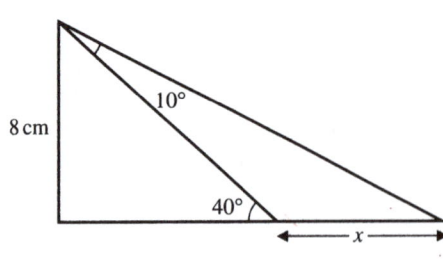

9. AB is a chord of a circle of radius 5 cm and centre O.
   The perpendicular bisector of AB passes through O and also bisects the angle AOB.
   If $A\hat{O}B = 100°$ calculate the length of the chord AB.

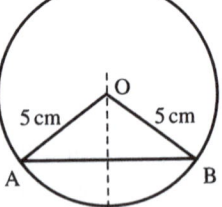

10. A ship is due South of a lighthouse L. It sails on a bearing of 055° for a distance of 80 km until it is due East of the lighthouse.

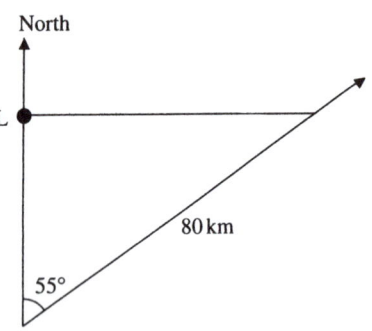

How far is it now from the lighthouse?

11. A ship is due South of a lighthouse. It sails on a bearing of 071° for a distance of 200 km until it is due East of the lighthouse. How far is it now from the lighthouse?

12. A ship is due North of a lighthouse. It sails on a bearing of 200° at a speed of 15 km/h for five hours until it is due West of the lighthouse. How far is it now from the lighthouse?

13. From the top of a tower of height 75 m, a guard sees two prisoners, both due East of him.

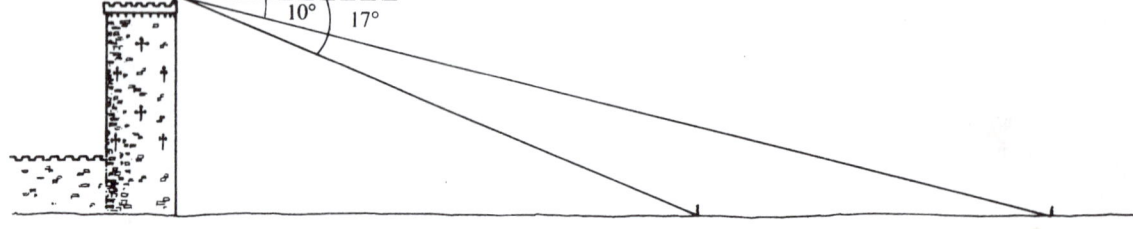

If the angles of depression of the two prisoners are 10° and 17°, calculate the distance between them.

14. From a horizontal distance of 40 m, the angle of elevation to the top of a building is 35·4°. From a point further away from the building the angle of elevation is 20·2°.
What is the distance between the two points?

15. An isosceles triangle has sides of length 8 cm, 8 cm and 5 cm. Find the angle between the two equal sides.

16. The angles of an isosceles triangle are 66°, 66° and 48°. If the shortest side of the triangle is 8·4 cm, find the length of one of the two equal sides.

17. A regular pentagon is inscribed in a circle of radius 7 cm. Find the angle a and then the length of a side of the pentagon.

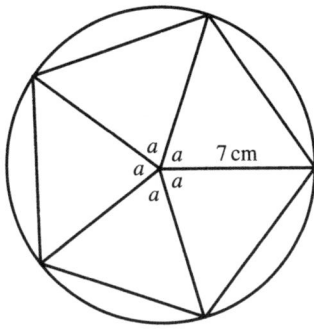

18. Find the acute angle between the diagonals of a rectangle whose sides are 5 cm and 7 cm.

Revision exercise 9A

1. Given BD = 1 m, calculate the length AC.

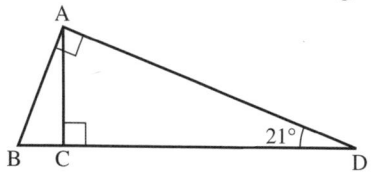

2. Calculate the side or angle marked with a letter.

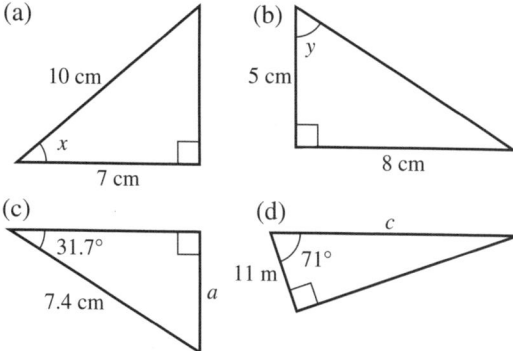

3. Rectangle B is an enlargement of rectangle A.
   Calculate the length x.

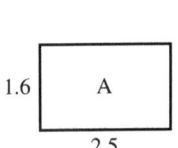
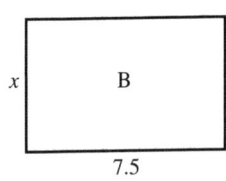

4. The pairs of shapes are similar. Find the sides marked with letters.

   (a)

   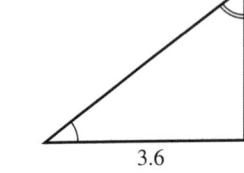

   (b)

   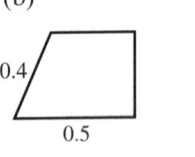

5. The sides of triangle ABC are each increased by 1 cm to form triangle DEF. Are triangles ABC and DEF similar?

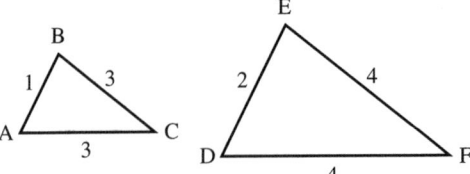

6. Calculate the length x.

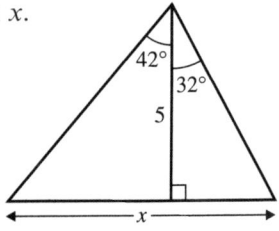

7. (a) Explain why triangles PQR and PST are similar.
   (b) Given that PQ = 8 cm, calculate the length QS.

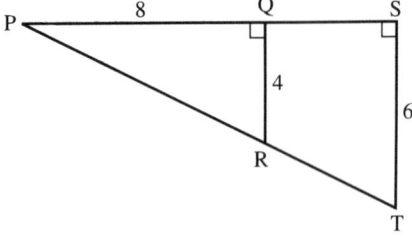

Examination exercise 9B

1.

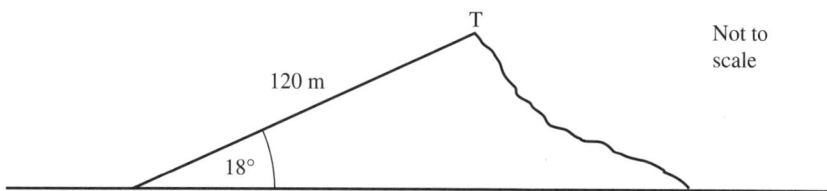

The diagram shows a sand dune in the desert.
The top of the sand dune, T, is 120 metres up a slope of 18°.
Calculate the vertical height of the sand dune.

[J 98 1]

2. Find the value of

(a) 8 sin 43·8°, (b) $\dfrac{7\cdot63 + 1\cdot28}{\cos 72°}$.

[J 97 1]

3. Calculate angle x.

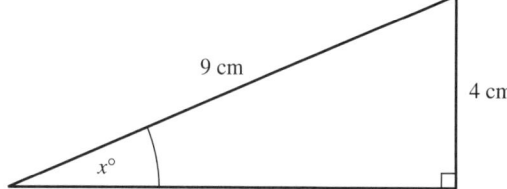

[J 95 1]

4. (a)

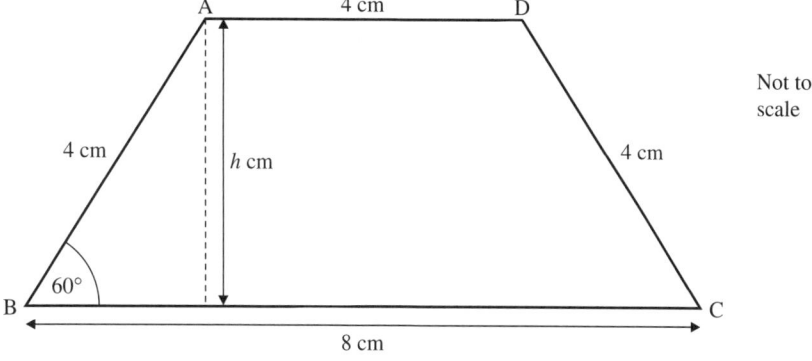

(i) Calculate the height, h cm, of the trapezium.
(ii) Find the area of the trapezium.
(b) The diagram on the right shows how three trapeziums, identical to the one in part (a), form an equilateral triangle.
(i) What would be the length of each side of the equilateral triangle?
(ii) What would be the area of the triangle?

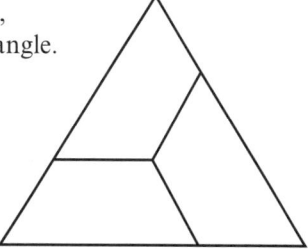

[J 96 3]

5.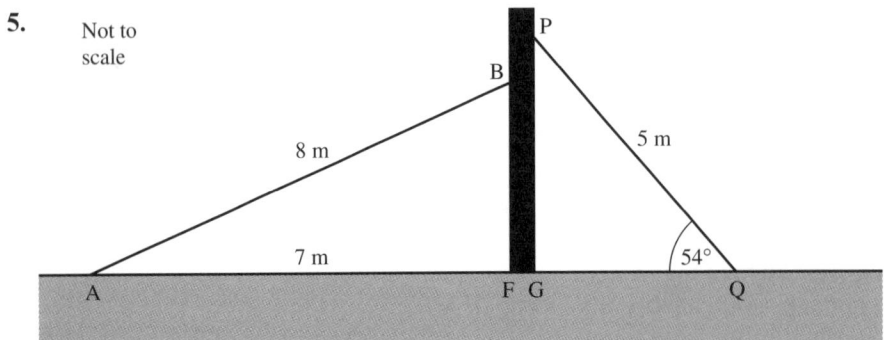

AB and PQ are two straight wires supporting a vertical pole on horizontal ground.
(a) A is 7 m from F, the foot of the pole. The length of the wire AB is 8 m. Calculate the angle BAF.
(b) The length of the wire PQ is 5 m and angle PQG = 54°. Calculate PG, the height of P above the ground.
(c) The width of the pole, FG, is 0.35 m. Calculate the distance between A and Q.

[N 96 3]

6. (a) The length of Enrico's stride is 75 centimetres.
   (i) He takes 114 strides to walk the length of a soccer pitch. What is the length of the soccer pitch? Give your answer in metres.
   (ii) Enrico now walks the width of the pitch, a distance of 50 metres. Calculate the number of full strides that he takes.
   (iii) Enrico's stride of 75 cm was measured to the nearest 5 cm. Copy and complete the inequality below.
   _____ cm ⩽ Enrico's stride < _____ cm
(b) In fact, the soccer pitch is 85 metres long and 50 metres wide.

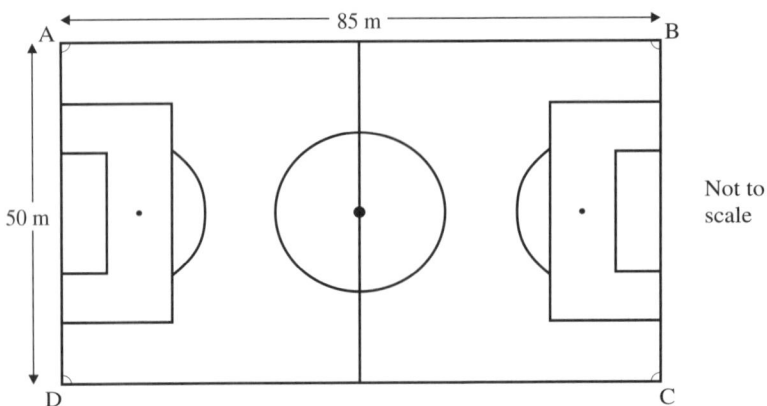

Calculate (i) the length of the diagonal AC,
          (ii) angle BAC.

[N 95 3]

10 NUMBER 3

10.1 Powers and roots

Indices

- Indices are used as a neat way of writing products.
  $2 \times 2 \times 2 \times 2 = 2^4$ [2 to the power 4]
  $5 \times 5 \times 5 = 5^3$ [5 to the power 3]
  $3 \times 3 \times 3 \times 3 \times 3 \times 10 \times 10 = 3^5 \times 10^2$
- Numbers like $3^2, 5^2, 11^2$ are *square numbers*.
  Numbers like $2^3, 6^3, 11^3$ are *cube numbers*.
- To work out $3 \cdot 2^2$ on a calculator, press $\boxed{3 \cdot 2} \; \boxed{x^2}$
  To work out 3^4 on a calculator, press $\boxed{3} \; \boxed{x^y} \; \boxed{4} \; \boxed{=}$

Exercise 1

Write in a form using indices.
1. $3 \times 3 \times 3 \times 3$
2. 5×5
3. $6 \times 6 \times 6$
4. $10 \times 10 \times 10 \times 10 \times 10$
5. $1 \times 1 \times 1 \times 1 \times 1 \times 1 \times 1$
6. $8 \times 8 \times 8 \times 8$
7. $7 \times 7 \times 7 \times 7 \times 7 \times 7$
8. $2 \times 2 \times 2 \times 5 \times 5$
9. $3 \times 3 \times 7 \times 7 \times 7 \times 7$
10. $3 \times 3 \times 10 \times 10 \times 10$
11. $5 \times 5 \times 5 \times 5 \times 11 \times 11$
12. $2 \times 3 \times 2 \times 3 \times 3$
13. $5 \times 3 \times 3 \times 5 \times 5$
14. $2 \times 2 \times 3 \times 3 \times 3 \times 11 \times 11$
15. Work out without a calculator:
    (a) 4^2 (b) 6^2 (c) 10^2 (d) 3^3 (e) 10^3
16. Use the $\boxed{x^2}$ button to work out:
    (a) 9^2 (b) 21^2 (c) $1 \cdot 2^2$ (d) $0 \cdot 2^2$ (e) $3 \cdot 1^2$
    (f) 100^2 (g) 25^2 (h) $8 \cdot 7^2$ (i) $0 \cdot 9^2$ (j) $81 \cdot 4^2$
17. Find the areas of these squares.
    (a) 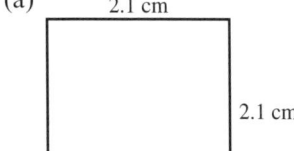 2.1 cm, 2.1 cm
    (b) 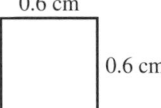 0.6 cm, 0.6 cm
    (c)  14 m, 14 m

18. Write in index form:
  (a) $a \times a \times a$
  (b) $n \times n \times n \times n$
  (c) $s \times s \times s \times s \times s$
  (d) $p \times p \times q \times q \times q$
  (e) $b \times b \times b \times b \times b \times b \times b$

19. Use the $\boxed{x^y}$ button to work out:
  (a) 6^3
  (b) 2^8
  (c) 3^5
  (d) 10^5
  (e) 4^3
  (f) $0 \cdot 1^3$
  (g) $1 \cdot 7^4$
  (h) $3^4 \times 7$
  (i) $5^3 \times 10$

20. A scientist has a dish containing 10^9 germs.
One day later there are 10 times as many germs.
How many germs are in the dish now?

21. A large garden has 2^8 daisies growing on the grass.
A weedkiller removes half of the daisies.
How many daisies are left?

22. A maths teacher won the National Lottery and, as a leaving present, she decided to set a final test to a class of 25 children. The person coming 25th won 2c, the 24th won 4c, the 23rd 8c, the 22nd 16c and so on, doubling the amount each time.
  (a) Write 2, 4, 8, 16 as powers of 2.
  (b) How much, in dollars, would be given to the person who came first in the test?

23. Abdul says 'If you work out the product of any four consecutive numbers and then add one, the answer will be square number.'
For example: $1 \times 2 \times 3 \times 4 = 24$
  $24 + 1 = 25$, which is a square number.
Is Abdul right? Test his theory on four (or more) sets of four consecutive numbers.

Square roots and cube roots

A square has an area of $529 \, \text{cm}^2$.
How long is a side of the square?
In other words, what number *multiplied by itself* makes 529?

The answer is the **square root** of 529.

On a calculator press $\boxed{\sqrt{}}$ $\boxed{529}$ $\boxed{=}$

[On older calculators you may need to press $\boxed{529}$ $\boxed{\sqrt{}}$]

The side of the square is 23 cm.

A cube has a volume of $512 \, \text{cm}^3$.
How long is a side of the cube?

The answer is the **cube root** of 512.

On a calculator press $\boxed{\sqrt[3]{}}$ $\boxed{512}$ $\boxed{=}$

The side of the cube is 8 cm. [Check $8 \times 8 \times 8 = 512$]

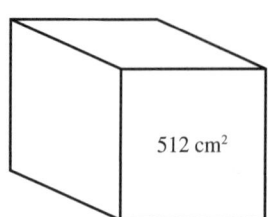

529 cm²

?

512 cm²

Exercise 2

1. Work out, without a calculator:
   (a) $\sqrt{16}$ (b) $\sqrt{36}$ (c) $\sqrt{1}$ (d) $\sqrt{100}$

2. Find the sides of the squares.
   (a) 81 cm²   (b) 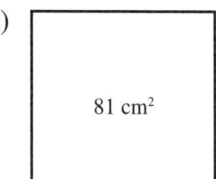 49 cm²   (c) 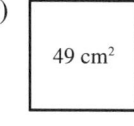 144 cm²

3. Use a calculator to find the following, correct to 1 d.p.
   (a) $\sqrt{10}$ (b) $\sqrt{29}$ (c) $\sqrt{107}$ (d) $\sqrt{19.7}$
   (e) $\sqrt{2406}$ (f) $\sqrt{58.6}$ (g) $\sqrt{0.15}$ (h) $\sqrt{0.727}$

4. A square photo has an area of 150 cm². Find the length of each side of the photo, correct to the nearest mm.

5. A square field has an area of 20 hectares. How long is each side of the field, correct to the nearest metre?
   [1 hectare = 10 000 m²]

6. The area of square A is equal to the sum of the areas of squares B and C. Find the length x, correct to 1 d.p.

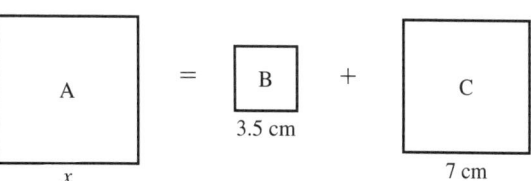

7. Find the following:
   (a) $\sqrt[3]{64}$ (b) $\sqrt[3]{125}$ (c) $\sqrt[3]{1000}$

8. A cube has a volume of 200 cm³. Find the length of the side of the cube, correct to 1 d.p.

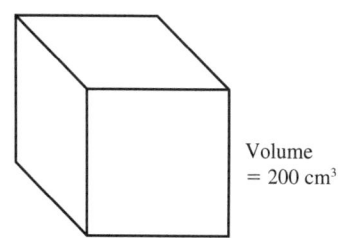

Volume = 200 cm³

Negative indices and the zero index

- Look at this sequence.

  2^4 2^3 2^2 2^1 2^0 2^{-1} From left to right the index goes down by one each time.

  $16 \longrightarrow 8 \longrightarrow 4 \longrightarrow 2 \longrightarrow \boxed{1} \longrightarrow \boxed{\tfrac{1}{2}}$ Also we divide by two each time.

  we see that $2^0 = 1$
  and that $2^{-1} = \tfrac{1}{2}$

- In general $x^0 = 1$ for any value of x which is not zero.
  In general $x^{-1} = \dfrac{1}{x}$
  Also $2^{-3} = \dfrac{1}{2^3}$ $\qquad 3^{-2} = \dfrac{1}{3^2}$
- The *reciprocal* of 3 is $\dfrac{1}{3}$. The reciprocal of 10 is $\dfrac{1}{10}$.
- The reciprocal of n is $\dfrac{1}{n}$ (which can be written n^{-1}).

Exercise 3

In Questions **1** to **12**, work out the value of the number given.

1. 3^{-1}
2. 4^{-1}
3. 10^{-1}
4. 1^{-4}
5. 3^{-2}
6. 4^{-2}
7. 10^{-2}
8. 8^0
9. 7^{-2}
10. $(-6)^0$
11. 9^{-2}
12. 1^{-7}

In Questions **13** to **32** answer 'true' or 'false'.

13. $2^3 = 8$
14. $3^2 = 6$
15. $5^3 = 125$
16. $2^{-1} = \frac{1}{2}$
17. $10^{-2} = \frac{1}{20}$
18. $3^{-3} = \frac{1}{9}$
19. $2^2 > 2^3$
20. $2^3 < 3^2$
21. $2^{-2} > 2^{-3}$
22. $3^{-2} < 3^3$
23. $1^9 = 9$
24. $(-3)^2 = -9$
25. $5^{-2} = \frac{1}{10}$
26. $10^{-3} = \frac{1}{1000}$
27. $10^{-2} > 10^{-3}$
28. $5^{-1} = 0 \cdot 2$
29. $10^{-1} = 0 \cdot 1$
30. $2^{-2} = 0 \cdot 25$
31. $5^0 = 1$
32. $16^0 = 0$

Multiplying and dividing

Example

To multiply powers of the same number *add* the indices.

$3^2 \times 3^4 = (3 \times 3) \times (3 \times 3 \times 3 \times 3) = 3^6$
$2^3 \times 2^2 = (2 \times 2 \times 2) \times (2 \times 2) = 2^5$
$7^3 \times 7^5 = 7^8$ [add the indices]

To divide powers of the same number *subtract* the indices.

$2^4 \div 2^2 = \dfrac{2 \times 2 \times 2 \times 2}{2 \times 2} = 2^2$

$\left. \begin{array}{l} 5^6 \div 5^2 = 5^4 \\ 7^8 \div 7^3 = 7^5 \end{array} \right\}$ [subtract the indices]

Exercise 4

Write in a more simple form.

1. $5^2 \times 5^4$
2. $6^3 \times 6^2$
3. $10^4 \times 10^5$
4. $7^5 \times 7^3$
5. $3^6 \times 3^4$
6. $8^3 \times 8^3$
7. $2^3 \times 2^{10}$
8. $3^6 \times 3^{-2}$
9. $5^4 \times 5^{-1}$
10. $7^7 \times 7^{-3}$
11. $5^{-3} \times 5^5$
12. $3^{-2} \times 3^{-2}$
13. $6^{-3} \times 6^8$
14. $5^{-2} \times 5^{-8}$
15. $7^{-3} \times 7^9$
16. $7^4 \div 7^2$
17. $6^7 \div 6^2$
18. $8^5 \div 8^4$
19. $5^{10} \div 5^2$
20. $10^7 \div 10^5$
21. $9^6 \div 9^8$
22. $3^8 \div 3^{10}$
23. $2^6 \div 2^2$
24. $3^3 \div 3^5$
25. $7^2 \div 7^8$
26. $3^{-2} \div 3^2$
27. $5^{-3} \div 5^2$
28. $8^{-1} \div 8^4$
29. $5^{-4} \div 5^1$
30. $6^2 \div 6^{-2}$
31. $3^4 \div 3^4$
32. $5^2 \div 5^2$
33. $\dfrac{3^4 \times 3^5}{3^2}$
34. $\dfrac{2^8 \times 2^4}{2^5}$
35. $\dfrac{7^3 \times 7^3}{7^4}$
36. $\dfrac{5^9 \times 5^{10}}{5^{20}}$

Further rules of indices

To raise a power of a number to a further power, **multiply** the indices.

Example 1
$(x^2)^3 = x^2 \times x^2 \times x^2 = x^6$ $\qquad (a^4)^2 = a^4 \times a^4 = a^8$

Example 2
$3x^2 \times 4x^5 = 12x^7$
$\qquad\quad (3 \times 4) \quad (2+5)$

$4a^7 \times 5a^2 = 20a^9$
$\qquad\quad (4 \times 5) \quad (7+2)$

$12x^5 \div 3x^2 = 4x^3$
$\qquad (12 \div 3) \quad (5-2)$

$(3a^2) = 3^3 \times a^6 = 27a^6$

Exercise 5

Write in a more simple form.

1. $(3^3)^2$
2. $(5^4)^3$
3. $(7^2)^5$
4. $(8^2)^{10}$
5. $(x^2)^3$
6. $(a^5)^3$
7. $(n^7)^2$
8. $(y^3)^3$
9. $(2^{-1})^2$
10. $(3^{-2})^2$
11. $(7^{-1})^{-2}$
12. $(x^3)^{-1}$
13. $2a^2 \times 3a^3$
14. $4n^3 \times 5n^1$
15. $7x^4 \times 2x$
16. $8y^5 \times 3y^2$
17. $5n^3 \times n^4$
18. $6y^2 \times 2$
19. $3p^3 \times 3p^2$
20. $2p \times 5p^5$
21. $(2x^2)^3$
22. $(3a^2)^3$
23. $(4y^3)^2$
24. $(5x^4)^2$

Solve the equations for x.

25. $x^2 = 9$
26. $x^5 = 1$
27. $x^3 = 27$
28. $x^5 = 0$
29. $2^x = 8$
30. $3^x = 3$
31. $5^x = 25$
32. $10^x = 1000$
33. $2^x = \frac{1}{2}$
34. $4^x = \frac{1}{4}$
35. $7^x = 1$
36. $3x^3 = 24$
37. $10x^3 = 640$
38. $2x^3 = 0$
39. $10^x = 0 \cdot 1$
40. $5^x = 1$

10.2 Standard form

When dealing with either very large or very small numbers, it is not convenient to write them out in full in the normal way. It is better to use standard form. Most calculators represent large and small numbers in this way.

This calculator shows $2 \cdot 3 \times 10^8$.

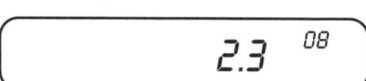

The number $a \times 10^n$ is in standard form when $1 \leq a < 10$ and n is a positive or negative integer.

Example

Write the following numbers in standard form:

(a) $2000 = 2 \times 1000 = 2 \times 10^3$

(b) $150 = 1 \cdot 5 \times 100 = 1 \cdot 5 \times 10^2$

(c) $0 \cdot 0004 = 4 \times \dfrac{1}{10\,000} = 4 \times 10^{-4}$

Exercise 6

Write the following numbers in standard form:

1. 4000
2. 500
3. 70 000
4. 60
5. 2400
6. 380
7. 46 000
8. 46
9. 900 000
10. 2560
11. 0·007
12. 0·0004
13. 0·0035
14. 0·421
15. 0·000 055
16. 0·01
17. 564 000
18. 19 million

19. The population of China is estimated at 1 100 000 000. Write this in standard form.

20. A hydrogen atom weighs 0·000 000 000 000 000 000 000 001 67 grams. Write this weight in standard form.

21. The area of the surface of the Earth is about 510 000 000 km². Express this in standard form.

22. A certain virus is 0·000 000 000 25 cm in diameter. Write this in standard form.

23. Avogadro's number is 602 300 000 000 000 000 000 000. Express this in standard form.

24. The speed of light is 300 000 km/s. Express this speed in cm/s in standard form.

25. A very rich oil sheikh leaves his fortune of $3·6 × 10⁸ to be divided between his 100 relatives.

How much does each person receive? Give the answer in standard form.

Example 1

Work out $1500 \times 8\,000\,000$.

$$1500 \times 8\,000\,000 = (1·5 \times 10^3) \times (8 \times 10^6)$$
$$= 12 \times 10^9$$
$$= 1·2 \times 10^{10}$$

Notice that we multiply the numbers and the powers of 10 separately.

Example 2
Many calculators have an [EXP] button which is used for standard form.

(a) To enter 1.6×10^7 into the calculator:

press [1.6] [EXP] [7]

(b) To enter 3.8×10^{-3}

press [3.8] [EXP] [3] [+/−]

(c) To calculate $(4.9 \times 10^{11}) \div (3.5 \times 10^{-4})$:

[4.9] [EXP] [11] [÷] [3.5] [EXP] [4] [+/−] [=]

The answer is 1.4×10^{15}.

Exercise 7

In Questions **1** to **22**, give the answer in standard form.

1. 5000×3000
2. $60\,000 \times 5000$
3. $0.000\,07 \times 400$
4. $0.0007 \times 0.000\,01$
5. $8000 \div 0.004$
6. $(0.002)^2$
7. 150×0.0006
8. $0.000\,033 \div 500$
9. $0.007 \div 20\,000$
10. $(0.0001)^4$
11. $(2000)^3$
12. $0.005\,92 \div 8000$
13. $(1.4 \times 10^7) \times (3.5 \times 10^4)$
14. $(8.8 \times 10^{10}) \div (2 \times 10^{-2})$
15. $(1.2 \times 10^{11}) \div (8 \times 10^7)$
16. $(4 \times 10^5) \times (5 \times 10^{11})$
17. $(2.1 \times 10^{-3}) \times (8 \times 10^{15})$
18. $(8.5 \times 10^{14}) \div 2000$
19. $(3.3 \times 10^{12}) \times (3 \times 10^{-5})$
20. $(2.5 \times 10^{-8})^2$
21. $(1.2 \times 10^5)^2 \div (5 \times 10^{-3})$
22. $(6.2 \times 10^{-4}) \times (1.1 \times 10^{-3})$

23. If $a = 512 \times 10^2$
    $b = 0.478 \times 10^6$
    $c = 0.0049 \times 10^7$
    arrange a, b and c in order of size (smallest first).

24. If the number 2.74×10^{15} is written out in full, how many zeros follow the 4?

25. If the number 7.31×10^{-17} is written out in full, how many zeros would there be between the decimal point and the first significant figure?

26. If $x = 2 \times 10^5$ and $y = 3 \times 10^{-3}$, find the values of:
    (i) xy
    (ii) $\dfrac{x}{y}$

27. Oil flows through a pipe at a rate of $40\,\text{m}^3/\text{s}$. How long will it take to fill a tank of volume $1.2 \times 10^5\,\text{m}^3$?

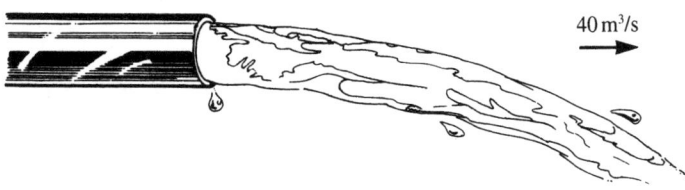

40 m³/s

28. Given that $L = 2\sqrt{\dfrac{a}{k}}$, find the value of L in standard form when $a = 4\cdot 5 \times 10^{12}$ and $k = 5 \times 10^{7}$.

29. A light year is the distance travelled by a beam of light in a year. Light travels at a speed of approximately 3×10^5 km/s.
(a) Work out the length of a light year in km.
(b) Light takes about 8 minutes to reach the Earth from the Sun. How far is the Earth from the Sun in km?

30. Percy, a rather mean gardener, is trying to estimate the number of seeds in a 50 gram packet. He counts 30 seeds from the packet and finds their weight is 6×10^{-2} grams.

Use his sample to estimate the total number of seeds in the packet.

10.3 Fractions

Common fractions are added or subtracted from one another directly only when they have a common denominator.

Example

(a) $\dfrac{3}{4} + \dfrac{2}{5} = \dfrac{15}{20} + \dfrac{8}{20}$
$= \dfrac{23}{20}$
$= 1\dfrac{3}{20}$

(b) $2\dfrac{3}{8} - 1\dfrac{5}{12} = \dfrac{19}{8} - \dfrac{17}{12}$
$= \dfrac{57}{24} - \dfrac{34}{24}$
$= \dfrac{23}{24}$

(c) $\dfrac{2}{5} \times \dfrac{6}{7} = \dfrac{12}{35}$

(d) $2\dfrac{2}{5} \div 6 = \dfrac{12}{5} \div \dfrac{6}{1}$
$= \dfrac{12}{5} \times \dfrac{1}{6} = \dfrac{2}{5}$

Exercise 8

Work out and simplify where possible.

1. $\dfrac{1}{3} + \dfrac{1}{2}$
2. $\dfrac{1}{3} \times \dfrac{1}{2}$
3. $\dfrac{1}{3} \div \dfrac{1}{2}$
4. $\dfrac{3}{4} - \dfrac{1}{3}$
5. $\dfrac{3}{4} \times \dfrac{1}{3}$
6. $\dfrac{3}{4} \div \dfrac{1}{3}$
7. $\dfrac{2}{5} + \dfrac{1}{2}$
8. $\dfrac{2}{5} \times \dfrac{1}{2}$
9. $\dfrac{2}{5} \div \dfrac{1}{2}$
10. $\dfrac{3}{7} + \dfrac{1}{2}$
11. $\dfrac{3}{7} \times \dfrac{1}{2}$
12. $\dfrac{3}{7} \div \dfrac{1}{2}$
13. $\dfrac{5}{8} - \dfrac{1}{4}$
14. $\dfrac{5}{8} \times \dfrac{1}{4}$
15. $\dfrac{5}{8} \div \dfrac{1}{4}$
16. $\dfrac{1}{6} + \dfrac{4}{5}$
17. $\dfrac{1}{6} \times \dfrac{4}{5}$
18. $\dfrac{1}{6} \div \dfrac{4}{5}$
19. $\dfrac{3}{7} + \dfrac{1}{3}$
20. $\dfrac{3}{7} \times \dfrac{1}{3}$
21. $\dfrac{3}{7} \div \dfrac{1}{3}$
22. $\dfrac{4}{5} - \dfrac{1}{4}$
23. $\dfrac{4}{5} \times \dfrac{1}{4}$
24. $\dfrac{4}{5} \div \dfrac{1}{4}$
25. $\dfrac{2}{3} - \dfrac{1}{8}$
26. $\dfrac{2}{3} \times \dfrac{1}{8}$
27. $\dfrac{2}{3} \div \dfrac{1}{8}$
28. $\dfrac{5}{9} + \dfrac{1}{4}$
29. $\dfrac{5}{9} \times \dfrac{1}{4}$
30. $\dfrac{5}{9} \div \dfrac{1}{4}$
31. $2\dfrac{1}{2} - \dfrac{1}{4}$
32. $2\dfrac{1}{2} \times \dfrac{1}{4}$
33. $2\dfrac{1}{2} \div \dfrac{1}{4}$
34. $3\dfrac{3}{4} - \dfrac{2}{3}$
35. $3\dfrac{3}{4} \times \dfrac{2}{3}$
36. $3\dfrac{3}{4} \div \dfrac{2}{3}$
37. $\dfrac{\frac{1}{2}+\frac{1}{5}}{\frac{1}{2}-\frac{1}{5}}$
38. $\dfrac{\frac{3}{4}-\frac{1}{3}}{\frac{3}{4}+\frac{1}{3}}$
39. $\dfrac{2\frac{1}{4} \times \frac{4}{5}}{\frac{3}{5}-\frac{1}{2}}$
40. $\dfrac{3\frac{1}{2} \times 2\frac{2}{3}}{\frac{1}{2}+1\frac{1}{18}}$

Exercise 9

1. Arrange the fractions in order of size:
   (a) $\frac{7}{12}, \frac{1}{2}, \frac{2}{3}$
   (b) $\frac{3}{4}, \frac{2}{3}, \frac{5}{6}$
   (c) $\frac{1}{3}, \frac{17}{24}, \frac{5}{8}, \frac{3}{4}$
   (d) $\frac{5}{6}, \frac{8}{9}, \frac{11}{12}$

2. Find the fraction which is mid-way between the two fractions given:
   (a) $\frac{2}{5}, \frac{3}{5}$
   (b) $\frac{5}{8}, \frac{7}{8}$
   (c) $\frac{2}{3}, \frac{3}{4}$
   (d) $\frac{1}{3}, \frac{4}{9}$
   (e) $\frac{4}{15}, \frac{1}{3}$
   (f) $\frac{3}{8}, \frac{11}{24}$

3. In the equation on the right, all the asterisks stand for the same number. What is the number?
   $$\left[\frac{*}{*} - \frac{*}{6} = \frac{*}{30}\right]$$

4. Work out one-half of one-third of 65% of $360.

5. Find the value of n if
   $(1\frac{1}{3})^n - (1\frac{1}{3}) = \frac{28}{27}$

6. A rubber ball is dropped from a height of 300 cm. After each bounce, the ball rises to $\frac{4}{5}$ of its previous height. How high, to the nearest cm, will it rise after the fourth bounce?

7. Steve Braindead spends his income as follows:
   (a) $\frac{2}{5}$ of his income goes in tax,
   (b) $\frac{2}{3}$ of what is left goes on food, rent and transport,
   (c) he spends the rest on cigarettes, and computer games.
   What fraction of his income is spent on cigarettes, and computer games?

8. A formula used by opticians is
   $$\frac{1}{f} = \frac{1}{u} + \frac{1}{v}$$
   Given that $u = 3$ and $v = 2\frac{1}{2}$, find the exact value of f.

9. A set of drills starts at $\frac{1}{8}$ cm and goes up to $\frac{5}{8}$ cm in steps of $\frac{1}{16}$ cm.
   (a) How many drills are there in the full set?
   (b) Which size is half-way between $\frac{1}{4}$ cm and $\frac{3}{8}$ cm?

10. A fraction is equivalent to $\frac{2}{3}$ and its denominator (bottom number) is 8 more than its numerator (top number). What is the fraction?

11. When it hatches from its egg, the shell of a certain crab is 1 cm across. When fully grown the shell is approximately 10 cm across. Each new shell is one-third bigger than the previous one. How many shells does a fully grown crab have during its life?

12. Figures 1 and 2 show an equilateral triangle divided into thirds and quarters. They are combined in Figure 3. Calculate the fraction of Figure 3 that is shaded.

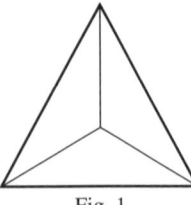
Fig. 1

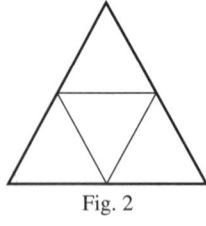
Fig. 2

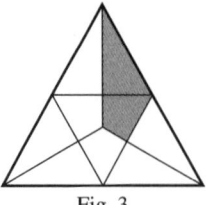
Fig. 3

13. Glass A contains 10 ml of water and glass B contains 100 ml of wine.

    A 10 ml spoonful of wine is taken from glass B and mixed thoroughly with the water in glass A. A 10 ml spoonful of the mixture from A is returned by B. Is there now more wine in the water or more water in the wine?

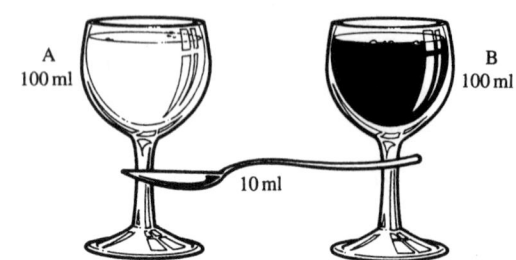

10.4 Negative numbers

- For adding and subtracting use the number line.

Example

Find: (a) $-1 + 4$ (b) $-2 - 3$ (c) $4 - 6$

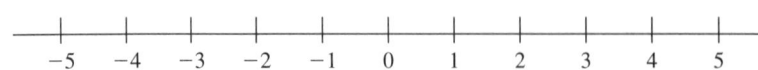

(a) $\quad$ −1 $\quad$ + $\quad$ 4 $\qquad\qquad$ $-1 + 4 = 3$
     start here $\quad$ go right $\quad$ 4 places

(b) $\quad$ −2 $\quad$ − $\quad$ 3 $\qquad\qquad$ $-2 - 3 = -5$
     start here $\quad$ go left $\quad$ 3 places

(c) $\quad$ 4 $\quad$ − $\quad$ 6 $\qquad\qquad$ $4 - 6 = -2$
     start here $\quad$ go left $\quad$ 6 places

When you have two (+) or (−) signs together use this rule:

$\quad$ ++ = + $\qquad$ +− = −

$\quad$ −− = + $\qquad$ −+ = −

Example

(a) $3 - (-6) = 3 + 6 = 9$

(b) $-4 + (-5) = -4 - 5 = -9$

(c) $-5 - (+7) = -5 - 7 = -12$

Exercise 10

Work out:

1. $-6 + 2$
2. $-7 - 5$
3. $-3 - 8$
4. $-5 + 2$
5. $-6 + 1$
6. $8 - 4$
7. $4 - 9$
8. $11 - 19$
9. $4 + 15$
10. $-7 - 10$
11. $16 - 20$
12. $-7 + 2$
13. $-6 - 5$
14. $10 - 4$
15. $-4 + 0$
16. $-6 + 12$
17. $-7 + 7$
18. $2 - 20$
19. $8 - 11$
20. $-6 - 5$
21. $-3 + (-5)$
22. $-5 - (+2)$
23. $4 - (+3)$
24. $-3 - (-4)$
25. $6 - (-3)$
26. $16 + (-5)$
27. $-4 + (-4)$
28. $20 - (-22)$
29. $-6 - (-10)$
30. $95 + (-80)$
31. $-3 - (+4)$
32. $-5 - (+4)$
33. $6 + (-7)$
34. $-4 + (-3)$
35. $-7 - (-7)$
36. $3 - (-8)$
37. $-8 + (-6)$
38. $7 - (+7)$
39. $12 - (-5)$
40. $9 - (+6)$

When two directed numbers with the same sign are multiplied together, the answer is positive.

Example

(a) $+7 \times (+3) = +21$
(b) $-6 \times (-4) = +24$

When two directed numbers with different signs are multiplied together, the answer is negative.

Example

(a) $-8 \times (+4) = -32$
(b) $+7 \times (-5) = -35$
(c) $-3 \times (+2) \times (+5) = -6 \times (+5) = -30$

When dividing directed numbers, the rules are the same as in multiplication.

Example

(a) $-70 \div (-2) = +35$
(b) $+12 \div (-3) = -4$
(c) $-20 \div (+4) = -5$

Exercise 11

1. $-3 \times (+2)$
2. $-4 \times (+1)$
3. $+5 \times (-3)$
4. $-3 \times (-3)$
5. $-4 \times (2)$
6. $-5 \times (3)$
7. $6 \times (-4)$
8. $3 \times (2)$
9. $-3 \times (-4)$
10. $6 \times (-3)$
11. $-7 \times (3)$
12. $-5 \times (-5)$
13. $6 \times (-10)$
14. $-3 \times (-7)$
15. $8 \times (6)$
16. $-8 \times (2)$
17. $-7 \times (6)$
18. $-5 \times (-4)$
19. $-6 \times (7)$
20. $11 \times (-6)$
21. $8 \div (-2)$
22. $-9 \div (3)$
23. $-6 \div (-2)$
24. $10 \div (-2)$
25. $-12 \div (-3)$
26. $-16 \div (4)$
27. $4 \div (-1)$
28. $8 \div (-8)$
29. $16 \div (-8)$
30. $-20 \div (-5)$
31. $-16 \div (1)$
32. $18 \div (-9)$
33. $36 \div (-9)$
34. $-45 \div (-9)$
35. $-70 \div (7)$
36. $-11 \div (-1)$
37. $-16 \div (-1)$
38. $1 \div (-\frac{1}{2})$
39. $-2 \div (\frac{1}{2})$
40. $50 \div (-10)$
41. $-8 \times (-8)$
42. $-9 \times (3)$
43. $10 \times (-60)$
44. $-8 \times (-5)$
45. $-12 \div (-6)$
46. $-18 \times (-2)$
47. $-8 \div (4)$
48. $-80 \div (10)$
49. $-16 \times (-10)$
50. $32 \div (-16)$

Questions on negative numbers are more difficult when the different sorts are mixed together. The remaining questions are given in the form of three short tests.

Test 1

1. $-8 - 8$
2. $-8 \times (-8)$
3. -5×3
4. $-5 + 3$
5. $8 - (-7)$
6. $20 - 2$
7. $-18 \div (-6)$
8. $4 + (-10)$
9. $-2 + 13$
10. $+8 \times (-6)$
11. $-9 + (+2)$
12. $-2 - (-11)$
13. $-6 \times (-1)$
14. $2 - 20$
15. $-14 - (-4)$
16. $-40 \div (-5)$
17. $5 - 11$
18. -3×10
19. $9 + (-5)$
20. $7 \div (-7)$

Test 2

1. $-2 \times (+8)$
2. $-2 + 8$
3. $-7 - 6$
4. $-7 \times (-6)$
5. $+36 \div (-9)$
6. $-8 - (-4)$
7. $-14 + 2$
8. $5 \times (-4)$
9. $11 + (-5)$
10. $11 - 11$
11. $-9 \times (-4)$
12. $-6 + (-4)$
13. $3 - 10$
14. $-20 \div (-2)$
15. $16 + (-10)$
16. $-4 - (+14)$
17. $-45 \div 5$
18. $18 - 3$
19. $-1 \times (-1)$
20. $-3 - (-3)$

Test 3

1. $-10 \times (-10)$
2. $-10 - 10$
3. $-8 \times (+1)$
4. $-8 + 1$
5. $5 + (-9)$
6. $15 - 5$
7. $-72 \div (-8)$
8. $-12 - (-2)$
9. $-1 + 8$
10. $-5 \times (-7)$
11. $-10 + (-10)$
12. $-6 \times (+4)$
13. $6 - 16$
14. $-42 \div (+6)$
15. $-13 + (-6)$
16. $-8 - (-7)$
17. $5 \times (-1)$
18. $2 - 15$
19. $21 + (-21)$
20. $-16 \div (-2)$

10.5 Substituting into formulas

When a calculation is repeated many times it is often helpful to use a formula. When a building society offers a mortgage it may use a formula like '$2\frac{1}{2}$ times the main salary plus the second salary'. Publishers use a formula to work out the selling price of a book based on the production costs and the expected sales of the book.

Example 1
A formula connecting velocities with acceleration and time is $v = u + at$.
Find the value of v when $u = 3$,
$a = 4$,
$t = 6$.

$v = u + at$
$v = 3 + (4 \times 6)$
$v = 27$

Example 2
A formula for the tension in a spring is $T = \dfrac{kx}{a}$.
Find the value of T when $k = 13$,
$x = 5$,
$a = 2$.

$T = \dfrac{kx}{a}$

$T = \dfrac{13 \times 5}{2}$

$T = 32\frac{1}{2}$

Exercise 12

1. A formula involving force, mass and acceleration is $F = ma$. Find the value of F when $m = 12$ and $a = 3$.

2. The height of a growing tree is given by the formula $h = 2t + 15$. Find the value of h when $t = 7$.

3. The time required to cook a joint of meat is given by the formula
   $T = \text{(mass of joint)} \times 3 + \frac{1}{2}$.
   Find the value of T when (mass of joint) $= 2\frac{1}{2}$.

4. An important formula in Physics states that $I = mu - mv$. Find the value of I when $m = 6$, $u = 8$, $v = 5$.

5. The distance travelled by an accelerating car is given by the formula $s = \left(\dfrac{u+v}{2}\right)t$. Find the value of s when $u = 17$, $v = 25$ and $t = 4$.

6. Einstein's famous formula states that $E = mc^2$. Find the value of E when $m = 0{\cdot}0001$ and $c = 3 \times 10^8$.

7. The height of a stone thrown upwards is given by $h = ut - 5t^2$.
   Find the value of h when $u = 70$ and $t = 3$.

8. The speed of an accelerating particle is given by the formula $v^2 = u^2 + 2as$. Find the value of v when $u = 11$, $a = 5$ and $s = 6$.

9. The time period T of a simple pendulum is given by the formula
   $$T = 2\pi\sqrt{\left(\frac{\ell}{g}\right)},$$
   where ℓ is the length of the pendulum and g is the gravitational acceleration. Find T when $\ell = 0\cdot65$, $g = 9\cdot81$ and $\pi = 3\cdot142$.

10. The sum S of the squares of the integers from 1 to n is given by $S = \frac{1}{6}n(n+1)(2n+1)$. Find S when $n = 12$.

Example

If $x = 3$, $y = -4$, work out the following.

(a) $2x + y$
      $= 6 + -4$
      $= 6 - 4$
      $= 2$

(b) $xy - y$
      $= -12 - -4$
      $= -12 + 4$
      $= -8$

Do some of the working in your head.

Exercise 13

If $a = -4$, $b = 5$, $c = -2$, work out:

1. $2a + 3$
2. $3b - 7$
3. $4a - 1$
4. $2b + c$
5. $5c - 2a$
6. $6a - 3$
7. $2c + b$
8. $3a - 2b$
9. $6c - 2b$
10. $3c + 4a$
11. $3c - 4$
12. $2a - 3c$
13. $7b + 3a$
14. $8a + 6c$
15. $2b - 4a$
16. $4b + 5$
17. $3a + 8$
18. $2c - a$
19. $5a - 2c$
20. $3b + 7$

If $n = 3$, $x = -1$, $y = 6$, work out:

21. $2x - 3$
22. $3y + 4n$
23. $5n + 2x$
24. $4y - x$
25. $7y - 2$
26. $3x + 2n$
27. $10x + 5$
28. $6x - y$
29. $4x - 5y$
30. $2y - 10$
31. $8n - 2y$
32. $7n + 3y$
33. $6y + 4$
34. $4n + 5x$
35. $2n + 3x$
36. $5y - 20$
37. $9y - n$
38. $8x + 2n$
39. $5x + 6$
40. $3n - 2x$

$a^2 = a \times a$
$a^3 = a \times a \times a$
$2a^2 = 2(a^2)$
$(2a)^2 = 2a \times 2a$
$a(b - c)$: Work out the term in brackets first
$\dfrac{a+b}{c}$: The division line works like a bracket, so work out $a + b$ first.

Example

If $y = -3$, $x = 2$, work out   (a) y^2 (b) $3x^2$

(a) $y^2 = -3 \times -3 = 9$

(b) $3x^2 = 3 \times 4 = 12$

Exercise 14

If $m = 2$, $t = -2$, $x = -3$, $y = 4$, work out:

1. m^2
2. t^2
3. x^2
4. y^2
5. m^3
6. t^3
7. x^3
8. y^3
9. $2m^2$
10. $(2m)^2$
11. $2t^2$
12. $(2t)^2$
13. $2x^2$
14. $(2x)^2$
15. $3y^2$
16. $4m^2$
17. $5t^2$
18. $6x^2$
19. $(3y)^2$
20. $3m^3$
21. $x^2 + 4$
22. $y^2 - 6$
23. $t^2 - 3$
24. $m^3 + 10$
25. $x^2 + t^2$
26. $2x^2 + 1$
27. $m^2 + xt$
28. my^2
29. $(mt)^2$
30. $(xy)^2$
31. $(xt)^2$
32. yx^2
33. $m - t$
34. $t - x$
35. $y - m$
36. $m - y^2$
37. $t + x$
38. $2m + 3x$
39. $3t - y$
40. $xt + y$
41. $3(m + t)$
42. $4(x + y)$
43. $5(m + 2y)$
44. $2(y - m)$
45. $m(t + x)$
46. $y(m + x)$
47. $x(y - m)$
48. $t(2m + y)$
49. $m^2(y - x)$
50. $t^2(x^2 + m)$

Exercise 15

If $w = -2$, $x = 3$, $y = 0$, $z = 2$, work out:

1. $\dfrac{w}{z} + x$
2. $\dfrac{w + x}{z}$
3. $y\left(\dfrac{x + z}{w}\right)$
4. $x^2(z + wy)$
5. $x\sqrt{(x + wz)}$
6. $w^2\sqrt{(z^2 + y^2)}$
7. $2(w^2 + x^2 + y^2)$
8. $2x(w - z)$
9. $\dfrac{z}{w} + x$
10. $\dfrac{z + w}{x}$
11. $\dfrac{x + w}{z^2}$
12. $\dfrac{y^2 - w^2}{xz}$
13. $z^2 + 4z + 5$
14. $\dfrac{1}{w} + \dfrac{1}{z} + \dfrac{1}{x}$
15. $\dfrac{4}{z} + \dfrac{10}{w}$
16. $\dfrac{yz - xw}{xz - w}$

17. Find $K = \sqrt{\left(\dfrac{a^2 + b^2 + c^2 - 2c}{a^2 + b^2 + 4c}\right)}$ if $a = 3$, $b = -2$, $c = -1$.

18. Find $W = \dfrac{kmn(k + m + n)}{(k + m)(k + n)}$ if $k = \tfrac{1}{2}$, $m = -\tfrac{1}{3}$, $n = \tfrac{1}{4}$.

10.6 Problems 3

Exercise 16

1. A maths teacher bought 40 calculators at $8.20 each and a number of other calculators costing $2.95 each. In all she spent $387. How many of the cheaper calculators did she buy?

2. The total mass of a jar one-quarter full of jam is 250 g. The total mass of the same jar three-quarters full of jam is 350 g.

   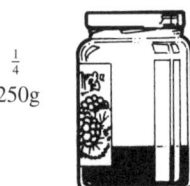 

   What is the mass of the empty jar?

3. I have lots of 1c, 2c, 3c and 4c stamps. How many different combinations of stamps can I make which total 5c?

4. 8% of 2500 + 37% of $P = 348$. Find the value of P.

5. Express 419 965 in terms of its prime factors.

6. A map is 278 mm wide and 445 mm long. When reduced on a photocopier, the copy is 360 mm long. What is the width of the copy, to the nearest millimetre?

7. How many prime numbers are there between 120 and 130?

8. You are given that $41 \times 271 = 11111$. Work out the following *in your head*.
   (a) 246×271
   (b) $22222 \div 271$

9. Booklets have a mass of 19 g each, and they are posted in an envelope of mass 38 g. Postage charges are shown in the table below

Mass (in grams) not more than	60	100	150	200	250	300	350	600
Postage (in cents)	24	30	37	44	51	59	67	110

   (a) A package consists of 15 booklets in an envelope. What is the total mass of the package?
   (b) The mass of a second package is 475 g. How many booklets does it contain?
   (c) What is the postage charge on a package of mass 320 g?
   (d) The postage on a third package was $1.10. What is the largest number of booklets it could contain?

Substituting into formulas 265

Exercise 17

1. A wicked witch stole a new-born baby from its parents. On the baby's first birthday the witch sent the grief-stricken parents 1 cent. On the second birthday she sent 2 cents. On the third birthday she sent 4 cents and so on, doubling the amount each time.
   How much did the witch send the parents on the twenty-first birthday?

2. The diagrams show magic squares in which the sum of the numbers in any row, column or diagonal is the same. Find the value of x in each square.

   (a)

	x	6
3		7
		2

   (b)

4	5	16	
x		10	
	7	11	2
1			13

3. Find a pair of positive integers a and b for which
   $18a + 65b = 1865$.

4. Work out $100 - 99 + 98 - 97 + 96 - \ldots + 4 - 3 + 2 - 1$.

5. The smallest three-digit product of a one-digit prime and a two-digit prime is

   (A) 102 (B) 103 (C) 104 (D) 105 (E) 106

6. Apart from 1, 3 and 5 all odd numbers less than 100 can be written in the form $p + 2^n$ where p is a prime number and n is greater than or equal to 2.

   e.g. $43 = 11 + 2^5$
   $27 = 23 + 2^2$

   For the odd numbers $7, 9, 11, \ldots 39$ write as many as you can in the form $p + 2^n$.

7. Evaluate   (a) $\frac{1}{3} \times \frac{2}{4} \times \frac{3}{5} \times \ldots \times \frac{9}{11} \times \frac{10}{12}$ (b) $[(-2)^{-2}]^{-2}$

8. What is the smallest number greater than 1000 that is exactly divisible by 13 and 17?

9. Find the smallest value of n for which
   $1^2 + 2^2 + 3^2 + 4^2 + 5^2 + \ldots + n^2 > 800$

10. The reciprocal of 2 is $\frac{1}{2}$. The reciprocal of 7 is $\frac{1}{7}$. The reciprocal of x is $\frac{1}{x}$.
    Find the square root of the reciprocal of the square root of the reciprocal of ten thousand.

Revision exercise 10A

1. $a = \frac{1}{2}$, $b = \frac{1}{4}$. Which one of the following has the greatest value?
   (i) ab (ii) $a+b$ (iii) $\dfrac{a}{b}$
   (iv) $\dfrac{b}{a}$ (v) $(ab)^2$

2. Given that $x = 4$, $y = 3$, $z = -2$, evaluate:
   (a) $2x(y+z)$
   (b) $(xy)^2 - z^2$
   (c) $x^2 + y^2 + z2$
   (d) $(x+y)(x-z)$

3. Work out:
   (a) $-6 - 5$ (b) $-7 + 30$
   (c) $-13 + 3$ (d) -4×5
   (e) -3×-2 (f) $-4 + -10$

4. Given $a = 3$, $b = -2$ and $c = 5$, work out:
   (a) $b + c$ (b) $a - b$
   (c) ab (d) $a + bc$

5. Given $a = 3$, $b = 4$ and $c = -2$, evaluate:
   (a) $2a^2 - b$ (b) $a(b - c)$
   (c) $2b^2 - c^2$

6. Throughout his life Mr Cram's heart has beat at an average rate of 72 beats per minute. Mr Cram is sixty years old. How many times has his heart beat during his life? Give the answer in standard form correct to two significant figures.

7. (a) Given that $x - z = 5y$, express z in terms of x and y.
   (b) Given that $mk + 3m = 11$, express k in terms of m.

8. Write in a form using indices:
   (a) $4 \times 4 \times 4 \times 4 \times 4$
   (b) $1 \times 1 \times 1 \times 1 \times 1 \times 1 \times 1$
   (c) $2 \times 2 \times 2 \times 5 \times 5$

9. Write in a more simple form:
   (a) $6^2 \times 6^3$ (b) $7^4 \times 7^4$
   (c) $3^{10} \div 3^3$ (d) $10^4 \div 10^1$
   (e) $5^{-2} \times 5^6$ (f) $2^4 \div 2^5$

10. Solve the equations for x.
    (a) $x^3 = 8$ (b) $3^x = 9$ (c) $2^x = 16$

11. Simplify:
    (a) $(x^2)^4$ (b) $(n^3)^3$ (c) $4a^2 \times 3a$

12. Write in standard form:
    (a) $50\,000$ (b) $610\,000$ (c) 0.0003
    (d) 0.0015 (e) 10 million

13. Use a calculator and give the answer in standard form:
    (a) $(2 \times 10^6) \times (1.5 \times 10^4)$
    (b) $(8 \times 10^9) \div (2 \times 10^5)$
    (c) $(4 \times 10^{-2}) \times (2 \times 10^8)$
    (d) $(1.5 \times 10^3) \times (3 \times 10^4)$

14. Work out:
    (a) $\frac{3}{5} + \frac{1}{3}$ (b) $\frac{3}{8} \times \frac{2}{3}$
    (c) $\frac{1}{5} - \frac{1}{10}$ (d) $\frac{2}{3} \div \frac{1}{4}$
    (e) $1\frac{1}{2} - \frac{2}{5}$ (f) $2\frac{1}{4} \times \frac{3}{4}$

15. If $H = \dfrac{1}{2}\left(\dfrac{1}{x} + \dfrac{1}{y}\right)$, find H when $x = 4$ and $y = 6$.

16. How many of the statements below are true?
    $5\% = \frac{1}{20}$, $5^{-1} = 0.5$, $\frac{1}{3} = 0.3$, $\frac{1}{2} \div \frac{1}{2} = \frac{1}{4}$

Examination exercise 10B

1. At the start of an experiment there is one cell in a dish.
   The number of cells in the dish doubles every five minutes.
   (a) Copy and complete the table below.

Time in minutes	0	5	10	15	20	25
Number of cells	1	2	4			

   (b) Write down, **as a power of 2**, the number of cells in the dish after one hour.
   (c) After how many hours would there be 2^{36} cells in the dish?
   (d) The experiment is stopped when there are 2^{40} cells.
   Half of these cells are then removed.
   Find, as a power of 2, the number of cells remaining in the dish. [J 97 3]

2. $$y = (x-1)(x-5)$$
   Calculate the value of y when: (a) $x = 5$ (b) $x = -2$ [J 96 1]

3. The diameter of the Sun is 1 390 000 kilometres.
   The diameter of the Earth is 12 700 kilometres.
   (a) Write the diameter of the Sun in standard form.
   (b) Calculate the value of $\dfrac{\text{the diameter of the Sun}}{\text{the diameter of the Earth}}$, giving your answer correct to the nearest whole number. [J 97 1]

4. (a) Write as decimals (i) $2 \cdot 1 \times 10^{-2}$ (ii) $2 \cdot 1 \times 10^{-3}$
   (b) Work out $2 \cdot 1 \times 10^{-2} - 2 \cdot 1 \times 10^{-3}$, giving your answer in standard form. [N 97 1]

5. (a) Work out $\frac{1}{3} + \frac{1}{12}$ as a single fraction in its lowest terms.
   (b) Find the integers p and q such that $\dfrac{1}{p} + \dfrac{1}{q} = \dfrac{5}{8}$. [J 96 1]

6. The length of a person's forearm (f cm) and the person's height (h cm) are approximately related by the formula
   $$h = \frac{10f + 256}{3}$$
   (a) Abdul's forearm is 32 centimetres long. Use the formula to estimate his height.
   (b) Bertha's height is 162 centimetres.
       (i) Use the formula to write down an equation in f.
       (ii) Solve your equation and hence estimate the length of Bertha's forearm.
   (c) Carl, who is 18 months old, is 72 centimetres tall. Show by calculation that the formula does not work in his case. [J 97 3]

7. In a quiz, a correct answer scores 3 and an incorrect answer scores -1. David guesses all the answers. He has 2 correct answers and 8 incorrect answers. Work out his total score. [N 97 1]

8. Copy and complete the spaces in the grid by answering the questions below.
Write one digit in each empty square.
The answer to question 2 (down) is 961 and has been written in the grid for you.

Across
1. A prime number between 30 and 70.
4. The number of days in 90 weeks.
6. The number of minutes between 07:00 and 02:00 the next day.

Down
2. 31 squared.
3. The number of millilitres in 3 litres.
5. A multiple of 17.
6. A factor of 72 but not a factor of 96.

[N 97 3]

11 Using and Applying Mathematics

11.1 Coursework tasks

There are a large number of possible starting points for investigations here so it may be possible to allow students to choose investigations which appeal to them. On other occasions the same investigation may be set to a whole class.

Here are a few guidelines for pupils:
(a) If the set problem is too complicated try an easier case;
(b) Draw your own diagrams;
(c) Make tables of your results and be systematic;
(d) Look for patterns;
(e) Is there a rule or formula to describe the results?
(f) Can you *predict* further results?
(g) Can you *explain* any rules which you may find?
(h) Where possible extend the task further by asking questions like 'what happens if ...'

1 Opposite corners

Here the numbers are arranged in 9 columns.

1	2	3	4	5	6	7	8	9
10	11	12	13	14	15	16	17	18
19	20	21	22	23	24	25	26	27
28	29	30	31	32	33	34	35	36
37	38	39	40	41	42	43	44	45
46	47	48	49	50	51	52	53	54
55	56	57	58	59	60	61	62	63
64	65	66	67	68	69	70	71	72
73	74	75	76	77	78	79	80	81
82	83	84	85	86	87	88	89	90

In the 2 × 2 square ...

```
| 6   7 |
| 15  16|
```

$6 \times 16 = 96$
$7 \times 15 = 105$

... the difference between them is 9.

In the 3 × 3 square ...

```
| 22  23  24 |
| 31  32  33 |
| 40  41  42 |
```

$22 \times 42 = 924$
$24 \times 40 = 960$

... the difference between them is 36.

Investigate to see if you can find any rules or patterns connecting the size of square chosen and the difference.

If you find a rule, use it to *predict* the difference for larger squares.

Test your rule by looking at squares like 8×8 or 9×9.

Can you *generalise* the rule?

[What is the difference for a square of size $n \times n$?]

Can you *prove* the rule?

Hint:

In a 3×3 square ...

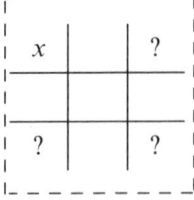

What happens if the numbers are arranged in six columns or seven columns?

1	2	3	4	5	6
7	8	9	10	11	12
13	14	15	16	17	18
19					

1	2	3	4	5	6	7
8	9	10	11	12	13	14
15	16	17	18	19	20	21
22						

2 Hiring a car

You are going to hire a car for one week (7 days).
Which of the firms below should you choose?

Gibson car hire	Snowdon rent-a-car	Hav-a-car
$170 per week unlimited travel	$10 per day 6·5c per km	$60 per week 500 miles without charge 22c per km over 500 km

Work out as detailed an answer as possible.

3 Half-time score

The final score in a football match was 3–2. How many different scores were possible at half-time?

Investigate for other final scores where the difference between the teams is always one goal. [1–0, 5–4, etc.]. Is there a pattern or rule which would tell you the number of possible half-time scores in a game which finished 58–57?

Suppose the game ends in a draw. Find a rule which would tell you the number of possible half-time scores if the final score was 63–63.

Investigate for other final scores [3–0, 5–1, 4–2, etc.].
Find a rule which gives the number of different half-time scores for *any* final score (say $a - b$).

4 An expanding diagram

Look at the series of diagrams below.

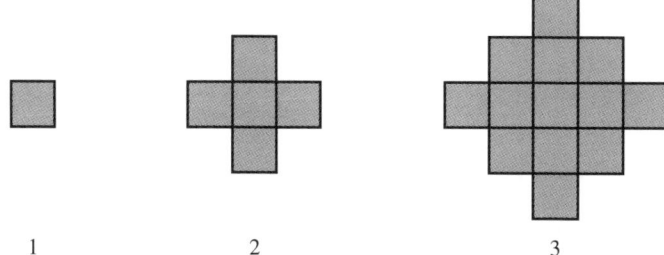

1 2 3

Continue the series by drawing the fourth, fifth and sixth diagrams in the sequence. Each new diagram is obtained by drawing squares all around the outside of the previous diagram. For each diagram count the number of squares it contains.
Using the results of the first six diagrams, can you predict the number of squares in the seventh diagram? See if you were right by drawing the diagram.
Can you predict the number of squares in the eighth diagram? Again draw the diagram to see if you were right.
Can you predict the number of squares in:
(a) the 12th diagram,   (b) the 20th diagram?
Try to find a rule which will enable you to predict the number of squares for any member of the sequence of diagrams.

5 Maximum box

(a) You have a square sheet of card 24 cm by 24 cm.
You can make a box (without a lid) by cutting squares from the corners and folding up the sides.
What size corners should you cut out so that the volume of the box is as large as possible?
Try different sizes for the corners and record the results in a table.

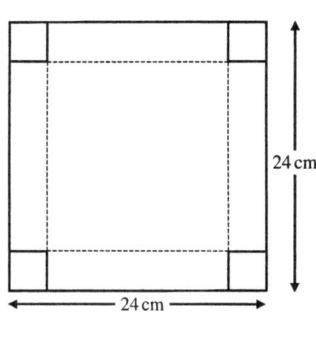

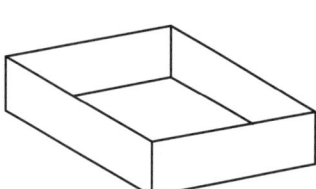

Length of the side of the corner square (cm)	Dimensions of the open box (cm)	Volume of the box (cm³)
1	22 × 22 × 1	484
2		
—		
—		

Now consider boxes made from different sized cards:
15 cm × 15 cm and 20 cm by 20 cm.
What size corners should you cut out this time so that the volume of the box is as large as possible?
Is there a connection between the size of the corners cut out and the size of the square card?

(b) Investigate the situation when the card is not square.
Take rectangular cards where the length is twice the width
(20 × 10, 12 × 6, 18 × 9 etc.).
Again, for the maximum volume is there a connection between
the size of the corners cut out and the size of the original card?

6 Timetabling

(a) Every year a new timetable has to be written for the school.
We will look at the problem of writing the timetable for one
department (mathematics). The department allocates the
teaching periods as follows:

        U6   2 sets (at the same times); 8 periods in 4 doubles.
        L6   2 sets (at the same times); 8 periods in 4 doubles.
Year 5   6 sets (at the same times); 5 single periods.
Year 4   6 sets (at the same times); 5 single periods.
Year 3   6 sets (at the same times); 5 single periods.
Year 2   6 sets (at the same times); 5 single periods.
Year 1   5 mixed ability forms; 5 single periods not
             necessarily at the same times.

Here are the teachers and the maximum number of maths
periods which they can teach.

    A   33   F   15   (Must be Years 5, 4, 3)
    B   33   G   10   (Must be Years 2, 1)
    C   33   H   10   (Must be Years 2, 1)
    D   20   I   5   (Must be Year 3)
    E   20

Furthermore, to ensure some continuity of teaching, teachers B
and C must teach the U6 and teachers A, B, C, D, E, F must
teach year 5.

Here is a timetable form which has been started

						U6 B, C	U6 B, C	
M	5							
Tu		5		U6 B, C	U6 B, C			
W					5			
Th						5	U6 B, C	U6 B, C
F		U6 B, C	U6 B, C		5			

Your task is to write a complete timetable for the mathematics
department subject to the restrictions already stated.

(b) If that was too easy, here are some changes.

U6 and L6 have 4 sets each (still 8 periods)
Two new teachers:
  J 20 periods maximum
  K 15 periods maximum but cannot teach on Mondays.

Because of games lessons: A cannot teach Wednesday afternoon
                          B cannot teach Tuesday afternoon
                          C cannot teach Friday afternoon

Also: A, B, C and E must teach U6
      A, B, C, D, E, F must teach year 5

For the pupils, games afternoons are as follows:
Monday year 2; Tuesday year 3; Wednesday year 5 L6, U6;
Thursday year 4; Friday year 1.

7 Diagonals

In a 4 × 7 rectangle, the diagonal passes through 10 squares.

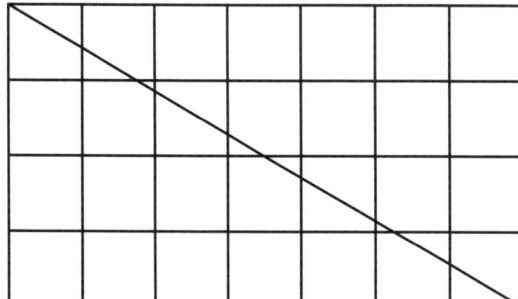

Draw rectangles of your own choice and count the number of squares through which the diagonal passes.
A rectangle is 640 × 250. How many squares will the diagonal pass through?

8 Painting cubes

The large cube on the right consists of 27 unit cubes.

All six faces of the large cube are painted green.

- How many unit cubes have 3 green faces?
- How many unit cubes have 2 green faces?
- How many unit cubes have 1 green face?
- How many unit cubes have 0 green faces?

Answer the four questions for the cube which is $n \times n \times n$.

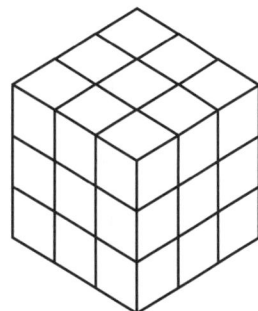

11.2 Puzzles and games

1 Crossnumbers

Draw a copy of the crossnumber pattern below and work out the answers using the clues. You can check your working by doing *all* the across and *all* the down clues.

Part A

Across
1. $327 + 198$
2. $245 \div 7$
5. $3146 - 729$
6. $248 - 76$
7. 2^6
8. $850 \div 5$
10. $10^2 + 1^2$
11. $3843 \div 7$
12. $1000 - 913$
13. $37 \times 5 \times 3$
16. $152\,300 \div 50$
19. 3^6
20. $100 - \left(\dfrac{17 \times 10}{5} \right)$

Down
1. $3280 + 1938$
2. $65\,720 - 13\,510$
3. $3 \cdot 1 \times 1000$
4. $1284 \div 6$
7. $811 - 127$
9. 65×11
10. $(12^2 - 8) \div 8$
11. $(7^2 + 1^2) \times 11$
12. $7 + 29 + 234 + 607$
14. $800 - 265$
15. $1 + 2 + 3 + 4 + 5 + 6 + 7 + 8 + 13$
17. $(69 \times 6) \div 9$
18. $3^2 + 4^2 + 5^2 + 2^4$

Part B Draw decimal points on the lines between squares where necessary.

Across
1. $4 \cdot 2 + 1 \cdot 64$
3. $7 \times 0 \cdot 5$
5. $20 \cdot 562 \div 6$
6. $(2^3 \times 5) \times 10 - 1$
7. $0 \cdot 034 \times 1000$
8. $61 \times 0 \cdot 3$
10. $8 - 0 \cdot 36$
11. 19×50
12. $95 \cdot 7 \div 11$
13. $8 \cdot 1 \times 0 \cdot 7$
16. $(11 \times 5) \div 8$
19. $(44 - 2 \cdot 8) \div 5$
20. $2^2 \times 3^2$

Down
1. $62 \cdot 6 - 4 \cdot 24$
2. $48 \cdot 73 - 4 \cdot 814$
3. $25 + 7 \cdot 2 + 0 \cdot 63$
4. $2548 \div 7$
7. $0 \cdot 315 \times 100$
9. $169 \times 0 \cdot 05$
10. $770 \div 100$
11. $14 \cdot 2 + 0 \cdot 7 - 5 \cdot 12$
12. $11 \cdot 4 - 2 \cdot 64 - 0 \cdot 18$
14. $0 \cdot 0667 \times 10^3$
15. $0 \cdot 6 + 0 \cdot 7 + 0 \cdot 8 + 7 \cdot 3$
17. $0 \cdot 73$ m written in cm
18. $0 \cdot 028 \times 200$

Part C

Across
1. Eleven squared take away six
3. Next in the sequence 21, 24, 28, 33
5. Number of minutes in a day
6. $2 \times 13 \times 5 \times 5$
7. Next in the sequence 92, 83, 74
8. 5% of 11 400
10. $98 + 11^2$
11. $(120 - 9) \times 6$
12. $1\frac{2}{5}$ as a decimal
13. $2387 \div 7$
16. $9 \cdot 05 \times 1000$
19. 8 m − 95 cm (in cm)
20. 3^4

Down
1. Write $18 \cdot 6$ m in cm
2. Fifty-one thousand and fifty-one
3. Write $3 \cdot 47$ km in m
4. $1\frac{1}{4}$ as a decimal
7. 7 m − 54 cm (in cm)
9. $0 \cdot 0793 \times 1000$
10. 2% of 1200
11. $\frac{1}{5}$ of 3050
12. $127 \div 100$
14. Number of minutes between 12:00 and 20:10
15. 4% of 1125
17. $7^2 + 3^2$
18. Last two digits of (67×3)

Part D

Across
1. $1\frac{3}{4}$ as a decimal
3. Two dozen
5. Forty less than ten thousand
6. $10^3 - 10^0$
7. 5% of 740
8. $10 - 0 \cdot 95$
10. $1 \cdot 6$ m written in cm
11. $5649 \div 7$
12. One-third of 108
13. $6 - 0 \cdot 28$
16. A quarter to midnight on the 24 h clock
19. $5^3 \times 2^2 + 1^5$
20. $3300 \div 150$

Down
1. $5 \times 7 \times 0 \cdot 37$
2. Four less than sixty thousand
3. 245×11
4. James Bond
7. Number of minutes between 09:10 and 15:30
9. $\frac{1}{20}$ as a decimal
10. 2^4
11. $8 \cdot 227$ to two decimal places
12. 4 m − 95 cm (in cm)
14. Three to the power 6
15. $20 \cdot 64$ to the nearest whole number
17. $(6\frac{1}{2})^2$ to the nearest whole number
18. Number of minutes between 14:22 and 15:14

2 Crossnumbers without clues

Here we have five cross number puzzles with a difference. There are no clues, only answers, and it is your task to find where the answers go.
(a) Copy out the crossnumber pattern.
(b) Fit all the given numbers into the correct spaces.
   Tick off the numbers from the lists as you write them in the square.

1.

2 digits	3 digits	4 digits	5 digits	6 digits
26	215	5841	21862	134953
41	427	9217	83642	727542
19	106	9131	21362	
71	872	1624	57320	
63	725	1506		
76	385	4214		
	156	5216		
	263	4734		
	234	2007		
	180	2637		

2.

2 digits	3 digits	4 digits	5 digits	6 digits
99	571	9603	24715	387566
25	918	8072	72180	338472
52	131	4210	54073	414725
26	328	3824	71436	198264
42	906	8916	82125	
57	249			
30	653			*7 digits*
53	609			8592070
14	111			
61	127			
	276			

The next three are more difficult but they are possible! Don't give up.

3.

2 digits	3 digits	4 digits	5 digits	6 digits
26	306	3654	38975	582778
28	457	3735	49561	585778
32	504	3751	56073	728468
47	827	3755	56315	
49	917	3819	56435	*7 digits*
52	951	6426	57435	8677056
70		7214	58535	
74		7315	58835	
		7618	66430	
		7643	77435	
		9847	77543	

4.

2 digits	3 digits	4 digits	5 digits	6 digits
11	121	2104	14700	216841
17	147	2356	24567	588369
18	170	2456	25921	846789
19	174	3714	26759	861277
23	204	4711	30388	876452
31	247	5548	50968	
37	287	5678	51789	
58	324	6231	78967	
61	431	6789	98438	
62	450	7630		*7 digits*
62	612	9012		6645678
70	678	9921		
74	772			
81	774			
85	789			
94	870			
99				

5.

2 digits	3 digits	4 digits	5 digits	6 digits
12 47	129	2096	12641	324029
14 48	143	3966	23449	559641
16 54	298	5019	33111	956782
18 56	325	5665	33210	
20 63	331	6462	34509	
21 67	341	7809	40551	
23 81	443	8019	41503	
26 90	831	8652	44333	*7 digits*
27 91	923		69786	1788932
32 93			88058	5749306
38 98			88961	
39 99			90963	
46			94461	
			99654	

3 Number messages

(a) Start at the box containing the letter 'Q'.

(b) Work out the answer to the question in the box.

(c) Look for the answer in the corner of another box.

(d) Write down the letter in the box and then work out the answer to the problem in the box.

(e) Look for the answer as before and continue until you arrive back at box 'Q'.

(f) Read the message.

1.

27	99	125	444
Q	**S**	**W**	**N**
$99 - 27$	$2212 \div 7$	$211 - 99$	110×9
766	112	615	25
I	**O**	**N**	**S**
$(18 - 13)^2$	$(21 - 18)^3$	18×20	$108 + 209$
317	990	72	118
T	**E**	**O**	**U**
$625 \div 5$	$840 \div 3$	$123 + 321$	$3^2 \times 11$
166	360	316	280
L	**E**	**O**	**P**
$19 + 99$	$1000 - 234$	$5 + 55 + 555$	$200 - 34$

2.

0·42 **Q** 8·1 ÷ 5	3·3 **R** 6·1 ÷ 5	4·1 **B** 19 − 13·7	10·5 **R** 14·5 − 3
5·3 **I** 3·24 ÷ 9	11·5 **S** 0·84 ÷ 4	1·22 **E** 11 − 8·95	0·01 **H** 4·2 × 0·1
2·05 **R** 0·313 × 100	31·3 **U** 8·8 + 9·9	13·1 **S** 8 − 3·7	0·21 **A** 0·33 × 10
4·3 **P** 2·4 + 7	0·36 **S** 10 − 9·99	18·7 **B** 8·2 × 0·5	9·4 **U** 2·1 × 5

3.

6 **Q** 10 + 3 × 2	13 **S** 22 + 20 ÷ 10	33 **R** 19 − 12 ÷ 6	71 **N** 7 × 4 − 15 ÷ 5
7 **E** 8 + 9 ÷ 3	53 **O** 39 − 17 × 2	25 **D** (25 + 23) ÷ 8	19 **E** 13 − 3 × 2
55 **H** 2 × 3 + 4 × 2	5 **U** 8 × 7 + 3 × 5	16 **T** 12 − 4 × 2	17 **T** (4 + 7) × 5
4 **H** 6 × 3 + 1	24 **R** 3 × 14 + 11	14 **I** 3 × 5 − 1 × 2	11 **A** 5 × 7 − 2

4.

50 **Q** 2·5 × 4 + 3	8·1 **O** 5 × 9 − 2 × 9	2·13 **N** 7 − 0·04 × 10	2 **N** 0·5 × 2 + 17
7·2 **L** 0·3 × 100 − 7	3·5 **O** 8 × 5 + 6 × 7	84 **G** 11 × 9 − 7 × 7	52·2 **G** 10 × (3·4 + 5)
6 **A** 1·7 + 3 ÷ 10	23 **A** 13 ÷ 100 + 2	13 **C** 8 − 0·2 × 10	7·24 **B** 8 + 1 ÷ 10
82 **U** 6·2 ÷ 5 + 6	27 **I** 8 − 0·4 × 2	6·6 **E** 3·2 + 7 × 7	18 **Y** 12·5 − 3 × 3

5.

-13 Q $-6+2$	-7 C $(-3)^2+4^2$	12 Y $12\div(-2)$	0 A $12\times(-10)$	-14 A $-8+17$
-120 R $16\div(-16)$	-8 H $-3-15$	-18 E $(-2)^2$	8 E $(-8)\div(-8)$	4 R $-3+7-9$
-6 T $-8-9$	13 E $-2+1-1$	-4 M $(-3)\times(-4)$	25 L $-7+20$	1 R $-3-2-8$
9 C $(-8)\div 1$	-5 S $0\times(-17)$	-2 V $6-(-2)$	-1 E $-2+6-11$	-17 E -2×7

6.

$3\cdot 62$ Q $12-8\cdot 99$	8 O $45\div 9-5$	25 U $90\times 2-5$	300 S $-8-6$	$1\cdot 3$ L $6+9\div 3$
-9 A $2\cdot 6\times 0\cdot 5$	6 Y $0\cdot 7\div 100$	$0\cdot 27$ R $(-1)^2+(-2)^2$	21 N $200-41$	159 G $25\cdot 34\div 7$
0 R $1\cdot 4+19$	$1\cdot 24$ A $9\times 5-3\times 7$	$3\cdot 01$ M $18-3\times 4$	5 O $6\times(11-7\cdot 5)$	175 L $6\cdot 2\div 5$
9 C $(-2)^2+21$	-14 W $2\cdot 7\times 0\cdot 1$	$20\cdot 4$ I $0\cdot 3\times 1000$	24 T $-7+15$	$0\cdot 007$ C $-36\div 4$

4 Calculator words

On a calculator the number 4915 looks like the word 'SIGH' when the calculator is held upside down.

Find the words given by the clues below.

1. $221\times 7\times 5$ (Sounds like 'cell')
2. $5\times 601\times 5\times 3$ (Wet blow)
3. 88^2-6 (Ringer)
4. $0\cdot 9\times 5900-1$ (Leaves)
5. $62^2-(4\times 7\times 5)$ (Nothing to it)
6. $0\cdot 88^2-\frac{1}{1000}$ (O Hell)
7. $(5\times 7\times 10^3)+(3\times 113)$ (Gaggle)
8. 44^4+ Half of $67\,682$ (Readable)
9. $5\times 3\times 37\times 1000-1420$ (Stick in mind)
10. $3200-1320\div 11$ (Woodwind)

11. $48^4 + 8929$ (Deceitful dame)
12. $31^2 \times 32^2 - 276^2 + 30$ (Not a twig)
13. $(130 \times 135) + (23 \times 3 \times 11 \times 23)$ (Wobbly)
14. $164 \times 166^2 + 734$ (Almost big)
15. $8794^2 + 25 \times 342 \cdot 28 + 120 \times 25$ (Thin skin)
16. $0 \cdot 08 - (3^2 \div 10^4)$ (Ice house)
17. $235^2 - (4 \times 36 \cdot 5)$ (Shiny surface)
18. $(80^2 + 60^2) \times 3 + 81^2 + 12^2 + 3013$ (Ship gunge)
19. $3 \times 17 \times (329^2 + 2 \times 173)$ (Unlimbed)
20. $230 \times 230\frac{1}{2} + 30$ (Fit feet)
21. $33 \times 34 \times 35 + 15 \times 3$ (Beleaguer)
22. $0 \cdot 32^2 + \frac{1}{1000}$ (Did he or didn't he?)
23. $(23 \times 24 \times 25 \times 26) + (3 \times 11 \times 10^3) - 20$ (Help)
24. $(16^2 + 16)^2 - (13^2 - 2)$ (Slander)
25. $(3 \times 661)^2 - (3^6 + 22)$ (Pester)
26. $(22^2 + 29 \cdot 4) \times 10;\ (3 \cdot 03^2 - 0 \cdot 02^2) \times 100^2$ (Four words) (Goliath)
27. $1 \cdot 25 \times 0 \cdot 2^6 + 0 \cdot 2^2$ (Tissue time)
28. $(710 + (1823 \times 4)) \times 4$ (Liquor)
29. $(3^3)^2 + 2^2$ (Wriggler)
30. $14 + (5 \times (83^2 + 110))$ (Bigger than a duck)
31. $2 \times 3 \times 53 \times 10^4 + 9$ (Opposite to hello, almost!)
32. $(177 \times 179 \times 182) + (85 \times 86) - 82$ (Good salesman)

5 The milk crate problem

You have 18 bottles to put into the crate below which has space for 24 bottles.

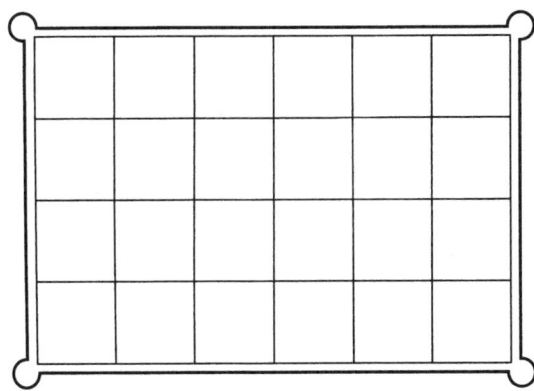

The only condition is that you have to put an *even* number of bottles into every row and every column. Good luck.

6 Estimating game

This is a game for two players. On squared paper draw an answer grid with the numbers shown.

Answer grid

891	7047	546	2262	8526	429
2548	231	1479	357	850	7938
663	1078	2058	1014	1666	3822
1300	1950	819	187	1050	3393
4350	286	3159	442	2106	550
1701	4050	1377	4900	1827	957

The players now take turns to choose two numbers from the question grid below and multiply them on a calculator.

Question grid

11	26	81
17	39	87
21	50	98

The number obtained is crossed out on the answer grid using the players' own colour.

The game continues until all the numbers in the answer grid have been crossed out. The object is to get four answers in a line (horizontally, vertically or diagonally). The winner is the player with most lines of four.

A line of *five* counts as *two* lines of four.
A line of *six* counts as *three* lines of four.

7 Creating numbers

Using only the numbers 1, 2, 3 and 4 once each and the operations $+, -, \times, \div, !$ create every number from 1 to 100.

You can use the numbers as powers and you must use all of the numbers 1, 2, 3 and 4.

[4! is pronounced 'four factorial' and means $4 \times 3 \times 2 \times 1$ (i.e. 24) similarly $3! = 3 \times 2 \times 1 = 6$
$5! = 5 \times 4 \times 3 \times 2 \times 1 = 120$]

Examples: $1 = (4 - 3) \div (2 - 1)$
$20 = 4^2 + 3 + 1$
$68 = 34 \times 2 \times 1$
$100 = (4! + 1)(3! - 2!)$

8 Pentominoes

A pentomino is a set of five squares joined along their edges. You probably know of the game of dominoes. A domino is just two squares joined together; there is only one possible shape because the two shapes here count as the same.

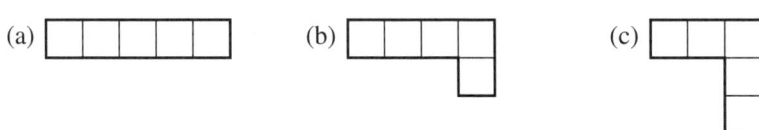

1. See how many different pentominoes you can design on squared paper. Here are a few.

   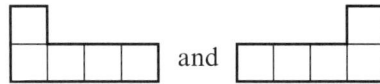

   You may find that some of your designs are really the same, for example

   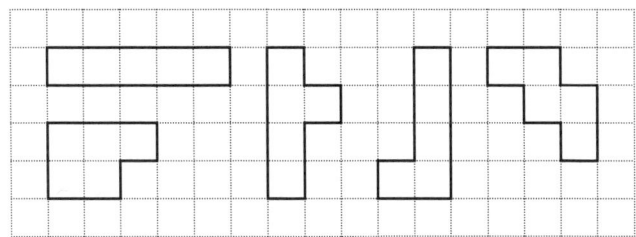

   You can use a piece of tracing paper to check if some of your designs are really the same or different.

   After about fifteen minutes, compare your designs with those of other people in your class. There are in fact twelve different pentomino shapes. Make a neat copy of these.

2. Fit these five pentominoes together to form a square.

3. On squared paper, draw a square having eight units on each side. Somewhere inside the square draw a small square having two units on each side and shade it.
   Now fill up the rest of the square with as many different pentominoes as you can. There should be no 'holes' left by the time you have finished.

   A start has been made in the diagram on the right.

   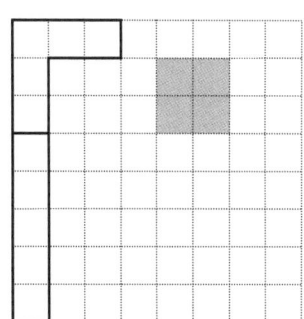

4. Take some more squared paper and draw a rectangle measuring 10 by 6. Fill up the rectangle with as many different pentominoes as you can. This problem is more difficult than the 8 by 8 square.

9 'I can read your mind'

Here is a trick where you can demonstrate your ability to read a friend's mind.

Start by writing any number between 1 and 50 on a card but do not let your friend see it.

Example

I will choose 31

Now ask your friend to do the following:

1. Write any number between 50 and 100.

    74 (say)

2. Add _____ to your number.
   [The number is 99 minus the number on *your* card]
   i.e. $99 - 31 = 68$

    Add 68
    $74 + 68 = 142$

3. Cross out the left-hand digit.
4. Add this digit to the number remaining.
5. Subtract this number from the number you chose at the start.
   (i.e. In Line 1 above)

    ~~1~~42
    $42 + 1 = 43$
    $74 - 43 = 31$

Now, with a flourish, show your friend your card with the correct number written on it.

10 The chess board problem

On the 4 × 4 square below we have placed four objects subject to the restriction that nowhere are there two objects on the same row, column or diagonal.

Subject to the same restrictions:
  (i) find a solution for a 5 × 5 square, using five objects,
  (ii) find a solution for a 6 × 6 square, using six objects,
  (iii) find a solution for a 7 × 7 square, using seven objects,
  (iv) find a solution for a 8 × 8 square, using eight objects.

It is called the chess board problem because the objects could be 'Queens' which can move any number of squares in any direction.

11 Miscellaneous puzzles

1. This shape can be divided into equal pieces in several ways. Each piece must be exactly the same size and shape.

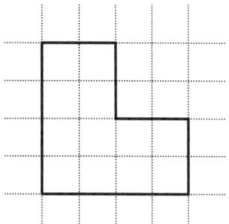

We can easily divide the shape into two equal pieces.
Draw the shape three times and show how it can be divided into:
(a) 3 pieces
(b) 6 pieces
(c) (harder) 4 pieces.

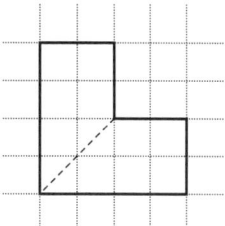

Draw this shape three times and show how it can be divided into:
(a) 3 pieces
(b) 6 pieces
(c) (harder) 8 pieces.

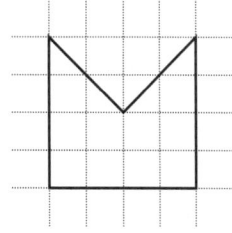

2. King John is given nine coins which look identical but in fact one of the coins is an underweight fake.
Describe how you can use a balance to find the fake in just two weighings.

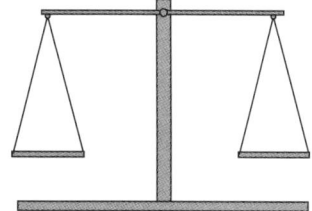

3. Here we have used 12 matches to enclose an area of 9 squares.
Draw four diagrams to show how 12 matches can be used to enclose areas of 8, 7, 6 and 5 squares.

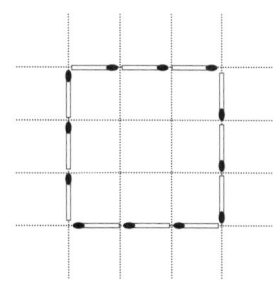

4. There is a fire in the kitchens of Gibson College and the principal, Mr Gibson, is stranded on the roof of the burning building.

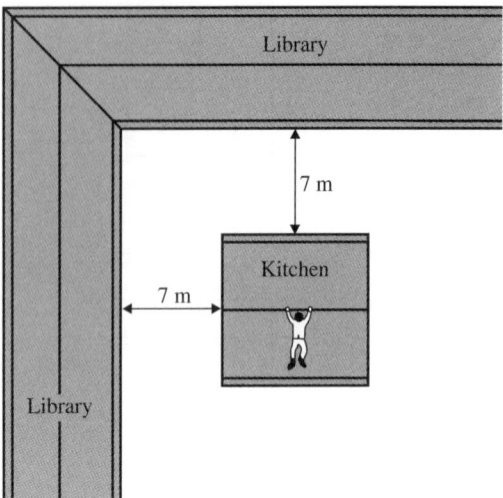

Firemen are on the roof of the library and they have two ladders each 6 m long.
The shortest distance from the library to the kitchen roof is 7 m.
How can the firemen rescue Mr Gibson?

5. Two coins have a total value of 60c. One of them is *not* a 50c coin. What are the two coins?

6. In a 24-hour day, from midnight to midnight, how many times are the hands of a clock at right angles to each other?

12 Multiple choice tests

Test 1

1. How many mm are there in 1 m 1 cm?
   - A 1001
   - B 1110
   - C 1010
   - D 1100

2. The circumference of a circle is 16π cm. The radius, in cm, of the circle is:
   - A 2
   - B 4
   - C $\dfrac{4}{\pi}$
   - D 8

3. In the triangle below the value of $\cos x$ is:
   - A 0·8
   - B 1·333
   - C 0·75
   - D 0·6

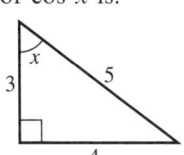

4. The line $y = 2x - 1$ cuts the x-axis at P. The coordinates of P are:
   - A $(0, -1)$
   - B $(\tfrac{1}{2}, 0)$
   - C $(-\tfrac{1}{2}, 0)$
   - D $(-1, 0)$

5. The mean weight of a group of 11 men is 70 kg. What is the mean weight of the remaining group when a man of weight 90 kg leaves?
   - A 80 kg
   - B 72 kg
   - C 68 kg
   - D 62 kg

6. A, B, C and D are points on the sides of a rectangle. Find the area in cm² of quadrilateral ABCD.
   - A $27\tfrac{1}{2}$
   - B 28
   - C $28\tfrac{1}{2}$
   - D cannot be found

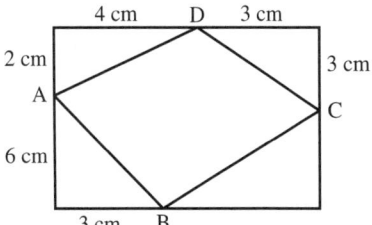

7. The formula $\dfrac{x}{a} + b = c$ is rearranged to make x the subject. What is x?
   - A $a(c - b)$
   - B $ac - b$
   - C $\dfrac{c - b}{a}$
   - D $ac + ab$

8. In standard form the value of $2000 \times 80\,000$ is:
   - A 16×10^6
   - B $1\cdot6 \times 10^9$
   - C $1\cdot6 \times 10^7$
   - D $1\cdot6 \times 10^8$

9. The sum of the lengths of the edges of a cube is 36 cm. The volume, in cm³, of the cube is:
   - A 36
   - B 27
   - C 64
   - D 48

10. In the triangle the size of angle x is:
    - A 35°
    - B 70°
    - C 110°
    - D 40°

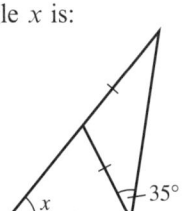

11. A man paid tax on $9000 at 30%. He paid the tax in 12 equal payments. Each payment was:
    - A $2·25
    - B $22·50
    - C $225
    - D $250

12. The approximate value of $\dfrac{3\cdot96 \times (0\cdot5)^2}{97\cdot1}$ is:
    - A 0·01
    - B 0·02
    - C 0·04
    - D 0·1

13. Given that $\dfrac{3}{n} = 5$, then $n = ?$
    - A 2
    - B -2
    - C $1\tfrac{2}{3}$
    - D 0·6

14. Cube A has side 2 cm. Cube B has side 4 cm. $\left(\dfrac{\text{Volume of B}}{\text{Volume of A}}\right) =$
    - A 2
    - B 4
    - C 8
    - D 16

15. How many tiles of side 50 cm will be needed to cover the floor shown?

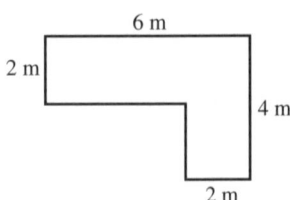

- A 16
- B 32
- C 64
- D 84

16. The equation $ax^2 + x - 6 = 0$ has a solution $x = -2$. What is a?

- A 1
- B -2
- C $\sqrt{2}$
- D 2

17. Which of the following is/are correct?
1. $\sqrt{0.16} = 0.4$
2. $0.2 \div 0.1 = 0.2$
3. $\frac{4}{7} > \frac{3}{5}$

- A 1 only
- B 2 only
- C 3 only
- D 1 and 2

18. How many prime numbers are there between 30 and 40?

- A 0
- B 1
- C 2
- D 3

19. A man is paid $180 per week *after* a pay rise of 20%. What was he paid before?

- A $144
- B $150
- C $160
- D $164

20. A car travels for 20 minutes at 45 km/h and then for 40 minutes at 60 km/h. The average speed for the whole journey is:

- A 52 km/h
- B 50 km/h
- C 54 km/h
- D 55 km/h

21. The point (3, −1) is reflected in the line $y = 2$. The new coordinates are:

- A (3, 5)
- B (1, −1)
- C (3, 4)
- D (0, −1)

22. Given the equation $5^x = 120$, the best approximate solution is $x =$

- A 2
- B 3
- C 4
- D 25

23. The rectangle ABCD is cut out of paper and the edges AB and DC are joined to make a cylinder. The radius of the cylinder in cm is:

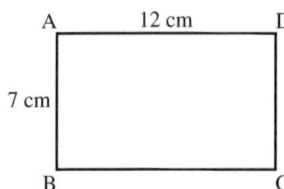

- A 6
- B 7
- C $\dfrac{6}{\pi}$
- D $\dfrac{12}{\pi}$

24. The shaded area in cm² is:

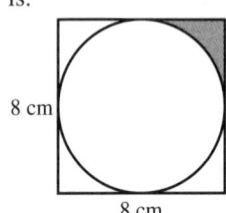

- A $16 - 2\pi$
- B $16 - 4\pi$
- C $\dfrac{4}{\pi}$
- D $64 - 8\pi$

25. What is the sine of 45°?

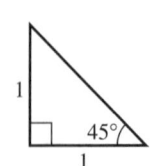

- A 1
- B $\dfrac{1}{2}$
- C $\dfrac{1}{\sqrt{2}}$
- D $\sqrt{2}$

Test 2

1. What is the value of the expression $(x - 2)(x + 4)$ when $x = -1$?

- A 9
- B −9
- C 5
- D −5

2. The perimeter of a square is 36 cm. What is its area?

- A 36 cm²
- B 324 cm²
- C 81 cm²
- D 9 cm²

3. $3(x - 3) + 2(2x + 1) =$

- A $5x - 7$
- B $7x - 7$
- C $7x + 11$
- D $5x - 1$

4. The shape consists of four semi-circles placed round a square of side 2 m. The area of the shape in m² is:

A $2\pi + 4$
B $2\pi + 2$
C $4\pi + 4$
D $\pi + 4$

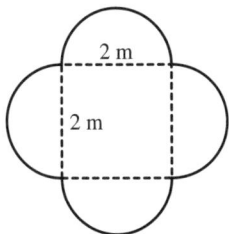

5. A firm employs 1200 people, of whom 240 are men. The percentage of employees who are men is:

A 40%
B 10%
C 15%
D 20%

6. A car is travelling at a constant speed of 30 km/h. How far will the car travel in 10 minutes?

A $\frac{1}{3}$ km
B 3 km
C 5 km
D 6 km

7. What are the coordinates of the point $(1, -1)$ after reflection in the line $y = x$?

A $(-1, 1)$
B $(1, 1)$
C $(-1, -1)$
D $(1, -1)$

8. $\frac{1}{3} + \frac{2}{5} = ?$

A $\frac{2}{8}$
B $\frac{3}{8}$
C $\frac{3}{15}$
D $\frac{11}{15}$

9. In the triangle the size of the largest angle is:

A 30°
B 90°
C 120°
D 80°

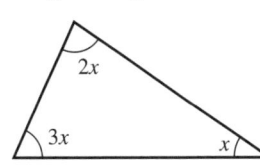

10. 800 decreased by 5% is:

A 795
B 640
C 760
D 400

11. Which of the statements is (are) true?
1. $\tan 60° = 2$
2. $\sin 60° = \cos 30°$
3. $\sin 30° > \cos 30°$

A 1 only
B 2 only
C 3 only
D 2 and 3

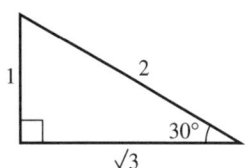

12. Given $a = \frac{3}{5}$, $b = \frac{1}{3}$, $c = \frac{1}{2}$ then:

A $a < b < c$
B $a < c < b$
C $a > b > c$
D $a > c > b$

13. The *larger* angle between South-West and East is:

A 225°
B 240°
C 135°
D 315°

14. In a triangle PQR, $\widehat{PQR} = 50°$ and point X lies on PQ such that $QX = XR$. Calculate $\widehat{QXR}$.

A 100°
B 50°
C 80°
D 65°

15. What is the value of $1 - 0.05$ as a fraction?

A $\frac{1}{20}$
B $\frac{9}{10}$
C $\frac{19}{20}$
D $\frac{5}{100}$

16. Find the length x.

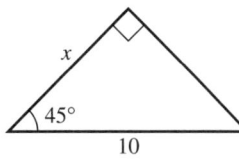

A 5
B 6
C 8
D $\sqrt{50}$

17. Given that $m = 2$ and $n = -3$, what is mn^2?

A -18
B 18
C -36
D 36

18. The graph of $y = (x - 3)(x - 2)$ cuts the y-axis at P. The coordinates of P are:

A (0, 6)
B (6, 0)
C (2, 0)
D (3, 0)

19. $240 is shared in the ratio 2:3:7. The largest share is:
A $130
B $140
C $150
D $160

20. Adjacent angles in a parallelogram are $x°$ and $3x°$. The smallest angles in the parallelogram are each:
A 30°
B 45°
C 60°
D 120°

21. When the sides of the square are increased by 10% the area is increased by:
A 10%
B 20%
C 21%
D 15%

22. The volume, in cm³, of the cylinder is:
A 9π
B 12π
C 600π
D 900π

23. A car travels for 10 minutes at 30 km/h and then for 20 minutes at 45 km/h. The average speed for the whole journey is:
A 40 km/h
B $37\frac{1}{2}$ km/h
C 20 km/h
D 35 km/h

24. Four people each toss a coin. What is the probability that the fourth person will toss a 'tail'?
A $\frac{1}{2}$
B $\frac{1}{4}$
C $\frac{1}{8}$
D $\frac{1}{16}$

25. What is the area in cm², of a circle of diameter 10 cm?
A 10π
B 25π
C 49π
D 100π

Test 3

1. The price of a T.V. changed from $240 to $300. What is the percentage increase?
A 15%
B 20%
C 60%
D 25%

2. Find the length x.

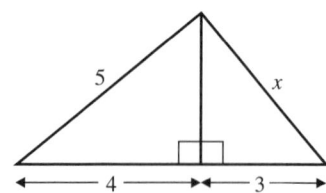

A 6
B 5
C $\sqrt{44}$
D $\sqrt{18}$

3. The bearing of A from B is 120°. What is the bearing of B from A?
A 060°
B 120°
C 240°
D 300°

4. Numbers m, x and y satisfy the equation $y = mx^2$. When $m = \frac{1}{2}$ and $x = 4$ the value of y is:
A 4
B 8
C 1
D 2

5. A school has 400 pupils, of whom 250 are boys. The ratio of boys to girls is:
A 5:3
B 3:2
C 3:5
D 8:5

6. A train is travelling at a speed of 30 km per hour. How long will it take to travel 500 m?
A 2 minutes
B $\frac{3}{50}$ hour
C 1 minute
D $\frac{1}{2}$ hour

7. The approximate value of $\dfrac{9.65 \times 0.203}{0.0198}$ is:
A 99
B 9.9
C 0.99
D 180

8. Which point does *not* lie on the curve $y = \dfrac{12}{x}$?
A (6, 2)
B ($\frac{1}{2}$, 24)
C (−3, −4)
D (3, −4)

9. $t = \dfrac{c^3}{y}$, $y = ?$
A $\dfrac{t}{c^3}$
B $c^3 t$
C $c^3 - t$
D $\dfrac{c^3}{t}$

10. The largest number of 1 cm cubes which will fit inside a cubical box of side 1 m is:
    A 10^3
    B 10^6
    C 10^8
    D 10^{12}

11. I start with x, then square it, multiply by 2 and finally subtract 3. The final result is:
    A $(2x)^2 - 3$
    B $(2x - 3)^2$
    C $2x^2 - 3$
    D $2(x - 3)^2$

12. Which of the following has the largest value?
    A $\sqrt{100}$
    B $\sqrt{\dfrac{1}{0.1}}$
    C $\sqrt{1000}$
    D $\dfrac{1}{0.01}$

13. Two dice numbered 1 to 6 are thrown together and their scores are added. The probability that the sum will be 12 is:
    A $\tfrac{1}{6}$
    B $\tfrac{1}{12}$
    C $\tfrac{1}{18}$
    D $\tfrac{1}{36}$

14. The length, in cm, of the minor arc is:
    A 2π
    B 3π
    C 6π
    D $13\tfrac{1}{2}\pi$

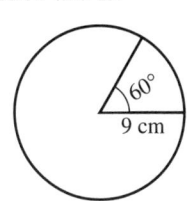

15. Metal of weight 84 kg is made into 40 000 pins. What is the weight, in kg, of one pin?
    A 0·0021
    B 0·0036
    C 0·021
    D 0·21

16. What is the value of x which satisfies both equations?
    $3x + y = 1$
    $x - 2y = 5$
    A -1
    B 1
    C -2
    D 2

17. What is the new fare when the old fare of $250 is increased by 8%?
    A $258
    B $260
    C $£270
    D $281·25

18. What is the area of this triangle?
    A $12x^2$
    B $15x^2$
    C $16x^2$
    D $30x^2$

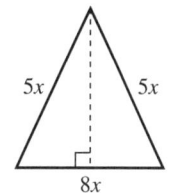

19. What values of x satisfy the inequality $2 - 3x > 1$?
    A $x < -\tfrac{1}{3}$
    B $x > -\tfrac{1}{3}$
    C $x > \tfrac{1}{3}$
    D $x < \tfrac{1}{3}$

20. A right-angled triangle has sides in the ratio $5:12:13$. The tangent of the smallest angle is:
    A $\tfrac{12}{5}$
    B $\tfrac{12}{13}$
    C $\tfrac{5}{13}$
    D $\tfrac{5}{12}$

21. To one significant figure, $\sqrt{0.1}$ is:
    A 0·01
    B 0·1
    C 0·3
    D 0·5

22. The number of letters in the word SNAIL that have line symmetry is:
    A 0
    B 1
    C 2
    D 3

23. The probability of an event occurring is 0·35. The probability of the event *not* occurring is:
    A $\dfrac{1}{0.35}$
    B 0·65
    C 0·35
    D 0

24. What fraction of the area of the rectangle is the area of the triangle?

A $\frac{1}{4}$
B $\frac{1}{8}$
C $\frac{1}{16}$
D $\frac{1}{32}$

25. On a map a distance of 40 km is represented by a line of 2 cm. What is the scale of the map?

A 1 : 2000
B 1 : 20 000
C 1 : 200 000
D 1 : 2000 000

Test 4

1. What is the value of x satisfying the simultaneous equations $3x + 2y = 13$, $x - 2y = -1$?

A 7
B 3
C $3\frac{1}{2}$
D 2

2. A straight line is 4·5 cm long. $\frac{2}{5}$ of the line is:

A 0·4 cm
B 1·8 cm
C 2 cm
D 0·18 cm

3. The mean of four numbers is 12. The mean of three of the numbers is 13. What is the fourth number?

A 9
B 12·5
C 7
D 1

4. How many cubes of edge 3 cm are needed to fill a box with internal dimensions 12 cm by 6 cm by 6 cm?

A 8
B 18
C 16
D 24

5. The value of 4865·355 correct to 2 significant figures is:

A 4865·36
B 4865·35
C 4900
D 49

6. The value of 5^0 is:

A 0
B 1
C 5
D 50

For Questions **7** to **9** use the diagram below.

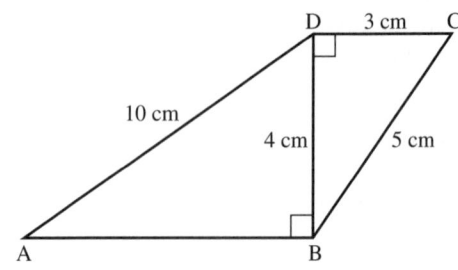

7. The length of AB, in cm, is:

A 6
B $\sqrt{116}$
C 8
D $\sqrt{84}$

8. The sine of angle DCB is:

A 0·8
B 1·25
C 0·6
D 0·75

9. The tangent of angle CBD is:

A 0·6
B 0·75
C 1·333
D 1·6

10. The area of a circle is 100π cm^2. The radius, in cm, of the circle is:

A 50
B 10
C $\sqrt{50}$
D 5

11. $4(x + 3) - 2(x - 5) = ?$

A $2x + 2$
B $2x - 2$
C $6x + 22$
D $2x + 22$

12. An estimate of the value of $\dfrac{204 \cdot 7 \times 97 \cdot 5}{1064 \cdot 2}$, to one significant figure is:

A 2
B 20
C 200
D 2000

13. The cube root of 64 is:

A 2
B 4
C 8
D 16

14. Here are four statements about the diagonals of a rectangle. The statement which is not *always* true is
    A They are equal in length
    B They divide the rectangle into four triangles of equal area
    C They cross at right angles
    D They bisect each other

15. Given $16^x = 4^4$, what is x?
    A -2
    B $-\frac{1}{2}$
    C $\frac{1}{2}$
    D 2

16. What is the area, in m², of a square with each side 0·02 m long?
    A 0·0004
    B 0·004
    C 0·04
    D 0·4

17. I start with x, then square it, multiply by 3 and finally subtract 4. The final result is:
    A $(3x)^2 - 4$
    B $(3x - 4)^2$
    C $3x^2 - 4$
    D $3(x - 4)^2$

18. How many prime numbers are there between 50 and 60?
    A 1
    B 2
    C 3
    D 4

19. What are the coordinates of the point $(2, -2)$ after reflection in the line $y = -x$?
    A $(-2, 2)$
    B $(2, -2)$
    C $(-2, -2)$
    D $(2, 2)$

20. The area of a circle is 36π cm². The circumference, in cm, is:
    A 6π
    B 18π
    C $12\sqrt{\pi}$
    D 12π

21. Here are some numbers: 7, 3, 1, 4, 6 The median is:
    A 1
    B 4
    C 4·2
    D 3·5

22. When all three sides of a triangle are trebled in length, the area is increased by a factor of:
    A 3
    B 6
    C 9
    D 27

23. Solve the equation: $2(x - 3) + 5 = 7$
    A 1
    B 2
    C 4
    D 8

24. A coin is tossed three times. The probability of getting three 'heads' is:
    A $\frac{1}{3}$
    B $\frac{1}{6}$
    C $\frac{1}{8}$
    D $\frac{1}{16}$

25. A triangle has sides of length 5 cm, 5 cm and 6 cm. What is the area, in cm²?
    A 12
    B 15
    C 18
    D 20

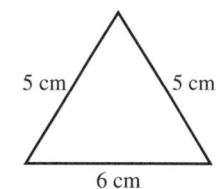

IGCSE Mathematics Specimen Paper 1

Specimen Paper 1 (Core; short questions)

1. Work out 4^5. [1]

2. Which of these is **not** a prime number?
$$31, \quad 41, \quad 51, \quad 61$$ [1]

3. Find the median of these five numbers:
$$5, \quad 2, \quad 11, \quad 2, \quad 8$$ [1]

4. Estimate the circumference of a tennis ball, in centimetres. [1]

5. Writing down your full calculator display, work out $\sqrt{\dfrac{2000}{\pi}}$. [1]

6. In a 100 metre race, the time of the winner was 10·57 seconds, and the time of the athlete who came third was 10·64 seconds. Write down a possible time for the athlete who came second. [1]

7. Find the volume of a cube with all its edges 2·7 cm long. [2]

8. Showing your working, simplify: (a) $\frac{2}{9} \times \frac{3}{5}$ (b) $\frac{2}{9} \div \frac{3}{5}$ [2]

9. A girl walks through a field so that she is always the same distance from each of two trees. Draw the locus of her walk. [2]

10. (a) Simplify: $5x - (2x - 7)$. [1]
    (b) Factorise fully: $5pq + 10p$. [2]

11. The populations of three Ethiopian villages are 2000, 2400 and 3600. During a food shortage, a charity sends 200 tonnes of grain. It is shared out in proportion to the population. How much grain should each village receive? [3]

12. Q is a point due North of a point P. A third point, R, is on a bearing of 045° from P. Angle PQR = 60°.
    (a) Sketch the triangle PQR, marking the given angles. [1]
    (b) Find the bearing of (i) R from Q   (ii) P from R. [2]

13. The statement $10 - 5 - 2 = 7$ is incorrect. If we put in brackets, the statement $10 - (5 - 2) = 7$ is correct. The following statements are all incorrect. Put in brackets to make them correct.
    (a) $6 \times 5 + 3 = 48$ [1]
    (b) $28 - 12 \div 4 = 4$ [1]
    (c) $9 - 3^2 = 36$ [1]

14.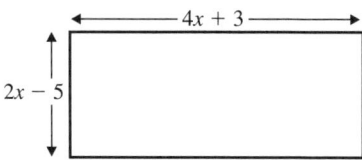

Write down, in its simplest form, an expression for the perimeter of this rectangle. [3]

15. (a) Divide this isosceles right-angled triangle into two congruent parts. [1]

(b) Divide this equilateral triangle into four congruent parts. [2]

16.

| Dishcloths | $0.75 | Buckets | $1.99 |
| Plastic bowls | $1.29 | Waste bins | $2.60 |

(a) What is the cost of two dishcloths and a bucket? [1]
(b) How much *more* would you pay for a waste bin than for a plastic bowl? [1]
(c) Waste bins are offered in the sales at a 30% discount. What will the price be then? [2]

17.

The diagram, which is drawn to scale, shows the principal exports of an African country.
(a) What percentage of the country's exports is cocoa? [2]
(b) What fraction of their exports is gold? Give your answer in its lowest terms. [2]

18. Draw an arc XY, which is a quarter of the circumference of a circle centre O, radius 3 cm. Extend YO to Z, so that OZ = 2 cm, and join XZ.
(a) Draw an accurate reflection of your diagram in the line YZ. [2]
(b) Draw an accurate rotation of the original diagram through 180° about O as centre. [2]

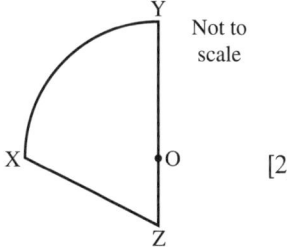

19. All four sides of this quadrilateral are equal.
    (a) What is its special name? [1]
    (b) How many lines of symmetry does
        the quadrilateral have? [1]
    (c) Find the other three angles of
        the quadrilateral. [2]

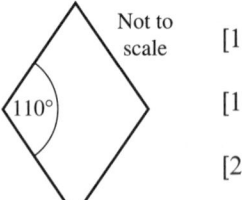

20. When the temperature is $t°C$, the number of times per minute (n) that a grasshopper chirps is given by the formula $n = 4t - 50$.
    (a) How many times a minute does a grasshopper chirp when the temperature is 22°C? [1]
    (b) At what temperature do grasshoppers stop chirping? [2]
    (c) Make t the subject of the formula $n = 4t - 50$. [2]

21. When the time in London is 12:00, the time in New York is 07:00 and the time in Tokyo is 21:00.
    (a) Copy the clock face and draw the hands to show the time 21:00. [1]
    (b) When the time in Tokyo is 12:00, what is the time in London? [2]
    (c) When the time in Tokyo is 12:00 on Wednesday, what is the time and day in New York? [2]

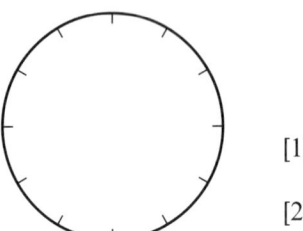

Total 56

Specimen Paper 2 (Core; structured questions)

1. (a) 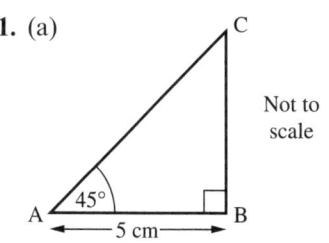 The diagram represents a set square AB = 5 cm and angle CAB = 45°.
   Find: (i) angle ACB [1]
   (ii) the length of BC [1]
   (iii) the length of AC. [2]

   (b) 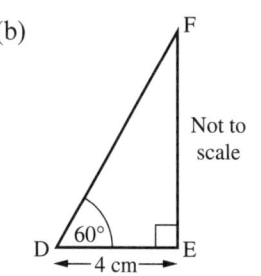 The diagram represents another set square DE = 4 cm and angle EDF = 60°.
   Find: (i) angle DFE [1]
   (ii) the length of EF [2]
   (iii) the length of DF. [2]

   (c) Which of the two triangles, ACB and DFE, has the larger area, and by how much? [3]

2. (a) Work out
$$9 \times 9 + 7$$
$$98 \times 9 + 6$$
$$987 \times 9 + 5$$
$$9876 \times 9 + 4$$
   [2]
   (b) Write down the next three lines in the sequence above and, in each case, work out and write down the answer. [2]
   (c) Complete: $987\,654\,321 \times 9 =$ .... [1]

3. The table shows the mid-day temperature on the first day of each month during one year at a settlement within the Arctic Circle.

Month	Jan	Feb	Mar	April	May	June	July	Aug	Sept	Oct	Nov	Dec
Temperature (°C)	−20	−17	−12	−3	3	12	14	13	8	−1	−12	−15

   (a) (i) Find the difference between the temperatures listed for October and November. [1]
   (ii) Find the difference between the highest and lowest listed temperatures. [2]
   (b) A month is selected at random. What is the probability that the temperature listed for it is greater than 0°C? [2]
   (c) For the list of temperatures find:
   (i) the mode [1]
   (ii) the median [2]
   (iii) the mean. [3]

4. The diagram shows a staircase. It has 11 'treads' and 12 'risers'. Each tread is 24 cm long, and each riser is 18 cm high.

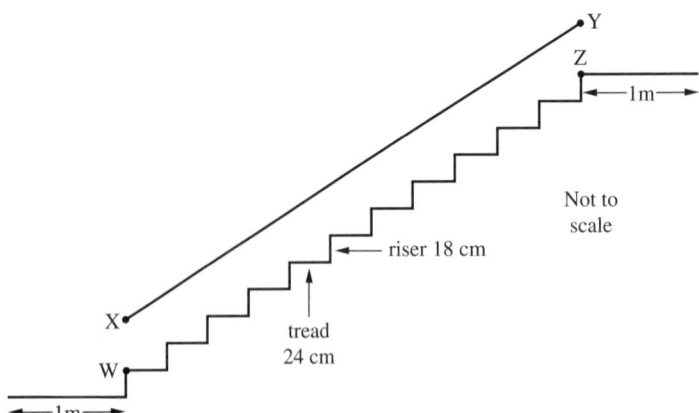

(a) A carpet is to be laid, to cover all the stairs and to extend a distance of 1 m at the bottom and 1 m at the top.
The carpet costs $8·40 per metre length.
Calculate: (i) the length of the carpet, in metres, [3]
(ii) the cost of the carpet, to the nearest dollar. [3]
(b) A handrail XY runs parallel to the stairs, such that the lines XW and YZ are vertical and equal in length. Calculate:
(i) the angle that the handrail makes with the horizontal [2]
(ii) the length of the handrail in metres (to the nearest cm). [3]

5. (a) Copy and complete this table of values below for the function $y = \dfrac{6}{x}$, where $x \neq 0$.

x	−6	−5	−4	−3	−2	−1½	−1	1	1½	2	3	4	5	6
y		−1·2				−4	−6	6						

[3]

(b) Draw x and y-axes from −6 to +6, using a scale of 1 cm to 1 unit in both directions. Plot the points in the table on your graph grid, and hence draw the two separate branches of the graph $y = \dfrac{6}{x}$. [4]

(c) (i) The graph has two lines of symmetry. Mark them clearly on your graph with broken lines, like this – – – – – – – – –. [1]
(ii) Does the curve have rotational symmetry? If so, describe it. [2]

(d) (i) Copy and complete the table of values below for the function $y = 3x − 1$. [2]

x	−1	0	1	2
y				

(ii) Draw the graph of $y = 3x − 1$ on the same graph grid used in parts (b) and (c). [2]

(e) Read off the coordinates of the points of intersection of the two graphs. [2]

6. A set of saucepans are *similar* to each other.
That is, the measurements of all the saucepans are in proportion.
(a) Copy and complete the table below.

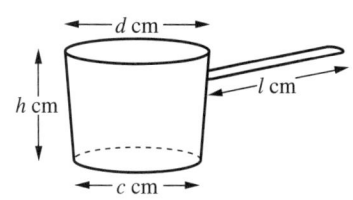

Saucepan	Diameter of top (d)	Diameter of base (c)	Height (h)	Length of handle (l)
W	10	8	6	9
X	15			
Y	$17\frac{1}{2}$			
Z	20			

[9]

(b) A formula for the volume of each saucepan is $V = \dfrac{\pi h(d^3 - c^3)}{12(d-c)}$.

Work out the volume of the smallest saucepan. [3]

7. (a) (i) The diagram shows a regular polygon.
What is its special name? [1]
(ii) Show by calculation that each interior angle of the regular polygon is 135°. [2]
(b) (i) Construct an isosceles triangle ABC with AB = AC = 6 cm and angle BAC = 135°. [2]
(ii) Measure the length of BC. [1]
(iii) Construct the bisector of angle ABC. [2]
(iv) The bisector of angle ABC cuts AC at D. Measure angle ABD. [1]

8. (a) Alice Adams grows fruit in her garden.
She kept the following record of her crops in 1999.
Choose an effective way to represent this data in a statistical diagram, and draw that diagram.

Fruit	Weight (in kg)
Apples	100
Pears	70
Plums	90
Raspberries	30
Strawberries	35

[5]

(b) Alice used the plums she had grown in the ways shown in the table below.

Sold	45 kg
Made into jam	15 kg
Made into fruit pies	10 kg
Put into freezer	20 kg

Showing clearly how you calculate the angles, draw a pie chart to represent this data. Use a circle of radius 6 cm. [5]

9. (a) Work out the circumference of a circle with a radius of 25 cm. [2]
(b) The circumference of a circular tree trunk is 286 cm.
Work out the diameter of the trunk. [3]
(c) Another tree trunk is cylindrical in shape, with a radius of 50 cm and a height of 12 m.
(i) Calculate the volume of the tree trunk, in cubic metres. [3]
[The volume of a cylinder of radius r and height h is $\pi r^2 h$.]
(ii) The weight of the wood from this tree is 0·75 tonnes per cubic metre. Calculate the weight of the tree trunk in tonnes. [2]

10. The nine digits 1, 2, 3, 4, 5, 6, 7, 8 and 9 can be arranged in triangles so that all three sides add up to the same total.
For example

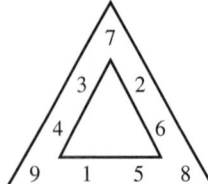

(a) (i) Starting with 1, 2 and 3 in the corners, place the other six digits so that all three sides add up to 17. [2]

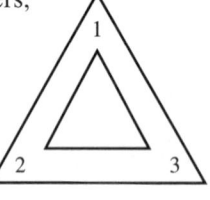

(ii) The problem in part (i) has two different correct solutions. Find the other one. [2]

(b) Starting with 4, 5 and 6 in the corners, place the other six digits so that all three sides add up to the same total. Write down that total. [4]

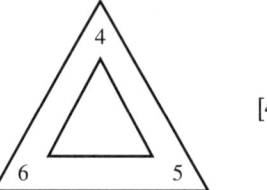

Total 104

ANSWERS

Shape and space 1

page 1 Exercise 1
1. 7·3 cm
2. 7·9 cm
3. 8·0 cm
4. 10·3 cm
5. 6·4 cm
6. 6·8 cm
7. 9·0 cm
8. 9·6 cm
9. 7·6 cm
10. 8·7 cm
11. 8·2 cm
12. 5·3 cm
13. $60\frac{1}{2}°$
14. $85\frac{1}{2}°$
15. 72°
16. 121°
17. 10 000 m²
18. 10 300–10 400 m²

page 3 Exercise 2
1. (a), (b), (d)
5. (a) triangular prism (b) square pyramid
7. (a) 6 (b) 4 (c) 10, 6, 10, 10 (d) 64 cm³

page 5 Exercise 3
1. 70°
2. 100°
3. 70°
4. 100°
5. 44°
6. 80°
7. 40°
8. 48°
9. 40°
10. 35°
11. $a = 40°, b = 140°$
12. $x = 108°, y = 72°$

page 6 Exercise 4
1. 50°
2. 70°
3. 29°
4. 30°
5. 70°
6. 42°
7. 40°
8. $a = 55°, b = 70°$
9. 60°
10. $x = 122°, y = 116°$
11. 135°
12. 30°
13. 154°
14. 75°
15. $x = 30°$
16. 28°

page 7 Exercise 5
1. 72°
2. 98°
3. 80°
4. 74°
5. 86°
6. 88°
7. $x = 95°, y = 50°$
8. $a = 87°, b = 74°$
9. $a = 65°, c = 103°$
10. $a = 68°, b = 42°$
11. $y = 65°, z = 50°$
12. $a = 55°, b = 75°, c = 50°$

page 8 Exercise 6
1. 108°
2. 50°
3. 76°
4. 270°
5. $a = 119°, b = 25°$
6. $c = 70°, d = 60°$
7. $a = 45°, b = 67\frac{1}{2}°$

page 9 Exercise 7
1. 42°
2. 68°
3. 100°
4. 73°
5. 120°
6. 52°
7. 100°
8. $a = 70°, b = 60°$
9. $x = 58°, y = 109°$
10. 66°
11. 65°
12. $e = 70°, f = 30°$
13. $x = 72°, y = 36°$
14. $a = 68°, b = 72°, c = 68°$
15. 4°
16. $28\frac{1}{2}°$
17. 20°
18. $x = 62°, y = 28°$
19. 34°
20. 58°
21. $x = 60°, y = 48°$
22. $a = 65°, b = 40°$
23. $x = 49°, y = 61°$
24. $a = 60°, b = 40°$
25. 136°
26. 80°
27. $x = 65°, y = 35°, z = 55°$
28. 26°

page 12 Exercise 8

1. (a) $a = 80°$, $b = 70°$, $c = 65°$, $d = 86°$, $e = 59°$ 2. (a) $a = 36°$ (b) $144°$
3. (a) (i) $40°$ (ii) $20°$ (iii) $8°$ (iv) $6°$ (b) (i) $140°$ (ii) $160°$ (iii) $172°$ (iv) $174°$
4. $p = 101°$, $q = 79°$, $x = 70°$, $m = 70°$, $n = 130°$ 5. 24   6. 9   7. 20   8. 20

page 13 Exercise 9

2. $90°$
3. $65°$
4. $45°$
5. $90°$
6. $e = 40°$, $f = 50°$,
7. $g = 30°$
8. $h = 90°$, $i = 60°$
9. $j = 49°$
10. $45°$
11. $l = 60°$, $m = 50°$
12. $n = 40°$
13. $50°$
14. semicircle

page 15 Exercise 10

1. (a) 1 (b) 1
2. (a) 1 (b) 1
3. (a) 4 (b) 4
4. (a) 2 (b) 2
5. (a) 0 (b) 6
6. (a) 0 (b) 2
7. (a) 0 (b) 2
8. (a) 4 (b) 4
9. (a) 0 (b) 4
10. (a) 4 (b) 4
11. (a) 6 (b) 6
12. (a) infinite (b) infinite

page 17 Exercise 12

1. 34·6 cm
2. 25·1 cm
3. 37·7 cm
4. 15·7 cm
5. 28·3 cm
6. 53·4 m
7. 44·6 m
8. 72·3 m
9. 13 mm
10. 8·48 m
11. 212
12. 400 m
13. 226 cm
14. (a) 823 m (b) 655
15. 643 cm
16. 23 or 24
17. 45 000

page 20 Exercise 13

1. $95·0 \text{ cm}^2$
2. $78·5 \text{ cm}^2$
3. $28·3 \text{ m}^2$
4. $38·5 \text{ m}^2$
5. 113 cm^2
6. 201 cm^2
7. $19·6 \text{ m}^2$
8. 380 cm^2
9. $29·5 \text{ cm}^2$
10. 125 m^2
11. $21·5 \text{ cm}^2$
12. 4580 g
13. 30; (a) 1508 cm^2 (b) 508 cm^2
14. (a) $40·8 \text{ m}^2$ (b) 6 15. 118 m^2

page 22 Exercise 14

1. 23·1 cm
2. 38·6 cm
3. 20·6 m
4. 8·23 cm
5. 28·6 cm
6. 39·4 m
7. 17·9 cm
8. 28·1 m
9. 24·8 cm
10. 46·3 m
11. 28·8 cm

page 23 Exercise 15

1. $35·9 \text{ cm}^2$
2. $84·1 \text{ cm}^2$
3. $37·7 \text{ cm}^2$
4. $74·6 \text{ cm}^2$
5. $13·7 \text{ cm}^2$
6. $25·1 \text{ cm}^2$
7. (a) $12·5 \text{ cm}^2$ (b) 50 cm^2 (c) $78·5 \text{ cm}^2$ (d) $28·5 \text{ cm}^2$

page 24 Exercise 16

1. 2·39 cm
2. 4·46 cm
3. 1·11 m
4. 4·15 cm
5. 3·48 cm
6. 3·95 m
7. 2·55 m
8. 4·37 cm
9. 4·62 cm
10. 5·75 cm
11. 15·9 cm
12. 5·09 cm
13. 9·2 m
14. 58·6 cm
15. 5·39 cm
16. 17·8 cm
17. 195 km
18. 395 cm
19. 215 m^2
20. 3·88 m
21. 575 m^2
22. 5·41 cm
23. 4·5 m

page 26 Exercise 17

1. 24 cm^2
2. 14 cm^2
3. 36 cm^2
4. 77 cm^2
5. 54 cm^2
6. 25 cm^2
7. 36 cm^2
8. 48 cm^2
9. 51 cm^2
10. 36 cm^2
11. 24 cm^2
12. 24 cm^2
13. 57 cm^2
14. 48 cm^2
15. 36 cm^2
16. 41 cm^2

page 27 **Exercise 18**
1. (a) 14·6 m (b) 6 (c) $19·20 (d) 11·22 m²
2. A (a) 13·2 m (b) 6 (c) $19·20 (d) 9·32 m²
   B (a) 19·4 m (b) 9 (c) $28·80 (d) 13 m²

page 28 **Exercise 19**
Questions **1** to **7** answers in square units.
1. (b) 10, 6, 3 (c) 36 (d) 17
2. (b) 5, 14, 6 (c) 42 (d) 17
3. $13\frac{1}{2}$ 4. $14\frac{1}{2}$ 5. 24 6. 22 7. 21
8. (a) 248 cm² (b) 120

page 29 **Exercise 20**
1. 42 cm² 2. 22 cm² 3. 103 cm² 4. 60·5 cm²
5. 143 cm² 6. 9 cm² 7. 47 cm² 8. 81·75 cm²
9. (a) 4 000 000 m²; 400 hectares (b) 314 hectares; 758 acres
10. $252

page 31 **Exercise 22**
1. 150 cm³ 2. 60 m³ 3. 480 cm³ 4. 300 cm³ 5. 56 m³
6. 280 cm³ 7. 145 cm³ 8. 448 cm³ 9. 108 cm³

page 32 **Exercise 23**
1. 62·8 cm³ 2. 113 cm³ 3. 198 cm³ 4. 763 cm³
5. 157 cm³ 6. 385 cm³ 7. 770 cm³ 8. 176 m³
9. 228 m³ 10. 486 cm³ 11. 113 litres 12. 141 cm³, 25·1 cm³

page 33 **Exercise 24**
1. 2400 cm³ 2. (a) 200 m² (b) 2400 m³ 3. 770 cm³
4. (a) 2·25 cm² (b) 0·451 cm³ (c) 4510 cm³ 5. 125
6. (a) 76 cm² (b) 30 400 cm³ (c) 237 kg (d) 33 7. 8 cm³
8. (a) 7 (b) 35, 6 (c) 1200 cm³, 14 000 cm³ (d) 48c, $5·60, $50·40 (e) 140
9. No 10. 1570 cm³, 12·6 kg 11. 53 times
12. 191 cm 13. 98 min 14. 144

page 37 **Revision exercise 1A**
1. (a) and (c) 2. (a) 91·5 cm² (b) 119 cm² 3. 17·7 cm
4. (a) 198 cm³ (b) 1357 mm³ (c) 145 5. Both arrive at the same time.
6. 74 m 7. (a) 500 m³ (b) 13 m 8. 3·43 cm², 4·57 cm²
9. 9·95 cm 10. 25 11. 5·14 cm²
12. 20 cm²

page 39 **Examination exercise 1B**
2. (a) 45° (ii) $67\frac{1}{2}°$ (iii) 135°
   (b) Sum of angles of quadrilateral EFGH = 360°, angle G + angle F = 270°, so angle H = angle E = 45°. So AHE = 135° − 45° = 90°.
3. No lines of symmetry; rotational symmetry order 3
4. (a) (i) 1 : 1 (ii) 8 cm²

5. (a) 32° (b) 90° (c) 122°
6. (a) One horizontal and one vertical line of symmetry
   (b) 2 (c) 314·2 cm² (d) 888·2 cm² (or 888·4 cm²) (e) 41·5%
7. (a) 28·3 cm² (b) (i) 22·0 cm² (ii) 4·4 cm³
8. (a) regular hexagon (b) isosceles (c) (i) 6 (ii) rotational symmetry order 6
   (d) (i) 60° (ii) 060°, 180°, 300°
9. (a) (i) 10 cm (ii) 314 cm² (iii) 78·5 cm² per $1
   (b) medium, area 452 cm², 90·4 cm² per $1, large, area 1963 cm², 78·5 cm² per $1.
   The medium size gives most pizza per $1.

Algebra 1

page 42 **Exercise 1**

1. (a) 17 (b) 27 (c) 48 (d) 30 (e) 12·5 (f) 121
2. (a) 11 (b) 16 (c) −1 (d) 2·4 (e) 11 (f) 0
3. (a) 7, 11, 18, 29, 47, 76, 123 (b) 12, 19, 31, 50
4. (a) $6 \times 7 = 6 + 6^2, 7 \times 8 = 7 + 7^2$ (b) $10 \times 11 = 10 + 10^2, 30 \times 31 = 30 + 30^2$
5. $5 + 9 \times 1234 = 11\,111$
   $6 + 9 \times 12\,345 = 111\,111$
   $7 + 9 \times 123\,456 = 1\,111\,111$
6. 63, 3968 **7.** 3, 5, 5 **8.** (a) Yes (b) (i) 5 (ii) 10 (iii) 1331
9. (b) $(1 + 2 + 3 + \ldots + 10)^2 = 55^2 = 3025$
10. (a) 16 (b) 15 (c) 26 (d) 25
    (e) 113 (f) (i) 90 (ii) 105 (iii) 199 (iv) 437
11. (a) (i) 24 (ii) 36 (iii) 75 (b) (i) 23 (ii) 35 (iii) 59
    (c) (i) 28 (ii) 39 (iii) 50 (iv) 88 (d) (i) 40 (ii) 21 (iii) 31 (iv) 50

page 44 **Exercise 2**

1. 4 kg **2.** 3 kg **3.** 3 kg **4.** 2 kg **5.** 4 kg **6.** 3 kg

page 45 **Exercise 3**

1. 12 **2.** 9 **3.** 18 **4.** 4 **5.** 17 **6.** −5 **7.** 6 **8.** −7 **9.** 4 **10.** 8
11. 17 **12.** −5 **13.** 5 **14.** 6 **15.** 2 **16.** $\frac{4}{5}$ **17.** $2\frac{1}{3}$ **18.** $7\frac{1}{2}$ **19.** $1\frac{5}{6}$ **20.** 0
21. $\frac{5}{9}$ **22.** 1 **23.** $\frac{1}{5}$ **24.** $\frac{2}{7}$ **25.** $\frac{3}{4}$ **26.** $\frac{2}{3}$ **27.** $1\frac{1}{4}$ **28.** $1\frac{1}{5}$ **29.** $1\frac{5}{9}$ **30.** $\frac{1}{3}$
31. $\frac{1}{2}$ **32.** $\frac{1}{10}$ **33.** $-\frac{3}{8}$ **34.** $\frac{9}{50}$ **35.** $\frac{1}{2}$ **36.** $\frac{3}{5}$ **37.** $-\frac{4}{9}$ **38.** 0 **39.** $4\frac{5}{8}$ **40.** $-1\frac{3}{7}$
41. $2\frac{1}{3}$ **42.** $\frac{3}{4}$ **43.** 1 **44.** $3\frac{3}{5}$ **45.** $\frac{1}{3}$ **46.** $2\frac{1}{14}$ **47.** −1 **48.** $-\frac{5}{6}$ **49.** $8\frac{1}{4}$ **50.** −55

page 45 **Exercise 4**

1. $2\frac{3}{4}$ **2.** $1\frac{2}{3}$ **3.** 2 **4.** $\frac{1}{5}$ **5.** $\frac{1}{2}$ **6.** 2 **7.** $5\frac{1}{3}$ **8.** $1\frac{1}{5}$ **9.** 0 **10.** $\frac{2}{9}$
11. $1\frac{1}{2}$ **12.** $\frac{1}{6}$ **13.** $1\frac{1}{3}$ **14.** $\frac{6}{7}$ **15.** $\frac{4}{7}$ **16.** 7 **17.** $\frac{5}{8}$ **18.** 5 **19.** $\frac{2}{3}$ **20.** $\frac{1}{3}$
21. 4 **22.** −1 **23.** 1 **24.** $\frac{6}{7}$ **25.** $1\frac{1}{4}$ **26.** 1 **27.** $\frac{7}{9}$ **28.** $-1\frac{1}{2}$ **29.** $\frac{2}{9}$ **30.** $-1\frac{1}{2}$

page 46 **Exercise 5**

1. 3 **2.** 5 **3.** $10\frac{1}{2}$ **4.** −8 **5.** $\frac{1}{3}$ **6.** $-4\frac{1}{2}$ **7.** $3\frac{1}{3}$ **8.** $3\frac{1}{2}$ **9.** $3\frac{2}{3}$ **10.** −2
11. $-5\frac{1}{2}$ **12.** $4\frac{1}{5}$ **13.** $\frac{3}{7}$ **14.** $\frac{7}{11}$ **15.** $4\frac{4}{5}$ **16.** 5 **17.** 9 **18.** $-2\frac{1}{3}$ **19.** $\frac{2}{5}$ **20.** $\frac{3}{5}$
21. −1 **22.** 13 **23.** 9 **24.** $4\frac{1}{2}$ **25.** $3\frac{1}{3}$

Answers 305

page 46 **Exercise 6**
1. $\frac{3}{5}$ 2. $\frac{4}{7}$ 3. $\frac{11}{12}$ 4. $\frac{6}{11}$ 5. $\frac{2}{3}$ 6. $\frac{5}{9}$ 7. $\frac{7}{9}$ 8. $1\frac{1}{3}$ 9. $\frac{1}{2}$ 10. $\frac{2}{3}$
11. 3 12. $1\frac{1}{2}$ 13. 24 14. 15 15. -10 16. 21 17. 21 18. $2\frac{2}{3}$ 19. $4\frac{3}{8}$ 20. $1\frac{1}{2}$
21. $3\frac{3}{4}$ 22. $1\frac{1}{3}$ 23. $3\frac{3}{5}$ 24. 2 25. $\frac{5}{8}$ 26. $\frac{7}{19}$ 27. $-\frac{3}{5}$ 28. -24 29. -70 30. $8\frac{1}{4}$
31. 220 32. -500 33. $-\frac{98}{99}$ 34. 6 35. 30 36. $1\frac{1}{2}$ 37. 84 38. 6 39. $\frac{5}{7}$ 40. $\frac{3}{5}$

page 47 **Exercise 7**
1. 2 2. 3 3. 2 4. 2 5. 2 6. 3 7. 6 8. 1

page 48 **Exercise 8**
1. 3 2. $\frac{3}{4}$ 3. $4\frac{1}{2}$ 4. $-\frac{3}{10}$ 5. $-\frac{1}{2}$ 6. $17\frac{2}{3}$
7. $\frac{1}{6}$ 8. 5 9. 12 10. $3\frac{1}{3}$ 11. $4\frac{2}{3}$ 12. -9

page 49 **Exercise 9**
1. $\frac{3}{4}$ 2. $\frac{1}{4}$ 3. $1\frac{3}{8}$ 4. $1\frac{1}{4}$ 5. 7 6. (a) $3\frac{3}{5}$ (b) $\frac{3}{4}$
7. (a) 41 (b) 31 8. 29 9. (a) 53 (b) 65 10. 55, 56, 57
11. 41, 42, 43, 44 12. (a) (i) $x-3$ (ii) $2(x-3)$ (b) $x=12\frac{1}{2}$ 13. $x=8$, perimeter $=60$ cm
14. 11 15. £6 16. $x=3$ 17. $x=47$ 18. 27 cm

page 53 **Exercise 11**
14. (a) $10 \cdot 7$ cm^2 (b) $5 \cdot 3 \times 1 \cdot 7$ (c) $12 \cdot 25$ cm^2 (d) $3 \cdot 5 \times 3 \cdot 5$

page 56 **Exercise 12**
1. (a) $3 \cdot 6/3 \cdot 7$ and $-1 \cdot 6/-1 \cdot 7$ (b) $2 \cdot 4, -0 \cdot 4$ (c) $-1, 3$
2. (a) $2 \cdot 4, -0 \cdot 4$ (b) 0, 2 3. (a) 0, 3 (b) $3 \cdot 8, -0 \cdot 8$
4. (a) $-1 \cdot 6, 3 \cdot 6$ (b) $2 \cdot 4, -0 \cdot 4$ 5. (a) $6 \cdot 5, 0 \cdot 5$ (b) No intersection

page 57 **Revision exercise 2A**
1. (a) 30, 37 (b) 12, 10 (c) 7, 10 (d) 8, 4 (e) 26, 33
2. (a) 9 (b) 11 (c) 3 (d) 7
3. (a) 7 (b) $\frac{1}{4}$ (c) $\frac{4}{5}$
4. (a) 9 (b) 50 (c) $7 \times 11 - 6 = 72 - 1$
5. (a) 4 (b) 19
6. (a) $1+2+3+4+5+4+3+2+1 = 5^2$ (b) $\ldots + 4 + \ldots + 9 + \ldots + 1 = 9^2$
   $1+\ldots+6+\ldots+1 = 6^2$
7. A $y=6$, B $y=\frac{1}{2}x-3$, C $y=10-x$, D $y=3x$
8. $4\frac{1}{6}$ sq. units 9. $(0,7), (0,-2), (4\frac{1}{2}, 2\frac{1}{2})$ 10. (a) $6x+15 < 200$ (b) 29

page 58 **Examination exercise 2B**
1. (a) $44 - 4 \times 7 = 44 - 28 = 16 = 4^2$ (b) $55 - 5 \times 6 = 5^2$
   (c) $121 - 11 \times 0 = 11^2$ $66 - 6 \times 5 = 6^2$
   (d) 13 $77 - 7 \times 4 = 7^2$
2. $\frac{2}{3}$ 3. $-\frac{3}{4}$ 4. 2
5. (a) (i) 1, 4, 9, 16 (ii) square numbers (iii) $(11+13+15+17+19) \div 3 = 25$
   (b) (i) 36, 49, 64, 81 (ii) 9 (iii) $2^2 + 3^2 + 6^2 = 7^2$
6. (a) $-4, 5, -1 \cdot 25, -4$ (c) $-3 \cdot 2, 1 \cdot 2$ (e) -4 or 1
7. (a) 2, 11, 2 (c) $4 \cdot 3$ or $-2 \cdot 3$ (e) $(-2 \cdot 9, -3 \cdot 9)$ and $(3 \cdot 9, 2 \cdot 9)$

Number 1

page 59 **Exercise 1**

1. 20
2. 400
3. 80
4. 6
5. 6000
6. 20 000
7. 5 000 000
8. 800 000
9. 200
10. 70
11. 10
12. 800
13. 6000
14. 60
15. 400
16. 70 000, 70
17. (a) 720 (b) 5206 (c) 16 430 (d) 500 000 (e) 300 090 (f) 8500
18. (a) 8753 (b) 3578
19. (a) four thousand, six hundred and twenty (b) six hundred and seven
    (c) twenty-five thousand, four hundred (d) six million, eight hundred thousand
    (e) twenty-one thousand, four hundred and twenty-five
20. (a) 75 423 (b) 23 574 21. (a) 257 (b) 3221 (c) 704
22. (a) 1392 (b) 26 611 (c) 257 900 23. (a) 5-0 (b) 52 000
24. (a) 2058, 2136, 2142, 2290 (b) 5029, 5299, 5329, 5330 (c) 25 000, 25 117, 25 171, 25 200, 25 500
25. 100
26. 10
27. $a = 100$, $b = 7$
28. $p = 1000$, $q = 10$

page 61 **Exercise 2**

1. 3497
2. 2435
3. 785
4. 68 521
5. 212
6. 41
7. 859
8. 208
9. 270
10. 5000
11. 365
12. 856
13. 2528
14. 64 568
15. 85
16. 324
17. 639
18. 325
19. 52
20. 52
21. 2018
22. 4569
23. 7
24. 1080
25. 1492
26. 524
27. 5800
28. 188
29. 1641
30. 365
31. 254
32. 21 200

page 61

	Test 1	Test 2	Test 3	Test 4
1.	22	22	40	35
2.	45	27	40	18
3.	8	54	10	83
4.	58	45	81	8
5.	77	143	98	32
6.	48	9	90	89
7.	36	5	6	29
8.	9	1300	35	12
9.	110	198	52	100
10.	42	50	190	154
11.	48	57	5	55
12.	7	21	8	11
13.	116	49	110	5000
14.	21	37	195	225
15.	900	12	32	63

page 62 **Exercise 3**

1. (a)   285
       + 514

         799

   (b)   637
       + 252

         889

   (c)   635
       + 344

         979

2. (a)   356
       + 526

         882

   (b)   224
       + 537

         761

   (c)   388
       + 425

         813

3. (a) 48 × 3 = 144 (b) 33 × 7 = 231 (c) 321 × 5 = 1605
4. (a) 150 (b) 15 (c) 9 (d) 552
5. (a) 445 + 285 = 730 (b) 427 + 177 = 604 (c) 535 + 264 = 799
6. (a) 35 × 7 = 245 (b) 58 (c) 4 (d) 950
7. (a) 72 (b) 108 (c) 889 − 346 = 543 (d) 335 − 218 = 117
9. (a) 4 × 4 − 4 (b) 8 ÷ 8 + 8 (c) 8 × 8 + 8
10. (a) − (b) ÷ (c) × (d) ÷ (e) +   **11.** (a) + (b) −, − (c) +

page 64 **Exercise 4**

1. T   **2.** F   **3.** T   **4.** T   **5.** T   **6.** F   **7.** T   **8.** T
9. $50 + 7 + \frac{2}{10}$
10. (a) 235·1 (b) 67·23 (c) 98·32 (d) 3·167
11. 0·2, 0·31, 0·41   **12.** 0·58, 0·702, 0·75   **13.** 0·41, 0·43, 0·432
14. 0·6, 0·609, 0·61   **15.** 0·04, 0·15, 0·2, 0·35   **16.** 0·18, 0·81, 1·18, 1·8
17. 0·061, 0·07, 0·1, 0·7   **18.** 0·009, 0·025, 0·03, 0·2   **19.** CARWASH
20. (a) 32·51 (b) 0·853 (c) 1·16
21. (a) 5·69 (b) 0·552 (c) 1·30
22. (a) $3·50 (b) $0·15 (c) $0·03 (d) $0·10 (e) $12·60 (f) $0·08
23. (a) T (b) F (c) T (d) T

page 65 **Exercise 5**

1. 4·3   **2.** 0·7   **3.** 9·4   **4.** 1·2   **5.** 16   **6.** 10·7
7. 17·4   **8.** 128   **9.** 375   **10.** 0·24   **11.** 1·92   **12.** 5·2
13. 0·06   **14.** 1·76   **15.** 3·16   **16.** 105   **17.** 50   **18.** 125

page 66 **Exercise 6**

1. 6·34   **2.** 8·38   **3.** 81·5   **4.** 7·4   **5.** 7245
6. 32   **7.** 6·3   **8.** 142   **9.** 4·1   **10.** 30
11. 710   **12.** 39·5   **13.** 0·624   **14.** 0·897   **15.** 0·175
16. 0·236   **17.** 0·127   **18.** 0·705   **19.** 1·3   **20.** 0·08
21. 0·007   **22.** 21·8   **23.** 0·035   **24.** 0·0086   **25.** 95
26. 111·1   **27.** 0·32   **28.** 70   **29.** 5·76   **30.** 9·99
31. 660   **32.** 1   **33.** 0·042   **34.** 6200   **35.** 0·009
36. 0·0555   **37.** (a) 0 (b) (i) 5, 2 (ii) 5, 2, 0 (iii) 0, 5, 2 and ·

page 67 **Exercise 7**

1. 10·14   **2.** 20·94   **3.** 26·71   **4.** 216·95   **5.** 9·6
6. 23·1   **7.** 9·14   **8.** 17·32   **9.** 0·062   **10.** 1·11
11. 4·36   **12.** 2·41   **13.** 1·36   **14.** 6·23   **15.** 2·46
16. 8·4   **17.** 2·8   **18.** 10·3   **19.** 0·18   **20.** 4·01
21. 6·66   **22.** 41·11   **23.** 3·6   **24.** 6·44

page 67 **Exercise 8**
1. 0·06
2. 0·15
3. 0·12
4. 0·006
5. 1·8
6. 3·5
7. 1·8
8. 0·8
9. 0·36
10. 0·014
11. 1·26
12. 2·35
13. 8·52
14. 3·12
15. 0·126
16. 127·2
17. 0·17
18. 0·327
19. 0·126
20. 0·34
21. 0·055
22. 0·52
23. 1·3
24. 0·001

page 68 **Exercise 9**
1. 2·1
2. 3·1
3. 4·36
4. 4
5. 4
6. 2·5
7. 16
8. 200
9. 70
10. 0·92
11. 30·5
12. 6·2
13. 12·5
14. 122
15. 212
16. 56
17. 60
18. 1500
19. 0·3
20. 0·7
21. 0·5
22. 3·04
23. 5·62
24. 0·78
25. 0·14
26. 3·75
27. 0·075
28. 0·15
29. 1·22
30. 163·8
31. 1·75
32. 18·8
33. 12
34. 88
35. 580

page 68 **Cross-numbers**

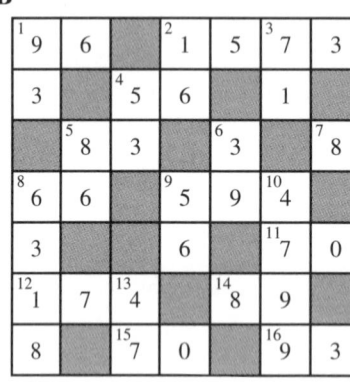

A, B, C grids

page 69 **Exercise 10**
1. (a) 11, 22, 11, 33   (b) 12, 24, 13, 39   (c) 7, 14, 28, 17, 51
   (d) 9, 16, 32, 21, 63   (e) 11, 18, 36, 25, 75   (f) 13, 20, 40, 29, 87
2. (a) 6, 12, 27, 20, 5   (b) 3, 6, 21, 14, $3\frac{1}{2}$ (c) 8, 16, 31, 24, 6
   (d) 10, 20, 35, 28, 7   (e) 1, 2, 17, 10, $2\frac{1}{2}$ (f) 12, 24, 39, 32, 8
3. (a) 7, 22, 44, 22, $5\frac{1}{2}$ (b) 10, 25, 50, 28, 7   (c) 16, 31, 62, 40, 10
   (d) $\frac{1}{2}$, $15\frac{1}{2}$, 31, 9, $2\frac{1}{4}$ (e) 100, 115, 230, 208, 52   (f) 24, 39, 78, 56, 14
4. (a) 4, 16, 48, 38, 19   (b) 5, 25, 75, 65, $32\frac{1}{2}$ (c) 6, 36, 108, 98, 49
   (d) 8, 64, 48, 38, 19   (e) 1, 1, 3, −7, $-3\frac{1}{2}$ (f) 10, 100, 300, 290, 145
5. ×4, square root, −10, × − 2   6. reciprocal, +1, square, ÷3   7. +3, cube, ÷−2, +100

page 71 **Exercise 11**
1. (a) 1, 2, 3, 6   (b) 1, 3, 5, 15   (c) 1, 2, 3, 6, 9, 18
   (d) 1, 3, 7, 21   (e) 1, 2, 4, 5, 8, 10, 20, 40
2. 2, 3, 5, 7, 11, 13, 17, 19   3. $2 + 5 = 7$ $2 + 11 = 13$ etc.
4. 101, 151, 293 are prime
5. (a) $36 = 2 \times 2 \times 3 \times 3$ (b) $60 = 2 \times 2 \times 3 \times 5$ (c) $216 = 2 \times 2 \times 2 \times 3 \times 3 \times 3$
   (d) $200 = 2 \times 2 \times 2 \times 5 \times 5$ (e) $1500 = 2 \times 2 \times 3 \times 5 \times 5 \times 5$

6. $1200 = 2 \times 2 \times 2 \times 3 \times 5 \times 5$
7. (a) 3, 6, 9, 12 (b) 4, 8, 12, 16 (c) 10, 20, 30, 40 (d) 11, 22, 33, 44 (e) 20, 40, 60, 80
8. (a) 32 (b) 56 **9.** 12, 24, etc. **10.** (a) even (b) odd (c) even

11.

	Prime number	Multiple of 3	Factor of 16
Number > 5	7	9	8
Odd number	5	3	1
Even number	2	6	4

12. (a) 7 (b) 50 (c) 1 (d) 5

page 73 **Exercise 12**

1. 805 **2.** 459 **3.** 650 **4.** 1333 **5.** 2745
6. 1248 **7.** 4522 **8.** 30 368 **9.** 28 224 **10.** 8568
11. 46 800 **12.** 66 281 **13.** 57 602 **14.** 89 516 **15.** 97 525

page 73 **Exercise 13**

1. 32 **2.** 25 **3.** 18 **4.** 13 **5.** 35
6. 22 r 2 **7.** 23 r 24 **8.** 18 r 10 **9.** 27 r 18 **10.** 13 r 31
11. 35 r 6 **12.** 23 r 24 **13.** 64 r 37 **14.** 151 r 17 **15.** 2961 r 15

page 73 **Exercise 14**

1. $47·04 **2.** 46 **3.** 7592 **4.** 21, 17c change **5.** 8
6. $80·64 **7.** $14 million **8.** $85 **9.** $21 600

page 74 **Exercise 15**

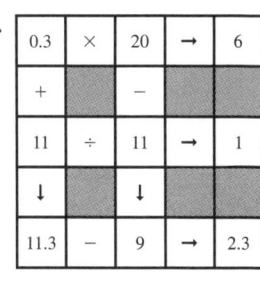

7.

7	×	0.1	→	0.7
÷		×		
4	÷	0.2	→	20
↓		↓		
1.75	+	0.02	→	1.77

8.

1.4	+	8	→	9.4
−		×		
0.1	×	0.1	→	0.01
↓		↓		
1.3	+	0.8	→	2.1

9.

100	×	0.3	→	30
−		×		
2.5	÷	10	→	0.25
↓		↓		
97.5	+	3	→	100.5

10.

3	÷	2	→	1.5
÷		÷		
8	÷	16	→	$\frac{1}{2}$
↓		↓		
$\frac{3}{8}$	+	$\frac{1}{8}$	→	$\frac{1}{2}$

11.

$\frac{1}{4}$	−	$\frac{1}{16}$	→	$\frac{3}{16}$
×		×		
$\frac{1}{2}$	÷	4	→	$\frac{1}{8}$
↓		↓		
$\frac{1}{8}$	+	$\frac{1}{4}$	→	$\frac{3}{8}$

12.

0.5	−	0.01	→	0.49
+		×		
3.5	×	10	→	35
↓		↓		
4	÷	0.1	→	40

13.

5.2	−	1.8	→	3.4
−		÷		
4.56	×	5	→	22.8
↓		↓		
0.64	+	0.36	→	1

14.

0.7	×	30	→	21
×		−		
16	−	−19	→	35
↓		↓		
11.2	−	49	→	−37.8

15.

−12	×	−6	→	72
÷		+		
4	+	7	→	11
↓		↓		
−3	+	1	→	−2

page 76 **Exercise 16**
1. $12   2. $8   3. $10   4. $3   5. $2·40   6. $24   7. $45
8. $72   9. $244   10. $9·60   11. $42   12. $88   13. 8 kg   14. 12 kg
15. 272 g   16. 45 m   17. 40 km   18. $710   19. 4·94 kg   20. 60 g   21. $204

page 76 **Exercise 17**
1. $0·28   2. $1·16   3. $1·22   4. $2·90   5. $3·57   6. $0·45   7. $0·93
8. $37·03   9. $16·97   10. $0·38   11. $0·79   12. $1·60   13. $13·40   14. $50
15. $2·94   16. $11·06   17. $1·23   18. $4·40   19. $11·25   20. $22·71   21. $9·19

page 77 **Exercise 18**
1. $63   2. $736   3. $77·55   4. $104   5. $1960   6. $792   7. $132
8. $45·75   9. $110·30   10. $42   11. $12·03   12. $9·49   13. $7·35   14. $7·01
15. $12·34   16. $16·92   17. $31·87   18. $9·02   19. $8·88   20. $14·14

page 77 **Exercise 19**
1. $35·20   2. $5724   3. $171·50   4. $88·35   5. 2·828 kg   6. $58·50
7. 24   8. 59 400   9. $9·52   10. 3·348 kg   11. 13·054 kg   12. $2762·50

page 78 **Exercise 20**
1. $17·51   2. $40·66   3. $77·96   4. $185·34
5. (a) $28   (b) $21   6. (a) $480   (b) (i) $16·20   (ii) $1053

page 80 **Exercise 21**

1. (a) $216 (b) $115·50 (c) 2 years (d) 5 years **2.** $2295 interest; $9045
3. 7·5% annual rate

page 81 **Exercise 22**

1. 200 m **2.** 500 m **3.** (b) 200 m (c) 1 km (d) 0·6 km
4. 63 m **5.** 24 km **6.** 120 m
7. (a) 2·8 km (b) 3·25 km (c) 2·7 km

page 81 **Exercise 23**

1. 150 cm **2.** 125 cm **3.** 28 cm **4.** 5·9 cm
5. (a) 60 cm (b) 84 cm (c) 56 cm (d) 140 cm (e) 100 cm **6.** 2·5 cm

page 82 **Exercise 24**

1. $10, $20 **2.** $45, $15 **3.** 330 g, 550 g **4.** $480, $600 **5.** 36, 90
6. $10, $20, $30 **7.** $70 **8.** $50 **9.** 3250

page 83 **Exercise 25**

1. 8 **2.** 5 **3.** 9 **4.** 30 g zinc, 40 g tin
5. 24 **6.** 2·4 kg **7.** 6 **8.** 18 cm
9. 22·5 cm **10.** 7·2 cm **11.** 300 g **12.** 5:3
13. $200 **14.** 42c **15.** $175 000 **16.** $\frac{1}{4} m^3$

page 85 **Exercise 26**

1. $28 **2.** $6 **3.** $3 **4.** 400 **5.** 10 min **6.** $4·80
7. $8·40 **8.** 12 days **9.** 12 hours **10.** 1 day **11.** 9 hours **12.** 24 men
13. 20 hours **14.** (a) 800 (b) 2400 (c) $1\frac{1}{2}$ hours (d) 100

page 86 **Exercise 27**

1. $3·66 **2.** $19·04 **3.** 12 litres **4.** 10 hours **5.** 10 days
6. 28 min **7.** 6 hours **8.** 3655 g **9.** 400 bottles **10.** 165 min
11. 11 grapefruit **12.** 315 francs **13.** 5 men **14.** 55 litres
15. (a) 180 hens (b) 9 days (c) 10 hens (d) 6 days
16. 7500 batteries **17.** 1 h 15 min **18.** 115·2 min **19.** $2n$ hours

page 88 **Exercise 28**

1. (a) $2\frac{1}{2}$ hours (b) $3 h 7\frac{1}{2} min$ (c) 75 seconds (d) 4 hours
2. (a) 20 m/s (b) 30 m/s (c) $83\frac{1}{3}$ m/s (d) 108 km/h (e) 79·2 km/h
  (f) 1·2 cm/s (g) 90 m/s (h) 25 mph (i) 0·03 miles per second
3. (a) 75 km/h (b) 4·52 km/h (c) 7·6 m/s (d) 4000 km/s (e) $2·5 \times 10^6$ m/s
  (f) 200 km/h (g) 3 km/h
4. (a) 110 000 m (b) 10 000 m (c) 56 400 m (d) 4500 m (e) 80 m
  (f) 80 m (g) 96 000 m
5. (a) $3 h 7\frac{1}{2} min$ (b) 76·8 km/h
6. (a) 4 hours 27 minutes (b) 23·6 km/h **7.** 46 km/h

page 90 **Exercise 29**

1. 2·35	2. 0·814	3. 26·2	4. 35·6	5. 113	6. 211
7. 0·825	8. 0·0312	9. 5·9	10. 1·2	11. 0·55	12. 0·72
13. 0·14	14. 1·8	15. 25	16. 31	17. 486·7	18. 500·4
19. 2·889	20. 3·113	21. 0·071 54	22. 3·041	23. 2464	24. 488 900
25. 0·513	26. 5·8	27. 66	28. 587·6	29. 0·6	30. 0·07
31. 5·84	32. 88	33. 2500	34. 52 700	35. 0·006	36. 7000

page 90 **Exercise 30**

1. 5·38	2. 11·05	3. 0·41	4. 0·37	5. 8·02	6. 87·04	7. 9·01
8. 0·07	9. 8·4	10. 0·7	11. 0·4	12. 0·1	13. 6·1	14. 19·5
15. 8·1	16. 7·1	17. 8·16	18. 3·0	19. 0·545	20. 0·0056	21. 0·71
22. 6·83	23. 0·8	24. 19·65	25. 0·0714	26. 60·1	27. −7·3	28. −5·42

29. (a) 5·9 cm by 3·3 cm; 5·1 cm by 2·9 cm   (b) 19·5 cm^2, 14·8 cm^2

page 91 **Exercise 31**

1. 0·57	2. 3·45	3. 431	4. 19·3	5. 0·22	6. 3942·7
7. 53	8. 18·4	9. 0·059	10. 1·1	11. 6140	12. 127·89
13. 20·3	14. 47·6	15. 599·1	16. 0·16		

page 92 **Exercise 32**

1. 0·85 m	2. 2400 m	3. 63 m	4. 0·25 m	5. 0·7 cm
6. 20 mm	7. 1200 m	8. 700 cm	9. 580 m	10. 0·815 m
11. 0·65 km	12. 2·5 cm	13. 5000 g	14. 4200 g	15. 6400 g
16. 3000 g	17. 800 g	18. 0·4 kg	19. 2000 kg	20. 0·25 kg
21. 500 kg	22. 620 kg	23. 0·007 t	24. 1·5 kg	25. 0·8 *l*
26. 2000 ml	27. 1 *l*	28. 4500 ml	29. 6000 ml	30. 3000 cm^3
31. 2000 *l*	32. 5500 *l*	33. 900 cm^3	34. 0·6 *l*	35. 15 000 *l*
36. 0·24 *l*	37. 0·28 m	38. 550 cm	39. 0·305 kg	40. 46 m
41. 0·016 *l*	42. 0·208 m	43. 2·8 cm	44. 0·27 m	45. 0·788 km
46. 14 000 kg	47. 1300 g	48. 0·09 m^3	49. 2900 kg	50. 0·019 *l*

51. (For discussion)

page 92 **Exercise 33**

(For discussion)

1. (a) Nelson's Column 56 m   (b) Empire State Building 450 m   (c) Mount Everest 8700 m
2. (a) No   (b) No   3. (a) No   (b) No
4. (a) No   (b) Probably   5. (a) Yes   (b) about 54 times

page 93 **Exercise 34**

1. 4c	2. 11c	3. 9c	4. 10c	5. 4c	6. 18c	7. 6c
8. 13c	9. $1·75	10. 36c	11. 2·5c	12. $7·25	13. 15c	14. 5c
15. 16c	16. $0·89	17. 14c	18. 2c	19. $3·60	20. 15c	

page 94 **Exercise 35**

1. 582	2. $5·12	3. 130 years	4. $28·50	5. 1455
6. 15 h 5 min	7. $10·35	8. $21·10	9. 3854	10. $725·33

page 95 **Exercise 36**
1. $3·25, £1·80, 7, $17·10   2. 6c   3. (a) double 18   (b) £11 111
4. 140   5. 4, 15   6. m, 9, z
7. 24   8. Both same (!)   9. 1·50 m

page 96 **Exercise 37**
1. 9   2. (a) 5 m (b) 50 m (c) 6 km   3. 51·4°
4. (a) 40 hectares   (b) 15 hectares   (c) 10%, 30%, 37·5%, 22·5%
5. 78   6. $184·50   7. $2518·50   8. $5·85
9. (a) $99 + \frac{9}{9}$ (b) $6 + \frac{6}{6}$ (c) $55 + 5$ (d) $55 + 5 + \frac{5}{5}$ (e) $\frac{7+7}{7+7}$ (f) $\frac{88}{8}$
10. From left to right   (a) 7, 3   (b) 4, 3   (c) 7, 8, 6   (d) 3, 7, 0   (e) 3, 6   (f) 6, 8, 0

page 98 **Exercise 38**
1. $3·26   2. $1·70   3. (a) 108 m^2 (b) 3
5. 100 m   6. (a) $3200 (b) 8%   7. 10 h 30 min
8. (a) 0·54 (b) 40 (c) 0·004 (d) 2·2 (e) £9 (f) £40   9. 260 million
10. (a) 4, 3 (b) 7, 6 (c) 8, 4 (d) 24, 2

page 99 **Exercise 39**
1. (a) 69 (b) 65   2. 120   3. 360 000 kg
4. 0·012, 0·021, 0·03, 0·12, 0·21   5. 16   7. 64 km/h
8. (a) Yes (b) No (c) Yes (d) Yes (e) Yes (f) Yes (g) Yes (h) No

page 100 **Revision exercise 3A**
1. 95c for 1 lb   2. (a) 0·005 m s (b) 1·6 s (c) 173 km
3. 43·1 litres   4. (a) 1 : 50 000 (b) 1 : 4 000 000
5. (a) $143 000   (b) 198   (c) $715   (d) $141 570   (e) $1430 less
6. (a) (i) 13, 49, 109 (ii) 4, 49 (iii) 13, 109
   (b) (i) 27 (ii) 33   (c) 148, 193   (d) 94, 127
7. (a) 2 cm (b) 8 m
8. 12 km   9. (a) $100 (b) 500 (c) $44 profit
10. $8   11. $184
12. (a) 1810 s (b) 72·4 s   13. 0·8 cm
14. $25·60, $6·70, 4, total $55·30   15. 17 kg
16. $33\frac{1}{3}$ km/h   17. (a) $13 (b) $148 (c) $170

page 102 **Examination exercise 3B**
1. 13, 7, 9, 23   2. 43 Prime, $45 = 3^2 \times 5$, 47 Prime, $49 = 7^2$ 3. $550 000
4. (a) mm   (b) 1460 mm   (b) 1·46 m
5. (a) 20%   (b) 11 550   (c) 123 million   (d) 1 : 4 or $\frac{1}{4}$
6. (a) 16, 25, 36   (b) 15, 21
   (c) (i) $1 + 3 + 5 = 9$, $1 + 3 + 5 + 7 = 16$ (ii) square numbers (iii) $10^2 = 100$ (iv) $210^2 = 44 100$
   (d) (i) $3 + 6 = 9$
           $6 + 10 = 16$
       (ii) $10 + 15 = 25$
            $15 + 21 = 36$
            square numbers

Handling data 1

page 104 **Exercise 1**

1. (a) $425 (b) $150 (c) $250 (d) $75
2. (a) $13 333·30 (b) $15 000 (c) $6666·70 (d) $10 000 (e) $12 000
3. (a) $21 600 000 (b) $8 000 000 (c) $1 000 000
4. (a) 8 min, 34 min, 10 min (b) 18°

page 105 **Exercise 2**

1. (a) (i) 45° (ii) 200° (iii) 110° (iv) 5°   2. (a) $\frac{3}{10}, \frac{4}{10}, \frac{1}{5}, \frac{1}{10}$
3. $x = 60°, y = 210°$ 4. Barley 60°, Oats 90°, Rye 165°, Wheat 45°
5. (a) 180° (b) 36° (c) 90° (d) 54°

page 107 **Exercise 3**

1. (a) 5 (b) 19 (c) 23 (d) 55 (e) $\frac{6}{23}$
3. (a) £3000 approx.
   (b) Profits increase in months before Christmas. Very few sales after Christmas.

page 109 **Exercise 4**

1. (a) 5 (b) 24 (c) 35 (d) Expect this shape.
2. (a) D (b) A (c) A (d) C (e) C (f) B
3. No significant change.

page 112 **Exercise 5**

1. (a) (i) $2·50 (ii) $2 (iii) $3 (b) (i) £0·80 (ii) £2·80 (iii) £2
2. (a) (i) 2·5 kg (ii) 3·6 kg (iii) 0·9 kg (b) (i) 4·4 lb (ii) 6·6 lb (iii) 3·3 lb (c) 2·2 lb (d) 3·2 kg
3. (a) DM 0·6 less (b) 25%   4. (a) 10°C (b) 68°F (c) −18°C

page 120 **Exercise 7**

1. (a) mean = 6, median = 5, mode = 4   (b) mean = 9, median = 7, mode = 7
   (c) mean = 6·5, median = 8, mode = 9   (d) mean = 3·5, median = 3·5, mode = 4
2. 2°C   3. (a) 3 (b) 3   5. 70·4, 73·25, No   6. 6
7. (a) 1·6 m (b) 1·634 m   8. (a) 51 kg (b) 50 kg
9. (a) 7·2 (b) 5 (c) 6
10. (a) mean = $47 920, median = $22 500, mode = $22 500
    (b) The mean is skewed by one large number.
11. (a) mean = 157·1 kg, median = 91 kg
    (b) mean. No: over three quarters of the cattle are below the mean weight.
12. (a) mean = 74·5 cm, median = 91 cm (b) Yes

page 125 **Exercise 8**

2. (a) 25 (b) 90
4. (a) 62
   (b) Sport B has more heavy people. Sport A has a much smaller range of weights compared to sport B.
5. (a) Plants with fertilizer are significantly taller (b) No significant effect

page 127 **Revision exercise 4A**
1. (a) 5·89 (b) 6 (c) 7 2. 1·55 m
3. (a) (i) 560 kg (ii) 57 kg (b) 50 kg 4. (a) 84 (b) 19·2
5. (a) 25 (b) 75 (c) 20
6. Spain 108°, France 45°, Greece 90°, Portugal 136°, USA 81°
7. (a) 29 (b) 23 (c) wrong 8. (a) F (b) possible (c) possible

page 128 **Examination exercise 4B**
1. (a) (i) 6 (ii) Frequencies: 9, 5, 6, 3, 1 (iii) 5 (iv) 6 (v) 6·25 (vi) 75°
2. (a) Frequencies: 5, 7, 13, 14, 5, 4
   (b) (i) 42 (ii) 41 (iii) 41·40 (2 d.p.) (c) 42 (d) 43

Shape and space 2

page 130 **Exercise 2**
2. (d) $(7, -7), (-5, 5), (5, 7)$ 3. (d) $(7, 5), (-5, 7), (5, -7)$
4. (g) $(-3, 6), (-6, 6), (-6, 4)$ 5. (g) $(3, 1), (7, 1), (7, 3)$
6. (a) $y = 0$ (x-axis) (b) $x = 1$ (c) $y = 1$ (d) $y = -x$

page 132 **Exercise 3**
7. Shape 1: C, 90° CW; Shape 2: B, 180°;
   Shape 3: A, 90° ACW; Shape 4: B, 90° CW; Shape 5: F, 180°

page 133 **Exercise 4**
2. (e) $(-2, 1), (2, 1), (1, -2)$ 3. (e) $(-2, 2), (0, 0), (-2, -2)$

page 135 **Exercise 6**
1. (a) Yes (b) No (c) Yes (d) Yes 2. 78 mm
3. $y = 24$ mm, $z = 67·5$ mm 7. $OA' = 2 \times OA$, $OB' = 2 \times OB$
9. (b) Scale factor $= 1\frac{1}{2}$

page 139 **Exercise 7**
7. (e) $(3, 0), (-5, -1), (3, -1)$
8. (e) $(3, 3), (-6, -1), (3, -3)$
9. (e) $(3, -1), (2, -1), (5, -7)$

page 142 **Exercise 9**
1. (a) $\begin{pmatrix} 4 \\ 6 \end{pmatrix}$ (b) $\begin{pmatrix} 6 \\ 4 \end{pmatrix}$ (c) $\begin{pmatrix} 6 \\ 0 \end{pmatrix}$ (d) $\begin{pmatrix} 6 \\ 0 \end{pmatrix}$ (e) $\begin{pmatrix} 5 \\ -2 \end{pmatrix}$
   (f) $\begin{pmatrix} 1 \\ 2 \end{pmatrix}$ (g) $\begin{pmatrix} -2 \\ 5 \end{pmatrix}$ (h) $\begin{pmatrix} 2 \\ -2 \end{pmatrix}$ (i) $\begin{pmatrix} -4 \\ -3 \end{pmatrix}$ (j) $\begin{pmatrix} 2 \\ -6 \end{pmatrix}$
   (k) $\begin{pmatrix} 1 \\ -8 \end{pmatrix}$ (l) $\begin{pmatrix} -6 \\ -1 \end{pmatrix}$ (m) $\begin{pmatrix} 0 \\ -4 \end{pmatrix}$ (n) $\begin{pmatrix} 6 \\ 1 \end{pmatrix}$

page 142 **Exercise 10**

1. (a) Reflection in $y = 0$, Translation $\begin{pmatrix} -7 \\ 0 \end{pmatrix}$ (b) Yes

2. Enlargement scale factor 2. Reflection in $y = -x$

page 144 **Exercise 11**

1. (a) 115° (b) 90° (c) 80°
3. C(−3, −3), D(−4, 2)
4. (a) 34° (b) 56°
5. (a) 35° (b) 35°
6. (a) 72° (b) 108° (c) 80°
7. (a) 40° (b) 30° (c) 110°
8. (a) 116° (b) 32° (c) 58°
9. (a) 55° (b) 55°
10. (a) 26° (b) 26° (c) 77°
11. (a) 52° (b) 64° (c) 116°
12. 110°
13. (a) 54° (b) 72° (c) 36°
14. (a) 60° (b) 15° (c) 75°

page 146 **Exercise 12**

1. A 035°, B 070°, C 155°, D 220°, E 290°, L 340°
2. A 040°, B 065°, C 130°, D 160°, E 230°, F 330°

page 147 **Exercise 13**

1. (a) $147\frac{1}{2}°$ (b) 122° (c) 090°
2. (a) 286° (b) 225° (c) 153°
3. (a) 061° (b) $327\frac{1}{2}°$
4. (a) 302° (b) 344° (c) 045°

page 149 **Exercise 16**

1. 11·5 km
2. 14·1 km
3. 12·5 km, 032°
4. 6·9 km
5. 8·5 km, 074°
6. 8·4 km, 029°
7. (b) 5·2 h
8. No

page 155 **Exercise 18**

1. 10 cm
2. 4·12 cm
3. 10·6 cm
4. 5·66 cm
5. 4·24 cm
6. 990
7. 4·58 cm
8. 5·20 cm
9. 9·85 cm
10. 7·07 cm
11. 3·46 m
12. 40·3 km
13. 9·49 cm
14. 32·6 cm
15. 5·39 units
16. Yes
17. 6·63 cm
18. 5·57
19. 8·72
20. 5·66
21. 6·63 cm
22. 2·24
23. (a) (i) 13 (ii) 25 (iii) 9
24. (a) 5 cm (b) 7·81 cm
25. (a) 8·06 cm (b) 9 cm
26. Philip

page 157 **Exercise 19**

1. 113 litres
2. 17·3 litres
3. (a) $\frac{1}{3}$ (b) $\frac{4}{9}$ (c) 25 cm²
4. 2500
5. 1100 m
6. (a) 24 cm² (b) 35 cm²
7. 740 cm³
8. 2·4 cm
9. (a) 2·5 cm (b) 3·25 cm
10. 40
11. 100
12. 900
13. (a) 384 cm² (b) 80 cm
14. (a) 6 (b) 12 (c) 8 (d) 1

page 160 **Revision exercise 5A**

1. 4·1 cm
2. (a) 40° (b) 100°
3. (a) 14·1 cm, 48·3 cm square (b) 1930 cm²
4. (a) $1\frac{2}{3}$ (b) 20 cm
5. (a) reflection in the x-axis (b) reflection in $x = -1$ (c) reflection in $y = x$
 (d) rotation, centre (0, 0), 90° clockwise (e) reflection in $y = -1$
 (f) rotation, centre (0, −1), 180°

Answers 317

6. (a) enlargement; scale factor $1\frac{1}{2}$, (1, −4)
   (b) rotation 90° clockwise, (0, −4)
   (c) reflection in $y = -x$
   (d) translation $\begin{pmatrix} 11 \\ 10 \end{pmatrix}$ (e) enlargement; scale factor $\frac{1}{2}$, (−3, 8)
   (f) rotation 90° anticlockwise, $(\frac{1}{2}, 6\frac{1}{2})$
   (g) enlargement; scale factor 3, (−2, 5)
7. (c) △2 (6, 0); △3 (2, −8); △4 (−8, 2); △6 (1, −5); △7 (−1, 3)
8. (b) 85·5 km (±1·5 km)
9. (a) 7·2 cm   (b) 9·2 cm   (c) 7·3 cm
10. (a) 220°   (b) 295°

page 162 **Examination exercise 5B**

1. (a) (i) △P is (−5, −1), (−2, −4), (−1, −1)   (b) $\begin{pmatrix} 8 \\ -4 \end{pmatrix}$
       (ii) △Q is (1, 5), (4, 2), (1, 1)
       (iii) arc, centre (0, 0)
       (iv) △R is (3, −3), (7, −3), (6, 0)
2. (a) an arc, radius is length of thread, centre the fixed point
   (b) (perpendicular bisector of line joining AB)
3. (a) 110°   (b) 70°   (c) 14 km
4. 255°
5. (a) (i) circle, radius 3 cm, centre A   (ii) perpendicular bisector of AB
   (b) P and Q are the points of intersection of two circles, each radius 3 cm, one with centre A, the other with centre B.
6. (a) reflection in $x = 3$
   (b) rotation 90° anticlockwise about (0, 0)
   (c) (i) △D is at (−5, −1), (−1, −1), (−5, −3)
       (ii) △E is at (2, 1), (4, 1), (4, −3)
       (iii) △F is at (−3, −5), (−1, −1), (−1, −5)
       (iv) △G is at (−5, 3), (−5, 4), (−3, 3)
7. (a) (i) 7·5 cm²   (ii) 150 cm³   (iii) 132 g   (b) 5·8 cm
8. (a) (i) 4   (ii) C
   (b) (i) reflection in $y = 0$ (ii) reflection in $y = x$ (iii) rotation 180° about (0, 0)

Algebra 2

page 167 **Exercise 1**

1. $w = b + 4$ 2. $w = 2b + 6$ 3. $w = 2b - 12$
4. $m = 2t + 1$ 5. $m = 3t + 2$ 6. $s = t + 2$
7. (a) $p = 5n - 2$ (b) $k = 7n + 3$ (c) $w = 2n + 11$
8. (a) $y = 3n + 1$ (b) $h = 4n - 3$ (c) $k = 3n + 5$
9. $m = 8c + 4$

page 170 **Exercise 2**

1. (a) (3, 7) (b) (1, 3) (c) (11, −1)   2. (2, 4)   3. (2, 3)
4. (3, 1)   5. (1, 5)   6. (5, 3)
7. (a) (4, 0) (b) (1, 6) (c) (−2, −3) (d) (8, −1) (e) (−0·6, 1·2)

page 172 Exercise 3

1. $x = 2, y = 1$
2. $x = 4, y = 2$
3. $x = 3, y = 1$
4. $x = -2, y = 1$
5. $x = 3, y = 2$
6. $x = 5, y = -2$
7. $x = 2, y = 1$
8. $x = 5, y = 3$
9. $x = 3, y = -1$
10. $a = 2, b = -3$
11. $a = 5, b = \frac{1}{4}$
12. $a = 1, b = 3$
13. $m = \frac{1}{2}, n = 4$
14. $w = 2, x = 3$
15. $x = 6, y = 3$
16. $x = \frac{1}{2}, z = -3$
17. $m = 1\frac{15}{17}, n = \frac{11}{17}$
18. $c = 1\frac{16}{23}, d = -2\frac{12}{23}$

page 173 Exercise 4

1. $x = 2, y = 4$
2. $x = 1, y = 4$
3. $x = 2, y = 5$
4. $x = 3, y = 7$
5. $x = 5, y = 2$
6. $a = 3, b = 1$
7. $x = 1, y = 3$
8. $x = 1, y = 3$
9. $x = -2, y = 3$
10. $x = 4, y = 1$
11. $x = 1, y = 5$
12. $x = 0, y = 2$
13. $x = \frac{5}{7}, y = 4\frac{3}{7}$
14. $x = 1, y = 2$
15. $x = 2, y = 3$
16. $x = 4, y = -1$
17. $x = 3, y = 1$
18. $x = 1, y = 2$
19. $x = 2, y = 1$
20. $x = -2, y = 1$

page 173 Exercise 5

1. $5\frac{1}{2}, 9\frac{1}{2}$
2. 6, 3 or $2\frac{2}{5}, 5\frac{2}{5}$
3. 4, 10
4. 10·5, 7·5
5. $a = 2, c = 7$
6. $m = 4, c = -3$
7. $a = 30, b = 5$
8. TV $200, video $450
9. w 2 g, b $3\frac{1}{2}$ g
10. 2c × 15, 5c × 25
11. 10c × 14, 50c × 7

page 174 Exercise 6

1. (a) 40 km (b) 60 km (c) Gap, Sisteron (d) 15 min
   (e) (i) 11:00 (ii) 13:45 (f) (i) 40 km/h (ii) 60 km/h (iii) 100 km/h
2. (a) 25 km (b) 15 km (c) 09:45 (d) 1 h
   (e) (i) 26·7 km/h (ii) 5 km/h (iii) 30 km/h (iv) 40 km/h
3. (a) (i) 14:00 (ii) 13:45 (b) (i) 15:45 (ii) towards Aston
   (c) (i) 15 mph (ii) 40 mph (iii) 40 mph (iv) 20 mph (d) $16:07\frac{1}{2}$
4. (a) 45 min (b) 09:15 (c) 60 km/h (d) 47 km (e) 57·1 km/h
5. (a) 09:15 (b) 64 km/h (c) 37·6 km/h (d) 47 km (e) 80 km/h
6. 11:05 7. 12:42 8. 12:35

page 177 Exercise 7

1. (a) 740c (b) $280 (c) $14 000 (d) $11 000
4. (a) 30 l (b) (i) 8 km/l (ii) 6 km/l (c) 6·7 km/l, 30 litres
5. 180 km 6. 2·5 h

page 180 Exercise 8

1. B
2. D
3. (a) C (b) A (c) D (d) B
4. (a) (i) B (ii) A (b) 8 s to 18 s (c) about 15 s
   (d) about 9 s (e) B (f) A
6. (a) runners slow down for takeover (b) baton dropped at third takeover

page 182 Exercise 9

1. $3x + 9$
2. $4x - 8$
3. $10x + 5$
4. $4a + 28$
5. $12x + 6$
6. $50 - 10x$
7. $12x + 15$
8. $27 + 9x$
9. $5y - 10$
10. $7a - 14$
11. $22x - 11y$
12. $24x + 16y$

page 182 **Exercise 10**
1. $2(3x + 2y)$
2. $3(3x + 4y)$
3. $2(5a + 2b)$
4. $4(x + 3y)$
5. $5(2a + 3b)$
6. $6(3x - 4y)$
7. $4(2u - 7v)$
8. $5(3s + 5t)$
9. $8(3m + 5n)$
10. $9(3c - 8d)$
11. $4(5a + 2b)$
12. $6(5x - 4y)$
13. $3(9c - 11d)$
14. $7(5u + 7v)$
15. $4(3s - 8t)$
16. $8(5x - 2t)$
17. $12(2x + 7y)$
18. $4(3x + 2y + 4z)$
19. $3(4a - 2b + 3c)$
20. $5(2x - 4y + 5z)$
21. $4(5a - 3b - 7c)$
22. $8(6m + n - 3x)$
23. $7(6x + 7y - 3z)$
24. $3(2x^2 + 5y^2)$
25. $5(4x^2 - 3y^2)$
26. $7(a^2 + 4b^2)$
27. $9(3a + 7b - 4c)$
28. $6(2x^2 + 4xy + 3y^2)$
29. $8(8p - 9q - 5r)$
30. $12(3x - 5y + 8z)$

page 183 **Exercise 11**
1. $e - b$
2. $m + t$
3. $a + b + f$
4. $A + B - h$
5. y
6. $b - a$
7. $m - k$
8. $w + y - v$
9. $\dfrac{b}{a}$
10. $\dfrac{m}{h}$
11. $\dfrac{a+b}{m}$
12. $\dfrac{c-d}{k}$
13. $\dfrac{e+n}{v}$
14. $\dfrac{y+z}{3}$
15. $\dfrac{r}{p}$
16. $\dfrac{h-m}{m}$
17. $\dfrac{a-t}{a}$
18. $\dfrac{k+e}{m}$
19. $\dfrac{m+h}{u}$
20. $\dfrac{t-q}{e}$
21. $\dfrac{v^2+u^2}{k}$
22. $\dfrac{s^2-t^2}{g}$
23. $\dfrac{m^2-k}{a}$
24. $\dfrac{m+v}{m}$
25. $\dfrac{c-a}{b}$
26. $\dfrac{y-t}{s}$
27. $\dfrac{z-y}{c}$
28. $\dfrac{a}{h}$
29. $\dfrac{2b}{m}$
30. $\dfrac{cd-ab}{k}$
31. $\dfrac{c+ab}{a}$
32. $\dfrac{e+cd}{c}$
33. $\dfrac{n^2-m^2}{m}$
34. $\dfrac{t+ka}{k}$
35. $\dfrac{k+h^2}{h}$
36. $\dfrac{n-mb}{m}$
37. $2a$
38. $\dfrac{d-ac}{c}$
39. $\dfrac{e-mb}{m}$

page 184 **Exercise 12**
1. mt
2. en
3. ap
4. amt
5. abc
6. ey^2
7. $a(b+c)$
8. $t(c-d)$
9. $m(s+t)$
10. $k(h+i)$
11. $\dfrac{ab}{c}$
12. $\dfrac{mz}{y}$
13. $\dfrac{ch}{d}$
14. $\dfrac{em}{k}$
15. $\dfrac{hb}{e}$
16. $c(a+b)$
17. $m(h+k)$
18. $\dfrac{mu}{y}$
19. $t(h-k)$
20. $(z+t)(a+b)$
21. $\dfrac{e}{7}$
22. $\dfrac{e}{a}$
23. $\dfrac{h}{m}$
24. $\dfrac{bc}{a}$
25. $\dfrac{ud}{c}$
26. $\dfrac{m}{t^2}$
27. $\dfrac{h}{\sin 20°}$
28. $\dfrac{e}{\cos 40°}$
29. $\dfrac{m}{\tan 46°}$
30. $\dfrac{b^2c^2}{a^2}$

page 184 **Exercise 13**
1. $\dfrac{h+d}{a}$
2. $\dfrac{m-k}{z}$
3. $\dfrac{f-ed}{d}$
4. $\dfrac{d-ma}{m}$
5. $\dfrac{c-a}{b}$
6. $b - a$

7. $\dfrac{z}{y}$ 8. $e+c$ 9. $\dfrac{b+n}{m}$ 10. $\dfrac{b-a^2}{a}$ 11. $\dfrac{a}{d}$ 12. mt

13. mn 14. $\dfrac{y}{d}$ 15. $\dfrac{a}{t}$ 16. $\dfrac{d}{n}$ 17. $k(a+b)$ 18. $\dfrac{v}{y}$

19. $\dfrac{m}{c}$ 20. mb 21. $\dfrac{b-ag}{g}$ 22. $x^2 - h^2$ 23. $y - z$ 24. $\dfrac{c}{2m}$

25. $\dfrac{t-ay}{a}$ 26. $\dfrac{y^2 + t^2}{u}$ 27. $\dfrac{c-t}{3}$ 28. $k - m$ 29. $\dfrac{c-b}{a}$ 30. $\dfrac{c-am}{m}$

31. $pq - ab$ 32. $a^2 - t$ 33. $\dfrac{w}{v^2}$ 34. $c - t$ 35. $\dfrac{t}{x}$ 36. $k - n$

page 185   Revision exercise 6A

1. (a) $l = 2d - 4$ (b) 149
3. (a) A, swimmer; B, car ferry from Calais; C, hovercraft;
   D, train from Dover; E, marker buoy; F, car ferry from Dover
4. (a) $s = t(r+3)$ (b) $r = \dfrac{s-3t}{t}$ 5. (b) 1, 4, 9, 16   (c) square numbers   (d) 49
6. (a) $c = 5, d = -2$ (b) $x = 2, y = -1$
7. (a) (i) Consett   (ii) Durham   (iii) Consett   (b) (i) 55 km   (ii) 40 km
   (c) (i) 80 km/h   (ii) 55 km/h   (iii) 70 km/h   (iv) 80 km/h
   (d) $1\tfrac{3}{4}$ h
8. (a) $3 \to 14, 4 \to 18, 5 \to 22, 6 \to 26$ (c) (i) 42   (ii) 62   (d) $n = 4x + 2$

page 187   Examination exercise 6B

1. (a) 3   (b) (i) 5 min   (ii) 12 km/h   2. $7x + 8$ 3. $y = \dfrac{10 - 2x}{5}$
4. (a) 12   (b) 126   (c) 630 km/h   5. (a) $0.167 > \tfrac{1}{6}$ (b) $-2\tfrac{1}{4} > -2\tfrac{1}{2}$
6. (a) $19\tfrac{1}{4}$ (b) $h = \dfrac{A - c^2}{b}$
7. (a) $-2, -1, 0, 1, 2, 3$ (b) $6q + 5$ (c) $m = -2, n = 3$
8. (a) $x > y$ (b) $y > z$ (c) $x^2 < y^2$
9. (b) Number of white squares 4, 6, 8, 10, 12   (c) (i) 22   (ii) 24   (d) $y = 2x + 2$
10. (a) (i) 1982   (ii) $34 per barrel   (b) 1980–1981   (c) (i) $13   (ii) 46%
11. (b)

Triangle	Number of dots on perimeter	Number of dots inside	Column 2 + Column 3
1st	4	0	4
2nd	8	1	9
3rd	12	4	16
4th	16	9	25
5th	20	16	36
6th	24	25	49

   (c) 4 × triangle number   (d) (triangle number $-1)^2$ (e) 80, 361, 441
12. (b) 4·8 km   (c) $-24°$C   (d) $-20°$ (e) $-41°$ (f) 2 : 1
13. (a) (i) 16, 19   (ii) 162, 486   (iii) 76, 123
    (b) (i) 8·1   (ii) 98·01
    (c) (i) 36, 49   (ii) 225   (iii) n^2 (iv) $n^2 + 1$

Number 2

page 192 **Exercise 1**

1. 8%
2. 10%
3. 25%
4. 2%
5. 4%
6. $2\frac{1}{2}$%
7. 20%
8. 50%
9. 15%
10. 80%
11. 25%
12. 20%
13. $12\frac{1}{2}$%
14. $33\frac{1}{3}$%
15. 80%
16. 5%
17. 6%
18. 20%
19. 5%
20. $2\frac{1}{2}$%

page 193 **Exercise 2**

1. 36·4%
2. 19·0%
3. 19·4%
4. 22·0%
5. 12·2%
6. 9·4%
7. 14·0%
8. 17·4%
9. 32·7%
10. 10·2%
11. 7·7%
12. 35·3%
13. 30·8%
14. 5·2%
15. 14·1%
16. 14·5%
17. 19·1%
18. 3·6%
19. 31·1%
20. 6·5%

page 193 **Exercise 3**

1. 12%
2. 29%
3. 16%
4. 0·25%
5. 15%
6. 61·1%
7. 15%
8. 13·7%
9. 1·5%
10. 23·8%

page 194 **Exercise 4**

1. (a) 25c   (b) $12·80   (c) $2·80   (d) 28%
2. (a) $10   (b) (i) $4·20   (ii) 42%
3. (a) (i) 120 cm   (ii) 75 cm   (iii) 10 000 cm^2 (iv) 9000 cm^2 (b) 10%
4. (a) $50 000   (b) (i) $53 800   (ii) 7·6%
5. 250 m^2

page 196 **Exercise 5**

1. '$\frac{1}{3}$ off'
2. $\frac{1}{6}$ of $5000
3. 25%
4. 20%
5. (a) 0·25   (b) 0·4   (c) 0·375   (d) 0·4$\dot{1}\dot{6}$ (e) 0·1$\dot{6}$ (f) 0·$\dot{2}$8571$\dot{4}$
6. (a) $\frac{1}{5}$ (b) $\frac{9}{20}$ (c) $\frac{9}{25}$ (d) $\frac{1}{8}$ (e) $1\frac{1}{20}$ (f) $\frac{7}{1000}$
7. (a) 25%   (b) 10%   (c) 72%   (d) 7·5%   (e) 2%   (f) $33\frac{1}{3}$%
8. (a) $\frac{1}{4}$, 0·25, 25%   (b) $\frac{1}{5}$, 0·2, 20%   (c) $\frac{4}{5}$, 0·8, 80%   (d) $\frac{1}{100}$, 0·01, 1%
   (e) $\frac{3}{10}$, 0·3, 30%   (f) $\frac{1}{3}$, 0·$\dot{3}$, $33\frac{1}{3}$%
9. (a) 0·14625   (b) $15·84
10. (a) 45%, $\frac{1}{2}$, 0·6   (b) 4%, $\frac{6}{16}$, 0·38   (c) 11%, 0·111; $\frac{1}{9}$
11. 0·58
12. 1·42
13. 0·65
14. 1·61
15. 0·07
16. 0·16
17. 3·64
18. 0·60
19. 62·5%

page 197 **Exercise 6**

1. B
2. C
3. B
4. A
5. B
6. C
7. B
8. B
9. A
10. B
11. A
12. A
13. C (or B)
14. C
15. £5200
16. about 20
17. (a) True   (b) True   (c) True   (d) False   (e) False
    (f) True   (g) True   (h) False   (i) True

page 200 Exercise 7

1. B 2. A 3. C 4. B 5. C 6. A 7. B
8. B 9. A 10. C 11. B 12. A 13. A 14. C
15. C 16. B 17. C 18. A 19. B 20. B 21. C
22. B 23. B 24. A 25. B 26. B 27. A 28. Yes
29. Yes 30. He got it wrong. Correct answer is $10·45 each
31. (a) (Say) 200 g per paper: 3250 papers per tree (b) about 5×10^{11} (c) For discussion

page 202 Exercise 8

1. 195·5 cm 2. 36·5 kg 3. 3·25 kg 4. 95·55
5. 28·65 s 6. B 7. C 8. Not necessarily
9. 16·5, 17·5 10. 255·5, 256·5 11. 2·35, 2·45 12. 0·335, 0·345
13. 2·035, 2·045 14. 11·95, 12·05 15. 81·35, 81·45 16. 0·25, 0·35
17. 4·795, 4·805 18. 0·065, 0·075 19. 0·65, 0·75 20. 614·5, 615·5
21. 7·125, 7·135 22. 51·5 million, 52·5 million 23. 84·95, 85·05
24. to 31. For discussion

page 204 Test 1

1. $3·50 2. $4·95 3. 48 4. 10c, 10c, 20c 5. $6\frac{1}{2}$
6. $\frac{1}{100}$ 7. 56 8. 75% 9. 15 10. 56c 11. 50 min
12. 6·5 13. 130 m 14. 770 15. 11 16. 25 17. $1\frac{1}{4}$
18. $10 19. 10 20. 60·5 21. 55 22. 16 23. 1 h
24. $4\frac{1}{2}$ 25. 75 or 105 26. 20 27. $2·40 28. 82% 29. $4000
30. 48c

page 205 Test 2

1. 96 2. 19 3. 06:30 4. $2·75 5. $1·90 6. 95°
7. 5 018 001 8. 15 9. $6 10. 3·5c 11. 53 12. 800 g
13. 74 14. 28 km 15. 40 16. 4 17. 62 18. 5
19. 5 20. 480 21. 158 22. 95 23. 0·2 24. 0·7
25. $84 26. $2455 27. 64 28. 90c 29. 55 km/h 30. 28

page 206 Test 3

1. 70 2. 240 3. 900 4. 10 705 5. 10:45 6. 245
7. 20 8. $3·05 9. $1·76 10. 20, 20, 20, 1 or 50, 5, 5, 1 11. 0·75
12. 5 13. Tuesday 14. 1·5 kg 15. $150·50 16. 640 m 17. $722
18. $25 000 19. 4 20. $1·10 21. 12 000 22. 9 23. 91
24. $6 25. 98c 26. $4·46 27. $3·30 28. $42 29. 960
30. False

page 207 Test 4

1. $8·05 2. 75 3. 25 4. 0·1 cm 5. 24c 6. 104
7. 40c 8. $88 9. 5:50 10. $8·20 11. 4 km 12. 45 km
13. $4·25 14. 998 15. 20 16. 200 17. 22·5 cm 18. 75c
19. 10 20. 16 21. 20 22. $9·82 23. 22 min 24. 1540
25. $7·94 26. 70c 27. 200 28. 35% 29. 100 30. $2500

page 208 **Test 5**

1. 25 km
2. $4·40
3. $2·10
4. $26
5. 8 min
6. 25
7. 500 (± 50)
8. $\frac{1}{1000}$
9. 2·65
10. —
11. $15 000
12. $3·85
13. $27·50
14. 8
15. 84
16. 1200
17. 30 litres
18. 7 cm
19. 153
20. 4
21. 7
22. 105 m^2
23. 2 000 000
24. 51
25. 6
26. $6
27. 2300 g
28. 150
29. 133
30. Wednesday

page 210 **Test 6**

1. 60°
2. 0·05
3. 80%
4. 8000
5. $16·90
6. 0·7
7. 5 h 20 min
8. $12\frac{1}{2}$%
9. 6 cm
10. 0·001
11. 7, 8
12. $2
13. 1·8
14. 49·2
15. $12·50
16. 165
17. 72°
18. 240
19. 34c
20. $9
21. 60 km/h
22. 302
23. 50
24. 37
25. $1·11
26. $15
27. 12
28. 8, 9
29. $80
30. $13·80

page 211 **Test 7**

1. 82°
2. 72c
3. 0·25
4. 90 nautical miles
5. 8
6. 11
7. 325
8. $\frac{1}{12}$
9. $25 000
10. 49 000
11. 6·3
12. $8·70
13. $2·40
14. 5
15. $37·50
16. 13·55 cm
17. 10 cm
18. $9
19. 200
20. $1·20
21. 250
22. 500 m^2
23. $8·70
24. 0·025
25. 2550 g
26. $40 000
27. 150°
28. $150
29. 11
30. 9

page 213 **Exercise 9**

1. 19
2. 4
3. 3
4. 0
5. 35
6. 60
7. 16
8. 6
9. 13
10. 14
11. 23
12. 71
13. 20
14. 36
15. 9
16. 8
17. 32
18. 30
19. 4
20. 0
21. 6
22. 5
23. 1
24. 47
25. 6
26. 3
27. 16
28. 12
29. 52
30. 15
31. 87
32. 17
33. 23
34. 8
35. 2
36. 26

page 214 **Exercise 10**

1. $7 + 5 \times 4$
2. $3 \times 5 + 10$
3. $4 \div 2 + 3$
4. $11 + 3 \times 3$
5. $31 - 10 \times 2$
6. $10 + 6 \times 5$
7. $4 \times 8 - 7$
8. $12 + 9 \times 2$
9. $18 - 4 \times 4$
10. $28 - 10 \times 2$
11. $21 \div 3 - 5$
12. $7 + 3 \times 3$
13. $10 \div 2 + 3$
14. $10 \times 3 + 12$
15. $18 \div 3 + 7$
16. $31 + 40 \div 5$
17. $15 - 16 \div 4$
18. $15 + 8 \times 9$
19. $37 + 35 \div 5$
20. $11 \times 5 + 9$
21. $8 + 3 \times 2 - 4$
22. $12 - 3 \times 3 + 1$
23. $11 + 4 - 1 \times 6$
24. $15 \div 5 + 2 \times 4$
25. $7 \times 2 - 3 \times 3$
26. $12 - 2 + 3 \times 4$
27. $8 \times 9 - 6 \times 11$
28. $20 \div 20 + 9 \times 0$
29. $20 - 30 \div 10 + 8$
30. $30 + 6 \times 11 - 11$

page 214 **Exercise 11**

1. 1851
2. 6·889
3. 1·214
4. 0·4189
5. 7·889
6. 19·35
7. 0·049 47
8. 221·5
9. 24·37
10. 6·619
11. 3·306
12. 2·303
13. 41·73
14. 8·163
15. 0·1090
16. 0·5001
17. 20·63
18. 10·09
19. 6·191
20. 10·27
21. 8·627
22. 22·02
23. 1·093
24. 44·72
25. 45·66
26. 52·86
27. 22·51
28. 5·479
29. 5·272
30. 0·2116

page 215 Exercise 12

1. 14·52	**2.** 1·666	**3.** 1·858	**4.** 0·8264	**5.** 2·717	**6.** 4·840
7. 10·87	**8.** 7·425	**9.** 13·49	**10.** 0·7392	**11.** 1135	**12.** 13·33
13. 5·836	**14.** 86·39	**15.** 10·23	**16.** 5540	**17.** 14·76	**18.** 8·502
19. 57·19	**20.** 19·90	**21.** 6·578	**22.** 9·097	**23.** 0·082 80	**24.** 1855
25. 2·367	**26.** 1·416	**27.** 7·261	**28.** 3·151	**29.** 149·9	**30.** 74 020
31. 8·482	**32.** 75·21	**33.** 1·226	**34.** 6767	**35.** 5·964	**36.** 15·45
37. 25·42	**38.** 2·724	**39.** 4·366	**40.** 0·2194	**41.** 0·000 465 9	**42.** 0·3934
43. −0·7526	**44.** 2·454	**45.** 40 000	**46.** 3·003	**47.** 0·006 562	**48.** 0·1330

page 216 Exercise 13

1. SOIL	**2.** ISLES	**3.** HE LIES	**4.** SOS
5. HO HO HO	**6.** ESSO OIL	**7.** SOLID	**8.** SOLO
9. BOILED EGGS	**10.** HE IS BOSS	**11.** LODGE	**12.** SIGH
13. HEDGEHOG	**14.** GOSH	**15.** GOBBLE	**16.** BEG
17. BIG SLOB	**18.** SID	**19.** HILL	**20.** LESLIE
21. HOBBIES	**22.** GIGGLE	**23.** BIBLE	**24.** BIGGLES
25. BOBBLE	**26.** HEIDI	**27.** BOBBIE	**28.** HIGH
29. HELLS BELLS	**30.** GOD BLESS	**31.** SHE DIES	**32.** SOLEIL

page 217 Exercise 14

1. 42 kg **2.** $120
3. (a) 7·2 (b) 11·28 (c) 0·1 (d) 0·026 (e) 28·2 (f) 0·01
4. (a) 3·32 (b) 1·61 (c) 1·46 (d) 4·4 (e) 6·2 (f) 2·74
5. (a) 8 hectares (b) 24 tonnes
6. $345 **7.** (a) $6400 (b) $83 200
8. $1·80 **9.** (a) 600 (b) $204

page 219 Exercise 15

1. (a) 15 (b) (i) 20% (ii) 16% (iii) 70% (iv) 2%
2. (a) 177 147 (b) 1 594 323
3. (a) 36 (b) 24 (c) 240 (d) 240
4. $7\frac{1}{2}$ cm^2 **5.** (a) 15051 (b) 110 km **6.** Total charges = $59·11
7. $7400 **8.** 14·7

page 220 Exercise 16

1. (a) 410 (b) 704·5 **2.** (a) 64 (b) 1 (c) 100 (d) 3000 (e) 32 (f) 81
3. 20 cm^2 **4.** 000, 001, 010, 011, 100, 101, 110, 111
5. (a) $162 (b) 200 (c) F1000 **6.** 5 h 34 min
7. (a) $6^2 = 5^2 + 11$, $7^2 = 6^2 + 13$ (b) $11^2 = 60 + 5^2 + 6^2$, $13^2 = 84 + 6^2 + 7^2$
8. 120 000 000 m^3 **9.** 50 m **10.** 2520

page 222 Exercise 17

1. (a) 80 g (b) 5·2 (c) 416 **2.** $x, 5, t$
3. (a) 12 (b) (i) 8 (ii) 48 **5.** 200 litres
6. 0·006 25 cm **7.** (a) 5·4 km (b) 0·6 cm
8. (a) 3 cm^2 (b) 27 cm^2 (c) $A = \dfrac{C^2}{12}$ **9.** 16

page 223 **Revision exercise 7A**
1. (a) 55c (b) 760
2. (a) 2·088 (b) 3·043
3. (a) 0·340 (b) 4.08×10^{-6} (c) 64·9 (d) 0·119
4. (a) 600 (b) 9000 or 10 000 (c) 3 (d) 60
5. 2.1×10^{24} tonnes
6. (a) 0·5601 (b) 3·215 (c) 0·6161 (d) 0·4743
7. (a) $\frac{3}{5}$, 0·6, 60% (b) $\frac{3}{4}$, 0·75, 75% (c) $\frac{1}{20}$, 0·05, 5% (d) $\frac{1}{8}$, 0·125, $12\frac{1}{2}$%
8. about 90 g 9. about 3 g
10. (a) 18·72 (b) 89·18 (c) 63·99 (d) 144·78 (e) 31·16
    (f) 48·248 (g) 9·24 (h) 1·92 (i) 4·08
11. (a) $33\,333 \times 5 = 166\,665$ (b) $333\,333\,333 \times 5 = 1\,666\,666\,665$
    $333\,333 \times 5 = 1\,666\,665$
12. (a) $654\,321 \times 9 = 5\,888\,889$ (b) $87\,654\,321 \times 9 = 788\,888\,889$

page 224 **Examination exercise 7B**
1. (a) $8 + 7 - 5$ (b) $8 - 7 \times 5$ (c) $8 \times 7 \div 5 = 11.2$
2. (a) $\frac{1}{3}$ (b) 80% 3. $65 \leqslant l < 75$, $14.5 \leqslant w < 15.5$
4. (a) 238 693·75 (b) 240 000
5. (a) 5% (b) $\frac{6}{25}$ (c) 722 (d) 36°
6. (a) $5·80 (b) 55% (c) (i) 1857·60 (ii) 33·4%

Probability

page 227 **Exercise 1**
1. B 2. C 3. A 4. B or C 5. C or D 6. C
7. B 8. B 9. C 10. A 11. D 12. C or D

page 228 **Exercise 2**
1. (a) $\frac{3}{8}$ (b) $\frac{5}{8}$ 2. (a) $\frac{1}{9}$ (b) $\frac{1}{3}$ (c) $\frac{4}{9}$ (d) $\frac{2}{9}$
3. (a) $\frac{5}{11}$ (b) $\frac{2}{11}$ (c) $\frac{4}{11}$ 4. (a) $\frac{4}{17}$ (b) $\frac{3}{17}$
5. (a) $\frac{4}{17}$ (b) $\frac{8}{17}$ (c) $\frac{5}{17}$ 6. (a) $\frac{1}{10}$ (b) $\frac{3}{10}$ (c) $\frac{3}{10}$
7. (a) $\frac{3}{13}$ (b) $\frac{5}{13}$ (c) $\frac{8}{13}$ 8. (a) (i) $\frac{5}{13}$ (ii) $\frac{6}{13}$ (b) (i) $\frac{5}{12}$ (ii) $\frac{1}{12}$
9. $\frac{9}{20}$ 10. $\frac{1}{7}$
11. (a) (i) $\frac{1}{4}$ (ii) $\frac{1}{4}$ (iii) $\frac{1}{4}$ (b) $\frac{1}{4}$ (c) $\frac{6}{27} = \frac{2}{9}$

page 230 **Exercise 3**
1. (a) 150 (b) 50 (c) 25 2. 25 3. 50
4. 40 5. (a) $\frac{3}{8}$ (b) 25 6. (a) $\frac{1}{2}$ (b) $\frac{1}{2}$

page 232 **Exercise 4**
1. $\frac{4}{5}$ 2. (a) $\frac{7}{20}$ (b) $\frac{13}{20}$ 3. $\frac{35}{36}$ 4. 0·76
5. 0·494 6. (a) $\frac{1}{4}$ (b) $\frac{3}{4}$ (c) $\frac{1}{4}$ (d) $\frac{3}{4}$ (e) 0 (f) 1
7. (a) 0·3 (b) 0·9 8. (a) (i) 0·24 (ii) 0·89 (b) 575

page 233 Revision exercise 8A
1. (a) $\frac{3}{8}$ (b) $\frac{5}{8}$ 2. (a) $\frac{2}{11}$ (b) $\frac{5}{11}$ (c) $\frac{9}{11}$ 3. $\frac{1}{6}$
4. $\frac{5}{16}$ 5. (a) $\frac{1}{9}$ (b) $\frac{1}{12}$ (c) 0

page 234 Examination exercise 8B
1. Black, Red, Black; Black, Black, Red (b) $\frac{2}{3}$
2. (a) (i) $\frac{1}{3}$ (ii) $\frac{1}{2}$ (iii) 0 (b) $\frac{2}{5}$
3. (a) (i) $\frac{5}{16}$ (ii) $\frac{11}{16}$ (b) It is not black
4. (a) 28 (b) (i) $\frac{1}{2}$ (ii) $\frac{5}{28}$ (iii) 1 (c) 114

Shape and space 3

page 236 Exercise 1
1. C only 2. $m = 12$ 3. $x = 9$ 4. $a = 2\frac{1}{2}$, $e = 3$ 5. $x = 6.75$
6. $x = 3.2$ 7. $t = 5.25$, $y = 5.6$ 8. 7.7 cm 9. No
10. (a) Yes (b) No (c) No (d) Yes (e) Yes (f) No (g) No (h) Yes
11. (b) 11.2 (c) 4.2 12. $y = 6$ 13. $a = 6$ 14. $f = 4.5$
15. 16 m 16. 3.75 cm 17. 10.8 m 18. AO = 2 cm, DO = 6 cm

page 239 Exercise 2
1. 3.01 cm 2. 5.35 cm 3. 3.13 cm 4. 7.00 cm 5. 73.1 cm
6. 15.4 cm 7. 5.31 cm 8. 7.99 cm 9. 11.6 cm 10. 11.4 cm
11. 961 cm 12. 0.894 cm 13. 46.0 cm 14. 34.9 cm 15. 9.39 cm
16. 8.23 cm 17. 35.6 cm 18. 80.2 cm 19. 4.86 cm 20. 6.98 cm

page 240 Exercise 3
1. 18.4 2. 9.15 3. 10.7 4. 17.1 5. 13.7 6. 126
7. 6.88 8. 11.8 9. 17.6 10. 11.5 11. 5, 5.55 12. 13.1, 27.8
13. 4.26 14. 3.50 15. 26.2 16. 8.82

page 241 Exercise 4
1. 38.7° 2. 48.6° 3. 31.0° 4. 54.5° 5. 38.7°
6. 17.5° 7. 38.9° 8. 59.0° 9. 41.3° 10. 62.7°
11. 54.3° 12. 66.0° 13. 48.2° 14. 12.4° 15. 72.9°
16. 56.9° 17. 36.9° 18. 41.8° 19. 78.0° 20. 89.4°

page 243 Exercise 5
1. 68.0° 2. 3.65 m 3. 14.0 m 4. 20.6° 5. 56.7 m
6. 15.3 m 7. 90.3 cm 8. 4.32 cm 9. 7.66 cm 10. 65.5 km
11. 189 km 12. 25.7 km 13. 180 m 14. 37.3 m 15. 36.4°
16. 10.3 cm 17. $a = 72°$, 8.23 cm 18. 71.1°

page 245 Revision exercise 9A
1. 0.335 m 2. (a) 45.6° (b) 58.0° (c) 3.89 cm (d) 33.8 m 3. 4.8
4. (a) 1.2 (b) 1.6 5. No 6. 7.6 7. 4

page 247 **Examination exercise 9B**
1. 37·1 m
2. (a) 5·537 (b) 28·83
3. 26·4°
4. (a) (i) 3·46 cm (ii) 20·8 cm^2 (b) (i) 12 cm (ii) 62·4 cm^2
5. (a) 29° (b) 4·05 m (c) 10·3 m
6. (a) (i) 85·5 m (ii) 66 (iii) 72·5 cm $\leqslant$ stride $<$ 77·5 cm
   (b) (i) 98·6 m (ii) 30·5°

Number 3

page 249 **Exercise 1**
1. 3^4
2. 5^2
3. 6^3
4. 10^5
5. 1^7
6. 8^4
7. 7^6
8. $2^3 \times 5^2$
9. $3^2 \times 7^4$
10. $3^2 \times 10^3$
11. $5^4 \times 11^2$
12. $2^2 \times 3^3$
13. $3^2 \times 5^3$
14. $2^2 \times 3^3 \times 11^2$
15. (a) 16 (b) 36 (c) 100 (d) 27 (e) 1000
16. (a) 81 (b) 441 (c) 1·44 (d) 0·04 (e) 9·61
    (f) 10 000 (g) 625 (h) 75·69 (i) 0·81 (j) 6625·96
17. (a) 4·41 cm^2 (b) 0·36 cm^2 (c) 196 m^2
18. (a) a^3 (b) n^4 (c) s^5 (d) $p^2 \times q^3$ (e) b^7
19. (a) 216 (b) 256 (c) 243 (d) 100 000 (e) 64
    (f) 0·001 (g) 8·3521 (h) 567 (i) 1250
20. 10^{10}
21. 2^7
22. (a) $2^1, 2^2, 2^3, 2^4$ (b) 2^{25} cents = $335 544·32
23. Yes

page 251 **Exercise 2**
1. (a) 4 (b) 6 (c) 1 (d) 10
2. (a) 9 cm (b) 7 cm (c) 12 cm
3. (a) 3·2 (b) 5·4 (c) 10·3 (d) 4·4
   (e) 49·1 (f) 7·7 (g) 0·4 (h) 0·9
4. 12·2 cm
5. 447 m
6. 7·8 cm
7. (a) 4 (b) 5 (c) 10
8. 5·8 cm

page 252 **Exercise 3**
1. $\frac{1}{3}$
2. $\frac{1}{4}$
3. $\frac{1}{10}$
4. 1
5. $\frac{1}{9}$
6. $\frac{1}{16}$
7. $\frac{1}{100}$
8. 1
9. $\frac{1}{49}$
10. 1
11. $\frac{1}{81}$
12. 1
13. T
14. F
15. T
16. T
17. F
18. F
19. F
20. T
21. T
22. T
23. F
24. F
25. F
26. T
27. T
28. T
29. T
30. T
31. T
32. F

page 252 **Exercise 4**
1. 5^6
2. 6^5
3. 10^9
4. 7^8
5. 3^{10}
6. 8^6
7. 2^{13}
8. 3^4
9. 5^3
10. 7^4
11. 5^2
12. 3^{-4}
13. 6^5
14. 5^{-10}
15. 7^6
16. 7^2
17. 6^5
18. 8^1
19. 5^8
20. 10^2
21. 9^{-2}
22. 3^{-2}
23. 2^4
24. 3^{-2}
25. 7^{-6}
26. 3^{-4}
27. 5^{-5}
28. 8^{-5}
29. 5^{-5}
30. 6^4
31. 3^0
32. 5^0
33. 3^7
34. 2^7
35. 7^2
36. 5^{-1}

page 253 **Exercise 5**

1. 3^6
2. 5^{12}
3. 7^{10}
4. 8^{20}
5. x^6
6. a^{15}
7. n^{14}
8. y^9
9. 2^{-2}
10. 3^{-4}
11. 7^2
12. x^{-3}
13. $6a^5$
14. $20n^4$
15. $14x^5$
16. $24y^7$
17. $5n^7$
18. $12y^2$
19. $9p^5$
20. $10p^6$
21. $8x^6$
22. $27a^6$
23. $16y^6$
24. $25x^8$
25. 3
26. 1
27. 3
28. 0
29. 3
30. 1
31. 2
32. 3
33. -1
34. -1
35. 0
36. 2
37. 4
38. 0
39. -1
40. 0

page 254 **Exercise 6**

1. 4×10^3
2. 5×10^2
3. 7×10^4
4. 6×10
5. $2 \cdot 4 \times 10^3$
6. $3 \cdot 8 \times 10^2$
7. $4 \cdot 6 \times 10^4$
8. $4 \cdot 6 \times 10$
9. 9×10^5
10. $2 \cdot 56 \times 10^3$
11. 7×10^{-3}
12. 4×10^{-4}
13. $3 \cdot 5 \times 10^{-3}$
14. $4 \cdot 21 \times 10^{-1}$
15. $5 \cdot 5 \times 10^{-5}$
16. 1×10^{-2}
17. $5 \cdot 64 \times 10^5$
18. $1 \cdot 9 \times 10^7$
19. $1 \cdot 1 \times 10^9$
20. $1 \cdot 67 \times 10^{-24}$
21. $5 \cdot 1 \times 10^8$
22. $2 \cdot 5 \times 10^{-10}$
23. $6 \cdot 023 \times 10^{23}$
24. 3×10^{10}
25. $\$3 \cdot 6 \times 10^6$

page 255 **Exercise 7**

1. $1 \cdot 5 \times 10^7$
2. 3×10^8
3. $2 \cdot 8 \times 10^{-2}$
4. 7×10^{-9}
5. 2×10^6
6. 4×10^{-6}
7. 9×10^{-2}
8. $6 \cdot 6 \times 10^{-8}$
9. $3 \cdot 5 \times 10^{-7}$
10. 10^{-16}
11. 8×10^9
12. $7 \cdot 4 \times 10^{-7}$
13. $4 \cdot 9 \times 10^{11}$
14. $4 \cdot 4 \times 10^{12}$
15. $1 \cdot 5 \times 10^3$
16. 2×10^{17}
17. $1 \cdot 68 \times 10^{13}$
18. $4 \cdot 25 \times 10^{11}$
19. $9 \cdot 9 \times 10^7$
20. $6 \cdot 25 \times 10^{-16}$
21. $2 \cdot 88 \times 10^{12}$
22. $6 \cdot 82 \times 10^{-7}$
23. c, a, b
24. 13
25. 16
26. (i) 6×10^2 (ii) $6 \cdot 67 \times 10^7$
27. 50 min
28. 6×10^2
29. (a) $9 \cdot 46 \times 10^{12}$ km (b) 144 million km
30. 25 000

page 256 **Exercise 8**

1. $\frac{5}{6}$
2. $\frac{1}{6}$
3. $\frac{2}{3}$
4. $\frac{5}{12}$
5. $\frac{1}{4}$
6. $2\frac{1}{4}$
7. $\frac{9}{10}$
8. $\frac{1}{5}$
9. $\frac{4}{5}$
10. $\frac{13}{14}$
11. $\frac{3}{14}$
12. $\frac{6}{7}$
13. $\frac{3}{8}$
14. $\frac{5}{32}$
15. $2\frac{1}{2}$
16. $\frac{29}{30}$
17. $\frac{2}{15}$
18. $\frac{5}{24}$
19. $\frac{16}{21}$
20. $\frac{1}{7}$
21. $1\frac{2}{7}$
22. $\frac{11}{20}$
23. $\frac{1}{5}$
24. $3\frac{1}{5}$
25. $\frac{13}{24}$
26. $\frac{1}{12}$
27. $5\frac{1}{3}$
28. $\frac{29}{36}$
29. $\frac{5}{36}$
30. $2\frac{2}{9}$
31. $2\frac{1}{4}$
32. $\frac{5}{8}$
33. 10
34. $3\frac{1}{12}$
35. $2\frac{1}{2}$
36. $5\frac{5}{8}$
37. $2\frac{1}{3}$
38. $\frac{5}{13}$
39. 18
40. 6

page 257 **Exercise 9**

1. (a) $\frac{1}{2}, \frac{7}{12}, \frac{2}{3}$ (b) $\frac{2}{3}, \frac{3}{4}, \frac{5}{6}$ (c) $\frac{1}{3}, \frac{5}{8}, \frac{17}{24}, \frac{3}{4}$ (d) $\frac{5}{6}, \frac{8}{9}, \frac{11}{12}$
2. (a) $\frac{1}{2}$ (b) $\frac{3}{4}$ (c) $\frac{17}{24}$ (d) $\frac{7}{18}$ (e) $\frac{3}{10}$ (f) $\frac{5}{12}$
3. 5
4. $39
5. 3
6. 123 cm
7. $\frac{1}{5}$
8. $1\frac{4}{11}$
9. (a) 9 (b) $\frac{5}{16}$
10. $\frac{16}{24}$
11. 9
12. $\frac{5}{24}$
13. same

page 259 **Exercise 10**

1. -4
2. -12
3. -11
4. -3
5. -5
6. 4
7. -5
8. -8
9. 19
10. -17
11. -4
12. -5
13. -11
14. 6
15. -4
16. 6
17. 0
18. -18
19. -3
20. -11
21. -8
22. -7
23. 1
24. 1
25. 9
26. 11
27. -8
28. 42
29. 4
30. 15
31. -7
32. -9
33. -1
34. -7
35. 0
36. 11
37. -14
38. 0
39. 17
40. 3

page 260 **Exercise 11**

1. −6   **2.** −4   **3.** −15   **4.** 9   **5.** −8   **6.** −15   **7.** −24   **8.** 6
9. 12   **10.** −18 **11.** −21   **12.** 25 **13.** −60 **14.** 21   **15.** 48   **16.** −16
17. −42 **18.** 20   **19.** −42   **20.** −66 **21.** −4 **22.** −3   **23.** 3   **24.** −5
25. 4   **26.** −4   **27.** −4   **28.** −1 **29.** −2 **30.** 4   **31.** −16 **32.** −2
33. −4 **34.** 5   **35.** −10   **36.** 11 **37.** 16 **38.** −2   **39.** −4   **40.** −5
41. 64 **42.** −27 **43.** −600 **44.** 40 **45.** 2   **46.** 36   **47.** −2   **48.** −8
49. 160 **50.** −2

page 260 **Test 1**

1. −16 **2.** 64   **3.** −15   **4.** −2   **5.** 15   **6.** 18   **7.** 3   **8.** −6
9. 11   **10.** −48 **11.** −7   **12.** 9   **13.** 6   **14.** −18 **15.** −10 **16.** 8
17. −6 **18.** −30 **19.** 4   **20.** −1

page 260 **Test 2**

1. −16 **2.** 6   **3.** −13   **4.** 42   **5.** −4   **6.** −4   **7.** −12   **8.** −20
9. 6   **10.** 0   **11.** 36   **12.** −10 **13.** −7 **14.** 10   **15.** 6   **16.** −18
17. −9 **18.** 15   **19.** 1   **20.** 0

page 260 **Test 3**

1. 100 **2.** −20   **3.** −8   **4.** −7   **5.** −4   **6.** 10   **7.** 9   **8.** −10
9. 7   **10.** 35   **11.** −20   **12.** −24 **13.** −10 **14.** −7   **15.** −19 **16.** −1
17. −5 **18.** −13 **19.** 0   **20.** 8

page 261 **Exercise 12**

1. 36   **2.** 29   **3.** 8   **4.** 18   **5.** 84
6. 9×10^{12} **7.** 165   **8.** $\sqrt{181}$ **9.** 1·62   **10.** 650

page 262 **Exercise 13**

1. −5   **2.** 8   **3.** −17   **4.** 8   **5.** −2   **6.** −27   **7.** 1   **8.** −22
9. −22 **10.** −22 **11.** −10   **12.** −2 **13.** 23 **14.** −44 **15.** 26   **16.** 25
17. −4 **18.** 0   **19.** −16   **20.** 22 **21.** −5 **22.** 30   **23.** 13   **24.** 25
25. 40 **26.** 3   **27.** −5   **28.** −12 **29.** −34 **30.** 2   **31.** 12   **32.** 39
33. 40 **34.** 7   **35.** 3   **36.** 10 **37.** 51 **38.** −2   **39.** 1   **40.** 11

page 263 **Exercise 14**

1. 4   **2.** 4   **3.** 9   **4.** 16   **5.** 8   **6.** −8   **7.** −27   **8.** 64
9. 8   **10.** 16   **11.** 8   **12.** 16 **13.** 18 **14.** 36   **15.** 48   **16.** 16
17. 20 **18.** 54   **19.** 144   **20.** 24 **21.** 13 **22.** 10   **23.** 1   **24.** 18
25. 13 **26.** 19   **27.** 10   **28.** 32 **29.** 16 **30.** 144 **31.** 36   **32.** 36
33. 4   **34.** 1   **35.** 2   **36.** −14 **37.** −5 **38.** −5   **39.** −10 **40.** 10
41. 0   **42.** 4   **43.** 50   **44.** 4   **45.** −10 **46.** −4   **47.** −6   **48.** −16
49. 28 **50.** 44

page 263 **Exercise 15**

1. 7   **2.** −2   **3.** 0   **4.** $-4\frac{1}{2}$ **5.** 6   **6.** 2
7. 26   **8.** −9   **9.** $3\frac{1}{4}$ **10.** $-\frac{5}{6}$ **11.** 4   **12.** $2\frac{2}{3}$
13. $3\frac{1}{4}$ **14.** $-2\frac{1}{6}$ **15.** −13   **16.** 12   **17.** $1\frac{1}{3}$ **18.** $-\frac{5}{36}$

page 264 Exercise 16
1. 20
2. 200 g
3. 6
4. 400
5. $5 \times 7 \times 13 \times 71$
6. 225 mm
7. 1
8. (a) 66666 (b) 82 (c) 29
9. (a) 323 g (b) 67c

page 265 Exercise 17
1. $10 485·76
2. (a) 1 (b) 15
3. $a = 100, b = 1$
4. 50
5. E
7. (a) $\frac{1}{66}$ (b) 16
8. 1105
9. 13
10. 10

page 266 Revision exercise 10A
1. (iii) $\frac{a}{b}$
2. (a) 8 (b) 140 (c) 29 (d) 42
3. (a) −11 (b) 23 (c) −10 (d) −20 (e) 6 (f) −14
4. (a) 3 (b) 5 (c) −6 (d) −7
5. (a) 14 (b) 18 (c) 28
6. $2·3 \times 10^9$
7. (a) $z = x - 5y$ (b) $k = \dfrac{11 - 3m}{m}$
8. (a) 4^5 (b) 1^7 (c) $2^3 \times 5^2$
9. (a) 6^5 (b) 7^8 (c) 3^7 (d) 10^3 (e) 5^4 (f) 2^{-1}
10. (a) 2 (b) 2 (c) 4
11. (a) x^8 (b) n^9 (c) $12a^3$
12. (a) 5×10^4 (b) $6·1 \times 10^5$ (c) 3×10^{-4} (d) $1·5 \times 10^{-3}$ (e) 1×10^7
13. (a) 3×10^{10} (b) 4×10^4 (c) 8×10^6 (d) $4·5 \times 10^7$
14. (a) $\frac{14}{15}$ (b) $\frac{1}{4}$ (c) $\frac{1}{10}$ (d) $2\frac{2}{3}$ (e) $1\frac{1}{10}$ (f) $1\frac{11}{16}$
15. $\frac{5}{24}$
16. $5\% = \frac{1}{20}$ is true

page 267 Examination exercise 10B
1. (a) number of cells: 1, 2, 4, 8, 16, 32 (b) 2^{12} (c) 3 (d) 2^{39}
2. (a) 0 (b) 21
3. (a) $1·39 \times 10^6$ (b) 109
4. (a) (i) 0·021 (ii) 0·0021 (b) $1·89 \times 10^{-2}$
5. (a) $\frac{5}{12}$ (b) $p = 8$ and $q = 2$
6. (a) 192 cm (b) (i) $f = \dfrac{3h - 256}{10}$ (ii) 23 cm (c) when $h = 72$, f is negative
7. −2
8.

5	9		3
	6	3	0
1	1	4	0
8			0

Multiple choice tests

page 287 **Test 1**

1. C	**2.** D	**3.** D	**4.** B	**5.** C
6. C	**7.** A	**8.** D	**9.** B	**10.** B
11. C	**12.** A	**13.** D	**14.** C	**15.** C
16. D	**17.** A	**18.** C	**19.** B	**20.** D
21. A	**22.** B	**23.** C	**24.** B	**25.** C

page 288 **Test 2**

1. B	**2.** C	**3.** B	**4.** A	**5.** D
6. C	**7.** A	**8.** D	**9.** B	**10.** C
11. B	**12.** D	**13.** A	**14.** C	**15.** C
16. D	**17.** B	**18.** A	**19.** B	**20.** B
21. C	**22.** D	**23.** A	**24.** A	**25.** B

page 290 **Test 3**

1. D	**2.** D	**3.** D	**4.** B	**5.** A
6. C	**7.** A	**8.** D	**9.** D	**10.** B
11. C	**12.** D	**13.** D	**14.** B	**15.** A
16. B	**17.** C	**18.** A	**19.** D	**20.** D
21. C	**22.** C	**23.** B	**24.** B	**25.** D

page 292 **Test 4**

1. B	**2.** B	**3.** A	**4.** C	**5.** C
6. B	**7.** D	**8.** A	**9.** B	**10.** B
11. D	**12.** B	**13.** B	**14.** C	**15.** D
16. A	**17.** C	**18.** B	**19.** B	**20.** D
21. B	**22.** C	**23.** C	**24.** C	**25.** A

page 294 **Specimen Paper 1**

1. 1024 **2.** 51 **3.** 5
4. Any value between 18 cm and 28 cm **5.** 25·23132522...
6. Any number in $10·58 \leqslant x \leqslant 10·63$ **7.** 19·7 cm^3
8. (a) $\frac{2}{15}$ (b) $\frac{10}{27}$ **9.** Perpendicular bisector of the line joining the two trees
10. (a) $3x + 7$ (b) $5p(q + 2)$ **11.** 50, 60 and 90 tonnes
12. (b) (i) 120° (ii) 225°
13. (a) $6 \times (5 + 3) = 48$ (b) $(28 - 12) \div 4 = 4$ (c) $(9 - 3)^2 = 36$
14. $12x - 4$
15. (a) (b)   **16.** (a) $3·49 (b) $1·31 (c) $1·82
   17. (a) $62\frac{1}{2}\%$ (b) $\frac{1}{8}$
   18. (a)   (b)

19. (a) Rhombus (b) 2 (c) 110°, 70°, 70°
20. (a) 38 (b) $12\frac{1}{2}$°C (c) $t = \frac{1}{4}(n + 50)$
21. (b) 03:00 (c) 22:00 on Tuesday

page 297 **Specimen Paper 2**
1. (a) (i) 45° (ii) 5 cm (iii) 7·07 cm
   (b) (i) 30° (ii) 6·93 cm (iii) 8 cm
   (c) Triangle DEF by 1·36 cm²
2. (a) 88, 888, 8888, 88 888
   (b) $98\,765 \times 9 + 3 = 888\,888$, $987\,654 \times 9 + 2 = 8\,888\,888$, $9\,876\,543 \times 9 + 1 = 88\,888\,888$
   (c) 8 888 888 889
3. (a) (i) 11°C (or −11°C) (ii) 34°C (or −34°) (b) $\frac{5}{12}$
   (c) (i) −12°C (ii) −2°C (iii) −2·5°C
4. (a) (i) 6·80 metres (ii) $57 (b) (i) 36·9° (ii) 3·30 metres
5. (a) −1, (−1·2), −1·5, −2, −3, (−4), (−6), (6), 4, 3, 2, 1·5, 1·2, 1
   (c) (ii) order 2 (d) (i) −4, −1, 2, 5 (e) (1·6, 3·8), (−1·25, −4·8)
6. (a) X 12, 9, 13½; Y 14, 10½, 15¾; Z 16, 12, 18 (b) 383 cm³
7. (a) (i) Octagon (b) (ii) 11·1 cm (iv) 11°
8. (b) Angles 180°, 60°, 40°, 80°
9. (a) 157 cm (b) 91 cm (c) (i) 9·42 m³ (ii) 7·07 tonnes
10. (a)
```
        1                  1          (b) Either one of      4              or      4
     9     7            8     9                           8     9                9     7
   5         6        6         4                       3         1            2         3
  2   4   8   3     2   7   5   3                     5   7   2   6         5   8   1   6
```

Index

acceleration 261
addition, decimals 66–7
algebra 42–8, 166–91
angles 5–10
    bisectors 151
    in circles 13–14
    of depression 242–5
    of elevation 242–5
    polygons 8, 11–14
    triangles 6, 241–2
approximations 89–91
    measurements 201–3
area 26–31
    circles 19–21
    complex shapes 22–3
    problem solving 157–9
    surface 32–3
arithmetic 61–2
    mental 203–13
averages 119–22

bar charts 107–8
bearings 146–50
    relative 147–8
boxes, maximum 271–2
brackets 182

calculators 213–17
    memories 215–16
    operations 213–15
    standard forms 253, 255
    words on 216–17, 280–1
car hire 270
chess boards 284
circles 17–25
    angles in 13–14
    area 19–21
    circumference 17–19
    loci 151
    radius 23–5
    tangents to 13
circumference 17–19
class boundaries 123–4
continuous data 123
conversion graphs 112–13
cosine ratio 239
crossnumbers 68, 274–8
cube numbers 249
cube roots 250–1
cubes

construction 3
    painting 273
cuboids, volume 31–2
cylinders
    surface area 32–3
    volume 32–3

data
    continuous 123
    discrete 123
    displaying 104–13
    grouped 109–12
    handling 104–28
data collection, and probability 226–7
decimals 64–8, 195–7
    addition 66–7
    division 66, 67–8
    multiplication 66, 67
    places 89, 90–1
    significant figures 89, 90
    subtraction 66–7
diagonals, rectangles 273
diagrams
    expanding 271
    flow 69–70
    frequency 107–8
    see also graphs
discrete data 123
distance 87–9
distance–time graphs 174–7
division
    decimals 66, 67–8
    indices 252
    long 72–5
drawings, accurate 1–3

elimination method 172–3
enlargements 135–40
    centre of 138
    fractional scale factors 140–1
    scale factor 138
equations
    fractions in 46–7
    graphical solution of 55–6
    problem solving 48–51
    quadratic 55–6
    solving 44–51
    see also simultaneous equations
estimations 197–201, 282
    probabilities 226–7

events
- exclusive 231
- probabilities 226–7

factors 182
flow diagrams 69–70
formulae
- changing subject of 183–4
- substitution 261–3

fractions 195–7, 256–8
- in equations 46–7
- in formulae 183–4

frequency diagrams 107–8
frequency polygons 123–6

games 274–86
graphs
- conversion 112–13
- curved 53–4
- distance–time 174–7
- drawing 52–4
- equation solving 55–6
- interpretation 174–81
- simultaneous equation solving 169–71
- sketching 180–1
- straight line 52–3
- see also diagrams

grouped data 109–12

hypotenuse 238

indices 249–53
- division 252
- multiplication 252
- negative 251–2
- powers of 253
- reciprocal 252
- rules 253
- zero 251–2

interest, simple 79–80
inverse operations 62–3
investigations 269–73

kites, symmetry 143

length, units 91
line symmetry 15
loci 151–4

maps, scales 80–2
mass, units 91
mathematics, applications 269–86

mean 119
measurements, approximations 201–3
median 119
mental arithmetic 203–13
metric units 91–3
mid-points 124
milk crate problem 281
mind-reading 284
mode 119–20
multiplication
- decimals 66, 67
- indices 252
- long 72–5

negative numbers 258–60
nets 3–5
number messages 278–80
numbers 59–103, 192–225, 249–68
- creating 282
- cubic 249
- negative 258–60
- place value 59–60
- properties 71–2
- square 249
- standard forms 253–6

number squares, rules 269–70

operations
- calculators 213–15
- inverse 62–3

parallel lines, and angles 7
parallelograms
- area 29–30
- symmetry 143

patterns, square 30–1
pentominoes 283–4
percentages 76–80, 195–7
- changes 192–5

perimeter, complex shapes 22–3
perpendiculars, bisectors 151
pie charts 104–6
pi (p) 19, 20
place value 59–60
points, angles at 5
polygons
- exterior angles 11–13
- frequency 123–6
- interior angles 8
- properties 143–5

powers see indices
prisms, volume 31–2

probability 226–34
    estimations 226–7
    and symmetry 226
problem solving, equations 48–51
profits 93–4, 193
proportion 85–7
puzzles 212–13, 274–86
pyramids, construction 3–5
Pythagoras' theorem 154–7

quadratic equations, graphical solution 55–6
quadrilaterals
    angles 8
    properties 143–5
    similarity 235
    symmetry 143
questionnaires 114–18
    analysis 117
    checklists 115–16
    hypothesis testing 117–18

range 120
ratios 82–4, 195–7
    trigonometric 238–9
rectangles
    area 26–8
    diagonals 273
    symmetry 143
reflections 129–31
rhombus, symmetry 143
right-angled triangles 238–42
    Pythagoras' theorem 154–7
rotational symmetry 15
rotations 132–4
    centre of 134
rules, finding 166–8

scale readings 65
scales 80–2
scores, half-time 270
sequences 42–4
shapes 1–41, 129–65, 235–48
    complex 22–3
    similar 235–8
    transformations 129–43
significant figures 89, 90
similarity 235–8
simple interest 79–80
simultaneous equations 169–74
    algebraic solution 171–3
    elimination method 172–3
    graphical solution 169–71

    problem solving 173–4
    substitution method 171–2
sine ratio 239
sketch graphs 180–1
speed 87–9
square numbers 249
square roots 250–1
squares, symmetry 143
standard forms, numbers 253–6
straight line graphs, drawing 52–3
straight lines, angles at 5
substitution
    into formulae 261–3
    method 171–2
subtraction, decimals 66–7
surface area, cylinders 32–3
surveys, questionnaires 114–18
symmetry 15–16
    and probability 226
    quadrilaterals 143

tally charts 107
tangent ratio 239
tangents, to circles 13
tension 261
time 87–9, 261
timetabling 272–3
transformations
    combined 142–3
    shapes 129–43
translations 141–2
trapeziums
    area 29–30
    symmetry 143
travel graphs 174–7
triangles
    angles 6, 241–2
    area 26, 28
    length of sides 239–41
    right-angled 154–7, 238–42
    similarity 235–6
trigonometric ratios 238–9
trigonometry 238–45

units, metric 91–3

velocity 261
volume 31–8
    problem solving 157–9
    units 91

words, on calculators 216–17, 280–1